T0318431

The Social Psychology of Change Management

Changes are rarely accomplished by individuals. People are social animals and changes are social processes which have to be organized.

Social psychology is essential for the effectiveness and development of the field of change management. It is necessary to understand people in change processes. Social psychology also teaches us that meaning is key during change and intervention. Social psychology makes change management comprehensible to people and allows them to consider their actions in groups and the organization on their merits. They may seem obvious and self-evident, but practice and science, as well as the popular change management literature, show that it is not.

Drawing on the field of social psychology and based on primary research, *The Social Psychology of Change Management* presents more than forty social psychological theories and concepts that are relevant for the field of change management. The theories and concepts are analysed and categorized following Fiske's five core social motives: belonging, understanding, controlling, enhancing self and trusting. Each theory has an introduction in which its assumptions and relevance are explained.

By studying the scientific evidence, including meta-analytic evidence, the book provides practitioners, students and academics in the field of change management, organizational behaviour and business strategy the most relevant social psychological ideas and best available evidence, thereby further unleashing the potential of social psychology in order to feed the field of change management. By categorizing and integrating the relevant theories and concepts, change management is enriched and restructured in a prudent, positive and practical way.

The overarching goal, however, inspired by the ideas and perspective of leading thinkers like Kurt Lewin, James Q. Wilson and Susan T. Fiske, is to make the world a better place. Social psychologists (being social scientists) study practical social issues, in our case issues related to change management, and application to real-world problems is a key goal. Therefore, this book goes beyond the domain of organizational sciences.

Steven ten Have, PhD, is a full professor of strategy and change at the Vrije Universiteit Amsterdam, the Netherlands, chairman of the Foundation for Evidence Based Management, and partner at TEN HAVE Change Management, the Netherlands.

John Rijsman, PhD, is a full professor of social psychology at Tilburg University, the Netherlands. He obtained his PhD in experimental social psychology from the University of Louvain in 1970, and, after a short stay at the University of Southern Illinois, was asked in 1972 to become chair of social psychology at the new faculty of psychology in Tilburg, where he has stayed ever since.

Wouter ten Have, PhD, is a full professor of organization and change at the Vrije Universiteit Amsterdam, the Netherlands, visiting university lecturer of change management (MBA health-care management) at the Amsterdam Business School, the Netherlands and partner at TEN HAVE Change Management, the Netherlands.

Joris Westhof, MSc, is a business consultant at Zestgroup, the Netherlands.

Routledge Studies in Organizational Change & Development
Series Editor: Bernard Burnes

For a full list of available titles please visit: https://www.routledge.com/
Routledge-Studies-in-Organizational-Change—Development/book-series/
SE0690

The Social Psychology of Change Management

Theories and an Evidence-Based Perspective on Social and Organizational Beings

Steven ten Have, John Rijsman, Wouter ten Have and Joris Westhof

Routledge
Taylor & Francis Group

LONDON AND NEW YORK

First published 2019 by Routledge

2 Park Square, Milton Park, Abingdon, Oxon, OX14 4RN
605 Third Avenue, New York, NY 10017

Routledge is an imprint of the Taylor & Francis Group, an informa business

First issued in paperback 2020

Library of Congress Cataloging-in-Publication Data
Names: Have, Steven ten, author. | Rijsman, John, author. |
    Have, Wouter ten, author.
Title: The social psychology of change management : theories and an
    evidence-based perspective on social and organizational beings /
    Steven ten Have, John Rijsman, Wouter ten Have and Joris
    Westhof.
Description: New York City : Routledge, [2019] | Series: Routledge
    studies in organizational change & development | Includes
    bibliographical references and index.
Identifiers: LCCN 2018042986 | ISBN 9781138552081 (hardback) |
    ISBN 9781315147956 (ebook)
Subjects: LCSH: Organizational change. | Organizational behavior. |
    Social psychology.
Classification: LCC HD58.8 .H3888 2019 | DDC 658.4/06—dc23
LC record available at https://lccn.loc.gov/2018042986

ISBN: 978-1-138-55208-1 (hbk)
ISBN: 978-0-367-73218-9 (pbk)

Typeset in Sabon
by Apex CoVantage, LLC

Contents

Research Team

Lead Researcher

Hans van Emmerik, MSc, is a former consultant of TEN HAVE Change Management.

Researchers

Ruben ten Have, student of Philosophy, Politics and Economics (PPE) at the Vrije Universiteit Amsterdam, the Netherlands and research-assistant at TEN HAVE Change Management.

Lianne Ossenkoppele, MSc, is a former consultant of TEN HAVE Change Management.

Cornell Vernooij, MSc, is a consultant of TEN HAVE Change Management.

Tables and Figures

Tables

Figures

Foreword

This book is about human beings, being social and organizational beings. And change. Following John Rijsman (1997) we see human beings in social contexts, socii, as subjects, that is, as (co-) producers of knowledge and understanding and thereby meaning, and not as the products or objects of it. As a consequence, we aim at positioning the human being as on the one hand an individual being and on the other hand as a social being, in a prudent and balanced, yet clear and structured way. Reconciliation, Fons Trompenaars' way, is the preferred way; it's neither 'or-or', nor 'and-and', but 'through-through'. Several thinkers have recognized the duality of man, being an individual and social being. In 1956 William H. Whyte wrote 'The Organization Man'. Whyte saw good in both what he called the Protestant Ethic and a social ethic. The first perspective is about the idea that the "pursuit of individual salvation through hard work, thrift, and competitive struggle is the heart of American achievement". The second is about the idea that "of himself, [man] is isolated, meaningless; only as he collaborates with others does he become worthwhile, for by sublimating himself in the group, he helps produce a whole that is greater than the sum of its parts" (Whyte, 1956). That time, to Whyte, the central problem was that the organization men actually liked being organization men; the Protestant Ethic was losing ground to the Social Ethic. Therefore, Whyte argued for "individualism within organization life". Ten years before, Kurt Lewin was worried about the dynamic or development, the other way around. On the last night of his life, in 1947, Lewin told to his long-time colleague Ronald Lippitt that a person's competence should not be defined in terms of 'going it alone': "The American cultural ideal of the self-made man, of everyone standing on his own feet, is as tragic a picture as the initiative-destroying dependence on a benevolent despot. We all need each other. This type of interdependence is the greatest challenge to the maturity of individual and group functioning" (Whyte, 1956). Edgar H. Schein in 2013 agrees and motivates the use of 'humble inquiry' by stating that: "The world is becoming more technologically complex, interdependent, and culturally diverse, which makes the building of relationships more and more necessary to get things accomplished and, at the same time, more difficult" (Schein, 2013, p. pm). In characterizing different (national) cultures, Trompenaars and Hampden-Turner (2012) describe the individual versus group or social entity with their dimension of individualism versus communitarianism. This is: personal freedom and achievement versus the belief that the group is more important than the individual, people making their own decisions and taking care of themselves versus the group that provides help and safety in exchange for loyalty. They guide the way for people who have to deal in practice with the social psychology of and in organizations. The social and organizational being and the group or organization will benefit from reconciliation of the individual-group or individualism-communitarianism dilemmas. The two sides are necessary, helpful and ingredients for synergy when handled in the right way. Trompenaars' example with regard to teams and individuals is illustrative; reconcile by rewarding teams for individual creativity, reward individuals for teamwork. The two sides are individually and in combination addressed by numerous social psychological theories and concepts: for example, conformity, social exchange theory, self-determination theory, attachment theory and social reinforcement. The two sides, their interactions and the theories and concepts are related to what Fiske (2004) calls core social motives: belonging, understanding, controlling, enhancing self and trusting. Social psychology as a discipline and perspective is essential and helpful, if not necessary for organizations to understand and develop organizational behaviour and to craft their change management. The overarching goal, however, inspired by the ideas and perspective of leading thinkers like Kurt Lewin, James Q. Wilson, Edgar H. Schein and Susan T. Fiske, is to make the world a better place. Social psychologists (being social scientists) study practical social issues, in our case issues related to change management, and application to real-world problems is a key goal.

Social psychology is essential for the effectiveness and development of the field of organizations, organizational behaviour and change management. It is necessary to understand people in change processes. People are social animals and change in organizations is a social process. Social psychology also teaches us that meaning is key during change and intervention. Social psychology makes change management comprehensible to people and allows them to consider their actions in groups and the organization on their merits. They may seem obvious and self-evident, but practice and science, as well as the popular change management literature, show that it is not. Drawing on the field of social psychology and based on primary research, *The Social Psychology of Change Management*, more than forty theories and an evidence-based perspective on social and organizational beings, presents social psychological theories and concepts that are relevant for the field of change management. The theories and concepts are analysed and categorized following Fiske's five core social motives: belonging, understanding, controlling, enhancing self and trusting. Each theory has an introduction in which its assumptions and relevance are explained. By studying the scientific evidence, including meta-analytic evidence, the book provides practitioners, students and academics in the field of change management, organizational behaviour and business strategy the most relevant social psychological ideas and best available evidence, thereby further unleashing the potential of social psychology in order to feed the field of change management. By categorizing and integrating the relevant theories and concepts, change management is enriched and restructured in a prudent, positive and practical way.

Our research project was a journey of academics and practitioners. With this book we are at an 'inn', nothing more, nothing less; the journey continues. At the inn we tell our story and share our experiences, the insights and the evidence gathered with other 'travellers', so that they are possibly better prepared for the next stages of their scientific or practical journey. With regard to the next stages, the question from a research and methodological perspective could be 'what's next'? The short answer is: making more, better, relevant and useful evidence available for the science and practice related to change management. That is, additional evidence in terms of quantity, level (of evidence), specificity and fitness for purpose. So *The Social Psychology of Change Management* can be seen as a 'stopping place' and 'starting point' for the next stages of the journey toward effective change management to make better organizations that 'work' and contribute.

On behalf of our team of authors, I would like to thank the members of the research team: Hans van Emmerik, Cornell Vernooij, Lianne Ossenkoppele and Ruben ten Have. Together with Joris Westhof they collected and analysed the evidence, continuously and prudently separating wheat from the chaff. Hans van Emmerik was the lead researcher; his talent, energy and creativity were essential for the development of the research project and the finalization of the book. We have managed this project, ably assisted and with the strong support of our colleague Anna van Houwelingen. She was truly committed. The project was fully funded and wholeheartedly supported by TEN HAVE Change Management. We are very grateful for this and like to thank in particular Anne-Bregje Huijsmans (managing partner) and Ton Speet for their warm support and unconditional commitment.

Having the privilege to write this Foreword I am in the privileged position to thank John Rijsman, Joris Westhof and Wouter ten Have. They are authors, colleagues, friends and more. The real privilege has been working with the three of you. John, you are strong and humble, knowledgeable and open, wise and generous. You are an icon, an exceptional teacher and my guide. Your lessons and insights, the core of our true dialogues, are the foundation of this book. Joris, you have contributed to the project and book in a more than significant way. You are loyal, tireless, committed, and also clever, curious and creative. With you as co-pilot the 'flight' was safe, inspiring, purposeful and fun. Wouter, you are the archetype of the scientist-practitioner, a thought leader in our field. Your signature and footprint are unmistakeable. You are empathetic yet determined, professional and human, a strong and social personality, a master and a talent. You are my brother, my best friend. We had luck, but with the three of you as travel companions it wasn't (only) luck that brought us to the 'inn'.

Steven ten Have
8th August 2018

1   Social Psychology and Change Management[1]

Introduction

Social psychology can offer important insights into change, for instance that change and intervention are all about interaction and meaning. However, in change management the insights provided by social psychology are not used frequently enough. By understanding the perspective of social psychology, change management as a profession can continue to grow. Managers and advisers are working every day to change organizations and the behaviour of employees. At times they do so spontaneously by giving an encouraging or a disapproving response to the behaviour of a group or individual; at other times they do so as part of a well-thought-out plan to bring about a particular change. Either way they are dealing with 'social animals'. Aristotle once said that humans are social (and political) beings by nature: man is different from other social beings because he can distinguish between good and evil, and between justice and injustice (Aristotle, 328 BC). In a conscious approach to change, one might, for instance, want to change an organization's structure or its management style. The approach can also be more comprehensive. Take the Organization Development (OD) approach: 'A system-wide application of behavioural science knowledge with a planned development and reinforcement of organizational strategies, structures and processes to make the organization more effective' (Cummings & Huse, 1989, p. 1; our translation). In addition, from the point of view of strategy-structure-systems one can also focus unilaterally on the 'hard side', or from the point of view of target-process-people on the 'soft side' (Ghoshal & Bartlett, 1996). Those two points of view can also be integrated, as in an integral model for culture change (e.g. Claus, 1991).

Social psychologist Schein (1999) distinguishes between primary anchoring mechanisms and secondary articulation and culture-reinforcing mechanisms. *Primary* anchoring mechanisms can be seen in the way in which leaders react to critical situations—what do they pay attention to, what do they reject or implement? Other examples are conscious model behaviour and appointing role models. Some of the *secondary* mechanisms Schein indicates are organizational structures, systems and procedures, designing work areas, plus rituals and customs, stories and myths, and formal statements on the values of the organization. The approach 'limits' itself by focusing on 'people' at certain times, and on the 'system's side' at other times. From a people perspective, behaviour is considered a function of the knowledge, attitudes and assumptions of individuals and groups; in these cases, interventions refer to values, leadership, collaboration and communication. From a system's perspective, behaviour is a function of the organizational system with interventions aimed at, among other things, the content of strategy and policy, organizational structure, reward systems and accountability. Ultimately, change management always concerns the possibilities and difficulties that are connected to (and influence) behavioural change on individual, group and organizational levels. People are social animals. It is all about the behaviour of and between people in social contexts. That is precisely the domain of social psychology. That profession revolves around the influence that people have on the convictions, the feelings and the behaviour of others (Aronson, 2016). However, an analysis of more than fifty bestsellers on the subject of change management shows us that social psychology is conspicuous by its absence (ten Have et al., 2017). Some books still mention Albert Bandura (for instance Bandura, 1963) and his social-cognitive learning theory. 'groupthink' and group dynamics are referred to left and right (for instance Janis, 1982). The notion of 'social proof' is visible in opinions about model behaviour, 'significant others' and the dissemination of ideas (for instance Sherif, 1935; Cialdini et al., 1999). But that is about it. We are talking about the best-selling and most popular books about the profession. They often touch on the right subjects and issues, or at least the most recognizable ones from the field. At the same time, they clearly ignore an enormous amount of very relevant knowledge. Not only is that a shame, but also it is a professional irresponsibility, especially since change management usually concerns issues with a great organizational, emotional, economic and social impact. It concerns the right to exist, jobs, identity, prosperity and welfare. Notwithstanding the more widespread socio-psychological insights of eminences like Weick (1979, 1995), Lewin (1943a) and Schein (1985, 1999), from the perspective of change management the discipline of social psychology is still a sleeping giant. Given the challenges and issues that managers and advisers are faced with during change, plus the level of knowledge in the field, there is still a world to be conquered out there.

Social Psychology in the Practice of Change Management

The importance of social psychology for change management in the field became apparent, for example, when a multinational asked us to brainstorm with them about their methods and methodology for change management. In the past decade, this organization had rather successfully translated several environmental changes into strategic adjustments and organizational changes. Nevertheless, the leaders still wondered if their knowledge of change management was still sufficiently current and advanced, for now and for the future. We asked them to state the aspects of change for which, in their opinion, they had sufficient in-house knowledge. They mentioned strategic developments, economic analyses and management control, and they referred to what Bower (2000) calls the 'systemic culture'. The latter is about control as programmed in the system of mission, values, reward systems, performance guidance, tasks-responsibilities-competences, the process of resource allocation, selection and promotion, training and development of employees and adjustment—to name but a few.

A strongly developed system of control is a positive point, but when changing circumstances require a change of course, such a positive point can become a millstone around your neck. The adage that structure follows strategy is then turned upside down: strategy follows structure (Eppink & ten Have, 2008). Strikwerda (2011) points out that the majority of enterprises forget to translate a new strategy into an adjusted systemic culture. As a consequence the activities set out to execute the new strategy are not determined by that new strategy, but by the old systemic culture. Culture grows into a product of success and failure, of what can and cannot be rewarded or punished. Culture influences the system of control, which in turn further reinforces culture through socialization, indoctrination, stimulating or demanding appropriate behaviour. Schein defines culture as follows: '*A pattern of* **basic assumptions**—*invented, discovered or developed by a group as it solved its problems of* **external adaptation** *and* **internal integration**—that has worked well enough to be considered valid and, therefore, to be taught to new members as the correct way to perceive, think and feel in relation to those problems'* (Schein, 1985, p. 9, our translation). In the briefing of the aforementioned multinational it was noted that culture change would be a point of interest, which, with the help of what went before, is understandable. There is a successful business model that gave rise to a particular culture. Except that they are not sure that this current culture will remain the cornerstone of the organization, or whether they can come up with a new systemic context. This critical self-reflection of an indisputably successful company can certainly be called positive. In the context of this case, it is interesting to see what Strikwerda (2002) has to say about advice and advisers: 'Modern organization advisers must not only know the socio-psychological aspects of organizational change (knowledge that is rather superficial in many advisers); the modern adviser must also be well versed in institutional economic analyses (this is on a different level than the quantitative analyses for strategy) and management control in the modern sense to be able to serve clients'.[2] Considering what the organization that approached us did and did not experience as problematic, it mostly focused on the former. Even though behaviour and culture were discussed extensively in our first meeting, they failed to mention social psychology. This multinational is not the only one. A leading social psychologist who has been working for decades to release his insights into that discipline in order to feed change management is Edgar Schein, one of the founders of the change management profession. In an interview with Diane Coutu in 2002 he confessed at the age of 74: "When I left Walter Reed for my first job at MIT, my mentor Douglas McGregor said to me: 'Ed, we took you on as a social psychologist, not as a management expert. So find out what social psychology can do for the things that managers think are relevant' ".[3] Weick and Lewin have also done research on that. Thanks to their work, the field of social psychology has opened up to answer questions that are relevant to managers, and to contribute to the solutions of their problems. Strikwerda (2002) correctly stated that advisers must know the socio-psychological aspects of organizational change. The same obviously applies to managers and other participants in the field. Strikwerda also correctly noted that this knowledge is too superficial, if not entirely absent, in many advisers and managers. In other words, the available socio-psychological knowledge is insufficiently utilized. The socio-psychological knowledge being propagated is also responsible for this 'shortage'. The example of the more than fifty bestsellers on change management (ten Have et al., 2017) mentioned earlier clearly illustrates that the quality and availability and how they are presented leave a lot to be desired.

Social Psychology in Four Core Insights

The availability can be improved by employing four core insights. The first insight clearly shows why social psychology, 'tout court', is relevant to change management: it is about people and people are social beings. The second shows why cohesion and methodization are important: there are a number of psychological forces and factors at play during change and that requires a combination of a variety of theories and insights. In that context, Rijsman (1990) refers to 'an inventory of social influences'. The third is about the central mechanism in social systems during change, which is to assign meaning. For instance, a mission, values or a reward system as such do next to nothing. They only 'do', or accomplish, something if they are meaningful to the people involved. With meaning as a starting point it becomes clear why social psychology, which revolves around social interaction, is so relevant. The fourth insight pushes back on the optimistic rhetoric which is typical of the many books, gurus and consultants in the change management segment. People act and react in a variety of ways in social environments. Especially during change it is essential to be able to explain, understand and predict; social psychology is ideal for supplying people with the tools for that. The four core insights are explained in depth next.

Core Insight 1—People Are Social Animals and Change in Organizations Is a Social Process

An analysis of the most important manuals shows that there are literally more than 100 relevant socio-psychological theories and models for change management. There is a lot available, including the necessary evidence. However, what is missing is the overview, the categorization and the relevance in relation to change management. A theory like the one of social affirmation (Cohen & Sherman, 2014) has already been studied and 'translated' in relation to change. But this step has still not been taken for most theories, or at least not sufficiently. Take, for instance, cognitive dissonance, planned behaviour, expectations, social identity, equity, conformity and social justice. From the perspective of change management these theories do not rise above the level of data, in a manner of speaking. For the time being, it is about data without meaning (Bots & Jansen, 2013). It only becomes information once the relevance of a theory for change management has been determined and, as with social affirmation, the 'translation' has been made. Knowledge is only created once this information has been selected, interpreted, combined and valued and, consequently, has enabled people to complete particular tasks (in this case, a manager or an adviser who gives change form and content) (Bertrams, 1999).

Social psychology teaches us that people are social beings (Fiske, 2010) or social animals (Aronson, 2016) and that change is a social process (Weick, 1979). It lets people be people again and makes change human. People are no longer objects (a fulltime-equivalent, fte, an employee, a resource, a project officer), but subjects. A subject which has needs and shows reactions, creates meaning through coordinated (inter)action with other subjects (Rijsman, 1997). Lewin's work shows us that in a concrete change situation one must obtain insight into all the forces or factors that influence change in relation to one another. Especially in complex change situations, many of factors come into play. An initial step is to come to a first temporary 'static' order, an *inventory* of social influences (Rijsman, 1990). That inventory offers an overview of relevant factors, but not yet how it operates in the field. The question is, what should that order or that model be like? One possibility is to classify the theories on the basis of subject matters that are relevant to change, such as leadership, organization and communication. One can also decide to include distinctions between the individual, intra- and inter-groups and the organization. In relation to change, however, it seems to be more fruitful to have the concept of the social being link up with what mobilizes or inhibits people, and what helps or obstructs them.

In that context, Fiske introduced (2010, p. 14) the 'social core motives': 'fundamental, underlying psychological processes that determine the thoughts, feelings and behaviour of people in situations in which they have to deal with others'. The five motives of social animals are: belonging, understanding, controlling, trusting and enhancing self. *Belonging* stands for the idea that for people to survive psychologically and physically they need stable relationships with others. This need is linked to theories on, for instance, social cohesion, conformity and prosocial behaviour. *Understanding* refers to the desire of people to understand their environment, to predict and to assign meaning. The attribution theory and the social representation theory apply here. *Controlling* stimulates people to deal effectively with their environment. Relevant theories for this are, for instance, the expectations theory and the cognitive dissonance theory. *Trusting* is about seeing 'the world' or one's own context as a good, safe and trustworthy place. Relevant theories in this context include that of fair process, equity and moral disengagement. *Enhancing self* is about self-confidence, a positive self-image or being motivated to grow or to improve oneself. Relevant theories include that of self-efficacy ('action control'), social reinforcement and self-affirmation. The motives and the relevant theories and insights offer an initial overview of and insight into ideas that can be useful in identifying the behaviour of social beings in situations of change. That alone will probably already prevent rash qualifications and stigmatization, and help change management to advance.

Core Insight 2—Social Psychology Is Necessary to Understand People in Change Processes

Bower (2000) positions the systemic context as the determining factor in change. The system that includes mission, values, strategy, structure, systems and means aimed at development and socialization, such as training and courses, is a strong determining factor for the behaviour of organizations and groups. That system, which carries in it a 'dominant logic', is the result of behaviour learned earlier, often because of success. That is why Schein (2001, p. 37) defines the organization's culture as 'the sum of all commonly held assumptions that a group has learned during its lifetime'. If one wants to change, then one must change that dominant logic, the culture. Tinkering with the systemic context can seem an attractive option.

But it is not as easy as that. It is true that a change in the reward system, a new organizational structure, the introduction of 'Agile' or a new leader can achieve the desired behavioural effects. But if they are accomplished, these effects usually do not last long. An important initial explanation for this is that with this type of isolated or one-dimensional intervention the systemic context does not automatically change. A change of the systemic context requires *breadth*: factors such as mission, strategy and structure must be tackled in a complete and coordinated way, in other words, integrally. A second explanation has to do with *depth*: sweeping changes are not purely technical; they are adaptive (Heifetz, Grashow, & Linsky, 2009). These changes touch on what is essential and valuable to groups and individuals. They are concerned with basic assumptions, emotions, values and identity. The systemic context offers insight and comfort when it comes to the importance and the workings of integration and the 'breadth' of interventions. However, if we want to understand more about the 'depth', how change 'works' on and for the people involved, then more is required.

Social psychology and Lewin's field theory (1943a,b) certainly offer 'more'. Lewin states that if one does not understand the current situation, or which forces and factors maintain this situation, even the beginning of change is far off. The field theory helps individuals and groups to explore, understand and learn about themselves. In the process, subjects interact with subjects. It is all about participatory learning, a process in which groups and individuals are in fact 'seen' and involved. Lewin considered this type of learning as the beginning of a change process. He believes that real change demands that you determine which concrete forces or factors must be changed in a specific context, and what the (possible) effects of the forces or factors might be. In other words, the change manager will have to identify the various possible change options and analyse them, make a selection from them, and then proceed to implement the selected changes (Burnes & Cooke, 2012). It is for that reason that Lewin emphasizes the importance of group dynamics. His field theory offers a holistic, systemic perspective on the entire *psychological* environment of individuals and groups. It makes the earlier static list of social influences come alive, makes it dynamic and offers a view of how change can work in the field.

Core Insight 3—Social Psychology Teaches Us That Meaning Is Key During Change and Intervention

Like Lewin, Weick is inextricably connected to the socio-psychological perspective in change management. A central concept in this context is sense-making—creating meaning. What Weick means by this is the process in which and with which people as subjects give meaning to their collective experiences. With this he offers a socio-psychological alternative to the dominant, mostly sociological, perspective on organizations where decision-making is the core question and structure the key word. In the decision-making process the core question is connected to the answer: what is the best decision? In Weick's perspective it is connected to the question: what makes sense, what does it matter? This last question precedes the decision-making process. While the dominant perspective tries to limit uncertainty and a lack of clarity as much as possible beforehand, Weick embraces it. They are necessary to determine, in interaction, what matters, what has (which) meaning.

The process of creating meaning is endless, which is one of the reasons why Weick (1979) prefers to talk about organizing instead of organization. When he finally does define organization, he refers to it as 'a body of thought, thought by thinking thinkers' (Weick, 1979, p. 42); that is how meanings are created. Those meanings can be individual at first, but in the context of groups and organizations they ultimately become (partially) collective and are shared. Meaning creation is a social process (Weick, 1995). The interaction with the others is of great importance. At the same time, organizations are more than just the direct interaction among people. Organizations are—also—based on generic intersubjectivity that is reflected in structures, systems, policy, responsibilities and roles, to name but a few. Weick (1995) juxtaposes the generic with the intersubjective; he sees the coordination of the various realities that arise from the tension between these two as the heart of organizing. The generic relates to Bower's systemic context, the intersubjectivity of the field theory and Lewin's group dynamics.

Core Insight 4—Social Psychology Makes Change Management Comprehensible to People and Allows Them to Consider Their Actions in Groups and the Organization on Their Merits

This core insight could also have been described as: social psychology is necessary in order to understand people in change processes. Social animals are complex beings. This becomes quite apparent when these beings have to change. By analogy with a statement by the well-known organization adviser and later professor Berenschot, we can say: 'Change is easy, but the people. . . .' If managers and advisers want to be effective, they must know their business, including the people and the groups they will be dealing with. The 'first law' of social psychologist Aronson (2016) is: 'People who do mad things aren't necessarily mad' (p. 9). It is not productive to label divergent, unexpected, 'weird' or 'incomprehensible' behaviour as 'psychotic' or 'resistant'. It is much more useful to understand or influence the context, interactions and processes this behaviour produces. People are 'subjects', not 'objects'; they are not pawns or standard units but beings with their own particular emotions, eccentricities, talents, vulnerabilities, possibilities and limitations. Change management cannot and should not ignore this. In a sense, change management is a world of highs and lows: most publications on the topic focus first on the failure percentages and go on and on about the many things that can go wrong—only to subsequently introduce a new narrative or model that most certainly is successful. They are often presented with boastful titles and happy, positive messages. In doing so, gurus and consultants are betting in a very idealistic way on the ability to shape and develop people and organizations. Change is positive and should be exciting.

Change management is better served by evidence and realism, less so by superficial and naïve approaches. When it comes to that, social psychology offers comfort by showing what people are capable of in social contexts as well as in groups. It is not always 'nice'. Take Stanley Milgram's world-famous obedience experiments: a majority of the participants[4] followed the orders of legitimate authorities, even when they conflicted with their conscience. Diane Coutu[5] also points out that books about learning and change are full of 'optimistic rhetoric': in his interview with her, Schein says that learning and the change that comes with that is a complex process. No wonder that he keeps referring to his work with American soldiers that had been Korean prisoners of war when he talks about change, culture, learning and the dynamics between groups. He compares the indoctrination of prisoners of war by Chinese communists with the indoctrination methods and the coercive persuasion employed by companies such as IBM and GE. As a social psychologist, Schein makes sure that we take off our rose-coloured glasses. For example, the social bond that deals with strength and discipline influences resistance and the willingness to lie.

Unleashing the Change Management Potential of Social Psychology

In essence, change management is about behavioural change in individuals and groups. The core insights clearly show that, and how, one must look during change at the social process, the psychological environment, the process of giving meaning and people as social beings: subjects instead of objects. With these insights, the leaders of the multinational mentioned will from now on probably come up with strategies and approaches for change and interventions from the perspective of people as social animals who need to understand the situation, to belong somewhere, to grow, to have a grip on things and mutual trust. With these socio-psychological insights one can better understand that change is not primarily about the object-subject relationship—for instance, the one between a new organizational structure or a new work method such as 'Agile' and the employees. The primary focus is on the subject-subject relationship, on the interaction between the people involved and the meaning that it brings forth. In addition, the people in the multinational will focus more on 'seeing' the entire psychological field, and in doing so be better capable of looking more integrally at the change issues and be aware that they should not use the 'odd' intervention for complex changes. The systemic context, with factors such as the structure and the reward systems, will now be combined with attention to the psychological context, from a realization that people should be judged on their merits, with their strengths and weaknesses, and taking into account the light and dark sides. That does not tolerate optimistic rhetoric; it requires a vision and the right tools with which to 'take care of and tame where necessary' the social animals to serve the prosperity and welfare of all. To do that, the socio-psychology insights are essential. Although the insights of social psychologists like Lewin, Schein and Weick may have taken hold in the change management profession, there is still so much knowledge to discover in social psychology. Let us not only wake up social psychology's 'sleeping giant', but also let the change management profession itself wake up and embrace the giant's socio-psychological insights.

The Approach and Structure of the Book

This book is a mutual reach-out between social psychology and change management. We present approximately forty social psychological theories and models, ranging from attribution theory and expectancy theory to social dominance and social identity theory, and from social cohesion and social exchange theory to moral disengagement and the attachment theory. The theories are structured, categorized and related to one another by a model that results from the integration of Fiske's five core social motives and our change management methodology (ten Have et al., 2015; ten Have et al., 2016). From the perspective of change management and its practitioners and researchers, the theories are without exception inspiring, sometimes thought-provoking, insightful, informative, helpful and hence relevant. Almost without exception the models are 'classic' and based on well-founded empirical research. This constitutes an important reason and criterion to select them. A second criterion is the estimated potential and relevance from the perspective of change management. This book is evidence-based. The focus of this book and our research is on research and resulting evidence related to the application of theories in the field of change and organization, management and leadership. Research and evidence with regard to the theories as such is only presented for reasons of illustration, explanation and positioning (of the theories).

The next chapter focuses on the model and methodology used. The core social motives, the change methodology and the evidence-based perspective and method are further introduced. After Chapter 2, Chapters 3, 4, 5, 6 and 7 will present the social psychological theories and evidence related to the field of change and organization. Each chapter focuses on one of Fiske's core social motives and theories (primarily) related to them. Chapter 3 is about belonging and related theories such as social cohesion and conformity. Chapter 4 focuses on understanding; theories such as social representation theory and attribution theory are presented. In Chapter 5 the social motive of controlling is further introduced by using theories such as expectancy theory and the theory of planned behaviour. In Chapter 6 the perspective is that of trusting; concepts such as fair process, attachment theory and moral disengagement are presented. Chapter 7 concerns the fifth core social motive, self-enhancing, and its relationship with and relevance to change management. Theories such as social reinforcement, social facilitation and self-esteem are further introduced. The final chapter, 8, is dedicated to integration and reflection—what are the lessons and insights and their relationships from social psychology for the field of change management and what does a more evidence-based, systematic and integrative approach bring to practice and research.

Notes

1. This chapter is based on the article 'Naar een sociale psychologie voor gedragsverandering in organisaties' published in Holland Management Review (2018).
2. www.managementsite.nl/organisationalchange-opgesloten-verkeerde-modellen.
3. Interview by Diane Coutu, originally published under the title 'Edgar H. Schein: The Anxiety of Learning' in March 2002 in the *Harvard Business Review* and in *O&O* (2014, # 2) in a Dutch translation.
4. In the most famous experiment 66%, 43% over the entire series.
5. See note 2.

2   Model and Methodology

The highest activity a human being can attain is learning for understanding, because to understand is to be free.

—Baruch Spinoza (1632–1677, Epistles)

Introduction

To unleash the change management potential of social psychology, we have selected defining theories and models from the field of social psychology. Social psychology can be defined as the science explaining how people influence other people. Fiske (2004) points to the classic definition of Gordon Allport, one of social psychology's pioneers: "Social psychology is the scientific attempt to understand and explain how the thoughts, feelings and behaviours of individuals are influenced by the actual, imagined or implied presence of other human beings" (in: Allport & Lindzey, 1954, p. 5). For this book a 'longlist' of more than 100 theories has been assessed by using the criteria of prominence, relevance and evidence. In this way, we selected approximately forty 'leading' social psychological theories for change management. To categorize these theories, we embraced the five core social motives (which are also five unifying themes in social psychology) of Fiske (2004). The essential idea of Fiske (2004) is that "*a small number of essential, core social motives enhance people's survival in groups*" and that this "offers a unifying framework for understanding the field of social psychology" (p. 15). We add: and for making social psychology (better) available and (more) accessible from the perspective of organizations in general and change management in particular. In addition to the introduction of these five 'categories', we introduced our own visualization in order to combine categorization and integration; the five motives are related perspectives. Together these form a dynamic system in which motives interact and have (causal) relationships and dependencies (like the issues and topics they address and the social psychological theories and concepts to which they relate). For example, understanding can positively influence controlling and trusting can be a precondition for self-enhancing. Fiske also addresses the interactions and combinations of motives. She makes use of these to address important social psychological issues and concepts. For example, Fiske presents schemas and expectations by stating that 'people trust and understand the familiar'. Other examples: the concept of attachment is addressed by combining belonging and trusting, interdependence by controlling and trusting, and social norms by belonging and understanding. Discussing social influence and in particular compliance, Fiske uses three motives. She introduces compliance as: 'strategies to understand self, maintain belonging and control resources'. Obedience is also defined by combining (in this case four) social motives: 'belonging, controlling, trusting and understanding by doing what others say' (all examples: Fiske, 2004, p. xv).

After selecting and categorizing the theories, we applied a rapid evidence assessment (REA) to each of them. Based on this and the theory itself, we have described the importance, relevance and potential of each theory for the field of change management. The theory itself was discussed in our team in order to define the possible contribution to the field of change and organization. This was primarily a deductive process of consensual validation carried out by experienced practitioners and scientists. The REA was focused on specific research on the theories applied to the field of change and organization. This was primarily an inductive process carried out by a team of analysts that delivered the REAs to the team of authors.

In summary, the purpose of our research and this book is threefold. The first aim is to further unlock the potential contribution of social psychology as a source for change management as a discipline and practice in a comprehensive, systematic and structured way ('encyclopaedic'). The second aim is to assess the available social psychological theories, concepts and research and fuel change management with the evidence and insights found (evidence-based, scientific). The third aim is to present, categorize and integrate the theories and findings by using a framework based on five core social motives (Fiske, 2004) and our change management methodology (ten Have et al., 2015) (cohesive, systemic, practical). The overarching goal, however, inspired by the ideas and perspective of leading thinkers like Kurt Lewin, James Q. Wilson and Susan T. Fiske, is to make the world a better place. Social psychologists (being social scientists) study practical social issues, in our case issues related to change management, and application to real-world problems is a key goal. As Fiske (2004) states: "Social psychologists believe that if we understand how people influence one another, then perhaps we can understand and ameliorate some of the negative influences. Social psychology is in some ways a field for idealists" (p. 33). In addition, Fiske emphasizes that in the end social psychology searches for wisdom, not just knowledge. This provides valuable extra guidance for the way in which social psychology has to be applied to the set of social issues we call change management: "Wisdom may be considered knowledge about people and the world, combined with enduring moral, intellectual and societal concerns, that makes sense in the context of people's lived experience" (p. 33).

In this chapter, we describe and explain the model based on the five core social motives (cohesive, systemic, see the section 'A Dynamic and Integrative Model of Social Motives'), the selection of leading social psychological theories ('encyclopaedic', see the section 'A Selection of Leading Social Psychological Theories') and the evidence-based methodology, the REA and the formats used in order to describe the theories and their contribution to change management (evidence-based, scientific, see 2.4).

A Dynamic and Integrative Model of Social Motives

The famous Noam Chomsky, linguist, cognitive scientist and social critic, once stated: "There are no magic answers, no miraculous methods to overcome the problems we face, just the familiar ones: honest search for understanding, education, organization, action that raises the cost of state violence for its perpetrators or that lays the basis for institutional change—and the kind of commitment that will persist despite the temptations of disillusionment, despite many failures and only limited successes, inspired by the hope of a brighter future". He relates change to commitment and resilience, but above all to true learning. His perspective is not an individual one, but that of our world, societies, communities and groups. His audience consists of people who are not only individuals, but also, and maybe above all, social animals. Elliot Aronson (2016) introduced the social animal and as a consequence positioned social psychology (as extremely important) from an implicit, yet strong belief. This implicit or, as Aronson says, secret belief is that social psychologists are in a unique position to have a 'profound and beneficial impact on our lives'. This impact is carried by the increased knowledge and understanding of such important phenomena and concepts as trust, conformity, belongingness, social reinforcement, persuasion and cooperation. Social psychology can fuel a learning process. However, it is confronted with human beings who are not only *social* animals, but also '*learned* animals'. These learned animals are Janus-faced. Boorstein (1998) states: "If we are awed by the powers of man, the learned animal, we must also be appalled that he has been such a slow learner. And there has been no greater obstacle to his learning than the stock of accumulated learning that he has made for himself with his illusions of knowledge". The learned animal is developed by theories and concepts related to the social phenomena Aronson points to. The animal is hampered by biases (like the confirmation bias, the courtesy bias and the just world bias) *and* by outdated or incomplete knowledge and a limited awareness of and insight into the available evidence. To create the impact mentioned by Aronson, people have to be or become knowers *and* learners, together. David Boulton (1987, p. 1) underlines this: "And what of foundations, institutions, governments and social movements? Are they really any different? Unless their intent is to manipulate people, what is more important to their missions than learning about facilitating social learning? What is an elected official, but an elected social learner? Isn't it their jobs to find out what is really going on and what can be done to enhance individual and social quality of life? What school can ensure that their curriculum will prepare tomorrow's leaders for the swiftness of the ever-new complexities they will face daily? How can someone who was once an attorney or business person and is now newly elected to office come to understand the root causes of child abuse, welfare dependency, the ecological implications of factory X at location Y or the sweeping changes occurring in international relations? The most important characteristic of an effective leader is his or her ability to learn".

In Chapter 1, we built a first layer for the foundation of the knowledge transfer and learning process needed to be able to use social psychology as a source of impact. By introducing the four core insights, we described the importance and relevance of social psychology for change and change management. In this chapter, a second layer is constructed. The main ingredients or bricks are the more than 100 selected theories and concepts from social psychology. With regard to impact on specific change and change management, we have judged these ingredients to be fit for purpose. But from both a knowing and a learning perspective, not to mention application in practice, more than 100 ideas and angles are to say the least not that manageable. We have therefore chosen to categorize and to model them. The first categorization is based on Fiske's (2004) social core motives that have already been introduced: belonging, understanding, controlling, trusting and enhancing self. These motives are "fundamental, underlying psychological processes that impel people's thinking, feeling and behaving in situations involving other people" (Fiske, 2010, p. 14). The model that structures this book is based on these five core motives and their relative position, relationship or interaction and interdependency. But before we explain the model further, we discuss the value and functions of models as such and as learning aids.

The use of models as learning aids has two primary benefits (Gage & Berliner, 1992). The first benefit is that models provide "accurate and useful representations of knowledge that is needed when solving problems in some particular domain" (p. 314). In addition, a model makes the process of understanding a domain of knowledge easier because it is a visual expression of the topic. Research (Gage & Berliner, 1992) shows that students who study models before a lecture may recall as much as 57% more on questions concerning conceptual information. This is compared with students who receive instruction without the advantage of seeing and discussing models. Other studies, like Alessandrini (1981), who studied different pictorial-verbal strategies for learning, came to similar conclusions. A model can be seen as a 'mnemonic'.

A mnemonic is any learning technique that aids information retention or retrieval in the human memory. A mnemonic enables people to remember and mobilize longlists of information (Gazzaniga & Heatherton, 2006), like more than 100 social psychological ideas. The use of visual imagery is an especially effective mnemonic. A historical variant is related to monks placing specific knowledge in a systematic way in certain spaces in their monastery. This is the *method of loci*; placing objects like categories, subcategories or ideas in familiar locations, retrieving them by going back to these locations. A similar technique is learning a list of key words, or pegs, and then categorizing new words with these pegs by visualizing them together. Mnemonics help original information become associated with something more accessible or meaningful—which, in turn, provides better retention of the information. In this book, Fiske's social core motives are the five spaces in which, or the umbrellas under which, the more than a hundred ideas are organized in a meaningful and accessible way. In addition, these spaces are visualized and in a way construct a 'monastery' full of categorized and interrelated social psychological ideas.

According to Fiske (2004), the underlying principle of the model is oriented towards the (better) survival of 'the social animal': "All five motives orient toward making people fit better into groups, thus increasing their chances for survival" (p. 16). From this perspective, chance of survival or chance for change (in order to adapt to changing circumstances, contexts, conditions or demands) could be defined as the sum of its parts. The parts are the five social core motives: belonging, understanding, controlling, trusting and enhancing self. However, one can also see it as more (or even less) than the sum of its parts. The motives can be seen as interrelated, in positive or negative ways, in terms of synergies or trade-offs and antagonisms. One can imagine that there is a synergy between understanding and controlling, that a lack of trust can hamper a feeling of belongingness and that there could be a trade-off between controlling and trusting. From the perspective of the social animal and its biotope, the group (being a family, a team, etc.) or organization (being a company, a society, etc.), the motives cannot be separated in real life. They are interrelated and interdependent, together constituting the connective being that the social animal is in a dynamic way defining its biotope; its social environment in maybe even a more dynamic way. As illustrated in the first chapter, Fiske also combines and interrelates the social motives in order to define and make sense of social psychological concepts like obedience, social norms and compliance. Fiske (2004) defines her idea as a unifying framework for understanding the field of social psychology. In describing the relationships among core social motives, Fiske positions belonging as the principal motive and defines understanding and controlling as relatively cognitive motives and trusting and self-enhancing as relatively affective motives (Table 2.1).

Table 2.1 Relationships Among Core Social Motives (Fiske, 2010)

Belonging			
Need for Strong, Stable Relationships			
Relatively Cognitive Motives		*Relatively Affective Motives*	
Understanding	*Controlling*	*Trusting*	*Self-enhancing*
Need for shared meaning and prediction	Need for perceived contingency between behaviour and outcomes	Need for seeing others as basically benign	Need for viewing self as basically worthy or improvable

In a schematic way, one could envisage a cognitive and an affective axis, with belonging as the principal motive of the social animal or the quintessence at the very heart or crossing. To illustrate the interrelatedness or connectivity between the motives and the continuous interaction among the five motives and between the motives and specific contexts, one could introduce dynamism by using the lemniscate instead of the axis. The lemniscate shape bears an intrinsic dynamic component and entails continuously returning movements instead of linear lines. The uninterrupted lines, without a start and end point, can be equated to the iterative process that characterizes the positive or negative development of the social animal and its social relationships. The five social core motives and their mutual interconnectivity can be shown through two lemniscates and a connecting circle, a magnification of the central social motive, belonging (Figure 2.1).

In this way, we categorize *and* connect the motives and hence the theories. In the coming five chapters, we elaborate on each of the core social motives by relating them to the approximately forty (out of more than 100) theories and models that are most relevant from a change management perspective. There is an additional reason for using the introduced visualization or modelling. The basic, dynamic form was initially developed for and applied and tested in the field of change management (ten Have et al., 2015). This change competence model for purposive change is aimed at helping to answer the core question in addressing 'purposive change': 'What should it be, and how should it be accomplished?' (Bower, 2000). The first part is about the direction, idea or change vision, and the second part about the execution, the feasibility or change capacity (Figure 2.2).

Change vision is visualized as the vertical axis or lemniscate and is defined as the key factor for change rationale and effect in connection. Change capacity, the horizontal part, is construed in terms of focus and energy in connection. The combination of the two models, the social

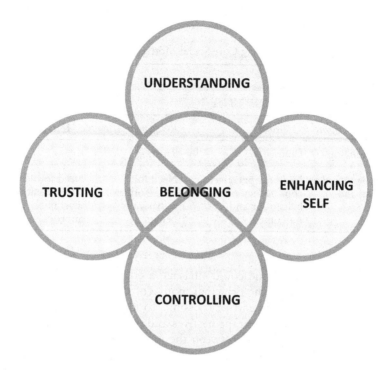

Figure 2.1 The Five Motives Ordered Using the Lemniscate

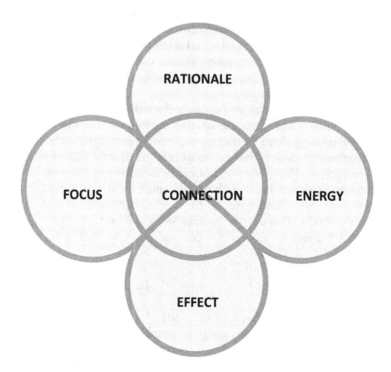

Figure 2.2 Change Competence Model

psychological model based on the five social motives and the change competence model based on the five key factors for change, which share at least the schematic, visual and conceptual similarities, may provide additional insights and learnings with regard to (toward) a social psychology of change management. We reflect on this in the final chapter (8), after the presentation of and discussion with regard to the insights and evidence on approximately forty social psychological theories in the context of organization and change (Chapters 3 to 7).

In addition to the categorization and positioning of the theories, each theory or model is assessed with the help of the most relevant and best available scientific evidence ('rapid evidence assessment', REA). For each theory or model and its evidence we describe the relevance, consequences or learnings for change management. In the chapters, the forty leading theories and models are combined with other also relevant theories and models and insights from the change management field and its most popular books. In this chapter, we give a first illustrative overview for each core social motive of relevant theories, models and insights.

We start with belonging as the principal core social motive. That is followed by the relatively cognitive motives, understanding and controlling. In addition, we illustrate and envisage the domains of the affective motives, trusting and self-enhancing. In doing this, and in the elaboration of the motives in the following chapters, there is mainly a static categorization and description of theories and models. Where relevant, the interaction or dynamics with other social motives or related theories is mentioned or discussed. The social psychological theories and models are attributed to the motive with the best or most relevant fit. Some theories and models can be related to more than one motive. For some others the relationship to more than one is in fact illustrative; these concern the relationships or interaction among core social motives.

A Selection of Leading Social Psychological Theories

Given the challenges of people and organizations in this world, change management is a discipline worth developing. In doing this, we can and must stand on the shoulders of giants like Lewin, Schein, Weick, Argyris and Oreg. They have built change management as a discipline primarily from the (social) psychological perspective. This is visible in the body of knowledge that characterizes change management and defining topics like leadership, employee behaviour, communication and organizational development. Again, social psychology is defined as a "scientific attempt to understand and explain how the thoughts, feelings and behaviours of individuals are influenced by the actual, imagined or implied presence of other human beings" (Allport & Lindzey, 1954, p. 5). Given this focus and its strong and fruitful research tradition, social psychology is a treasure house and provides change management with a very relevant and rich perspective. However, if we look at the literature available to and used by practitioners, scientists and students, the question could be whether the return of this perspective can be improved for science and practice. Our answer is 'yes', and more precisely: 'yes, by presenting social psychological concepts, insights and research which are or might be relevant to change management in an evidence-based, encyclopaedic and cohesive way and thus systematic, structured and accessible'. This contributes to filling the gap that is visible in popular management books on change. It also complements the insights provided by rich and relevant books like *The Routledge Companion to Organizational Change* (Boje, Burnes, & Hassard, 2012) and *The Psychology of Leadership, Change and Organizational Development* (Oreg, Michel, & Todnem, 2013). An analysis of the fifty-four most popular management books, listed in Table 2.2,

Table 2.2 Books and Book Chapters Reviewed and Analyzed

Allen, R. C. (2002). *Guiding change journeys: A synergistic approach to organization transformation.* San Francisco, CA: Jossey-Bass and Pfeiffer Publishers.

Anderson, L. A., & Anderson, D. (2010). *The change leader's roadmap.* San Francisco, CA: Jossey Bass Publishers.

Augustine, N. R. (1998). Reshaping an industry: Lockheed Martin's survival story. In: *Harvard business review on change* (pp. 159–187). Boston, MA: Harvard Business School.

Beer, M., & Nohria, N. (2000). *Breaking the code of change* (pp. 83–95). Boston, MA: Harvard Business School Press.

Belasco, J. A. (1990). *Teaching the elephant to dance. Empowering change in your organization.* New York, NY: Crown Publishers.

Blanchard, K., & Miller, M. (2014). *The secret: What great leaders know and do.* San Francisco, CA: Berrett-Koehler Publishers.

Bridges, W., & Mitchel, S. (2002). Leading transition: A new model for change. In F. Hesselbein & R. Johnson (Eds.), *On leading change* (pp. 33–47). San Francisco, CA: Jossey-Bass Publishers.

Bridges, W. (1991). *Managing transitions: Making the most of change.* Reading, MA: Perseus Books.

Brown, T. (2009). *Change by design: How design thinking transforms organizations and inspires innovation.* Broadway, NY: HarperCollins Publishers.

Cameron, K., & Quinn, R. (2011). *Diagnosing and changing organizational culture.* Reading, MA: Addison Wesley Longman.

Collins, J. C. (2001). *From good to great.* New York, NY: HarperCollins Publishers.

Collins, J. C. (2009). *How the mighty fall: And why some companies never give in.* New York, NY: Random House.

Collins, J. C., & Porras, J. I. (1996). Building your company's vision. *Harvard Business Review, 74*(5), 65.

Conner, D. (2006). *Managing at the speed of change.* New York, NY: Random House.

Connors, R., & Smith, T. (2011). *Change the culture, change the game: The breakthrough strategy for energizing your organization and creating accountability for results.* New York, NY: Random House.

Davidson, J. (2002). *The complete idiot's guide to change management.* Indianapolis: Alpha Books.

Duck, J. D. (1998). Managing change: The art of balancing. In: *Harvard business review on change* (pp. 55–83). Boston, MA: Harvard Business School.

Dupuy, F. (2002). *The chemistry of change.* New York, NY: John Wiley & Sons.

Eckes, G. (2001). *Making six sigma last: Managing the balance between cultural and technical change.* New York, NY: John Wiley and Sons.

Ghoshal, S, & Bartlett, C. A. (2000). Rebuilding behavioural context: A blueprint for corporate renewal. In: M. Beer & N. Nohria (Eds.), *Breaking the code of change* (pp. 195–222). Boston, MA: Harvard Business School.

Goleman, D. (2015). *On emotional intelligence.* Boston, MA: Harvard Business Review Press.

Goss, T., Pascale, R., & Athos, A. (1998). The reinvention roller coaster: Risking the present for a powerful future. In: *Harvard business review on change* (pp. 83–112). Boston, MA: Harvard Business School.

Heath, C., & Heath, D. (2010). *Switch: How to change things when change is hard.* New York, NY: Broadway Books.

Heifetz, R. A., Grashow, A., & Linsky, M. (2009). *The practice of adaptive leadership: Tools and tactics for changing your organization and the world.* Boston, MA: Harvard Business Press.

Heller, J. (1998). *Essential managers: Managing change.* New York: D. K. Publishing.

Hesselbein, F. (2000). The key to cultural transformation. In: F. Hesselbein & R. Johnston (Eds.), *A leader to leader guide* (pp. 1–6). San Francisco, CA: Jossey-Bass Publishers.

Hirschhorn, L. (2000). Changing structure is not enough: The moral meaning of organizational design. In: M. Beer & N. Nohria (Eds.), *Breaking the code of change* (pp. 161–176). Boston, MA: Harvard Business School.

Holman, P., & Devane, T. (Eds.). (1999). *The change handbook.* San Francisco, CA: Berrett-Koehler Publishers.

Humble, J., Molesky, J., & O'Reilly, B. (2015). *Lean enterprise: How high performance organizations innovate at scale.* Sebastopol, CA: O'Reilly Media.

Ibarra, H. (2015). *Act like a leader, think like a leader.* Boston, MA: Harvard Business Review Press.

Kanter, R. M. (2002). The enduring skills of change leaders. In F. Hesselbein & R. Johnston (Eds.), *On leading change* (pp. 47–61). San Francisco, CA: Jossey-Bass Publishers.

Kegan, R., & Lahey, L. (2001). *How the way we talk can change the way we work.* New York: John Wiley & Sons.

Kegan, R., & Lahey, L. (2009). *Immunity to change: How to overcome it and unlock the potential in yourself and your organization.* Boston, MA: Harvard Business Press.

Kimsey-House, K., & Kimsey-House, H. (2015). *Co-active leadership: Five ways to lead.* San Francisco, CA: Berrett-Koehler Publishers.

Kotter, J. P. (1996). *Leading change.* Boston, MA: Harvard Business Press.

Kotter, J. P. (1998). Leading change: Why transformation efforts fail. In: *Harvard business review on change* (pp. 1–21). Boston, MA: Harvard Business School.

Kotter, J. P., & Cohen, D. S. (2004). *The heart of change: Real-life stories of how people change their organizations.* Recording for the Blind & Dyslexic.

(Continued)

Table 2.2 (Continued)

Kouzes, J., & Posner, B. (2012). *The leadership challenge: How to make extraordinary things happen in organizations.* San Francisco, CA: Jossey-Bass Publishers.

Kriegel, R. J., & Brandt, D. (1996). *Sacred cows make the best burgers.* New York, NY: Warner Books, Inc.

Laloux, F. (2014). *Reinventing organizations: A guide to creating organizations inspired by the next stage of human consciousness.* Brussel, BE: Nelson Parker.

Langley, G. J., Moen, R., Nolan, K. M., Nolan, T. W., Norman, C. L., & Provost, L. P. (2009). *The improvement guide: A practical approach to enhancing organizational performance.* San Francisco, CA: Jossey-Bass Publishers.

Larkin, T., & Larkin, S. (1994). *Communicating change: Winning employee support for new business goals.* New York, NY: McGraw-Hill.

Lewis, L. K., Schmisseur, A. M., Stephens, K. K., & Weir, K. E. (2006). Advice on communicating during organizational change the content of popular press books. *Journal of Business Communication, 43*(2), 113–137.

Liedtka, J., & Ogilvie, T. (2011). *Designing for growth: A design thinking tool kit for managers.* New York, NY: Columbia University Press.

Lipman-Blumen, J. (2002). The age of connective leadership. In: F. Hesselbein & R. Johnston (Eds.), *On leading change* (pp. 89–102). San Francisco, CA: Jossey-Bass Publishers.

Martin, R. (1998). Changing the mind of the corporation. In *Harvard Business Review on change* (pp. 113–138). Boston, MA: Harvard Business School.

Maurer, R. (2010). *Beyond the wall of resistance: Why 70% of all changes still fail—And what you can do about it.* Austin, TX: Bard Press.

Miller, K. (2002). *The change agent's guide to radical improvement.* Milwaukee: American Society for Quality.

Mourier, P., & Smith, M. R. (2001). *Conquering organizational change. How to succeed where most companies fail.* Atlanta, GA: CEP Press.

Novak, D. (2012). *Taking people with you: The only way to make big things happen.* New York, NY: Portfolio and Penguin.

Oakley, E., & Krug, D. (1991). *Enlightened leadership: Getting to the heart of change.* New York, NY: Fireside.

Robertson, B. J. (2015). *Holacracy: The new management system for a rapidly changing world.* New York, NY: Henry Holt and Company.

Watkins, M. D. (2013). *The first 90 days: Proven strategies for getting up to speed faster and smarter, updated and expanded.* Boston, MA: Harvard Business Review Press.

Zaffron, S., & Logan, D. (2009). *The three laws of performance: Rewriting the future of your organization and your life.* San Francisco, CA: Jossey-Bass Publishers.

shows that subjects like people, change, leadership and group dynamics are more than present. However, the corresponding social psychological theories and research are almost absent. In some books Bandura is mentioned and from time to time one reads about groupthink and group dynamics. The idea of 'social proof' is visible in ideas about 'leading by example', 'significant others' and diffusion of ideas. That is all.

In the more scholarly, sound books mentioned earlier, social psychology is present (e.g. 'The Psychology of Leadership, Change and Organizational Development'—Leonard, Lewis, Friedman, & Passmore, 2013) or even central (e.g. 'The Psychology of Organizational Change'—Oreg et al., 2013). But even with their presence, a further return and progress of the social psychological perspective related to change management is possible and welcome. This notion is related to the three criteria mentioned earlier: encyclopaedic (this paragraph, 2.3), evidence-based (2.4) and cohesive (2.2).

Encyclopaedic

Oreg et al. (2013), for example, address a series of psychological and social psychological concepts and theories: positive change orientation, procedural justice, trust and social creativity, social exchange, social identity, social reciprocity, social support, etc. Leonard and Grobler (2006) introduce, among others, concepts and theories such as the social exclusion, social information-processing theory and social-learning theory. These authors have specific perspectives and themes such as leadership and justice (in relation to change) and select concepts and theories in order to address these themes. For example, Oreg et al. introduce social reciprocity to address the subject of justice and change. Leonard et al. use Bandura's social-learning theory to elaborate on the theme of leadership and change. In this way, an efficient and focused selection is made from social psychology; certain concepts and theories are included, others excluded. An interesting angle is also provided by thinkers and scientists who translate a basic social psychological theory into a concept that fits the context of organization and change (and thus becomes more relevant, insightful and helpful). A first example can be found in the work of Riketta (2005) on organizational identification, which has strong ties with self-categorization theory. Another example is Fugate's work (2008) on change appraisals, based on the stress appraisal theory. A fruitful alternative and potential complementary way can be found by working the other way around: first selecting the most important and potentially most relevant social psychological insights. This contributes to the creation and development of a more complete and complementary overview of ideas and insights from social psychology relevant to change management.

The collection, assessment and selection of the first more than 100 theories ('longlist') and subsequently approximately forty theories ('definitive list') was carried out by the four authors and by two members of the research team other than the four authors (one author was also a research team member). The (draft) 'definitive' list included three of the authors. Of these, two were full professors of change management—one being a social psychologist—who were also experienced management and change practitioners and had spent twenty-five years as a consultant and a manager. The other was a trained social psychologist (MSc) and consultant. The most experienced full professor—of social psychology—reviewed and reflected on the output. The longlist was drawn up by two of the authors (one professor) by reviewing and assessing the contents of leading manuals in the field of social psychology. The first criterion was the prominence of social psychological theory as such; the second was the potential or possible relevance of theory for the context of organization and change. The use of two frames of reference operationalized the second criterion. The first was the change competence model (ten Have et al., 2015). The second was a set of eighteen leading assumptions on change management (ten Have et al., 2016). Based on a team analysis, a set of change management topics was derived from these assumptions (Table 2.3):

Table 2.3 Change Management Topics

Change Management Topics		
Mission, vision, strategy	Performance management	Resistance
Leadership	Change capacity	Commitment
Culture	Change vision	Cooperation
Structure	Teams/team development	Participation
Systems	Communication	

Explanation Procedure Longlist and Final Selection of Theories

To thoroughly map the field of social psychology and all of its theories, the following handbooks were used to extract theories from:

- *Handbook of Theories of Social Psychology* (volume 1)
- *Handbook of Theories of Social Psychology* (volume 2)
- *Social Psychology and Organizations*

To further bolster our list of theories, we did a thorough internet search for the history of the field, social psychological glossaries and popular articles. The search resulted in a list of 106 social psychological theories, shown in Table 2.4.

During our research, we added one theory that was not on the longlist but was judged to be very relevant in the context of organization and change: self-discrepancy.

Table 2.4 Overview of All Listed Social Psychological Theories

1. A theory of heuristic and systematic information processing	24. Emotional response theory	47. Need-to-belong theory
2. A theory of individualism and collectivism	25. Equity theory	48. Optimal distinctiveness theory
3. Accessibility theory	26. Error management orientation, active feedback seeking	49. Persuasion
4. Action identification theory	27. Expectancy theory	50. Power increases abstract thinking
5. Action structure	28. Feelings as information theory	51. Power increases optimism and risk taking
6. Active goals and vision	29. Focus theory of normative conduct	52. Power, social connection and emotional identification
7. Ambiguity intolerance	30. Groupthink	53. Prejudice and discrimination
8. Assertive action (power)	31. Health belief model	54. Procedural fairness
9. Attachment theory	32. Heuristic processes	55. Reflective-impulsive model (RIM)
10. Attribution bias	33. Hot cognition	56. Regulatory focus theory
11. Attribution theory	34. Identity dissonance	57. Schemata theory
12. Balance theory	35. Implicit personality theories	58. Self-affirmation
13. Belongingness	36. Instrumental attention	59. Self-categorization theory
14. Broaden-and-built theory	37. Interdependence theory	60. Self-control theory
15. Cognitive dissonance theory	38. Investment model of commitment process	61. Self-determination theory
16. Cognitive theory of aggression	39. Justice theory	62. Self-enhancement
17. Cold cognition	40. Learned helplessness	63. Self-esteem
18. Conformity	41. Matching hypothesis	64. Self-perception theory
19. Cooperation	42. Mindset theory of action phases	65. Self-verification theory
20. Differential information theory and overconfidence	43. Minority influence theory	66. Sense of/illusion of control
21. Diffusion of innovation theory	44. Model of behavioural self-regulation	67. Shaping
22. Drive theory	45. Moral disengagement theory	68. Shared reality theory
23. Elaboration likelihood model	46. Motivation crowding theory	69. Social attentiveness

(*Continued*)

Table 2.4 (Continued)

70.	Social action theory	83.	Social identity theory
71.	Social behaviour/ Prosocial behaviour	84.	Social influence, compliance, identification, internalization, obedience
72.	Social category diversity, informational diversity	85.	Social information processing
73.	Social cognition	86.	Social norms, normative influences
74.	Social cognitive theory	87.	Social learning
75.	Social cohesion	88.	Social impact theory
76.	Social comparison theory	89.	Social penetration theory
77.	Social control	90.	Social reinforcement
78.	Social development theory	91.	Social representation theory
79.	Social dominance theory	92.	Social role theory
80.	Social equilibrium	93.	Socioemotional selectivity theory
81.	Social exchange theory	94.	Sociometer theory
82.	Social facilitation theory	95.	Stress appraisal theory / change appraisal

96.	System justification theory	101.	Theory of cooperation/competition
97.	Terror management	102.	Theory of planned behaviour
98.	The common ingroup identity model	103.	Triangular theory of love
99.	The linguistic category model	104.	Trust
100.	Theory of communal (and exchange) relationships	105.	Uncertainty identity theory
		106.	Workplace victimization, antisocial behaviour

Inclusion Criteria

Not all theories listed in Table 2.4 are included in the book. For the inclusion of theories, the following criteria were used:

1. **Core Theories**

   The main social psychological theories. These are important theories on which multiple other theories are based. They are found in multiple handbooks, glossaries and articles describing the history of social psychology.

2. **Popular Theories**

   Theories that are 'on top of mind'. These theories are frequently described and referred to. There is overlap with the main social psychological theories, as they are often both important and popular.

3. **Field of Change Management**

   Theories that are relevant from the perspective of change management. For example, justice theory, which has a direct link with organizational change.

4. **Research and evidence**

   Theories that are well-researched and with regard to which at least sufficient evidence is available.

Based on inclusion criteria, the following forty theories in Table 2.5 were included.

Table 2.5 Included Social Psychological Theories

1. Attachment theory	10. Groupthink	19. Self-discrepancy theory
2. Attribution theory	11. Justice theory	20. Self-esteem
3. Belongingness	12. Minority influence theory	21. Self-perception theory
4. Broaden-and-built theory	13. Moral disengagement theory	22. Self-verification theory
5. Change appraisal	14. Motivation crowding theory	23. Social behaviour/ Prosocial behaviour
6. Cognitive dissonance theory	15. Procedural fairness / justice	24. Social cognitive theory
7. Conformity	16. Self-affirmation	25. Social cohesion
8. Equity theory	17. Self-categorization theory	26. Social comparison theory
9. Expectancy theory	18. Self-determination theory	27. Social dominance theory

(*Continued*)

Table 2.5 (Continued)

28. Social exchange theory	33. Social learning theory	38. Theory of cooperation/ competition
29. Social facilitation theory	34. Social reinforcement	39. Theory of planned behaviour
30. Social identity theory	35. Social representation theory	40. Trust
31. Social impact theory	36. System justification theory	
32. Social judgement theory	37. Terror management	

The definitive list (Table 2.6) was categorized by using the five core social motives of Fiske (2004).

The first categorization was carried out by three of the four authors before the evidence assessment and based on the (formal) definitions of the theory plus initial additional research (where necessary) and a team analysis. After the evidence assessments (REAs), the three authors and the members of the research team assessed the categorization again. As a result, system-justification theory moved from the category 'trusting' (Chapter 6) to 'enhancing self' (Chapter 7). After the first evidence assessment, two theories already mentioned, self-categorization and stress appraisal theory, proved to be problematic in terms of the amount and level of evidence in the organizational context. First, consideration was given to removing it from the definitive selection. However, the potential and relevance were undisputed; additional research showed that the principles of theories were well researched under the labels of organizational identity and change appraisal, respectively. At least one concept can be viewed initially as problematic, but, notwithstanding that, is part of the definitive selection. This is 'groupthink' (Janis, 1972). The most important reason is that groupthink is a very popular and widespread concept, part of the daily language of people in organizational contexts. Fiske (2004) remarks that although there is some supportive descriptive evidence, 'groupthink experiments failed to pin it down clearly' (p. 496). She suggests that general models of group problem-solving are more useful. In this case we have chosen to stick to groupthink, given the reason mentioned, and to at least warn if the evidence indeed proves to be limited. Last but not least, the categorization is not 'absolute'; we have looked for the best fit. Several theories are relevant for or related to more than one core social motive. For example, attachment (theory) is located in the chapter on 'trusting', but clearly also strongly related to 'belonging'. This interrelatedness, this interdependency and these possible synergies and trade-offs between both core social motives and the related theories

Table 2.6 List of all included Social Psychological Theories Categorized Using the Five Core Social Motives (Fiske, 2004)

---

1. Belonging – Need for strong, stable relationships – fundamental core social motive
   Belongingness
   Broaden-and-built theory
   Conformity
   Prosocial behaviour
   Self-categorization theory ('Organizational identification')
   Social cohesion
   Social identity theory
   Terror management theory

2. Understanding – Need for shared meaning and prediction – first cognitive motive
   Attribution theory
   Social exchange theory
   Social impact theory
   Social judgement theory
   Social learning theory
   Social representation theory
   Theory of cooperation/competition

3. Controlling – Need for perceived contingency between behaviour and outcomes – second cognitive motive
   Stress appraisal ('Change appraisal')
   Expectancy theory
   Minority influence theory
   Motivation crowding theory
   Self-determination theory
   Self-perception theory
   Social cognitive theory (self-efficacy; SCCT)
   Social dominance theory
   Theory of planned behaviour

4. Trusting – Need for seeing others as basically benign – first affective motive
   Attachment theory
   Equity theory
   Groupthink
   Justice theory
   Moral disengagement theory
   Procedural fairness
   Trust

5. Self-enhancing – Need for viewing self as basically worthy or improvable – second affective motive
   Self-affirmation
   Social comparison theory
   Cognitive dissonance theory
   Self-discrepancy
   Self-esteem
   Self-verification theory
   Social facilitation theory
   Social reinforcement
   System justification theory

---

is also addressed by the dynamic modelling or visualization introduced in the first chapter and further explained in this chapter. In the final chapter (8) we reflect on the 'interrelatedness', and the potential and relevance (and possible complications) for the (further) development of a social psychology of change management.

For the selected social psychological theories as such, one can state that almost without exception the theories are based on well-founded empirical research. For practical reasons we had to 'limit' the selection of prominent social psychological theories with assessed relevance and potential for the organizational context, the field of change management, to around forty. There is a possibility that we missed or left out theories (from or outside the longlist) that are prominent and have the relevance and potential mentioned. Hopefully we can identify these theories or their 'offspring' in the organizational context (compare the examples of self-categorization and organizational identity, stress appraisal and change appraisal) and analyse and unleash them as well for the field of organization and change in the near future. In the coming chapters, we see and experience that with regard to the specific evidence on the around forty theories in the organizational context, the quantity and quality (level of evidence), and also the relevance (what it contributes to the field and practice) will vary between the theories. Without doubt, future research will provide more of this kind of evidence to the field and practice. This progress will be followed and included and integrated in future versions, as we already did with our earlier research and publications (ten Have et al., 2016; ten Have, ten Have, & Rijsman, 2018).

The Evidence-Based Methodology (REA)[1]

In our earlier research we applied the evidence-based methodology and more specifically the method of rapid evidence assessment (REA) with the purpose of 'myth busting' (ten Have et al., 2016). By confronting popular change management ideas with scientific evidence generated with the REAs, we found how popular evidence-based claims were. The purpose of this book is different. Here the REA is applied in order to generate the evidence available with regard to the application of social psychological theories in the field of change and organization. Evidence summaries come in many forms. One of the best-known is the conventional literature review which provides a general overview of the relevant scientific literature published on a given topic. However, a conventional literature review is not always entirely trustworthy: studies are selected based on the researcher's individual preferences rather than on explicit and objective criteria, and the research results are generally not subject to critical appraisal (Antman, 1992; Bushman & Wells, 2001; Chalmers, Enkin, & Keirse, 1993; Fink, 1998). Most conventional literature reviews are therefore prone to severe bias and are considered to be unsuitable for answering questions about the effectiveness of strategies or interventions.

This is why REAs are the preferred method for reviewing evidence in Evidence-Based Management. Such reviews address a focused question through a methodology that identifies the most relevant studies and only includes those studies that meet explicit quality and relevance criteria as determined by several researchers (Higgins & Green, 2006; Petticrew & Roberts, 2006). Unlike a conventional literature review, an REA is transparent, verifiable and reproducible and therefore less biased and more relevant.

To examine the evidence base of the X theories in relation to change and organization, we conducted a series of REAs that are presented in this book. Each of the REAs conducted involved the following nine steps:

1. Description
2. Inclusion criteria
3. Search strategy
4. Study selection
5. Data extraction
6. Critical appraisal
7. Main findings
8. Conclusion
9. Practical reflections

Description: What Is the Theory About and What Is the Basic Assumption?

First, a theory like social identity theory or attachment theory is described: what is the theory about and what are its basic assumptions. Both popular and academic literature is used to explain and illustrate the theory and its underlying assumptions.

Inclusion Criteria: Which Studies to Include?

This section specifies the criteria and justification for the inclusion (or exclusion) of particular studies. The following **inclusion criteria** were applied for all REAs:

1. Type of publication: Only articles published in peer-reviewed scholarly journals.
2. Language: Only articles in English.
3. Type of studies: Only quantitative studies.
4. Measurement: Only studies in which an effect of the theory was measured.
5. Context: Focus on studies relating the theory to organizations and/or change management.
6. Level of trustworthiness: Only studies that were graded level E or above (see 6).

Remark: To ensure thorough descriptions of the included theories, a wider range of articles were included. From the main findings and beyond, the inclusion criteria just stated were used.

Search Strategy: How Was the Research Evidence Sought?

The first search was done combining the theory with change management. The search was limited to the following three bibliographical databases:

- ABI/INFORM Global from ProQuest
- Business Source Premier from EBSCO
- PsycINFO from Ovid

If the first search yielded an insufficient number of studies, a second, broader search was carried out only including the name of the theory. To find relevant studies in other disciplines (than social psychology and change management), databases related to disciplines like health care and education were searched. Examples of these databases are PubMed (health care) and ERIC (education). In addition, generic databases like Google Scholar were used. The search steps are summarized in Figure 2.3.

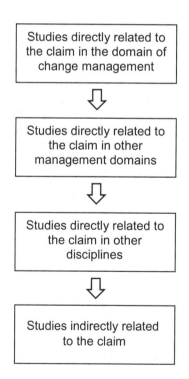

Figure 2.3 Overview of the Research Steps

Study Selection: How Were the Studies to Be Included Selected?

In most cases the search yielded many studies, sometimes several hundred. Some of the studies found were not directly relevant to the research question. Hence, two reviewers independently screened the titles and the abstracts of the studies identified for their relevance of the theory in relation to organizations. In the event of doubt, lack of information or disagreement, the study was included. The remaining studies for inclusion were then selected based on the full text of the article. Studies were excluded where they failed to meet the inclusion criteria. Again, two reviewers worked independently to identify which studies were to be included or excluded. Where the two reviewers disagreed on inclusion, a third reviewer assessed whether the study was appropriate for inclusion, with no prior knowledge of the initial reviewers' assessments. The decision of the third reviewer was final.

Data Extraction

Data extraction involved the collation of the results of the studies included. In this phase relevant data was extracted from the final set of studies. Specifically, this was data on year of publication, research design, sample size, population (e.g. industry, type of employees), possible moderators or mediators, outcome measures, main findings, effect sizes and limitations.

Critical Appraisal: How Was the Trustworthiness of the Evidence Appraised?

Methodological Appropriateness

A study's trustworthiness was first determined by its methodological appropriateness. The appropriateness was considered high when the design reflected the best way to answer the research question.

For cause-and-effect claims (i.e. if I do A, will it result in B?), a study that used both a control group and random assignment was regarded as the 'gold standard'. Non-randomized studies and before-after studies came next in terms of appropriateness. Cross-sectional studies (surveys) were regarded as having the greatest chance of showing bias in the outcome and therefore came lower down in the ranking in terms of appropriateness. Meta-analyses in which statistical analysis techniques were used to pool the results of controlled studies were therefore regarded as the most appropriate design.

Campbell and Petticrew's classification system (Shadish, Cook, & Campbell, 2002; Petticrew & Roberts, 2006) was used to determine the methodological appropriateness of the research design of the studies included on the basis of a systematic assessment. Any discrepancies were resolved through discussion or by consulting a third party where necessary. The following five levels of appropriateness were used for the classification (Table 2.7):

Table 2.7 Five Levels to Determine the Methodological Appropriateness of the Research Design of the Studies Included

Design	Appropriateness	Level
Systematic review and meta-analysis of randomized, controlled studies	Very high	A+
Systematic review and meta-analysis of controlled and/or before-after studies	High	A
Randomized, controlled studies		
Systematic review and meta-analysis of cross-sectional studies	Moderate	B
Non-randomized, controlled before-after studies		
Interrupted time series		
Controlled studies without a pretest and uncontrolled studies with a pretest	Limited	C
Cross-sectional studies	Low	D

Methodological Quality

The trustworthiness of a study, however, is also affected by its methodological quality, that is, how it was conducted. To determine methodological quality, all the studies included were systematically assessed based on explicit quality criteria, such as the PRISMA (Moher, Liberati, Tetzlaff, & Altman, 2009) and CONSORT(ref) statement, the CASP checklists (ref), the checklists of the EPPI Center (ref), and the critical appraisal criteria developed by the Center for Evidence-Based Management (ref). Based on a tally of the number of weaknesses, the trustworthiness was downgraded by one or more levels. To determine the final level of trustworthiness, the reviewers adopted the following rule of thumb:

- 1 weakness = no downgrade (i.e. we accept that nothing is perfect)
- 2 weaknesses = downgrade 1 level
- 3 weaknesses = downgrade 2 levels, etc.

Impact: Effect Sizes

An effect (association or difference) can be statistically significant but may not necessarily be of practical relevance: even a trivial effect can be statistically significant if the sample size is big enough. For this reason the effect size—a standard measure of the magnitude (strength) of the effect—of the studies included was assessed. To determine the magnitude of an effect, Cohen's rule of thumb (Cohen, 1988) was applied. According to Cohen (1988), a small effect is an effect that is only visible through careful examination. A medium effect, however, is one that is 'visible to the naked eye of the careful observer'. Finally, a large effect is an effect that anyone can easily see because it is substantial.

Main Findings: What Was Found?

This section provides an overview of the relevant main findings. The main evidence from the REA is presented for each finding, together with the level of trustworthiness and the effect size.

Conclusion: What Is the Added Value of the Theory?

This section presents the conclusions. The conclusion describes the added value of the theory in relation to organizations and the field of change management. These are based on the overall methodological appropriateness and quality of the studies that were included and the practical relevance of the effect sizes found.

Practical Reflections

As stated in the introduction, evidence-based practice is based on four sources of evidence. Evidence in the scientific literature alone is insufficient—we need the experience and expertise of practitioners to be able to determine whether the research findings will apply in a particular situation. Practitioner expertise is also necessary when the evidence is contradictory or lacking. This section therefore shows how the findings of the REA relate to the daily practice of change managers and discusses their implications in practice.

Limitations

A REA provides a balanced assessment of what is known in the scientific literature about a theory, by applying a systematic review method to search and critically appraise primary studies. However, for it to be 'rapid', concessions have been made in terms of the breadth and depth of the search process for the REAs in this book. These include the exclusion of unpublished research, the use of a limited number of databases and a main focus on meta-analyses and primary studies published over the past twenty years. As a consequence, some relevant studies may have been omitted. The critical appraisal also did not always include a comprehensive review of the psychometric properties of the tests, scales and questionnaires used in the studies included. Given these limitations, care must be taken not to accept the findings presented in this book as conclusive.

Report and Format Per Theory

The REA format as described in 2.4 is fully applied to each of the selected social psychological theories. However, given the purpose of this book and for practical reasons, the format used to report on each theory has been partly redesigned. To start with, four of the nine steps or parts of the procedure are general and only described in this chapter (2.4): (2) inclusion criteria, (4) study selection, (5) data extraction, and (6) critical appraisal. For this research and this book, one subparagraph has been added (2: 'relevance'). The format used for the social psychological theories in Chapters 3 to7 is:

1. What is (for example) social identity theory?
2. What is the relevance of social identity theory for organization and change?
3. Search strategy
4. Main findings
5. What is the conclusion?
6. Practical reflections

Under point 1, What is theory X?, the theory or concept, its history, background and development are primarily described from a social psychological background. Point 2 is about the relevance of a theory in the context of organization and change. The theory or concept is related and translated to the organizational context, management and change. By using the list of change management topics introduced earlier (such as mission, change vision, leadership, culture and change capacity), the potential and relevance of the theory is described. In this part, quotes from the selected and assessed list of popular change management literature may be used for illustration purposes. After the search strategy (point 3) and the main findings (point 4), the conclusion (point 5) is presented. Based on the (organizational) context-relevant (main) findings, the conclusion describes what the contributions and insights for the practice of management and change are or can be. In the conclusion, we often relate to the change management topics mentioned. An example of a conclusion (stress appraisal theory/change appraisal; 5.3.5): *Stress appraisal, as such, and its sibling the concept of change appraisal, are highly relevant and informative for the practice of management and change. The findings show that the appraisal of change is a key factor in change processes and the way people involved react to change, commit or resist. The concept underscores the important role of change history in change processes and the influence it has on the people involved. This appraisal is strongly related to the way people adjust to and cope with times of change.* Under point 6, practical reflections and guidelines for the practice of management and change may be given based on the evidence. For all theories addressed, the conclusion will be based on inductive element, empirical evidence, that is, the main findings (point 4). However, the conclusion can also be based partly on deductive elements, the (projected) relevance, the potential and the logical and theoretical explanatory power of the theory. For practical considerations, warnings or possible consequences of the findings and insights related to theory in the organizational context may also be given. In some cases, further illustration of the ideas and insights is given, by making use of the (popular) management literature.

Each search strategy led to a matrix in which the characteristics and findings of the included studies are described. In addition, a short description of excluded studies is part of the matrix. For practical reasons, the complete set of matrices is not included in the book. However, in Appendix B a theory plus matrix is included for each core social motive, leading to five examples.

Note

1. Based on Ten Have, S., Ten Have, W. D., Huijsmans, A.-B., & Otto, M. (2016). *Reconsidering change management: Applying evidence-based insights in change management practice.* New York, NY: Routledge.

3 Belonging, Organizational Behaviour and Change

A First Short Story of Belonging and Change

Being social animals, people have a desire to form and maintain social bonds. Social connectedness unifies and is stimulated by shared common goals and interests. Perceived cohesion influences the behaviour of the individual and the group. It has two dimensions: a sense of belonging and feelings of morale. Conformity is the convergence of individuals' thoughts, feelings or behaviour toward a social or group norm. Corporate visions and missions, shared senses of urgency, or core values are instrumental in developing such kinds of consensus or agreement. An individual's self-concept is partly derived from his knowledge of his membership in a social group (or groups) and the value or emotional significance attached to that membership. People have a personal identity and a social identity; psychological depersonalization of the self produces 'group behaviour' and emergent group processes such as influence, cooperation and cohesiveness. Belonging to a group stimulates prosocial behaviour toward the in-group. People function securely if they believe that they are contributing to a meaningful change or mission. Standards and goals have to be inviting and inclusive, including for minority groups within the organization. Negative stimuli such as threats and urgency can be effective in change, but positive ambitions, mirroring positive emotions and feelings, create more self-efficacy or action control in dealing with changes and challenges.

Belonging, the need for strong stable relationships, is the first core social motive and the most fundamental one (Fiske, 2004). The (perceived) presence or absence may influence loyalty, solidarity and cooperation in organizations and communities and the well-being and health of people as well as the organizational climate. This motive helps groups to survive and belonging to a group helps the social animal to survive. In times of organizational change the sense of belonging of certain individuals and groups may come under pressure. This may influence people's social (or organizational) identity (self-categorization) and the social cohesion. Change leading to scarcity or the reallocation of resources may, for example, decrease cohesion and prosocial behaviour. But it can also increase this, because as a result of the change people have and are inspired by a clear-shared objective ('broaden-and-build') or have to fight a common 'enemy' or threat ('terror management'). Belongingness is related to change and management topics like mission, leadership, organizational culture, resistance to change, commitment, compliance, change capacity and vision.

In this chapter the following theories and concepts are presented and assessed:

Belongingness
Social cohesion
Conformity
Social identity
Self-categorization
Prosocial behaviour
Terror management theory
Broaden-and-build theory

Belongingness

Being social animals, people have a desire to form and maintain social bonds. Social connectedness unifies and is stimulated by shared common goals and interests.

What Is Belongingness

Belonging is defined as the need for strong, stable relationships (Fiske, 2010). The need to belong is related to belongingness and is the desire for interpersonal attachments. It can be seen as a fundamental human motivation (Baumeister & Leary, 1995) or as a (first) core social motive (Fiske, 2010). In the need-to-belong theory "the motivation to form and sustain at least a minimum amount of social connections is one of the most powerful, universal and influential human drives. It shapes emotion, cognition and behaviour. It explains self-esteem as an internal measure of one's chances of having good relationships" (Van Lange et al., 2012, p. 121). Belongingness can have strong effects on emotional patterns and cognitive processes. The perspective provided by this need-to-belong theory shows that lack of attachments is linked to a variety of ill effects on health, adjustment and well-being. The need to belong is seen as "a powerful, fundamental and extremely pervasive motivation" (Baumeister & Leary, 1995, p. 497). Belongingness, the desire to form and maintain social bonds, can indeed be seen as a core social motive. The desire to form and maintain social bonds is among the most powerful human motives. This can be an important positive variable in change management, given the fact that a shared vision or a collective sense of mission is seen as a positive factor in realizing change. Research shows that a mere sense of social connectedness can lead to the acceptance or even internalization of the goals and drives of others (Walton, Cohen,

Cwir, & Spencer, 2012). This suggests that achievement motivation and self-identity are highly sensitive to minor cues of social connection. Social belonging factors are social feedback, validation, shared experiences and 'relevant others' (e.g. Cialdini & Goldstein, 2004). Shared common goals and interests with others help to develop positive social bonds and may enhance feelings of self-worth. Charismatic leaders inspire their people to go the extra mile, to contribute to the collective group instead of focusing on their own self-interest. In return, employees receive an identity and belongingness, while organizations benefit from the collective feeling of unity (Den Hartog, De Hoogh, & Keegan, 2007).

What Is the Relevance of Belongingness for Organization and Change?

Belongingness serves as an umbrella for multiple social psychological theories. It has links to the concepts and theories of conformity, group-think, social identity and social exchange. Individuals will conform to a certain degree in order to fit in a group (link with conformity). The desire to maintain harmony and conformity in the group can lead to groupthink (link with groupthink). Being part of a group also forms an individual's social identity (link with social identity). The intrinsic desire to be part of a group/multiple groups is so strong that people will always search for social contact and try to maximize the value of being part of a group, while minimizing risks and costs (link with social exchange). From the perspective of change and organization, it is relevant for the understanding of subjects like organizations as such, teams and team and group development, commitment and cooperation. Belongingness is also relevant for key themes in the field of organization and change, such as (a shared) vision and mission, organizational culture(s) and change capacity. With regard to change capacity, Heifetz, Grashow, and Linsky (2009) underline the importance of belongingness and a shared identity: "In an organization with a high capacity to adapt, people share responsibility for the larger organization's future in addition to their identification with specific roles and functions" (p. 103). In organizations with a strong culture there is often a strong sense of belonging. Vision, mission and leadership contribute to this sense and provide direction. "Culture is it!" says Belasco (1990, p. 201). He states that every organization has a culture that shapes behaviour, culture calls the tune, and the challenge is to create the culture you want—one that empowers using the vision.

Search Strategy

Relevant databases were searched using the term 'belonging' and 'belongingness' in combination with 'work', 'employee', 'theory' and 'organization'. The search yielded more than 500 studies. However, only three studies were relevant enough to be included. To strengthen our research, we carried out a snowball search and found two further relevant studies and a literature review.

Main Findings

1. *Interactional fairness positively predicts employees' sense of belongingness (Level D-).*

   "Consistent with expectations, the findings demonstrate that interactional fairness positively predicts employees' sense of belongingness, and employees show more helping behaviour (supervisor-rated) when they have a stronger sense of belongingness at work" (Kyei-Poku, 2013, p. 691).

   "Satisfying employees' need for belonging is an important aspect of organizational life and useful in promoting helping behaviours among co-workers; it is essential for organizations to, therefore, create a work culture of inclusiveness. It is prudent for organizations to also expend greater effort to maximize interactional fairness by introducing programmes intended for training organizational leaders how to be fair" (Kyei-Poku, 2013, p. 691).

2. *Lower levels of co-worker belonging increase interpersonally harmful behaviours and decrease interpersonally helpful behaviours (Level D-).*

   "As predicted, employees who perceived that their actual state of belonging with respect to their colleagues fell short of their desired level were reported by their supervisors as exhibiting more interpersonally harmful and fewer interpersonally helpful behaviours" (Thau, Karl, & Poortvliet, 2007, p. 844).

   "The need for belonging is among the most powerful sources of human motivation (Baumeister & Leary, 1995; Maslow, 1943), and the desire for its fulfilment is perhaps why many employees often prefer to work in groups rather than alone (Alderfer, 1972), why they cooperate with others (Kramer, 1993), and why they refrain from engaging in actions that harm their co-workers (Hollinger & Clark, 1982)" (Thau et al., 2007, p. 840).

What Is the Conclusion?

The claim that people have an intrinsic need to be part of a group is borne out. The claim that individuals have an intrinsic desire to belong to a group holds true. It can be stated that the field of social psychology as such is primarily based upon the idea that humans are social species, social beings or social animals who are always looking for social interaction and preventing loneliness and isolation. Belongingness is a key theory for social psychology and highly relevant from the perspective of organization and change. In addition, our specific research produced insights with regard to the sense of belonging and fairness and interpersonally harmful and helpful behaviours. These insights give important guidance for the way to organize and change.

Practical Reflections

Belongingness is at the core of change and organization; it is highly relevant to organizations, their leaders and their people. As Kyei-Poku (2013) states: "Satisfying employees' need for belonging is an important aspect of organizational life and useful in promoting helping behaviours among co-workers; it is essential for organizations to, therefore, create a work culture of inclusiveness. It is prudent for organizations to also expend greater effort to maximize interactional fairness by introducing programmes intended for training organizational leaders how to be fair" (p. 691). It should be noted that specific evidence with regard to the concept of belonging and also for its relationship with organization and change is relatively limited. However, for underlying theories such as social identity, fairness, support, conformity, social exchange and groupthink, the evidence is strong. The relative absence of this evidence for belongingness as such may well be because of the breadth of the theory, as well as the obvious fact that there is no need for further proof. Take, for example, gravity theory. Setting up an experiment to test the gravity theory might be very difficult if you ask participants to jump out of a window on the fifteenth floor of an apartment building to see what happens. People will at least think you are crazy, as the outcome of this experiment needs no further proof. To our knowledge, the experiment has never been done, and hopefully that will remain the case. We all know how gravity works, thanks to other experiments. Finally, it is difficult to study belongingness properly because of ethical reasons. Experimenting with the effects of isolation and loneliness and comparing these with people in a group is not very ethical. Furthermore, the negative effects of being lonely, for example, have already been examined thoroughly and findings show that loneliness can impair health, for example, increasing the chance of heart disease, increasing blood pressure and depressions, dementia and even suicide attempts (Hara et al., 2012;Holt-Lunstad, et al., 2015; Holwerda et al., 2012; Valtorta, Kanaan, Gilbody, Ronzi, & Hanratty, 2016).

Social Cohesion

Perceived cohesion influences the behaviour of the individual and the group. It has two dimensions: a sense of belonging and feelings of morale.

What Is Social Cohesion?

Related to belonging is the concept of social cohesion or group cohesion. This is about social groups defined by the fact that there are people who share some common characteristic(s), socially meaningful for themselves or for others. The origin of social cohesion can be traced back to the time of Emile Durkheim, one of the founding fathers of modern sociology. A key feature is that social cohesion is often analysed in relation to social integration, stability and disintegration (Chan, To, & Chan, 2006). Social psychologists also contributed to the term, introducing cohesion as a concept of its own, suggesting there are two perspectives on cohesion: objective and perceived (Bollen & Hoyle, 1990). Carron and Spink (1995) said: "It could be argued that the terms cohesion and group are tautological; if a group exists, it must be cohesive to some degree. Thus it is probably no surprise that even in collectives where minimal group characteristics are present, manifestations of cohesion are evident" (pp. 86–87). Group cohesion can be seen as the product of a deep sense of 'we-ness', or belonging to a group (Bollen & Hoyle, 1990).

From a social psychological perspective, cohesion is treated as a trait that combines with others in order to influence the way the group does things (sociologists, for example, primarily see cohesion as a structural issue; they focus on the way interlocking parts of the whole group interact to allow the group to function) (Bruhn, 2009). Perceived cohesion influences the behaviour of the individual and the group. It has two dimensions: a sense of belonging and feelings of morale (Bollen & Hoyle, 1990). The varying models of cohesion share two generic factors: attraction and bonding and self-disclosure and feedback (Braaten, 1991). Schiefer and colleagues (2016) define social cohesion in three core dimensions: the quality of social relations (including social networks, trust, acceptance of diversity and participation), identification with the social entity, and orientation toward the common good (sense of responsibility, solidarity, compliance with social order). Bottoni (2016) defined social cohesion in seven core dimensions: interpersonal trust, density of social relations, social support, openness, participation, legitimacy of institutions and institutional trust. Important factors that influence group cohesiveness include similarity of group members (Tajfel, 1982), group success (Zaccaro & McCoy, 1988) and external competition and threats (e.g. Rempel & Fischer, 1997). An important concept related to social or group cohesion is that of social norms. Social norms are generally accepted ways of thinking, feeling or behaving that group members agree on and endorse as right or just; they can be seen as the key to belongingness. A descriptive social norm states what a group thinks or feels; injunctive social norms state what they should think or feel (Smith, Thomas, & McGarty., 2015). Social norms, like standards of conduct, tend to keep a group working better together as long as these are uniformly enforced.

Here the important concept of conformity is introduced and is discussed in the next paragraph.

What Is the Relevance of Social Cohesion for Organization and Change?

From the perspective of organization and change, social or group cohesion is relevant to subjects such as culture, change vision, teams and team development, cooperation and also goal-setting performance. To illustrate this, social or group cohesion is often considered to be positively related to performance, because a cohesive group will be more motivated and will participate more in its activities (Evans & Dion, 1991). Looking at the dimensions of social cohesion with elements such as 'trust', 'social support' and 'identification', group cohesion is likely to have positive outcomes on multiple factors, for example: distributive justice, job satisfaction and affective commitment. With regard to teams and performance, task cohesion is likely to have more impact on the performance compared with social cohesion, because the task/product will ultimately be the factor determining the performance. "Highly cohesive groups emerge where interactions are required by the task-related activities of work group members to achieve common goals. Task interdependence and goal interdependence help to set up a work situation that is favourable to positive interaction and strong group identity; group cohesion is thus enhanced accordingly" (Chen, Tang, & Wang, 2009, p. 634). Social and group cohesion are at the core of change and performance as organizational efforts. These efforts demand commitment, more precisely collective or shared commitment. As Conner (1992) states: "Successful change is rooted in commitment. Unless key participants in a transition are committed to both attaining the goals of the change and paying the price those goals entail, the project will ultimately fail. In fact, most change failures trace back to this lack of commitment, with obvious symptoms like sponsors terminating projects and more subtle signs such as target apathy as leading indicators" (p. 147). And: "Given that committed people will devote the time, money, endurance, persistence, loyalty and ingenuity necessary, it is easy to see why commitment is critical for successful change. It is the glue that provides the vital bond between people and change goals. It is the source of energy that propels resilient people and organizations through the process at the fastest, most effective pace possible—the optimum speed of change" (p. 148).

Search Strategy

Relevant databases were searched using the terms 'social cohesion', 'group cohesion' and 'task cohesion' in combination with 'meta-analysis', 'systematic review' and 'studies'. The search yielded more than 500 articles. After screening the title and abstracts for relevance, two meta-analyses and eleven studies were included.

Main Findings

1. *Group cohesion has a moderate to large effect on performance, and cohesive groups are more productive than non-cohesive groups (Level C).*

   It was found that cohesive groups, on average, tend to be more productive and perform better than non-cohesive groups. The study used sports teams, experimental groups and military units, because these groups have measurable performance criteria. For organizations, these performance criteria are more difficult to develop. Still, the effect of group cohesion on performance is found in multiple studies, for example in the meta-analysis of Gully and colleagues (1995). These findings further support the idea that group cohesion and performance are positively related to each other.

2. *The nature of the task has a substantial influence on the cohesion-performance relationship (Level B).*

   When the task demands cooperation, coordination, communication and mutual performance among group members, cohesion and performance are more strongly related than when task interdependence is low (Gully, Devine, & Whitney, 1995). This can logically be explained by the fact that cohesion creates a bond and the more the team members must work together, the more the bond becomes important for the overall performance.

3. *Group cohesion is positively related to multiple factors that are beneficial for both organizations and change (Levels D, E).*

   According to multiple studies, group cohesion has a positive effect on: Organizational citizenship behaviour (extra-role performance), distributive justice, affective commitment, new product performance, job satisfaction, participation, team morale, social support, team effectiveness and communication (Andrews, Kacmar, Blakely, & Bucklew, 2008; Carless & De Paola, 2000; Chen et al., 2009).

4. *Both task cohesion and social cohesion have a positive effect on perceived subordinate performance, with task cohesion having the strongest effect (Level E).*

   It was found that both types of cohesion have a positive effect on perceived subordinate performance, with task cohesion having the strongest effect (Carless & De Paola, 2000).

5. *Task and group interdependence strengthen group cohesion, further leading to employees' willingness to engage in more organizational citizenship behaviour (Level D).*

   Task interdependence and goal interdependence indirectly affect employees' engagement in organizational citizenship behaviour through the mediation of group cohesion. Task and goal interdependence may strengthen group cohesion, further increasing organizational citizenship behaviour.

What Is the Conclusion?

Scientific literature supports the idea that social cohesion is an important part of group cohesion. Group cohesion consists of both social and task cohesion and has positive effects on multiple factors that are beneficial for both organizations as such and organizations in change. It is highly relevant from the perspective of organization and change. Research on cohesion provides helpful insights for leaders and their people with regard to, for example, performance, cooperation, communication and engagement and commitment.

Practical Reflections

In both running and changing the organization, and related behaviours, managers have to be aware of the importance and possible impact of social and group cohesion. They should not overlook the importance of group cohesion, for example by focusing only on the competence of individual-group members. Group cohesion, including task and social cohesion, has a positive influence on multiple beneficial factors for both 'running and changing', including: organizational citizenship behaviour (extra-role performance), distributive justice, affective commitment, new product performance, job satisfaction, participation, team morale, social support, team effectiveness and communication (Andrews et al., 2008; Carless & De Paola, 2000; Chen et al., 2009). So, the perspective of group cohesion can provide helpful interventions for running and changing organizations: "Managers can publicly promote the collective goals and provide feedback, as well as team-based rewards, to the employees to develop goal interdependence among them. Furthermore, recognition and involvement in challenging tasks arouse positive affect among employees" (Chen et al., 2009, p. 636). This kind of intervention positively affects the team cohesion, increasing the likelihood of change success and improving the everyday running of the organization.

Conformity

What Is Conformity?

Conformity is the convergence of individuals' thoughts, feelings or behaviour toward a social or group norm. Corporate visions and missions, shared senses of urgency, or core values are instrumental in developing such kinds of consensus or agreement.

Conformity is the convergence of individuals' thoughts, feelings or behaviour toward a social or group norm (Allen, 1965). Iconic studies by Asch (1951, 1955) and Sherif (1936) show that people are influenced by and often adopt the opinion of other group members. Above all, people conform to social norms because they expect that others see the world in the same way. People overestimate this and that leads to the false consensus effect (Ross, Greene, & House, 1977). The more important the connection, the stronger this effect is. People like to relate and to belong to a group. Consensus is instrumental to this. If there is dissensus or disagreement, people become uncertain, uncomfortable and vulnerable to social influence. Agreeing with others provides certainty and comfort; it assures people that they are in contact with a common reality. Corporate visions and missions, a shared sense of urgency, or core values are instrumental in developing such kinds of consensus or agreement.

Kelman (1958) distinguished three kinds of conformity: compliance, internalization and identification. Compliance occurs when a person agrees with the majority in order to get a specific reward or a favourable reaction from the group. The person does not have to agree with the group intrinsically. Internalization happens when the person agrees with the group because the ideas and actions of the group actually are in line with his intrinsic values. This is the highest level of conformity, in which a permanent change of behaviour is present. Identification occurs when a person conforms to the expectations of a specific role. Take, for example, a firefighter who puts out fires because that is what is expected of him/her. In the case of identification there does not have to be a change in a person's own opinion.

What Is the Relevance of Conformity for Organization and Change?

The basic assumption is that people want to belong to a group and by 'conforming' they change their behaviour so they optimally fit in and stay in the group; people go along with the norms/behaviour in the group; they change their behaviour or beliefs in order to fit in with a group. In a more negative way, conformity can be characterized as 'breaking under group pressure'. It strongly relates to the first core social motive of belonging; people have the desire to fit in a group, as it can provide them with security and fulfil social needs. In operating and changing, organizations have to reckon with this and can make use of it. Leadership, a shared vision and mission are instrumental in stimulating this conformity, as are role models and 'relevant others' in a group or team. The concept of conformity is related to subjects like change vision and capacity and commitment and engagement. The question of whether there is sufficient conformity to state an ambition, change goal or target is not a theoretical one and is highly relevant for practice. A lack of it may lead to disengagement or even harmful actions. Maurer (2010) considers the underestimation of the potential power of employee engagement as an important mistake in change processes. He points to the 'extensive research' of the Gallup organization: "In average organizations the ratio of engaged to actively disengaged employees is near 8:1. . . . Actively disengaged employees erode an organization's bottom line while breaking the spirits of colleagues in the process. Within the U.S. workforce, Gallup estimates this cost to be more than $300 billion in lost productivity alone" (p. 13). Langley et al. emphasize that people need to cooperate to make effective change, but the commitment to change is not a given: "People will usually have some reaction to change. This reaction can range from total commitment to open hostility" (p. 46).

Search Strategy

Relevant databases were searched using the term 'conformity' and 'social norms' in combination with 'organization', 'work', 'employee' and 'change'. 'Group' was also used in combination with norms and pressure. Lastly, 'social pressure' and 'peer pressure' were used. In total, the search yielded more than 558 articles. After screening the title and abstracts for relevance, twenty studies met the inclusion criteria. After thorough examination, another twelve studies were excluded. The evidence levels of the included studies had a wide range (Level E- to A-).

Main Findings

1. *Critical norms within a group improve the quality of decisions (Level A)*. Studies showed that norms of critical thinking about ideas within a group improved the overall quality of decision-making, whereas consensus norms within a group did not improve the quality. This effect was mediated with the perceived value of shared and unshared information. Therefore, the content of group norms is an important factor influencing the quality of group decision-making. In addition, the content of these norms is related to the proneness of the group to groupthink (Postmes, Spears, & Cihangir, 2001). Furthermore, a cross-sectional study (Level D-) found that cooperative group norms increase group creativity (Kim, 2015).
2. *Group membership does not lead to hostility to other groups (Level A-)*. Studies of third-party punishment found no evidence that group membership leads to hostility to other groups. This contradicts the longstanding thought in sociology and social psychology that mere membership of a group leads to hostility toward other groups (Goette, Huffman, & Meijer, 2006).
3. *Productivity is affected in a different way by peer pressure, when it comes to men and women (Level C)*. Results found that the productivity

of women was not so strongly affected by the level of peer pressure, when paid either a fixed wage or a piece rate. The productivity of men, however, was strongly affected by peer pressure, both with fixed wages and piece rates. High levels of peer pressure were found to have a significant negative effect on productivity. Moreover, conformism and self-motivation considerations appear to be muted when male workers are paid piece rates (Bellemare, Lepage, & Shearer, 2009).

What Is the Conclusion?

As stated previously, the claim that people have the desire or need to be part of a group is borne out. Conformity is an important and well-researched concept in relation to this 'need to belong'. Our specific research shows the impact of norms of critical thinking versus consensus norms in decision-making, in-group-out-group dynamics and productivity and peer pressure, including gender differences and the role of financial incentives in behavioural change. An excess of conformity that impedes critical thinking can have a negative impact on the overall quality of decision-making and might increase groupthink. Peer pressure, which can occur if a person wants to be or remain part of the group, can have negative effects on productivity for men (especially when they are paid fixed wages). Being part of a group does not have to be negative, as groups can fulfil the socially intrinsic human needs.

Practical Reflections

Conformity is instrumental in organizing and changing; it helps people to 'march to the same drummer'. This may also lead to a lack of reflection, poor feedback, groupthink and poor decision-making. Groups can increase the quality of decision-making by having critical norms within a group. These norms are very important in the case of change that can be very impactful for organizations and their people. Change cannot be taken for granted; it is not a 'given'. People should think critically and evaluate in order to make the right decisions for their organization and all the people involved. In addition, there is a risk of groupthink when people conform to certain group norms, which can have negative consequences. Awareness is key. Both managers and employees should be aware of the fact that conforming to a group can undermine change success. In Chapter 6 (concerning the core social motive of trusting and change), groupthink is discussed and the possible negative implications of too much conformity is illustrated together with interventions to prevent or correct them. Examples of these interventions are assigning the role of devil's advocate, using a critical reviewer, planning open sessions to reconsider alternatives and discussing group ideas with people outside the group.

Social Identity

An individual's self-concept is partly derived from his knowledge of his membership in a social group (or groups) and the value or emotional significance attached to that membership.

What Is Social Identity?

A key concept related to belonging is social identity. Based on research conducted by Tajfel in 1978, social identity theory was founded by Tajfel and Turner in 1979 and was originally developed to gain an understanding of the psychological basis of intergroup discrimination. The researchers tried to identify the minimal conditions that would let members of one group discriminate in favour of the in-group to which they belonged and against another out-group. Social identity was generally studied in the context of artificial groups or groups with shared attributes such as nationality. Research on this theory in a business context has been more prevalent in the last few years (Bergami & Bagozzi, 2000). Social identity can be explained as "that part of an individual's self-concept which derives from his knowledge of his membership in a social group (or groups) together with the value or emotional significance attached to that membership" (Tajfel, 1978, p. 63). Social identity theory implies that people classify themselves and others in diverse social groups based on prototypical characteristics of the members of the groups. For example, classifications could be organizational membership, religious conviction, gender or age (Tajfel & Turner, 1986. The classification process is relational and comparative, which means that a classification is always relative to other people (Ashforth & Mael, 1989). For example, the classification 'young' is only meaningful in relation to the category 'old'. Social identity can also be described as the sense a person has of who he is, based on being a member of a group. Social identity is described as the knowledge people have of their belongingness to given social groups, along with the emotional impact of this knowledge and the social valuation associated with it (Ashforth & Mael, 1989). In organizational settings, social identity is positively related to both job satisfaction and 'organizational citizenship behaviour' (OCB) (Topa, Morales, & Moriano, 2009). In summary: "1. Individuals strive to maintain or enhance their self-esteem: they strive for a positive self-concept; 2. Social groups or categories and the membership of them are associated with positive or negative value connotations. Social identity may be positive or negative according to the evaluations (which tend to be socially consensual, either within or across groups) of those groups that contribute to an individual's social identity; 3. The evaluation of one's group is determined with reference to specific other groups through social comparisons" (Tajfel & Turner, 1979, p. 40).

What Is the Relevance of Social Identity for Organization and Change?

Social identity consists of three processes in the following specific order: social categorization, social identification and social comparison (Tajfel & Turner, 1979). Social categorization as the first stage can be explained as categorizing yourself and other people to understand the social environment. Social identification as the second stage means adopting the identity of the group in which we have categorized ourselves. Finally, the social comparison stage follows the categorization of yourself into a group (in-group); there is a tendency to compare the in-group with other groups (out-groups). In this way, groups give a sense of belonging to a part of the social world, or, put another way: a social identity. Social identity and its three processes help in understanding how organizations form, develop and work. It is related to the concepts of culture and leadership and may help to explain how engagement and cooperation, commitment and resistance to change develop. A shared social identity may be an asset in the case of change. But one's social identity can also become a liability from a personal or organizational perspective when it is threatened by a change. A strong and shared social identity may be the heart of a strong organizational culture. This can also be an asset and in some cases a liability. Conner (1992) states: "Whenever a discrepancy exists between the current culture and the objectives of your change, the culture always wins" (p. 179). From the perspective of change, people's identification with organizations is highly relevant: "Organizational identification is the degree to which a member defines himself or herself by the same attributes that he or she believes define the organization" (Dutton, Dukerich, & Harquail, 1994, p. 239). The self-concept of highly identified employees is related to the organization and its attributes. The self-concepts may be confused if these attributes are changed, for example as a result of a merger or a rebranding. To further illustrate the relevance: "Van Knippenberg, Martin, and Tyler (2006) found that highly identified group members tend to emphasize the change *process*, whereas less identified group members tend to emphasize the change *outcomes*. Thus, highly identified employees may even agree to drastic change processes if they perceive them to be fairly managed" (Drzensky & Van Dick, 2013, p. 279). Research by Madsen, Miller, and John (2005) shows that organizational identification is positively related to readiness for change.

Search Strategy

Relevant databases were searched using the term 'social identity' in combination with 'organization', 'employee', 'change', 'meta-analysis' and 'systematic review'. The searched yielded close to 130 articles. After screening the title and abstracts for relevance, twenty-six studies met the inclusion criteria. After thorough examination, another sixteen studies were excluded.

Main Findings

1. *Social identity is positively related to both job satisfaction and OCB (Level C-).* In a non-controlled before-after measurement study, findings show that social identity is positively related to job satisfaction and organizational citizenship behaviour (OCB, also known as extra-role behaviour) (Topa et al., 2009). We also found that "cognitive identification had strong influences on both affective commitment and organization-based self-esteem. Affective commitment and self-esteem then motivated citizenship behaviours" (Bergami & Bagozzi, 2000, p. 574; Level D).
2. *Social identification enhances job performance (Level D).* The positive effects of social identification on job performance are likely to take the form of both task performance and OCB (Huang, 2013).
3. *During mergers, increased perceived identity threat is negatively associated with organizational identification and negatively influences common in-group identity (Level D)* (Amiot, Terry, & McKimmie, 2012).
4. *Members of the lower-status premerger organization perceived fewer similarities between the two premerger organizations and have increased perceived identity threat* (Boen, Vanbeselaere, & Cool, 2006; Amiot et al., 2012; *Levels D and E*), "These findings suggest that both perceived similarity and perceptions of identity threat are important mechanisms for the establishment of a new identity during times of organizational mergers" (Amiot et al., 2012).
5. *Organization identification (a specific form of social identification) mediates the relationship between leader-member exchange (LMX) and job satisfaction (Level D).* "As LMX has a direct effect on organizational identification and an indirect effect on job satisfaction, a high-quality supervisor-subordinate relationship is the crucial success factor for cultivating employees' strong identification with the organization and positive feelings about their jobs" (Loi, Chang, & Lam, 2014).
6. *Social identification has a positive effect on the perception of organizational support, which in turn reduces emotional exhaustion and lowers turnover intentions (Avanzi, Fraccaroli, Sarchielli, Ullrich, & Van Dick, 2014; Level E).* "Low and high status are based on hospital size (number of beds), with low status having the fewest number of beds".

What Is the Conclusion?

Social identity theory is well researched. It is highly relevant for organizations in general and for change in particular. The specific evidence shows that social identity has a positive effect on job performance, job satisfaction and organizational citizenship behaviour. These are important factors for the performance and change in organizations. In an organizational context, social identity is about organizational identification. This kind of identification has a positive influence on job satisfaction. During mergers, an increase in perceived identity threat has negative outcomes, as it lowers organizational identification and negatively influences common in-group identity. Furthermore, members of the smaller ('lower status') premerger organization perceived fewer similarities between the two premerger organizations and have an increased perceived identity threat.

These findings underline the importance of social identity theory for the understanding of processes of performance and change in organizations. They show, for example, that in the case of mergers, additional attention needs to be devoted to the employees of the smaller ('lower status') organization, as they are susceptible to the negative effects of an increase in perceived identity threat.

Practical Reflections

Social identity theory has high relevance for organizations and their change processes: "In line with past research we have shown that organizational identification is a key variable" (Avanzi et al., 2014, p. 284). The theory and the perspective it provides have important implications for organizational change and its design. Based on the evidence gathered we can formulate a set of guidelines that may help to develop or improve the social identity in organizational contexts:

- "Create environments in which employees can identify not only with the teams in which they are working but also with the organization's overall mission and vision" (Avanzi et al., 2014, p. 284).
- Creating "favourable conditions for intergroup contact by officially encouraging members of the groups to interact and ensuring that the premerger differences are acknowledged" (Amiot et al., 2012, p. 454).
- "At the organizational level, merging organizations should also be transparent about the extent to which the premerger identities will continue to exist within the new merged organization, keeping in mind that if the lower-status group remains salient and vibrant in the new merged organization, this is also likely to lead these employees to identify more strongly with the new merged organization and, hence, to increase organizational cohesion and performance" (Amiot et al., 2012, p. 454).
- "Transformational leadership seems to have a positive effect on organizational identification" (Huang, 2013). This form of leadership "can be incorporated into training courses to improve follower outcomes and yield better results in comparison to those achieved via eclectic leadership training (e.g. managerial skills surveys, 360-degree feedback instruments)" (Huang, 2013, p. 101).

Self-Categorization

People have a personal identity and a social identity. Psychological depersonalization of the self produces 'group behaviour' and emergent group processes such as influence, cooperation and cohesiveness.

What Is Self-Categorization?

Human beings are able to act as an individual and as a member of social groups. The process that leads to the social animal seeing itself as belonging to, being a member of a group is called *self-categorization* (SC) (Turner, Hogg, Oakes, Reicher, & Wetherell, 1987). Self-categorization theory "is a theory of the nature of the self that recognizes that perceivers are both individuals and group members, explains how and when people will define themselves as individual and group entities and the implications, and examines the impact of this variability in self-perception ('I' to 'we') for understandings of mind and behaviour" (Van Lange, Kruglanski, & Higgins, 2012b, p. 399). Self-categorization theory (SCT) shares its foundations with social identity theory (SIT). Turner (2012, p. 1) says: "People live, work and act in a socially structured system, where there are group-based regularities of perception, cognition and conduct and this reality has psychological consequences. SIT and SCT capture the socially embedded, situated, shared, social, group-located properties of human beings". SCT explains when a group is 'a group'. In particular this theory explains how the human mind works in, and is influenced by, constructing and defining human beings, not as mere individuals (or 'minds', a set of neurotransmitters), but as social animals. As Turner states: "Individuals, groups and intergroup relations exist. Human beings are both individuals and group members and therefore have both personal identity and social identity" (2012, p. 7). SCT teaches that the psychological depersonalization of the self produces 'group behaviour' and emergent group processes such as influence, cooperation and cohesiveness. Belonging to the same inclusive self-category also makes people feel the experiences of other members: 'What happens to others is also happening to themselves' (Turner, 1985). With regard to change capacity, Heifetz et al. (2009) illustrates the importance and potential of self-categorizations in situations of change: "In an organization with a high capacity to adapt, people share responsibility for the larger organization's future in addition to their identification with specific roles and functions" (p. 103).

What Is the Relevance of Self-Categorization Organization and Change?

Self-categorization theory (Turner, 1985) explains group behaviour and group processes, more specifically how and in which situations particular group memberships are meaningful or salient for the individual. Together with social identity theory, self-categorization is the basis of the social identity approach (SIA) (Drzensky & Van Dick, 2013). The two have similarities and do partly overlap. However, self-categorization, being less focused on intergroup relations specifically, has a broader explanatory scope. SCT also addresses the cognitive processes that are the basis for the behaviour it describes. In the context of organization and change, SIA is 'translated' into the concept of organizational identification (OI).

Self-categorization mechanisms may strengthen identity and conformity within groups, as they create a sense of belonging. Organizations with high self-categorization may profit from the group identification and cohesion and the commitment of group members. Self-categorization has the potential to increase job satisfaction, productivity and ultimately, performance.

Search Strategy

Relevant databases were searched using the term 'self-categorization', and 'self-categorization in combination with' meta-analysis or 'systematic review'. The searched yielded close to 200 articles. After screening the title and abstracts for relevance, seven studies met the inclusion criteria. After a critical appraisal, two studies were included. These two studies had a low evidence level (D-). The five excluded studies lacked relevance and/or methodological rigour. In addition, we searched for studies with regard to organizational identification (OI); five highly relevant studies (from A to B-) were found.

Main Findings

1. *Groups benefit from self-categorization when coping with stressful situations (Level D-).* Social identity can help consultants cope with stress as it creates a feeling of social inclusion. However, when consultants cannot meet the high occupational standards, social identity can backfire, provoking work stress (Mühlhaus & Bouwmeester, 2016).
2. *Cognitive organization identification[1] has strong positive effects on both affective commitment and group self-esteem (Level D-).* This instance of self-categorization had a positive effect on affective commitment and group self-esteem, linking the concept of self-categorization positively to commitment and self-esteem (Bergami & Bagozzi, 2000).

In addition to self-categorization as such, we have researched the concept of organizational identity (OI), which is based on self-organization and focused at the organizational context. The main findings with regard to OI are:

1. *Organizational Identification is correlated with a wide range of work-related attitudes, behaviours and context variables (Level A).*

   Organizational tenure, job scope/challenge, organizational prestige, intent to leave, and in-role and extra-role performance can plausibly be interpreted as either antecedents or consequences of Organizational Identification (Riketta, 2005, p. 373).

2. *Transformational leadership is more strongly associated with leader identification than with organizational identification or team identification (Level B-).*

   Transformational leadership is highlighted as an important tool to shape followers' identifications and provide substantial evidence in support of the social identity approach to leadership. Leader identification mediates the relationships between transformational leadership and collective identifications (i.e. organizational identification or team identification), illustrating that relational identification plays a crucial role in subsequently shaping collective identifications. (Horstmeier, Boer, Homan, & Voelpel, 2017, p. 280).

3. *Organizational identification is significantly associated with key attitudes and behaviours in organizations (Level B-).*

   Organizational identification is significantly associated with key attitudes (job involvement, job satisfaction and affective organizational commitment) and behaviours (in-role performance and extra-role performance) in organizations. Organizational identification has a direct effect on general behaviour above and beyond the effect of a general set of attitudes and behaviours. The effects of organizational identification are moderated by national culture, a higher-level social context wherein the organization is embedded, such that the effects are stronger in a collectivistic culture than in an individualistic culture. (Lee, Park, & Koo, 2015, p. 1).

4. *On average workgroup attachment is stronger than organizational attachment (Level B-).*

   Employees feel more identified with and committed to their workgroup than to the organization as a whole. Findings confirmed this hypothesis and thus were compatible with the arguments that workgroups (1) are the more salient social unit, (2) serve employee needs for optimal distinctiveness and (3) are the more important instances for socialization and control, particularly in times of more team-based working (Riketta & van Dick, 2005, p. 504).

5. *Results reveal a mean-weighted positive association between organizational identification and health (Level B).*

Evidence indicates that both workgroup and organizational identification are associated with individuals' experience of reduced strain and burnout as well as greater health and well-being. The findings suggest that social identifications in organizations are as important for individuals' health and well-being as they are for their productivity and performance (Steffens, 2017, p. 328).

What Is the Conclusion?

From the perspective of self-categorization two relevant studies were found. The two studies indicate that self-categorization has a direct or indirect positive effect on multiple factors such as commitment, group self-esteem and stress reduction, as self-categorization can, for example, create a feeling of social inclusion within groups. This may indicate that change management practitioners can benefit from self-categorization, because of the positive effects found. In addition to this perspective, evidence was gathered from the organizational identity (OI) perspective. The high-level evidence studies showed for example that OI is correlated with a wide range of work-related attitudes, behaviours and context variables like organizational tenure and prestige. In addition, there is a positive association between OI and health. The self-categorization related concept of OI is highly relevant and insightful and helpful in the organizational context.

Practical Reflections

Self-categorization theory has been influential for the academic field of social psychology. It has been applied to topics such as group cohesion, group polarization, social influence and collective action, leadership and personality. Together with social identity theory it forms the basis for the social identity approach (SIA). This approach is applied to change and organizations with the concept of organizational identity (OI) (see: Drzensky & Van Dick, 2013). OI is well researched (Riketta, 2005) and highly relevant for managers and organizations who care about the performance and change capacity and have to design and deploy change.

Prosocial Behaviour

Belonging to a group stimulates prosocial behaviour toward the in-group.

What Is Prosocial Behaviour?

Living (and working) in cooperative, highly interdependent groups results in significant fitness benefits (e.g. Leaky & Lewin, 1977). These benefits are associated with *ultrasociality* (Campbell, 1982). There-fore, one could expect that people have a profound need to belong (Baumeister & Leary, 1995). Prosocial behaviour helps to fulfil this need and belonging to a group stimulates prosocial behaviour toward the in-group ('in-group favouritism'). People do care more for in-group members than for out-group members when it comes to helping behaviour (e.g. Levine & Thomson, 2004). Defining each other in terms of the same social category, the experience of a shared identity or common fate and feelings of 'one-ness' or 'we-ness' stimulates in-group favouritism (Fiske, Gilbert, & Lindzey, 2010). If the self becomes an inclusive self, a 'we', then people can cooperate, care for each other and even be 'altruistic'; helping an in-group member is helping one-self (Onorato & Turner, 2004). Belonging, together with its benefits, including survival, can be seen as an economic, calculative or transac-tional phenomenon.

What Is the Relevance of Prosocial Behaviour for Organization and Change?

Change with its uncertainties and challenges can be uncomfortable, if not overwhelming, for human beings and social animals. Prosocial behaviour of leaders or group members in general, with its inclu-sive character and the focus on 'we-ness', can contribute to better and more human or social change processes. From an organizational perspective the fact that engaging in prosocial behaviour increases job satisfaction (of both the giver and receiver), as it fulfils social needs and makes work more enjoyable, illustrates the relevance of the concept. Prosocial behaviour will also increase job performance and commitment. The concept has high relevance and high potential for practice; prosocial behaviour can be beneficial in situations of both 'changing' and 'running' the organization. Prosocial behaviour can fuel organizational culture, team development and cooperation. When expressed in a sincere way, it can give a human face to leader-ship and performance management. With regard to capacity Connor (2006) states: "People can only change when they have the capacity to do so. *Ability* means having the necessary skills and knowing how to use them. *Willingness* is the motivation to apply those skills to a particular situation. If you lack either ability or willingness, it is unlikely that you will successfully adapt to a change" (p. 129). Kriegel and Brandt (1996) illustrate the motivational potential of prosocial behaviour of leaders in developing change capacity: "Emphasizing strengths builds esteem and encourages people to do better in eve-rything, including those things that give them trouble. When you're introducing change, remind people of their competence. Show them how the skills they already have will help them to excel in the new task" (p. 209).

Search Strategy

Relevant databases were searched using the terms 'prosocial', 'social' 'behaviour', 'organization', 'work', 'employee' and 'change', also in combination with 'meta-analysis' or 'systematic review'. The search yielded more than 500 articles. After screening the title and abstracts for relevance, fifteen studies were included. After thorough examination, four additional studies were excluded. Several of the eleven studies included were randomized, controlled experiments with before-after measurement and a high level of evidence (A-).

Main Findings

1. *Gratitude expressions increase prosocial behaviour by enabling individuals to feel socially valued (Level A-).*

    Expressions of gratitude, even in their smallest form, increase prosocial behaviour because individuals feel more socially valued (Grant & Gino, 2010).

2. *If individuals compare themselves socially with others, their prosocial behaviour will decrease (Level A-).*

    In two randomized, controlled experiments, the prosocial behaviour of individuals decreased significantly when they compared themselves socially with other individuals (Riyanto & Zhang, 2013), and it made no difference whether the social comparison was upward or downward (Yip & Kelly, 2013). In both types of comparison, prosocial behaviour will decrease. An explanation might be the reduction in empathy toward the other.

3. *Prosocial behaviour is positively related to organizational commitment and job performance and the behaviour itself increases overall well-being (Level D-).*

    Multiple studies found a positive link between prosocial behaviour and job performance (Baruch, O'Creevy, Hind, & Vigoda-Gadot, 2004; George & Bettenhausen, 1990; Matela & Ryan, 2016) and prosocial behaviour and organizational commitment (Baruch et al., 2004; Boundenghan, Desrumaux, Léoni, & Nicolas, 2012). It is still unclear whether prosocial behaviour increases organizational commitment or organizational commitment increases prosocial behaviour. Furthermore, engaging in prosocial behaviour increases overall well-being (Level D-) (Matela & Ryan, 2016).

4. *Prosocial behaviour increases group cohesiveness (Level D-)* (George & Bettenhausen, 1990).

5. *Prosocial behaviour can be increased by procedural justice and commitment (Level D-)* (Boundenghan et al., 2012).

What Is the Conclusion?

Engaging in prosocial behaviour is valuable, beneficial and helpful for organizations. It increases organizational commitment and job performance of individuals. Even expressing the smallest forms of gratitude can increase prosocial behaviours, as employees will feel more socially valued. When people compare themselves socially with others, prosocial behaviour decreases. During change, prosocial behaviour can be the engine that keeps the process going, as change can be hard and sometimes even depressing. It also bolsters group cohesiveness, which has multiple positive outcomes (see Chapter 3.2 on social cohesion). Helping colleagues through the difficult times of change can be crucial for change success.

Practical Reflections

Given the potential positive effects of prosocial behaviour, it is relevant to find ways to increase the context of organizations and change. Based on the research it is possible to define some guidelines which can be helpful in achieving that increase. First of all, make use of (small) expressions of gratitude as it makes employees feel socially valued. In addition, increase procedural justice during organizational change, for example by managing more equitably. Being aware that social comparison might decrease prosocial behaviour can also be helpful. Finally, create a learning environment with managerial support for employees, including constructive forms of feedback.

Terror Management Theory

People function securely if they believe they are contributing to a meaningful change or mission. Standards and goals have to be inviting and inclusive, also for minority groups within the organization.

What Is Terror Management Theory?

Belonging can also be seen as an existential, normative or transformational phenomenon. Terror management theory puts survival, the desire to stay alive, in a central position in explaining individual and social behaviour. The theory is related to the concept of mortality salience—the awareness by an individual that his or her death is inevitable. Terror management (TM) proposes that, being aware of death, almost all human activity is driven by the fear of death, thus creating anxiety. To cope with the fear of death, humans have evolved defence mechanisms. "TM asserts that defence mechanisms take one of two paths: the proximal system that distracts and distances one from increased consciousness of loss; and the distal system that uses existential buffers to prevent this awareness from reaching consciousness" (Bailey & Raelin, 2015, p. 128). Solomon, Greenberg and Pyszczynski developed this theory in 1984 in order to answer two basic questions: Why do people need self-esteem? Why do different cultures have such a difficult time coexisting peacefully? They were inspired by the ideas of the anthropologist Becker, who wrote 'The Denial of Death' (1974) and integrated insights from a variety of (social) sciences like sociology and psychology. People are able to realize that they are mortal and vulnerable and experience existential terror. As a result, they are very much aware of possible threats and they look for significant contributions to a meaningful setting, like a team, a company, a religious order or society. This terror management function can be served, for example, by an organizational culture that provides organizational members with 'meaningfulness' and self-esteem (e.g. Greenberg, Solomon, & Pyszczynski, 1997). Leaders may exploit this function in managing change by articulating external threats related to competitors, other 'cultures' or economic developments. Thus, they create a 'sense of urgency', an impetus for change; sometimes they formulate an 'enemy mission' or 'target mission' in order to materialize the existential threats and possibilities to enhance self-esteem. Terror management theory also provides an additional perspective with regard to belonging, or more specifically the in-group/out-group issue. Other people, with other paradigms and convictions, call into question the validity of your own (Solomon, Greenberg, & Pyszczynski, 1991). To deal with the threat of other views, one may ridicule, derogate, fight or even destroy them. Research into terror management can show change leaders that followers function securely if they believe they are contributing to a meaningful change or mission. In managing change, leaders have to deal with varying formal and informal groups. From terror management research one could learn that a feeling of belongingness and harmony can be facilitated by norms. Standards and goals must not be too narrow or unavailable to certain groups; instead they must be inviting and inclusive, also for minority groups within the organization.

What Is the Relevance of Terror Management Theory for Organization and Change?

Terror management theory puts survival and the desire to stay alive in a central position. This perspective is related to the ideas of 'burning platforms' and the so-called sense of urgency that are popular in the literature and practice of change management. This relates to (the kind of) change vision, leadership style, culture and also resistance and commitment to change. Jonas, Kauffeld, Sullivan & Fritsche (2011) illustrates the reliance on the theory for organizational culture: "Our results suggest that the many aspects of corporate culture—including underlying values and the more directly tangible artefacts of a company—all play a role in terror management defences" (p. 2877). In bestsellers on change management the concept of urgency and survival is popular and also discussed. Conner (2006) states that the urgency of burning-platform situations creates motivation to undertake major change. Urgency can be generated by the high price of unresolved problems or the high cost of missed opportunities. Novak (2012) points at the tendency to 'sugarcoat' things; Kriegel (1996) considers urgency to be one of the four keys to lighting a firestorm in your organization (the other three are inspiration, ownership and rewards and recognition). Heifetz, Grashow and Linsky also discuss urgency, in particular the negative or crisis variant and give a warning. They state: "There is a myth that drives many change initiatives into the ground: that the organization needs to change because it is broken" (p. 17). Heath and Heath (2010) also give a warning. There is a cliché that "the bar must be raised" to motivate people to perform and to change. But they emphasize that you need to lower the bar and 'shrink the change' to motivate reluctant people. However, Bridges (1991) emphasizes the importance of conveying the problem and the necessity of change: people do not act if they do not see, acknowledge and understand the problem. From the perspective of terror management, the urgency or the terror that derives from the psychological conflict mentioned earlier has an impact on employees. The fear of death/loss seems relevant during organizational changes, because in change employees can literally lose their job or feel a sense of loss because their job description has changed. Although this might seem far-fetched, there is substantial evidence linking terror management to organizational change.

Search Strategy

Relevant databases were searched using the term "terror management". The search yielded 220 articles. After screening the title and abstracts, five articles were included. Three studies had a very high level of evidence.

Main Findings

1. *Organizations act as a psychological shield against death-related thoughts (Level A-).*

   The workplace, as well as other institutions, seems important to employees as it can serve as a life-structuring sense of purpose and a feeling of group membership. These characteristics make the organization a key psychological shield against death-related thoughts (Jonas et al., 2011).

2. *Reminding people of their mortality is positively related to defending recent organizational changes against criticism (Level A).*

   When employees are reminded of their own death, they are more inclined to defend recent organizational changes against criticism. It seems that the psychological shield is so important that employees are willing to defend 'their shield' against criticism (Jonas et al., 2011).

3. *People react more strongly to perceived and procedural fairness when asked to think about their mortality (Level A).*

Research points in the direction that thinking about death (mortality salience) leads people to react more negatively toward violation and more positively toward fairness. This might explain why fairness is important to people and why people react more strongly to perceived and procedural fairness when asked to think about their mortality (Van den Bos & Miedema, 2000).

4. *Reminding people of their mortality is positively related to escalation of commitment (Level A).*

Mortality salience leads to an escalation of commitment. "Escalation of commitment refers to the phenomenon observed when people continue following the course set by a prior decision and even increase their investment in it, despite new evidence suggesting that the decision was probably wrong" (Yen & Lin, 2012, p. 52).

5. *Reminding people of their mortality is positively related to describing leaders in more agentic terms (Level C).*

Mortality salience has a positive effect on describing leaders in more agentic terms (stereotyping). In the media, the constant bombardment of images of war, terrorism and disasters change the way people see and describe their effective leaders, making them more agentic and masculine. This favours male leaders over female leaders. With sufficient motivation and practice, people can unlearn stereotyped associations and overcome prejudiced thoughts (Hoyt, Simon, & Innella, 2011).

What Is the Conclusion?

From the perspective of organization and change, terror management theory and its evidence provide useful insights. It also helps in understanding how the creation of a sense of urgency and a change vision that focuses on 'survival' might work. The evidence supports the idea that terror management has an effect on several factors applicable to situations of change and issues related to performance, commitment and leadership style, for example.

Practical Reflections

It might seem far-fetched to combine the fear of death with organizational outcomes, but the scientific evidence suggests otherwise. Thinking about mortality leads to stronger reactions with regard to fairness, contributes to the escalation of commitment and results in leaders being described increasingly in more agentic terms. Note that only the first outcome is positive for both organization and employee, with escalation of commitment being negative. Increasing stereotyping can be negative in the case of female leaders. In relation to change, thinking about death can be beneficial for the organization. People who were reminded of mortality tend to defend recent organizational change. Organizations in general work as an important psychological shield against death-related thoughts. They provide the 'social animal, with its uncertainties and vulnerability' with a 'safe haven' or a meaningful context.

Broaden-and-Build Theory

Negative stimuli such as threats and urgency can be effective in change, but positive ambitions, mirroring positive emotions and feelings, create more self-efficacy or action control in dealing with changes and challenges.

What Is the Broaden-and-Build Theory?

Fighting mortality may provide a positive impetus for change, but is in fact negative. An alternative, positive perspective is provided by the so-called broaden-and-build theory (e.g. Fredrickson, 1998). Fighting mortality is narrow and negative, but may result in effective action in cases of threatened survival. The alternative is broader and positive and may lead to more flexibility, a more adaptive repertoire and more sustainable change (e.g. Fredrickson & Branigan, 2005). The positive emotions related to this alternative provide people with a broader scope of attention, more openness and behavioural variety, thereby creating more self-efficacy or action control in dealing with changes and challenges. These insights do not rule out the possible stimulating effects of fear appeals or a sense of urgency; instead they articulate an alternative that may be more effective, attractive and sustainable in a lot of situations.

What Is the Relevance of the Broaden-and-Build Theory for Organizations and Change?

The broaden-and-build theory of positive emotions suggests that positive emotions (i.e. positive affect) are more than just rewards for favourable behaviours and circumstances. Instead, positive emotions are adaptive, and individuals experience them so that they can help prepare for future challenges by developing key resources. Specifically, when individuals experience positive emotions such as joy or contentment, their thought-action possibilities are broadened, which then creates physical and psychological resources (Fredrickson, 2001). Frequent experiences of positive affect increase approach-oriented behaviour (Elliot & Thrash, 2002), meaning that individuals are more likely to engage with their environments, allowing them to learn more, pursue new goals and develop more skills. This is in contrast to negative affect, which is associated with withdrawal behaviours, protection of resources, prevention of harm and quick reactions, all of which may be adaptive in life-threatening situations but may detract from an individual's experience when not in life-threatening situations (Fredrickson, 2001). The theory suggests that managers' first tendency in managing change should be to formulate a positive ambition, mirroring positive emotions and feelings, instead of trying to kick-start change by cultivating possible threats, adversaries or enemies. This illustrates the relevance of the theory and its relationships with organization- and change-related subjects such as leadership, performance management, culture, resistance and commitment and change vision. Several management thinkers illustrate the importance and potential of the theory and its perspective by emphasizing the need for and role of a vision or change vision. Ibarra points to the importance of having a clear and inspiring vision. She states that "across studies and research traditions, vision has been found to be a defining feature of leadership" (p. 41). Bridges (1991) emphasizes the importance of clarifying the purpose: What is the idea behind what you're doing? People need a picture of how the outcome will look; participation requires imagination. Bridges attributes terrible obstacles in change processes to having no discernible purpose behind the proposed changes. Belasco (1990) says his experience tells him that an energizing, inspiring vision is the key to mobilizing support: "This vision is the picture that drives all action" (p. 11). Belasco defines the vision as the focus and inspiration that empower people to change.

Search Strategy

Relevant databases were searched using the term 'broaden-and-build'. The search yielded 196 results of which ten seemed relevant in a study of the abstract. After thorough examination, seven studies were included.

Main Findings

1. *The results from two experiments support the premise that happy moods broaden and build general managers' (GM)s' knowledge by helping GMs move beyond initial preferences and focus on the full range of information that each GM can provide (Level B).*

   Moreover, the data indicate a mechanism for which mood might alter group performance. Specifically, within the current experiments, the results were due to mood influencing GMs' focus on the unique/critical information relative to the common/non-critical information. Thus, if a group's goal is to combine various pieces of information into a comprehensive understanding of the problem, this research indicates that it may be best to be in a happy mood, rather than a sad mood (Bramersfeld & Gasper, 2008).

"The current experiments clarify the role of mood in group decision-making and provide evidence for a broaden-and-build explanation, rather than the accessible-knowledge explanation, for the effects of mood on group-level information processing" (Bramersfeld & Gasper, 2008, p. 302).

2.   *Findings from a study support the broaden-and-build theory (Level D).*

There is support for Fredrickson's (2001) broaden-and-build theory, showing that experience of positive emotions that comes from engaging in Organization Citizenship Behaviour (OCB) relates to decreased depressed mood and increased satisfaction with health and life. As such, receiving help in the form of social support is indeed an important pathway by which relationships with co-workers relate to health and well-being, but giving help may be another important pathway to help explain employee health and well-being (Baranik & Eby, 2016).

"In particular, findings from the current study support mood regulation (Tice and Bratslavsky, 2000) and Fredrickson's (2001) broaden-and-build model of positive emotions, showing that the experience of positive emotions that comes from engaging in OCB-Is relates to decreased depressed mood and increased satisfaction with health and life" (Baranik & Eby, 2016, p. 363).

3.   *A systematic review of fifteen studies supports the contribution of the broaden-and-build theory to the creation of a healthy workplace by fostering positive emotions in employees (Level C).*

Positive emotions were found to be pivotal in enhancing employee performance, encouraging innovation and creativity that result in sustainable business practices, helping organizations make good decisions, facilitating workflow and motivation, developing authentic and charismatic leadership styles, job enrichment, better team performance and satisfactory customer relations. A link between positive emotions and an upward spiral of personal and organizational resources has also been established where positive self-evaluation, development of resilience, a climate of social support, the setting of clearer goals, high-quality social interaction, good health and productivity of workers have been found to promote effective coping (Glass, 2009).

"To review, this paper has considered the ground-breaking broaden-and-build theory of Barbara Frederickson and posited it as an explanation of how the mechanisms of Solution Focus (SF, added by the authors) operate inside our heads to produce useful outcomes in navigating the world" (Glass, 2009, p. 39).

4. *Leader membership exchange (LMX) predicts employees' change-oriented behaviours (Level B).*

"LMX predicts employees' change-oriented behaviours through two sequential paths: (a) the positive affect mediates the relationship between LMX and employee psychological capital, and (b) psychological capital mediates the relationship between positive affect and employees' creative performance and taking charge" (Lin, Kao, Chen, & Lu, 2016, p. 399).

"Our results provide a logical explanation of the 'broadening' and 'building' mechanisms through which LMX enhances employees' change-oriented behaviours" (Lin et al., 2016, p. 399; Level B).

5. *Collective positive emotions can be considered as antecedents of team resilience (Level D-).*

"This paper contributes to the literature on positive emotions by examining the mechanism (i.e. team resilience) underlying the relationships between collective positive emotions and team performance" (Meneghel, Salanova, & Martínez, 2016, p. 248).

"The findings of this study offer important implications and provide support for the B&B theory of positive emotions as an effective theoretical framework to explain how collective positive emotions influence team resilience in the work context" (Meneghel et al., 2016, p. 252).

6. *The experience of positive emotions builds hope over time (Level D-).*

"So, the findings of the current study are in line with B&B theory (Fredrickson, 1998) in that the experience of positive emotions builds hope over time—either through a broadened mindset (Fredrickson & Branigan, 2005) or by cognitively evaluating the experienced positive emotions (Weiss & Cropanzano, 1996)—which, in turn, is related to work engagement" Ouweneel, Le Blanc, Schaufeli, & Wijhe, 2012, p. 1145).

"Positive emotions and hope—as a personal resource—seem to predict vigour, dedication, and absorption at work, either indirectly or directly" (Ouweneel et al., 2012).

What Is the Conclusion?

The findings support Frederickson's (2001) broaden-and-build theory, by showing that: if a group's goal is to combine various pieces of information into a comprehensive understanding of the problem, the group may best be in a happy mood, rather than a sad mood (Bramersfeld & Gasper, 2008). Positive emotions were found to be pivotal in enhancing employee performance, helping organizations make good decisions, facilitating workflow and motivation, and developing authentically and charismatically. They also influence leadership styles, job enrichment, better team performance and satisfactory customer relations (Glass, 2009). In addition, collective positive emotions can be considered as antecedents of team resilience (Meneghel et al., 2016) and positive emotions build hope over time (Ouweneel et al., 2012).

Practical Reflections

Multiple high-level studies provide support for the broaden-and-build theory. The findings give important guidance for leaders and organizations in running and changing. Positive emotions can literally energize a person, increasing individual and team performance, decision-making, motivation and leadership development. Furthermore, it also benefits customer relations and it relates positively to health and well-being.

This theory seems to be so beneficial for both employer and employee that organizations must make use of it. Enhancing and nurturing the positive instead of the negative can bring so much to the organization. In our societies, we often focus on the negative. What did we do wrong? What can we do better next time? This is also true for the field of (social) psychology. Positive psychology, here in particular the broaden-and-build theory, shows us the importance and benefits of emphasizing the positive.

Note

1. This component was defined as the self-awareness of one's membership in the organization, which is an instance of self-categorization.

4 Understanding, Organizational Behaviour and Change

A First Short Story of Understanding and Change

Understanding is about understanding as the social need for shared meaning and prediction. A social representation is the ensemble of thoughts and feelings being expressed in verbal and overt behaviour of actors that constitutes an object for a social group. Social representations frame objects or issues in socially recognizable ways, in socially shared schemas. People are motivated to explain and understand the causes of events and behaviours. As a form of sense-making they assign causes to behaviour of themselves and others. Judgments are grounded in and based on people's attitudes; in order to understand or to make sense, people will compare the position advocated by an idea with their own position regarding that idea. Most of the behaviours that people display are the result of social learning, either deliberately or inadvertently, through modelling, the influence of example. The presence of others causes social impact, an influence that can be real or perceived, direct or indirect (implied), experienced or imagined. How group members believe their goals are related impacts their dynamics and performance significantly. Social contexts are 'forums of transaction', with social exchange as the market mechanism. Individuals voluntarily act in favour of another person or an organization, motivated by individuals' expectations of reciprocity.

Understanding, the need for shared meaning and prediction, is the second core social motive and one of the two (relatively) cognitive motives (the other is controlling). Shared understanding enables the functioning and survival of people in groups. Group meaning is instrumental in decision-making and helps to coordinate with other group members (Fiske, 2004). In organizations, understanding is present or visible in, for example, 'a sense of mission', the way people 'strategize', the organizational culture and values. Social learning, for example, is a vehicle for (shared) understanding in the organizational context and visible in, for example, socialization processes, the phenomenon of 'lead by example' and the role models that 'significant others' are. Shared understanding may hamper change when a current 'joint view of reality' is incongruent or in competition with a new 'reality' related to the change. Understanding is related to change and management topics like mission, leadership, organizational culture, and change vision and resistance to change.

In this chapter the following theories and concepts are presented and assessed:

Social representation
Attribution theory
Social judgment theory
Social learning theory
Social impact theory
Theory of cooperation/competition
Social exchange

Social Representation

A social representation is the ensemble of thoughts and feelings being expressed in verbal and overt behaviour of actors that constitutes an object for a social group. Social representations frame objects or issues in socially recognizable ways, in socially shared schemas.

What Is Social Representation?

Social representation stands for values, ideas, beliefs, practices and metaphors shared among members. A social representation can be seen as the collective elaboration "of a social object by the community for the purpose of behaving and communicating" (Moscovici, 1963, p. 251). The building blocks of social representations are shared knowledge and understanding of common reality, which enables communication between individuals and groups. Fiske (2010) defines understanding as the need for shared meaning and prediction. A way to create shared meaning is by providing a 'frame of reference' (Cantril, 1941, p. 20), generating a point of view that directs interpretations. Smircich and Morgan (1982) talk about the 'management of meaning' or 'framing'; "creating a point of reference against which some kind of action can emerge" (p. 258). Shared meaning is created in an interactive, social process, a process of sense-making (Weick, 1995). Rijsman (1997) talks about "the necessary social criterion of truth, namely consensus" (p. 144). He points to the logic that Festinger (1950) applied in his classic theory of social communication: "he (*Festinger*) said that people who do not know the world objectively will speak with each other and will try to arrive at consensus, to construct at least a social (although quasi-objective, for not based on a correct individual processing of objective information) sense of truth' (Rijsman, 1997, p. 144). People often relate understanding primarily to the individual mind. However, Rijsman (1997) introduces a '*social* ontology of mind' and states that without intersubjective co-ordination there is no meaning: "meaning is referential reality that follows from the co-ordinated activity between subjects" (p. 146). Weick (1993) illustrates this perspective by stating that designs do not create social systems; they are created by social systems. The people or minds that constitute these social systems are "always" determined by the limitation in their individual capacity to process all information correctly (like in the 'bounded rationality' concept of Herbert Simon). Therefore, they have to 'compensate' with the only thing that is left to them in practice, namely communicating and creating consensus. Rijsman (1977) illustrates this perspective in a vivid way. He reflects: "Such a view on meaning and communication, however, is like the old biblical image of fallen angels, or the image in which human beings only speak with each other and must constantly resolve contradictions, because they lost their original (angelic) capacity to see the world 'as it is'. Real angels, in contrast, are doomed to peace, for with their perfect minds, all replicas of the ideal mind, they only see truth and, thus, agree" (p. 144). For 'fallen angels' organization and change are not 'just that'; both are what Weick (1979) calls 'a body of thought, thought by thinking thinkers' (p. 42).

Weick's idea is related to social representation theory that provides very relevant insights with regard to the core social motive of understanding. Social representations are both the process and the result of social construction, being elaborated and changing over time. Weick's 'body of thought' can be seen as a set of social representations that are constantly converted into a social reality while continuously being reinterpreted, rethought, represented (e.g. Jovchelovitch, 2007). These representations are dynamic elements of knowledge resulting from a social, interactive process. The fundamental aim of social representations is to 'make the unfamiliar familiar' (Moscovici, 1984). Moscovici, inspired by Durkheim's collective representations, coined the term in 1961. He defines social representations as "systems of values, ideas and practices with a two-fold function: first, to establish an order which will enable individuals to orientate themselves in their material and social world and to master it; secondly, to enable communication to take place amongst members of a community by providing them with a code for social exchange and a code for naming and classifying unambiguously the various aspects of their world and their individual and group history" (Moscovici, 1973, p. xiii). Wagner and Lepine (1999) summarize: "a social representation is the ensemble of thoughts and feelings being expressed in verbal and overt behaviour of actors which constitutes an object for a social group" (p. 96). Social representations frame issues or objects in socially recognizable ways, in socially shared schemas (Moscovici, 1988). These representations are instrumental in making the unfamiliar familiar. The processes of anchoring and objectification are essential in realizing this. Anchoring is about giving meaning to new phenomena, such as objects, relations, experiences, practices and changes. These phenomena are related to or integrated in already known frames or worldviews so they can be interpreted from that which is familiar (Hoijer, 2011). Objectification is the process of filling a new phenomenon with familiar images by giving it an iconic form. It entails two stages: a new, abstract representation becomes more concretized and after that the elaborated representation achieves independence from the original context and becomes accepted as a 'conventional' reality (Moscovici, 1984). In social representations, objects, subjects and activities are linked (Jovchelovitch, 1996). This idea is elaborated in the 'Toblerone model of social representations' (Bauer & Gaskell, 1999). In this model there is a relationship between subjects, being the carriers of the representation; objects, being the activity or idea that is represented; and projects of a social group within which the representations makes sense.

What Is the Relevance of Social Representation for Organization and Change?

By making use of anchoring and objectification, people make a social representation familiar and abstract ideas become concrete. For example, the social object 'fair trade' is given a specific meaning by the Western world to help producers in developing countries achieve better trading conditions and to promote sustainable farming. The term by itself has no meaning, as fair is a subjective norm. However, we gave meaning to it as a group (Western world). In an organizational setting, members can be seen as a group of employees, for example a work team or a department. It is also argued that people in an organization think of decision and decision-making as realities and that both decision and decision-making can be defined as social representations: "They influence organizations' members' ways of understanding and behaving in organizations" (Laroche, 1995, p. 62). The social construction of meaning is an important process in organizations. Leaders can and must facilitate this; they have to take care of the 'management of meaning' (Smircich & Morgan, 1982). In organizational settings, meaning is given to and by certain social objects such as a mission statement, sense of urgency, a corporate vision, corporate values or a corporate strategy. These meanings can differentiate between and within organizations, between individuals or teams, for example. The importance of social representations such as vision and missions seems to be undisputed; management experts and gurus emphasize time after time the role and importance of them in organization and change. For example, Ibarra points to the importance of having a clear and inspiring vision. She states, "Across studies and research traditions, vision has been found to be a defining feature of leadership" (p. 41). Bridges (1991) emphasizes the importance of clarifying the purpose: What is the idea behind what you're doing? People need a picture of how the outcome will look; participation calls for imagination. Bridges attributes terrible obstacles in change processes to having no discernible purpose behind the proposed changes. Belasco (1990) says his experience tells him that an energizing, inspiring vision is the key to mobilizing support: "This vision is the picture that drives all action" (p. 11). Belasco defines the vision as the focus and inspiration that empower people to change. However, as Moscovici shows, to be effective they need to be socially 'shared' and 'recognized'. It is for this reason that the importance and necessity of a *shared* vision and a *'sense* of mission', for example, is emphasized (Campbell & Nash, 1992; also, Campbell & Yeung, 1990). In addition to a *sense* of mission, one can point to a *sense* of urgency as an example of social representations being relevant and instrumental in managing and changing organizations and behaviour. A sense of urgency is often seen as a prerequisite for effective change. To illustrate this, Kotter (2012) states: "By far the biggest mistake people make when trying to change organizations is to plunge ahead without establishing a high enough sense of urgency in fellow managers and employees" (p. 4). Social representations are relevant to organizational and change topics such as vision, mission, the impetus to change, culture, leadership and communication.

Search Strategy

Relevant databases were searched using the term 'social' and 'representation' in combination with 'meta-analysis' or 'systematic review'. The search yielded more than 400 articles (!). After screening the title and abstracts for relevance, fifty-two studies met the inclusion criteria. After thorough examination, we included only five articles because of relevance and methodological problems, with an evidence level ranging from B- to E.

Main Findings

1. *There is no universal approach to social representation theory, and it is often used in a very broad form (Level B-).*

    A meta-analysis found that 40% of the included articles regarding Social Representation Theory (SRT) used Moscovici's grand theory. A total of 10% used different theories and approaches, like Arbic's central nucleus theory and Doise's societal approach. About one third (31%) did not specify their approach and 19% just cited the theory, but did not make use of it in any way. Most articles used SRT in a very broad form, lacking in-depth discussions and sometimes using SRT incorrectly (Martins-Silva, Silva-Junior, Peroni, De Medeiros, & Vitória, 2016). "This data causes concern, because it shows that SRT is being used indiscriminately, without promoting a deeper discussion or reflection on this theory, which does not contribute to the development of this theoretical framework" (Martins-Silva et al., 2016, p. 911).

2. *Social representation influences the manner in which people obey and/or break rules (Level D-).*

The way in which people socially represent certain situations influences their behaviour. In some cases, they may even break the law and (socially) justify it. The study found a difference in which rules are broken and how they are justified: "we found three separate dimensions concerning acceptable reasons for running a red light, whereas there was only one dimension for tax evasion. This latter difference in results might reflect the fact that although all the respondents were familiar with traffic lights, not everybody was familiar with taxes" (Verkuyten, Rood-Pijpers, Elffers, & Hessing, 1994, p. 495).

3. *Social representation is an important factor in strategically aligning knowledge management systems (KMS) (Level E).*

Many organizations try to derive more business value from internal organizational knowledge. However, they often underestimate the challenges relating to social interactions and the employees' perception of new information systems (Dulipovici, 2013). Employee groups develop different views of KMS, which may eventually lead to strategic misalignment. "Since users generate social representations of KMS within their local work practices, managers should try to understand how groups anchor their social representations and how objectification mechanisms guide their behaviour" (Dulipovici & Robey, 2013, p. 124).

What Is the Conclusion?

Social representations and interactions and processes to share them and to make sense of them are relevant, if not essential, for the field of organization and change. A complication could be related to the lack of a clear-cut universal approach. The concept of social representation is fundamental and helpful to the understanding of the role of missions, culture and strategy, for example, and the way they work in organizations. Specific evidence related to the field of organization and change provides additional insights and guidance for practitioners. For example, the way people obey and break rules is related to their social representations. The same applies to decisions and decision-making, influencing behaviour of employees. In aligning knowledge management systems (KMS), managers should try to understand how groups use anchoring and objectification, as this guides their behaviour. Social representations can be instrumental in changing individual and group behaviour. Hence they can play an important role in the success and failure of organizational change and the understanding of it.

Practical Reflections

Social representations occur in understanding and working with instruments like corporate visions and mission statements. The concept is more than visible in the work of scientists and gurus like Morgan (Smircich & Morgan, 1982) and Weick (1979) and their concepts of 'framing', the management of meaning and 'enactment'. The same goes for well-known ideas with regard to culture and leadership like those of Schein (1985). Practitioners such as managers and consultants as well as the people involved in 'their' processes, such as employees or members of transition management teams (TMTs) (Duck, 1993), can benefit from the understanding of the concept. In fact, the concept of social representations is the 'software' of concepts such as culture and mission and the processes in which they come into being and become (socially) effective. At a more operational level, managers who unravel and assess social representations that employees make, construct or coproduce will have a better understanding of, for example, the reasons why they obey or break organizational rules. The latter can lead to employees stealing from their boss, scandals or even corruption.

Attribution Theory

People are motivated to explain and understand the causes of events and behaviours. As a form of sense-making they assign causes to behaviour of themselves and others.

What Is Attribution Theory?

Another perspective that sheds light on understanding, the way we make sense of the world, is provided by the attribution theory. This theory attempts to explain why people do what they do. Heider (1958) believed that people are naïve psychologists trying to make sense; they are motivated to explain and understand the causes of events and behaviours. In social psychology, attribution theory is basically the assigning of causes to behaviour of yourself and others. The theory addresses how and why people explain the things as they do. As a form of sense-making it links the causes and effects of behaviour. In attribution theory the two central questions are: "Why do I do what I do?" and "Why do others do what they do?" Most of our attributions are driven by emotional or motivational impulses, for example anger and commitment. The starting point of attribution theory was in 1958, when the well-known psychologist Fritz Heider published his book *The Psychology of Interpersonal Relations.* Heider (1958) described two types of attribution: internal attribution and external attribution. The first type is about attributing "the locus of causality to factors within the individual such as personality traits, skill and effort" (Gok, Deshpande, Deshpande, & Hunter, 2012, p. 2578). The second type is about attributing "the locus of causality to situational factors beyond the control of the individual, such as task difficulty and luck" (Gok et al., 2012, p. 2578). Heider's theory is criticized for being too mechanistic and for assuming that people think rationally, logically and systematically. This criticism can be refuted by the explanation that both emotional and motivational responses are seen as attributions. Recently, a third type of attribution, relational attribution, has been introduced by researchers (Eberly, Holley, Johnson, & Mitchell, 2017). "Our findings identify the circumstances under which relational attributions are likely to be formed and indicate that relational attributions are related to relational improvement behaviours, particularly when employees are of the same sex as their relationship partner and perceive sufficient time and energy to engage in relational improvement efforts" (Eberly et al., 2017). Their research has a low evidence level (D-), and future research is needed to further explore this finding.

Kelley (1967) shows that people acting as naïve scientists in explaining someone else's behaviour (the attribution process) look for three pieces of information: consistency, consensus and distinctiveness. Consistency concerns the question of whether an actor always behaves in this manner, in other times and situations. Consensus relates to the question of whether people other than the actor behave in the same way in the same situation. Distinctiveness of the action concerns the question of whether the actor is the only one who behaves in this manner. The way in which we use information to make attributions, to make sense of our context, is important in decision-making. The way in which we evaluate consensus and distinctiveness information is very important in making decisions such as whether to follow a leader, or to commit oneself to a change process or new strategy. However, this kind of rational thought is not a given in daily life, for ordinary people. We are 'fallen angels' (Rijsman, 1977); we do not possess a "God's-eye" view of the world; we are not all-knowing and free from bias (Aronson, 1995). It is impossible to evaluate each piece of information systematically. Therefore we use shortcuts. Fiske and Taylor (2013) state that human beings are programmed to be cognitive misers; information-processing capacity is limited, so we look for strategies that simplify complex problems and reduce complexity. For example, we ignore certain information or overuse other information in order to circumvent the search for other information. We use 'pattern recognition', stereotypes, models and 'benchmarks' to evaluate people and situations in an efficient and also simplified way. This can indeed be very efficient, but may also lead to serious errors and biases.

As Aronson (2016) shows: "Our propensity for bias and error, then, can be a significant barrier to interpersonal and intergroup understanding" (p. 120). People tend to go beyond the information given. That may be efficient, functional and even accurate. However, causal attributions may also be erroneous, dysfunctional and counterproductive. An illustration is related to what Pettigrew (1979) coined as the ultimate attribution error; in ambiguous situations, people tend to make attributions consistent with their prejudices.

What Is the Relevance of Attribution for Organization and Change?

People in organizations confronted with change initiatives or new policies, for example, will try to make sense of them. Attribution theory shows that they will be hampered or 'bounded' by not having complete information, let alone a "God's eye" (Aronson, 1995). The concept of attribution also emphasizes the importance of biases and causal mechanisms in organizational processes such as those of decision-making and sense-making. It helps to understand, explain and possibly influence organizational behaviour and attitudes toward change. It helps leaders to understand their followers: leaders' "attributions about the causes of subordinate performance can affect the way in which a leader subsequently interacts with subordinates" (Offermann, Schroyer, & Green, 1998, p. 1135). Attribution theory is relevant to the organization as a whole, as it affects relations and performance, and specifically to change management, as different attributions can be given to the reason for change, which in turn may affect the outcome of the change. Understanding attribution can also be instrumental in understanding something like resistance to change. Confronted with possible change, people will start thinking about causes and effects. It is helpful to understand these and the underlying processes in order to be better able to deal with factual or possible resistance. Bridges (1991) also emphasizes the importance of understanding resistance and its causes: "It's the process of letting go that people resist, not the change itself. Their resistance can take the form of foot-dragging or sabotage, and you have to understand the pattern of loss to be ready to deal with the resistance and keep it from getting out of hand" (p. 15).

Search Strategy

Relevant databases were searched using the term 'attribution theory', and 'attribution theory' in combination with 'meta-analysis' or 'systematic review'. The search yielded more than 600 articles. After screening the title and abstracts for relevance, one meta-analysis and six studies were included.

Main Findings

1. *When making economic decisions, people make use of causal attributions (Level B-).*

   ". . . what this research shows is that when people make economic decisions they may 'violate' expectations based on rational considerations such as these predicted by rational choice theory. However, their decisions are not arbitrary but rather crafted according to predictable rules complying with social motivation considerations such as these reflected by attribution theory" (Gurevich, Kliger, & Weiner, 2012).

2. *When groups perform poorly due to low effort, leaders make more negative comments than when performance is poor because of ability or luck (Level A).*

   When leaders perceive that group performance is poor because of low effort, leaders tend to make more negative comments than when they perceive the performance is low because of ability or luck. Furthermore, leaders were most verbally active when their groups succeeded because of good luck (Offermann et al., 1998).

3. *Individually focused attributions for past success caused groups to consider more divergent alternatives prior to making a shared decision, facilitated the sharing of unique information and improved decision-making (Level A).*

   This implies that focusing on the individual achievement is important for group performance, as it has positive effects for the group as a whole (described previously). Increasing emphasis on teamwork and the attribution of success to team effort may have negative effects on creativity and can ultimately lower the quality of group decision-making (Goncalo & Duguid, 2008).

4. *Internal attributions to favourable events have a positive effect on performance; external attributions to favourable events a negative effect (Level C).*

   This implies that internal attributions are important for success, as they positively affect performance (Harvey, Madison, Martinko, Crook, & Crook, 2014).

5. *Individuals learn more from their own success than from their own failure, but they learn more from the failures of others than from others' successes (Level D).*

   Focusing on own successes and others' failures is the best way for individuals to enhance learning (KC, Staats, & Gino, 2013).

What Is the Conclusion?

Attribution theory is a well-researched theory. It helps to understand human beings in their processes of interpreting, understanding and deciding in social contexts such as the organizational context. It helps leaders to understand followers and followers to understand their leaders. It sheds light on the way in which information, for example about a new strategic direction or a culture change, is processed. It helps raise awareness of the biases and tendencies plus the causal mechanisms that rule the way people interpret and decide as a basis for their intended or 'real' behaviour. In addition, attribution theory is key in understanding the culture, habits and routines and causal mechanisms in organizations. People use 'pattern recognition', stereotypes, models and 'benchmarks' to evaluate others, stimuli such as a change initiative or statement made by a leader, and situations. This can be efficient or helpful, but also hampering and frustrating in situations where changing and organizing are important or necessary. Attribution theory helps us, in an organizational context, to design and develop well-thought-out and contextual, sensitive and sensible 'paths to change'. Evidence shows that attribution theory is important for and helpful to (change) management. Attribution theory is a valuable concept in organizing and changing in the right way. Evidence shows that attributions can influence, among other things, performance, decision-making, economic decisions and learning in organizations.

Practical Reflections

The insights related to the concept of attributions can be instrumental in developing the mutual understanding of people who are involved together in change and have to cooperate in an organizational context. Practitioners can benefit from the concept because it gives them awareness of and insight into the motives, background, causal mechanisms and also biases and limitations (e.g. in scope, information and knowledge, leading to 'bounded rationality'). It can also provide the insights and hence foundations for better cooperation and a better 'return' on collective, social efforts. This is illustrated by Goncalo and Duguid (2008): "When attributions for group success focused on the contributions made by each individual, groups subsequently considered more alternatives prior to reaching consensus and the alternatives considered were also more divergent than those considered by groups who attributed their success to the group as a whole. In addition, individually focused attributions for success also increased the sharing of unique information and raised the likelihood of reaching the correct solution" (p. 40).

Social Judgment Theory

Judgments are grounded in and based on people's attitudes; in order to understand or to make sense, people will compare the position advocated by an idea with their own position regarding that idea.

What Is Social Judgment?

Social judgment is a form of social thinking: how we think about ideas, issues, persons or groups is dependent on its context. Social judgment theory (SJT) (Sherif & Hovland, 1961) can be defined as the perception and evaluation of an idea by comparing it with current attitudes. To understand or make sense, people will compare the position advocated by that idea with their own position regarding that idea. That latter position, their own, is dependent on people's most preferred position (their anchor point), their judgment of alternatives (latitude of acceptance, rejection, non-commitment) and the level of ego involvement with the idea and position advocated (e.g. Sherif, Kelly, Rodgers, Jr, Sarup, & Tittler, 1973). Brehmer (1988) defines social judgment theory as a meta-theory which gives direction to research on judgment. He states "SJT is the result of a systematic application of Brunswik's probabilistic functionalism to the problem of human judgment in social situations. Brunswik's theory of perception is also called 'cue theory'. According to such a theory, a person does not have access to any direct information about the objects in the environment. Instead, perception is seen as an indirect process, mediated by a set of proximal cues" (p. 13). Social judgment theory teaches that judgments are grounded in and based on people's attitudes. True attitudes are fundamental to self-identity, and they are complex and therefore may be hard to change. To understand a person's full attitude one has to understand a person's own position combined with what that person finds acceptable or unacceptable with regard to other positions (Nebergall, 1966). Sherif and Hovland (1961) consider attitudes to be amalgams or compound creatures, a combination of three latitudes, those of acceptance, rejection and non-commitment. Together they envisage the full spectrum of a person's attitude. Acceptance is related to positions on issues that are acceptable to this person. Rejection is related to positions that are objectionable from a person's perspective. In the case of non-commitment the positions are neither acceptable nor objectionable. Changes or messages of change that fall within a person's latitude of rejection will probably not persuade that person. In addition, the more ego-involved a person is, or the more important it is to that person, the larger the latitude of rejection will be. Changes in that latitude will be contrasted and, as a consequence, appear to be further away from a person's anchor point. It is unlikely that the person will be persuaded to accept or to commit to the change. Changes falling within the latitude of acceptance, on the contrary, will be assimilated; they appear closer to a person's anchor point than they objectively are. Persuasion is probable. In the case of non-commitment, a person has neither a positive nor a negative feeling with regard to a certain change message. It is possible to persuade a person in that position if that person is provided with information or arguments on which a judgment can be based (e.g. O'Keefe, 1990). Involvement can be seen as the core concept of social judgment theory. People who have a low ego involvement are likely to accept more and varying ideas or opinions. People with a high ego involvement are likely to evaluate all possible positions in a disciplined way. This will decrease the latitude of non-commitment. People who care deeply or have strong opinions have a large latitude of rejection and are probably not willing to change. Highly involved people probably have a limited, precise latitude of acceptance. Highly involved people who are confronted with changes outside their strict zone of acceptance are likely to resist change and be difficult to persuade. Ego-involvement concerns the importance of an issue to a person. This importance can be determined by the person's earlier experiences and wider background, but is often related to the membership of a group with an outspoken position with regard to specific issues. The level of (ego) involvement is dependent on how someone evaluates or appreciates an issue, for example whether it arouses an intense attitude or is seen as primarily a factual matter (Sherif & Hovland, 1961), or whether it is experienced as a more technical or as an adaptive challenge (Heifetz & Laurie, 2001). The immediate social environment can influence attitude change. In the interpersonal domain, people tend to shift their attitudes to align with those of their significant or relevant others. The general picture of social influence thus remains one of conformity and alignment attitudes (Ledgerwood et al., 2007). Brehmer (1976) states that social judgment theory applies to the analysis of interpersonal conflicts caused by cognitive differences. Cognitive factors are sufficient to explain certain forms of conflict, as well as why the conflicts are not resolved, and that the analysis of conflict will have to take into account not only the persons in conflict, but also the nature of the task facing them. Related to the theory and also focusing on attitude and attitude change, is the social judgment-involvement approach (Sherif, Sherif, & Nebergall, 1965). Johnson and Eagly (1989) elaborate on this and define involvement as a motivational state induced by an association between an activated attitude and the self-concept. Their research provides insights and a vocabulary which are relevant to behavioural and organizational change. Based on their research Johnson & Eagly state: "Integration of the available research suggests that the effects of involvement on attitude change depended on the aspect of message recipients' self-concept that was activated to create involvement: (a) their enduring values (value-relevant involve-ment), (b) their ability to attain desirable outcomes (outcome-relevant involvement), or (c) the impression they make on others (impression-relevant involvement). Findings showed that (a) with value-relevant involvement, high-involvement subjects were less persuaded than low-involvement subjects; (b) with outcome-relevant involvement, high-involvement subjects were more persuaded than low-involvement subjects by strong arguments and (somewhat inconsistently) less per-suaded by weak arguments; and (c) with impression-relevant involve-ment, high-involvement subjects were slightly less persuaded than low-involvement subjects" (p. 290).

What Is the Relevance of Social Judgment for Organization and Change?

Social judgment theory is a theory about the process of communication, about attitudes and attitude change. Central to it is people's perception and evaluation of an idea by comparing it with current attitudes. It learns that persuasion is difficult to accomplish and how opinions toward pro-posal or change are formed (like opposing, supporting, ambivalent and indifferent). The theory has relevance for the organizational context and relates to topics like organizational culture, leadership, resistance to change and commitment. It also has relevance for cooperation and team development (including group dynamics) as well as for socialization given the focus on conformity and alignment attitudes.

Search Strategy

Relevant databases were searched using the term 'social judgment' and 'human judgment*'. The searched yielded 179 articles. After screen-ing the title and abstracts for relevance, no studies met the inclusion criteria.

Main Findings

Not applicable.

What Is the Conclusion?

Social judgment theory (SJT) provides a perspective that is relevant for the organizational context and change management. Notwithstanding the fact that specific relevant evidence is not available, SJT conveys a per-spective, addresses issues and provide a vocabulary that may be relevant and useful for change management. Therefore, we concluded that it is worthwhile to present the theory in this book.

Practical Reflections

For organizational and change management, social judgment theory provides at least 'something to think about'. It gives a frame of reference and insights which are helpful in understanding how people evaluate change and react to persuasion. It also helps to understand the role of involvement in organizational and change processes. SJT also helps to understand the phenomena of resistance to change and organizational commitment.

Social Learning Theory

Most of the behaviours that people display are the result of social learning, either deliberately or inadvertently, through modelling, the influence of example.

What Is Social Learning?

Social learning theory aims to understand psychological functioning in terms of a continuous reciprocal interaction between behaviour and its controlling (social) conditions (Bandura, 1971). Social learning theory combines cognitive learning theory (which posits that learning is influenced by psychological factors) and behavioural learning theory (which assumes that learning is based on responses to environmental stimuli). In the '60s Albert Bandura developed the social learning theory by what became known as the Bobo doll experiments. In these experiments, children watched adults behave violent or passive (nonviolent) toward a toy called Bobo doll. What the children saw influenced how they subsequently interacted with the dolls. Children who observed violent behaviour were verbally and physically aggressive toward the dolls. Children who witnessed nonviolent behaviour behaved less aggressively toward the dolls. Bandura concluded that children learn through observation of the behaviour of others. Social learning theory acknowledges the complexity of human responsiveness and thus provides a critical alternative to the psychodynamic perspective (Bandura, 1963). The process of differential reinforcement is essential to social learning; successful modes of behaviour are selected from exploratory and unsuccessful modes. In explaining and understanding the causes of human behaviour, Bandura emphasizes the roles played by vicarious, symbolic and self-regulatory processes. The vicarious process focuses on man's capacity to learn by observation of others. Traditional learning theories envisage learning primarily or solely as the result of the direct experience of response consequences. Social-learning theory adds the perspective of the vicarious process; people also learn through observation of *other* people's behaviour and its consequences for them. The symbolic process is related to the superior cognitive capacity of human beings that enables insightful and fore-sightful behaviour. They are able to guide their actions by symbolic representations (instead of external influences in a direct way), to solve problems symbolically and foresee or project probable consequences of different behaviours and alter their behaviour accordingly. The self-regulatory process enables people to control their behaviour to some degree. Human beings are able to create self-regulative influences, for example by producing consequences for their own actions. For animals, including the human being, simple behaviour and performance can be altered through reinforcement without any real awareness of the relationship between actions and outcomes. However, unlike unthinking organisms, the human being is capable of more; superior cognitive skills help the human being to profit more from experience. This experience is based on response consequences that can be inform-ative, motivating and reinforcing. First of all, people gather informa-tive feedback by observing the differential consequences of their behaviour. Based on that, they develop 'hypotheses' about successful and unsuccessful behaviour. Consequences are not only informative, but also potentially motivating. Human beings are able to antici-pate and as a result conditions of reinforcement also have incentive-motivational effects. By making symbolic representations, people can convert future consequences into current motivators that influence behaviour. Response consequences can also be reinforcing, in particu-lar in performances that are not too complicated: "Responses can be automatically strengthened through selective reinforcement operating below the level of awareness" (Bandura, 1971, p. 5). In essence, social learning theory shows that learning is not purely behavioural; it is a cognitive process in a social context. Human beings as learners are not passive recipients of information. Social learning is about recipro-cal determinism; cognition, context and behaviour mutually influence one another (Grusec, 1992). Social learning theory teaches that learn-ing can benefit from, but is not solely dependent on, rewarding and punishing consequences and trial-and-error. People also learn through modelling: "it is difficult to imagine a socialization process in which the language, mores, vocational activities, familial customs, and the educational, religious and political practices of a culture are taught to each new member by selective reinforcement of fortuitous behaviours, without the benefit of models who exemplify the cultural patterns in their own behaviour. Most of the behaviours that people display are learned, either deliberately or inadvertently, through the influence of example" (Bandura, 1971, p. 5). In summary: "Under most circum-stances, a good example is (therefore) a much better teacher than the consequences of unguided actions" (Bandura, 1971, p. 5). So, model-ling is not so much about specific stimulus-response associations. It is about observers acquiring mainly symbolic representations of modelled activities (Bandura, 1969). The modelling process is based on four interrelated sub-processes (Bandura, 1972):

- Attention: to learn, learners must pay attention to modelled behaviour. Attention is influenced by observer characteristics such as cognitive abilities, arousal and personal history and background, and characteristics of the behaviour or event that provide the modelling context such as relevance, novelty and functional value.
- Retention: remembering observed behaviour and its features is conditional to reproducing it. Observer and event characteristics (like complexity and comfort) also influence the retention process.
- Reproduction: behavioural reproduction is the process of implementing the models observed and remembered. This reproduction is achieved by putting together a given set of responses according to the modelled patterns. Cognitive skills and also sensorimotor capabilities are essential. Feedback is important in order to improve performance.
- Reinforcement and motivation: reproducing or refraining from behaviour depends on the incentives or sanctions provided, the drives and expectations of the observer. If modelling does not occur, behaviour is not reproduced, there is a lack of matching behaviour following exposure to modelling influences and a variety of determinants must be considered, like failure to observe the relevant activities, retention decrements and motoric deficiencies.

Social learning theory provides a rich but not exclusive perspective on the way people learn in general and in social contexts in particular. As Thyer and Myers (1998) state: "There is no assumption in social learning theory that *all* behaviour is learned, rather the view is that much of it *is* acquired via respondent, operant and observational learning processes, and that it is a viable perspective to empirically ascertain to what extent they may be operative, as this may afford valuable etiological and interventive leads" (p. 47).

What Is the Relevance of Social Learning for Organization and Change?

In organizations people copy behaviour of others, for instance from their leaders and also from 'relevant others'. Social learning is related to a concept like 'lead by example' and socialization in organizations and therewith organizational culture. In the context of management and change it can also be related to, for example, change capacity and cooperation. *For a further explanation of the relevance of Bandura's thinking and theories see: 5.2.2 (Social-Cognitive Theory).*

Search Strategy

Relevant databases were searched using the term 'learning theory', 'employ*', 'organi*' and 'change'. The searched yielded 115 articles. After screening the title and abstracts for relevance, no studies met the inclusion criteria.

Remark: With the social learning theory (1977) and the related experiments ('the Bobo doll experiments' in 1961 and 1963) Bandura demonstrated the relevance of learning from others, social learning; the value of modelling for acquiring new or additional behaviours. With the social cognitive theory Bandura (1986) has elaborated and renamed social learning theory. Social cognition further attributes to the understanding of the social core motive understanding. However, social cognition is included in Chapter 5 under the core social motive of controlling (5.2). The further development and renaming may be a part of the explanation for the fact that we found no studies to be included for social learning theory. However, it should be noted that also for social cognitive theory the output was very limited. For that reason we have extended our research to 'self-efficacy' and 'social cognitive career theory' (see Chapter 5, Social Cognitive theory).

Main Findings

Not applicable

What Is the Conclusion?

See Chapter 5, Conclusion, Social Cognitive Theory.

Practical Reflections

See Chapter 5, Practical Reflections, Self-Determination Theory

Social Impact Theory

The presence of others causes social impact, an influence that can be real or perceived, direct or indirect (implied), experienced or imagined.

What Is Social Impact?

Building on Lewin's Field Theory and theorizing in terms of social forces by analogy with physical forces like light and gravity, Latané (1981) developed the Law of Social Impact. He proposed "that we think of the individual exposed to social influences as operating in a social force field, which determines what he does in lawful ways" (Brown, 1986, p. 18). According to Latané, a social impact is any influence on the feelings, thoughts or behaviours of an individual resulting from the social context of that individual. The presence of others that causes that influence can be real or perceived, direct or indirect (implied), experienced or imagined. Social forces on an individual are like light bulbs that cast light on a surface. Just as the total amount of light depends on factors such as the wattage and number of bulbs, the total social impact of a set of individuals on a single target individual is by analogy determined by a set of factors. Latané mentions the strength and number of the individuals and their immediacy (to the target individual). Strength is defined by status, age, experience, expertise and the quality of the relationship (with the target individual). Immediacy is not only proximity in a literal sense (e.g. distance in time and space), but also determined by the presence or absence of intervening barriers or filters (Brown, 1986). The formal statement of the Law of Social Impact is $I = f(SIN)$. The intensity of social impact increases with the strength of each source, the immediacy of sources and the number of sources. Total intensity is the result of multiplying the three values together. In fact, Latané uses (formulas based on) the three variables (SIN) to define three laws: that of social forces, the psychosocial law and the law of multiplication/divisions of impact. The first, that of social forces, or the first Law of Social Impact $[I = f(SIN)]$, has already been introduced. The second, the psychosocial law, is about the idea that the size of the psychological increase decreases as *n* increases; one person added to two persons is more impactful on a target individual than one added to a hundred persons. The third law of social impact concerns multiplication or divisions of impact and relates to the diffusion of responsibility. It states that the strength, immediacy and number of *targets* play a role in social impact. In short, social impact will be more divided among all of the targets with more strength and immediacy and an increasing number of targets in a social situation. For example, in an emergency, individuals will feel less responsible if more people are present at the scene.

As a result of some shortcomings or limitations of social impact theory (like the absence of explanations of the nature of influencing processes related to variables like immediacy, individual differences), the application is complicated. For that reason, in applying social impact theory, the idea of persuasiveness and supportiveness is introduced.[1] Persuasiveness concerns 'the ability to induce someone with an opposing position to change'. Supportiveness is 'the ability to help those who agree with someone's point of view to resist the influence of others'. Together they can produce change. In this perspective an individual's likelihood of change and being influenced is defined as a direct function of strength (persuasiveness), immediacy and the number of advocates. In addition, the likelihood is a direct inverse function of strength (supportiveness), immediacy and the number of advocates.

Based on social impact theory (SIT), Latané, Nowak, and Liu (1994) developed the 'dynamic' SIT. Social structures, societies, organizations and groups are seen as complex and dynamic systems, never static, always changing, as a result of social influences. Social structures and cultures are seen to result from "individuals, differing in their ability to influence each other in a dynamic iterative process of reciprocal and recursive influence" (Latané, 1996, p. 13). Latané (1996) defines culture as "the entire set of socially transmitted beliefs, values and practices that characterize a given society at a given time" (p. 13). Cultures are patterns of related ideas similar to the social representations of Moscovici (1984); they are a shared, social reality to guide our actions. In dynamic SIT, cultures are complex and dynamic systems that are characterized by a process with four forms of self-organization, namely: clustering, correlation, consolidation and continuing diversity. These four patterns are the basis for group dynamics to operate and the diffusion of ideas within social structures and help us to understand cultures and their development (Latané & Bourgeois, 2001). The overall process of self-organization and its properties "can lead initially random distributions of social attributes to become clustered in space and correlated, with less popular elements becoming consolidated or reduced in frequency but surviving in minority subgroups" (Latané, 1996, p. 13). From a culture perspective, consolidation means that patterns of related ideas become more and more uniform over time through interaction, thereby spreading the dominant culture, a dynamic phenomenon, from the majority to the minority, which decreases in size. Clustering is the social process that results from the tendency of individuals to interact with clusters of group members with similar opinions, in close proximity, rather than with members who have different views and are more distant. This may result in majorities, dominant groups and minorities, cultures and subgroups and subcultures with shared but different views and beliefs compared with the majority. The third process is correlation; over time group members' opinions converge and correlate with one another. This holds true for issues discussed *and* issues that are not discussed. Notwithstanding the processes of consolidation, clustering and correlation, there may be a continuing diversity within a group. Minority group members may cluster together and may resist the majority in interaction processes. Diversity may increase as a result of a very strong or intrusive majority or the (physical) isolation of minority members from one another.

What Is the Relevance of Social Impact for Organization and Change?

From the perspective of organization and change, social impact relating to leadership, culture, communication and teams and team development, among other subjects, is a very relevant and helpful concept. Social impact theory helps to understand how the relationship and interaction between leaders and followers develop. It explains the underlying mechanisms of concepts like 'relevant others', group dynamics, 'lead by example', 'tone at the top' and role models. The relevance of the concept of social impact for the organizational context is illustrated by Oc and Bashur (2013): "A combination of SIT, the work of Asch (1951, 1956) and some of the arguments we make here can provide valuable clues as to how followers can exercise their social influence in relative safety. Be aware of the needs of your leader. Build your strength accordingly (e.g. be persistent, show integrity and composure and have some positional or informational power), increase your immediacy (reduce social distance) and find safety in numbers (find a confederate, build coalitions)" (p. 931). With regard to organizational culture and the change of it, social impact theory provides possible explanations for the difficulties with it and possible interventions to change it. It helps to understand the way change agents, 'leading coalitions' or 'gideon gangs' might work. It also sheds light on the dynamics and possible problems related to dominant groups and cultures and majorities on the one hand and other groups, subcultures and minorities on the other hand. Those dynamics, problems and possibilities, and the underlying mechanisms, are very relevant for organizations as such and organizations in change in particular. In the context of change, social impact is also highly relevant in understanding resistance and its producers or 'bearers'. Focusing on resistance to change, Kriegel (1996) points to the classic paper "How to Deal with Resistance to Change" (1954) of Harvard Business School professor Paul Lawrence. Lawrence describes "how failing to understand workers' resistance can sabotage the whole effort" (p. 187). Heifetz (2009) pleas for the protection of the voices of dissent. He states: "The voices of dissent are the naysayers, the sceptics, who not only question this initiative but question whatever is on the agenda of today. They are princes of darkness, often resting on the negative. But they are valuable for implementing adaptive change because they are canaries in the coal mine, early-warning systems, and because in addition to being unproductive and annoying much of the time, they have the uncanny capacity for asking the really tough key question that you have been unwilling to face up to yourself or that others have been unwilling to raise. In many organizations, dissenters get marginalized, silenced, or even fired, which deprives the organization of their valuable, if unpopular service" (p. 145).

Search Strategy

Relevant databases were searched using the terms 'social impact theory' and combining 'social impact' with 'work', 'employee', 'organization' and 'change'. The search yielded more than 100 articles. After screening the title and abstracts for relevance, eight studies met the inclusion criteria. After thorough examination, one meta-analysis and three studies remained.

Main Findings

1. *Group size and relational distance affect customers' response to group service recovery strategies (Level A).*

   In a randomized, controlled before-after study, evidence found supports both group size and the relational distance in social impact theory, as it has an effect on the customer's response to group service recovery. "Specifically, private economic recovery creates less consumer satisfaction as group size increases, whereas consumers with a distant social relationship are more satisfied with public recovery for both economic recovery and social recovery. However, consumers with close relationships are more satisfied with public economic recovery and private social recovery" (Zhou, Tsang, Huang, & Zhou, 2014, p. 2480). Examples of economic recovery include monetary compensation, partial refunds and discounts for future purchases. Social recovery includes explanation and apology that can comfort customers and compensate for their psychological distress.

   "This study further enriches social impact theory by investigating the moderating effects of the social forces in the theory. We operationalized these forces into applicable concepts for group service recovery to provide further evidence supporting the validity and practicality of social impact theory" (Zhou et al., 2014, p. 2484).

2. *There is limited evidence for the social impact theory, as the effects are rather weak and inconsistent (Level B-).*

   A meta-analytical study found limited evidence for the social impact theory, as research regarding both strength and immediacy show weak correlations and inconsistencies (Mullen, 1985).

   "In the meantime, social psychologists might be cautious in their application of Social Impact Theory. The distinguishing attribute of Social Impact Theory has been its treatment of strength and immediacy. The present analyses reveal that these effects are rather weak and inconsistent and may very well be the result of methodological artefact (i.e. demand characteristics)" (Mullen, 1985, p. 1465).

3. *Leaders' emotion perceptions enhance employees' job performance and the strength of this relationship depends upon the task interdependence and the power distance (Vidyarthi, Anand & Liden, Level D-).*

   "Thus, consistent with social impact theory, we reason that leaders' influence on employees may diminish when employees independently work on their tasks. This is because high task interdependence requires more direct and frequent contact between the leader and employees for the purpose of coordinating the interrelated tasks, whereas substantially less contact between leaders and followers is needed when their tasks are independent of one another" (Vidyarthi, Anand, & Liden, 2014, p. 239).

What Is the Conclusion?

Social impact theory is a fruitful and—in the context of change and organization—highly relevant and very insightful concept. It relates to leadership and leader-follower interaction, organizational culture and culture change, group dynamics and resistance to change, among others. Having said that, some caution is required; studies show inconsistencies regarding social impact theory. The included meta-analysis states that the correlations are weak and studies show different results. However, this meta-analysis originates from 1985. Since 1985, more research on social impact theory has taken place, with more positive results. For example, high task interdependence can enhance leaders' influence on employees, as they have more direct and frequent contact. This targets the strength and immediacy of social impact theory.

Practical Reflections

In the context of change and organization, making decisions, influencing people and seeking guidance and orientation are important factors. Social impact theory sheds light on the underlying mechanisms and dynamics underlying those factors. As stated, some caution is required; the relevant evidence is mixed and limited. The evidence (partially) supports the social impact theory. The evidence is limited and not directly linked to organizational functioning or change management. Still, social impact theory can have added value in terms of the strength, immediacy and number of sources mentioned that are relevant to the factors and processes, such as decision-making. Evidence does indicate that these sources are important in leader-employee relationships and can be used to increase followers' social influence. This insight, like insights into social impact theory in a broader sense, can be helpful in designing and exhibiting role model and 'lead by example' behaviours.

Cooperation/Competition (Social Interdependence Theory)

How group members believe their goals are related impacts their dynamics and performance significantly.

What Is Cooperation/Competition, What Is Social Interdependence?

The interrelated concepts of cooperation and competition are essential for the understanding and control of social processes. With his 'Theory of Cooperation and Competition' (1949), Deutsch proposed that the way in which group members believe their goals are related impacts their dynamics and performance significantly. His ideas are related to the social interdependence theory. Social interdependence exists when the accomplishment of each individual's goals is affected by the actions of others (Johnson & Johnson, 1989). No interdependence results if individuals perceive that they can reach their goal regardless of whether others in the situation attain their goals or not (Johnson, Johnson, & Smith, 2007). Deutsch describes cooperation and competition as a positive and a negative type of social interdependence: "To put it colloquially, if you're positively linked with another, then you sink and swim together; with negative linkage, if the other sinks, you swim, and if the other swims, you sink" (Deutsch, 2012, pp. 278–279). Positive interdependence can result, for example, from the need to share a resource, being rewarded for a joint achievement or mutual sympathy. Negative interdependence can result from factors like disliking one another and rewards stimulating zero-sum games. In addition to the interdependence among goals, Deutsch also defines two basic types of action by an individual: effective actions and bungling actions. Effective actions improve the actor's chances of obtaining a goal and bungling actions worsen these chances. Deutsch (2012) combines these types of interdependence and action to posit how they affect three basic social psychological processes: substitutability, cathexis and inducibility. These processes are vital in understanding cooperation and competitions and their psychology. Substitutability permits you to accept the activities of others in the fulfilment of your needs; it is about how a person's action can satisfy another person's intentions. Substitutability is essential for the functioning of social institutions like companies and schools and conditional for role specializations and the division of labour. Cathexis is about evaluation; it "refers to the predisposition to respond evaluatively, favourably or unfavourably to aspects of one's environment or self" (Deutsch, 2012, p. 280). Based on this evaluation and as a result of evolution, living creatures have the ability to respond positively to stimuli that are beneficial and negatively to stimuli that are harmful. Deutsch (2012) states: "This inborn tendency to act positively toward the beneficial and negatively to the harmful is the foundation on which the human potentials for cooperation and love as well as for competition and hate develop" (p. 280). Inducibility is the complement of substitutability. It is about the readiness to accept another's influence to do what that other one wants. You are willing to engage in helpful, but not in harmful actions of another person. The theory of cooperation and competition makes further predictions with regard to intrapersonal, interpersonal, intragroup and intergroup processes. If the assumption is that actions are more frequently effective than bungling, then the theory predicts that cooperative relations with goals of the parties involved that are predominantly positively interdependent show more positive characteristics, such as the exhibition of effective communication, friend-liness, helpfulness, and lessened obstruction, fair treatment as a principle, influence based on persuasion and positive inducements, coordination of effort and willingness to enhance the other's power. The opposite effects, such as impaired, misleading communication, lack of helpfulness and obstruction and not valuing fairness to the other, characterize competitive processes (Deutsch, 2012).

What Is the Relevance of Cooperation/Competition for Organization and Change?

The theory of cooperation/competition might well be the nature/nurture discussion of social psychology. Is competition better for group performance, as it might increase the effort people put in, as winners are seen as successful in our society? Or is it cooperation that is the better way of working, increasing job satisfaction and ultimately performance by doing things as a team? Cooperative goal structures are today seen as more effective in motivating groups compared with competitive goal structures. Kistruck and his colleagues (2016) state: "There is a growing consensus that cooperative goal structures are more effective at motivating groups than competitive goal structures. However, such results are based largely on studies conducted in highly controlled settings where participants were provided with the necessary resources to accomplish their assigned task" (p. 1174). In the popular management literature, most concepts related to topics such as organizational structure, teams and leadership also advocate the 'cooperation-paradigm'; cooperation and shared goals are assumed, competition (within the team or organization) is often not addressed, nor is the problematic side of conflict. This is illustrated by Laloux (2014) providing us with 'A Guide to Creating Organizations Inspired by the Next Stage of Human Consciousness' and considers self-management (structures) and self-managing teams as defining elements. The so-called team-based organization (TBO) is often described in very positive, attractive terms. An example can be found in the 'Business Dictionary'[2]: "Non-traditional, innovative work environment relying on teams to achieve its objectives. Taboo's major characteristics include (1) mutual trust, (2) employee empowerment in planning, organization and goal-setting, (3) shared responsibility for self-management, (4) shared accountability for performance, and (5) shared leadership". We can also observe the awareness that one has to strike a balance between cooperation and competition. Both are probably necessary factors in developing organizations, leadership styles and change capacity of organizations. The competition perspective is (at least indirectly) visible in ideas about performance management, goal-setting and feedback. Mourier and Smith (2001) underline the importance of measurement, feedback and consequences: "Provide positive recognition when expectations are met and negative consequences when expectations aren't met" (p. 32). Kouznes and Posner (2012) state: "People need to know if they're making progress toward the goal or simply marking time. Their motivation to perform a task increases only when they have a challenging goal and receive feedback on their progress" (p. 282).

Search Strategy

Relevant databases were searched using the terms 'cooperation' and 'competition' in combination with 'meta-analysis' or 'systematic review'. The search yielded more than 600 (!) articles. After screening the title and abstracts for relevance, twenty studies and one meta-analysis met the inclusion criteria. After a thorough examination of the included studies, nine were excluded. Most of the included studies were randomized, controlled experiments with a high level of evidence (A or A-).

Main Findings

1. *Intragroup cooperation outperforms intragroup competition (Level A-).*

   A meta-analysis among students found that intragroup cooperation has a stronger positive effect on performance than intragroup competition, but the effect size found (medium) is smaller than earlier research that reported a high effect. The meta-analysis further found that intragroup cooperation is more effective for psychology and sociology students compared with business and accounting students (Na'im, 2004).

2. *In teams, cooperative rewards promote accuracy; competitive rewards promote speed (Level A).*

   Both cooperation and competition can have positive effects on the team performance, but it depends what is needed. When a task is urgent and speed is required, adding competition can increase the speed. When the task requires accuracy, cooperation is preferred. The randomized, controlled, before-after study also found that when a team is ".composed of extroverted and agreeable members, a cooperative reward structure is a very effective choice" (Beersma et al., 2003, p. 587).

3. *A combination of cooperation and competition is the most effective (Level A-).*

   Intergroup competition (or competition between groups where individuals in groups work cooperatively) has a positive effect on enjoyment and performance. This randomized, controlled experiment is conducted in a basketball setting with children as participants. Nevertheless, it is an interesting finding that might also be relevant in an organizational setting (Tauer, 2004).

4. *Individual competition leads to a decrease in the willingness of individuals to cooperate (Level B-), and intergroup competition itself does not increase within group cooperation (Level B).*

   Adding competitive elements can reduce the willingness of individuals to cooperate (Canegallo, Ortona, Ottone, Ponzano, & Scacciati, 2008). This can have detrimental effects on organizational functioning and change success, as they both often require teams to complete certain tasks. In a non-randomized, controlled, before- after study, researchers found that it is not intergroup competition itself, but setting certain threshold levels (such as winning an extra prize when a certain amount of in-group cooperation is reached) that is the most important factor determining why teams cooperate. This threshold does not have to be competitive, as social thresholds are equally effective (Jordan, Jordan, & Rand, 2017).

What Is the Conclusion?

With regard to organization and change, cooperation/competition is relevant for subjects like teams and team development, goal-setting and feedback, leadership and culture, change capacity and, of course, cooperation and commitment. The related theory is well researched as such and in addition there is a high level (A, B) of specific evidence with regard to the organizational context. The evidence shows that both cooperation and competition are relevant and effective in organizations, leading to, for example, (higher, better) performance and climates. A combination of the two is the most effective, each one promoting specific qualities, such as accuracy and speed. For leaders the relevance and importance of the concept of cooperation/competition is undisputed. Specifically where far-reaching changes and significant improvements are on the agenda, striking the right balance is essential. It is illustrative that Collins, in talking about great leadership, promotes a mix of elements related to the cooperation and competition, with regard to both the leadership style itself and the message to the followers. Based on his research, Collins (2001) defines five levels of executive capabilities. On 'Level 3' we find the so-called competent manager, who organizes people and resources toward the effective and efficient pursuit of pre-determined objectives. Their perspective is mainly a transactional one. On the higher levels of the 'effective leader' (4) and ideal typical 'executive' (5) we find the leaders who are (more) transformational. They, in particular the Level 5 one, are the leaders whose companies 'make the leap', where 'others don't'. The 'Level 5' leader "builds enduring greatness through a paradoxical blend of personal humility and professional will" (p. 20). On 'Level 4' is the 'effective leader' who "catalyses commitment to and vigorous pursuit of a clear and compelling vision, stimulating higher performance standards" (p. 20).

Practical Reflections

Cooperation is naturally related to the social animal, as is competition. Without cooperation, organizational functioning and the capacity to change will eventually suffer. Without competition, organizations, teams and individuals lack a natural stimulus to perform and to strive for the best. The combination of cooperation and competition is operationalized in the concepts of goal-setting and feedback. One could characterize cooperation as the 'mother', emphasizing togetherness, taking care of each other, and the social dimension as prerequisites for performance and health. Competition is the 'father', highlighting the importance of being sharp and competent, aware of who you are competing against or who may threaten you and your group, stressing the business perspective and survival as reasons to perform. The change management literature devotes a lot of (positive) attention to the cooperation perspective. The completion perspective has a less self-evident, 'natural' position in the literature. However, several practitioners and management thinkers illustrate the 'father' or competition perspective. Novak (2012), author and famous CEO, teaches us that "recognizing the behaviours you want and those you don't is essential to keeping your people on track toward achieving your Big Goal. It's important to do this formally, with things like performance reviews and raises, but even informal recognition can have a big impact" (p. 193). Mourier and Smith (2001) underline the importance of measurement, feedback and consequences: "Provide positive recognition when expectations are met and negative consequences when expectations aren't met" (p. 32). Kouznes and Posner (2012) state: "People need to know if they're making progress toward the goal or simply marking time. Their motivation to perform a task increases only when they have a challenging goal and receive feedback on their progress" (p. 282). Heller (1998) addresses measuring results and providing feedback as ways to influence or change employee behaviour by presenting the concept of 'goal setting'. He advises: "Set personal objectives for people so they focus their minds on performance; reaching the goals will reinforce their enhanced drive" (p. 51). On feedback: "Commend people, publicly or privately, to strengthen commitment. Be sure to set high standards, and never ignore mistakes" (p. 51). Watkins (2013) also advocates the definition and monitoring of goals and performance metrics: "On the push side, establishing—and sticking to—clear and explicit performance metrics is the best way to encourage accountability" (p. 183). Without cooperation between people in groups (organizations and teams), tasks that require multiple people become very difficult to complete. This is the case in particular in situations of change where tasks and assignments are significant, routines not sufficient to do the job and people often become insecure or even anxious. As illustrated, competition is also helpful, in particular in combination with cooperation. Research on children playing basketball showed that intergroup competition (or competition within and between groups) leads to a positive effect on enjoyment and performance. Another finding that is useful for practitioners and their management and change practice is that promoting people to work together in a group, setting clear goals for groups and having groups compete against one another gives employees the feeling they belong to a secure group (their own group). It also gives them an incentive to perform well (competition between groups). Obviously, this is contingent or situational in its eventual effect; it is easier to do in companies with sales and commercial drive than in hospitals, as sales provide an easier target from a competitive standpoint. Based on the high-quality scientific literature found, intergroup competition is the best of both worlds. Cooperation is an essential part of organizations and change management success; making smart use of competition in addition to cooperation can enhance this even further.

Social Exchange

Social contexts are 'forums of transaction' with social exchange as the market mechanism. Individuals voluntarily act in favour of another person or an organization, motivated by individuals' expectations of reciprocity.

What Is Social Exchange?

Social exchange theory is considered to be one of the most influential paradigms on organizational behaviour (Cropanzano & Mitchell, 2005). The theory's core is reciprocity; it explains why people in social contexts help and support one another (Blau, 1968; Gouldner, 1960). Social change and stability represent a process of cost-benefit analyses between the parties involved. From this perspective social groups are seen as a series of interactions between people that are based on estimates of rewards and punishments. The cost-benefit model and process are used to evaluate rewards (approval) or punishment (disapproval) that we expect to receive from others. The results of these (conscious or subconscious) evaluations determine our interactions. Central to this theory is the idea that interactions that elicit approval from others are more likely to be repeated than those that elicit disapproval. According to social exchange theory, the formula for predicting the behaviour of an individual in a social situation is: Behaviour (profits) = Rewards of interaction − Costs of interaction.

Examples of rewards are social recognition, money and a smile. Examples of punishments are public humiliation, a downgrade or reprimand. Social exchange theory is rooted in disciplines like anthropology, sociology and social psychology. These disciplines and their theorists agree that social exchange involves a series of interactions that generate obligations (Emerson, 1976). Social exchange theory explains in terms of reciprocity why people such as neighbours, colleagues and visitors to an event help one another in social situations. Following social exchange theory, Michel and Gonzalez-Morales (2013) describe organizations as 'forums of transaction'. The exchange can take many forms, such as work engagement and effort being exchanged for pay or another form of acknowledgement by one's supervisor. As Michel and Gonzalez-Morales (2013) state: "Taken together, social exchange describes the voluntary action of an individual in favour of another person or an organization. This action is motivated by individuals' expectations of reciprocity. Therefore, it is important that the exchange between the parties is reciprocal in terms of a balanced outcome of efforts invested (i.e. costs) and rewards received (i.e. benefits)" (pp. 80–81). Social exchange theory helps to explain why the fair implementation of change is related to favourable employees' reactions (Michel & Gonzalez-Morales, 2013). Participation, voice and fair process are perceived by employees as a form of reward, signs of appreciation and support. From an exchange perspective it is likely that employees reciprocate this by behaving in favour of the organization, thereby increasing employee-organization value congruence (Michel, Stegmaier, Meiser, & Sonntag, 2009). In the process of social exchange, individuals or units take several elements or dimensions into account, at least: reciprocity, rationality, altruism or social responsibility, group gain, status, consistency and competition or rivalry (Walczak, 2015; Meeker, 1971).

What Is the Relevance of Social Exchange for Organization and Change?

Social exchange theory proposes that an exchange process is the underlying factor for social behaviour. The purpose of this exchange process is to maximize benefits and minimize (potential) costs. "According to this theory, people weigh the potential benefits and risks of social relationships. When the risks outweigh the rewards, people will terminate or abandon that relationship" (Kendra, 2017). In deciding what is fair, people constantly compare the relationship using a give/take ratio. According to the social exchange theory, rewarding employees with recognition in the form of compliments, money or other benefits, will make employees engage in behaviour that benefits the organization. This 'exchange' is beneficial for both the employee (rewards) and the organization (performance). Furthermore, social exchange relationships should bolster employees, making them more satisfied with their job and more committed to the organization. Social exchange can take many forms. An example is that work engagement and effort is exchanged for acknowledgement by one's supervisor (Michel & Gonzalez-Morales, 2013). Being in a way 'transactional', the perspective of social exchange theory helps to counterbalance the ideological and idealistic one-sided emphasis and appreciation of leadership and management behaviour from a transformational and positive psychology perspective. Evidence shows that supervisory support is critical for the success of change (ten Have et al., 2016). The supportive style is often described and valued from an idealistic, normative perspective as the preferred one. Exhibiting this style makes you 'good', and 'good' people favour this style. Apart from the question of context and contingencies, there is an alternative interpretation. Social exchange theory teaches that giving support (or acknowledgement) can be or is part of an exchange, a transaction. This may lead to a more realistic and balanced appreciation of 'giving support'. It is not exclusively related to a supervisor who chooses to give support, let alone because he is or must be a 'good' human being. From the social exchange perspective, leaders and followers exchange in social situations, they do a 'transaction', hopefully with mutual benefit and for the greater good. In the case of change, another part of the 'deal' could be that leaders provide clarity, or more specifically are clear on what will change and what will *not* change. In this way, they exchange their part that reduces the anxiety or uncertainty of followers for commitment to the change. Kriegel (1996), noting that people distort how much change is involved in change, elaborates on this. He says, in order to correct the distortion: "Leaders should not point out just what will be altered but also what will stay the same. That bi-focus puts a more balanced spin on plans for change and reduces anxiety" (p. 225). Kouzes and Posner (2012) describe a social exchange in which a favourable organizational climate and facilitating control (self-efficacy) are exchanged for commitment and ownership. In their example they emphasize the importance of supervisory support focused on creating a climate in which people are fully engaged and feel in control of their own lives. "In a climate of competence and confidence, people don't hesitate to hold themselves personally accountable for results, and they feel profound ownership for their achievements" (p. 243). Kouzes and Posner also emphasize that a leader must "invest in strengthening the capacity and the resolve of everyone in the organization" (p. 256), especially in situations of change. Exemplary leaders strive to create conditions in which people perform effortlessly and expertly despite the challenging or even difficult situation. Social exchange also repositions and revaluates transactional leadership, based on exchanges between leaders and employees, with rewards and punishments as key motivators. A lot of people favour its counterpart; transformational leadership that focuses on higher-order goals seeks "to satisfy higher needs, and engage the full person of the follower" (Burns, 1978, p. 4). This is a useful contribution of social exchange theory for leaders in practice, because evidence demonstrates the importance of both leadership styles for different areas of organizational change (ten Have et al., 2017). Social exchange theory can also be related to the subject of participation and fair process, which are highly relevant for change management and the design and development of change processes (ten Have et al., 2017).

Search Strategy

Relevant databases were searched using the term 'social exchange', and 'social exchange' in combination with 'organization', 'employee', 'change', 'work', 'meta-analysis' and 'systematic review'. The search yielded more than 250 articles. After screening the title and abstracts for relevance, fifteen studies met the inclusion criteria. After thoroughly examining the studies, another eight were excluded.

Main Findings

1. *Engaging in social exchange (relationships) has a positive relationship with organizational commitment (Level C).*

    In multiple included studies, social exchange (relationships) has a positive effect on organizational commitment (Byrne, Pitts, Chiaburu, & Steiner, 2011; Jayawardana & O'Donnell, 2010; Yigit, 2016).

2. *Social exchange relationships have a positive effect on both trust in the organization and organizational citizenship behaviour (Level D-).*

    Employees that engage in social exchange relationships generally have more trust in the organization. They also demonstrate more organizational citizenship behaviour, known as extra-role performance (Bal, Chiaburu, & Jansen, 2010). This finding is important, because it positively affects organizational change.

3. *High-quality social exchange relationships can compensate for potentially negative consequences of certain personality traits, such as low conscientiousness and low agreeableness (Level D-).*

    Certain personality traits can have a negative effect on, for example, task performance. High-quality social exchange relationships can compensate for these potentially negative consequences (Kamdar & Van Dyne, 2007).

What Is the Conclusion?

Social exchange theory is a well-researched theory with high relevance to the field of management and change. Specific evidence provides useful insights for practitioners who focus on, for example, leadership, change, organizational culture and climate, and performance management. Michel and Gonzalez-Morales (2013) suggest "that social exchange theories provide the theoretical foundation to explain why the fair implementation of change is related to favourable employees' reactions" (p. 81). They illustrate: "For example, sufficient participation in planned changes and fair decision-making processes are perceived by employees as signs of management's appreciation and support. In turn, it is likely that employees reciprocate fair treatment by behaving in favour of the organization (Michel et al., 2009)" (p. 81).

Practical Reflections

Based on their research, Michel and Gonzalez-Morales (2013) state that: "With respect to social exchange, findings suggest that change managers should monitor the event characteristics and manage the change process by informing employees frequently and comprehensively, providing participation and voice opportunities and enacting effective leadership behaviours. Such actions positively influence employees' perception of fairness and organizational support, trust in management, commitment and increased employee-organization value congruence" (p. 83). The management thinkers Kriegel and Ibarra also emphasize the importance of the change *process*, involvement and fairness. Kriegel (1996) states: "The way you introduce change makes a world of difference in how people feel about it" (pp. 218–2019). He explains that if major changes are implemented, employees will be less resistant when they understand the decision in context and feel that they are treated honestly. However, in practice a fair process is often lacking and employees experience major changes as if a bombshell has been dropped. According to Kriegel: "Many companies simply announce a downsizing scheme like it was a new health plan or accounting procedure. No input. No Q&A. No dialogue. It's not just the bad news, but the form of delivery that bends employees out of shape. No wonder people feel victimized and disrespected. The rumour mills start racing and the resistance starts rising" (p. 219). He emphasizes the importance of providing a structure for employees to express their natural disappointment and sense of loss. This is not the same as involving people in the creation of change, but helps them move to acceptance. It is about the acknowledgement of their feelings and processing them. Ibarra (2015) points to the importance of engaging people in the change by developing supportive processes: "Naïve leaders act as if the idea itself is the ultimate selling point. Experienced leaders, on the other hand, understand that the process is just as important, if not more so" (p. 45).

In addition to the clear guidelines of Michel and Gonzalez-Morales, based on the studies included by us, the following practical guidelines can be provided. To increase social exchange (relationships): "Managers seeking to promote social exchange relationships with their employees need to focus on creating opportunities for job enrichment, enhanced transparency in decision-making and improved involvement for line employees in workplace level decision-making" (Jayawardana & O'Donnell, 2010, p. 25). In addition: "Leaders and practitioners should incorporate policies that value the integrity of managers, such as those grounded in fairness principles. By offering ongoing training, companies can boost their managers' ability level, a contributing factor to trustworthiness of the manager" (Byrne et al., 2011, p. 119). And: "Employees equipped with the best skills should be chosen; socialization processes of employees should be supported and it should be understood that organizations are a means of social exchange for employees" (Yigit, 2016, p. 47).

Notes

1. https://en.wikipedia.org/wiki/Social_impact (retrieved: 06–03–18)
2. www.businessdictionary.com/definition/leadership.html

5 Controlling, Organizational Behaviour and Change

A First Short Story of Controlling and Change

Individuals will act in a certain way based on the expectation that the act will be followed by a given outcome. People learn by observing others. People's emotions are extracted from their evaluations of events. These appraisals or estimates will lead to individual variances of emotional reactions to the same stimulus or event. Individuals come to 'know' their own attitudes, emotions and other internal states partially by inferring them from observations of their own overt behaviour and/or the circumstances in which this behaviour occurs. People are not only moulded by their social contexts, but also they are inherently active, intrinsically motivated and oriented toward developing naturally through integrative processes. People are part of group-based social hierarchies in which concepts like stereotyping and group oppression are instrumental to the maintenance and stability of those hierarchies. A person's attitude toward behaviour, subjective norms and perceived behavioural control in combination shape that person's behavioural intentions and behaviours. A strongly held and consistently expressed minority view can have extensive influence on the majority, as most majority members just follow the rest and lack strongly held views. External motivators may undermine the intrinsic motivation of individuals.

Controlling, the need for perceived contingency between behaviour and outcomes, is the third core social motive and one of the two (relatively) cognitive motives (the other is understanding). The social motive to control "encourages people to feel competent and effective in dealing with their environment and themselves. . . . People want to be effective, to have some sense of control and competence, and a lack of control provokes information seeking, in an effort to restore control" (Fiske, 2004, p. 20). 'Effectance', the need for control and competence, is important for effective organizational behaviour and change. In times of change the existing sense of control and competence may be challenged or threatened. Routines, habits, cultural patterns and cognitive schemes often have to be replaced or significantly adjusted. Existing control mechanisms may be the reason that organizational and behavioural change is needed *and* difficult. As a consequence of change people may have to unlearn and learn in order to regain control. Changes may lead to breach of psychological contract and the related expectancies. In times of change people may experience serious stress; the way they react may be a result of the way they appraise the change. Controlling is related to change and management topics like change capacity, culture, resistance to change, commitment and performance management.

In this chapter the following theories and concepts are presented and assessed:

Expectancy theory
Social cognitive theory
Stress appraisal theory
Self-perception theory
Self-determination theory
Social dominance theory
Theory of planned behaviour
Minority influence theory
Motivation crowding theory

Expectancy Theory

Individuals will act in a certain way based on the expectation that the act will be followed by a given outcome.

What Is Expectancy Theory?

Controlling as the third core social motive is described by Fiske (2010) as the need for perceived contingency between behaviour and outcomes. A first related theory is the expectancy theory. The theory helps to understand controlling as a social motive. Expectancy theory is a motivational theory and explains the processes that an individual undergoes to make certain choices. Expectancy theory can be defined as a theory that "predicts that an individual will act in a certain way based on the expectation that the act will be followed by a given outcome. . . . Simply put, the theory states that the actions of an individual are driven by expected consequences" (Renko, Kroeck, & Bullough, 2012, pp. 668–669). This motivation theory is first proposed by Vroom and asserts "that motivation is based on people's beliefs about the probability that effort will lead to performance (*expectancy*), multiplied by the probability that performance will lead to reward (*instrumentality*), multiplied by the perceived value of the reward (*valence*)" (Greenberg & Baron, 2008, p. 269). According to Holford and Lovelace-Elmore (2001, p. 8), Vroom stated: "Intensity of work effort depends on the perception that an individual's effort will result in a desired outcome".

The expectancy theory, or 'the expectancy theory of motivation', is related to drive theory (Hull, 1943; Spence, 1958), which stated that behaviour is determined by Drive × Habit and incentives, and a competing theory, which stated that behaviour is directed by Expectancy × Value (Atkinson, 1957). Drive theory is discussed in Chapter 7, which deals with the fifth core social motive, enhancing self. Expectancy theory here is related to controlling because Vroom asserts that "intensity of work effort depends on the perception that an individual's effort will result in a desired outcome" (Holford & Lovelace, 2001, p. 8). Expectancy is the belief that the right effort will lead to the desired performance. It is in most cases based on self-efficacy, goal difficulty and perceived control (e.g. Chiang, Jang, Canter, & Prince, 2008), the belief that one is able to successfully perform a certain behaviour in a certain context; the belief that goals or desired performance are attainable or not unattainable; and the belief that one has the ability to influence, has a certain control over the expected outcome. Expectancy theory defines motivation as a multiplicative function of expectancy, instrumentality and valence. If they are all high, motivation will be high. If one of the three components is zero, the motivation will be zero. Given the core social motive, controlling people want a (perceived) contingency between (their) behaviour and outcomes. In organizations, managers want the right performance and contributions to change. Therefore, in accordance with the principles of expectancy theory, the following things have to be done to motivate employees: clarify people's expectancies that their effort will lead to performance; administer rewards that are positively valent to employees and clearly link valued reward and performance (Greenberg & Barron, 2008).

What Is the Relevance of Expectancy Theory for Organization and Change?

Expectancy theory explains the motivation to work (e.g. effort and intensity). When people have certain expectations about the outcome that they desire, they will work harder and longer to achieve that specific outcome. For example, an athlete who desperately wants to take part in the Olympic Games and expects that he or she will be able to reach that goal by training long hours every day will train these hours because of the expected and desired outcome. This motivation can also be used in organizational settings, based on intrinsic (e.g. ambition, interest) and/or extrinsic (e.g. money, goods) outcomes. When employees expect the effort they put in to result in the desired outcome, whether intrinsic and/or extrinsic, this will motivate employees to work harder and for longer hours. This can backfire when people work harder but do not get the expected outcomes, resulting in a decline in motivation and work ethic. From an organizational and change perspective, expectancy theory is strongly related to goal-setting and feedback and the debate about extrinsic motivation, for example financial incentives, as a part of performance management.

Watkins (2013) advocates the definition and monitoring of goals and performance metrics: "On the push side, establishing—and sticking to—clear and explicit performance metrics is the best way to encourage accountability" (p. 183). With regard to managing changes, Bridges (1991) links feedback to reinforcement through consistency and reward: "It is common and always disastrous to tell people to act and react in new ways—and then to reward them for the old actions and reactions. You won't manage to hold a new beginning for long if you preach teamwork and then reward individual contribution, if you preach customer service and then reward following the rules, if you preach risk taking and then reward no mistakes. . . ." (pp. 61–62). These insights are built on and can be better understood in terms of the principles and mechanisms central to expectancy theory. Regarding financial incentives and reward as a way to reinforce commitment to change, Heller (1998) advises very clearly: "Be willing to pay generously for achievement. People may change their behaviour radically for significant pay rewards" (p. 51). He explains: "People want to feel that their reward will match their efforts; if it does, this will reinforce their commitment to the new ways" (p. 51). Kriegel is also very straightforward: "The most obvious way to motivate employees to get excited about your plans is through rewards" (p. 260). But he is also more specific: "There are two kinds of rewards: extrinsic incentives, like the corner office, money, gifts and titles, and intrinsic rewards, which appeal to more abstract personal needs. People do things not just to get an object or the cash to buy it. They're also motivated by such intangibles as recognition, fairness, flexibility, creativity, meaningfulness and freedom. These internal factors have more impact on readiness for change than traditional extrinsic rewards do" (p. 261). Connor (2006) states: "A lack of willingness stems from a shortage of motivation and should be addressed through consequence management (the combination of rewards and punishments)" (p. 129).

Search Strategy

Relevant databases were searched using the term 'expectancy theory', and 'expectancy theory' in combination with 'organization', 'employee', 'change', 'meta-analysis' and 'systematic review'. The search yielded more than 200 articles. After screening the title and abstracts for relevance, fourteen studies met the inclusion criteria. After thorough examination, another eight studies were excluded, leaving six relevant studies with a highest evidence level of C.

Main Findings

Most included studies find positive relationships between expectancy and variables like motivation, effort, performance and quantity of work.

Two studies found a positive relationship between expectancy and (job) satisfaction (Ferris, 1977, Level E; Futrell, Parasuraman, & Sager, 1983, Level D-). Furthermore, three studies describe a positive relationship between expectancy and work motivation and effort (Chian & Jang, 2008, level E; Hackman & Porter, 1968, Level E-; Renko et al., 2012, Level C). Hackman and Porter (1968, Level E-) even found positive relationships between expectancy and multiple variables (e.g. quantity of work, ability to learn and sales). However, Ferris (1977, Level E) found positive relationships only between expectancy and satisfaction, not between expectancy and performance. Reinharth and Wahba (1975; Level D-) do not find any support for the classical expectancy model, but find that "at best the expectancy model accounts for less than 10 percent of the variance in effort and performance, and in most cases for only one percent to five percent of the variance" (Reinharth & Wahba, 1975, p. 530). This might sound insignificant, but a 10% increase in performance can be the difference between being a very successful organization and bankruptcy. Even an increase of 5% in performance can be valuable for an organization.

What Is the Conclusion?

Five of the six included studies point in the same direction: organizations and change can benefit from expectancy theory and the underlying principles and mechanisms when used properly. These five studies show one or more positive relationships between expectancy and multiple factors like motivation, effort and performance. Expectancy theory translated into organizational and managerial instruments and concepts such as goal-setting, feedback, performance appraisals and reward systems may help to increase satisfaction, performance and effort.

Practical Reflections

Expectancy theory can be used to promote and support change, especially by operationalizing and rewarding or appreciating new desired behaviours. In addition, expectancy theory can also be helpful in understanding how people become frustrated during change processes. They may have learned that certain behaviours and performance lead to appreciation and when these are rewarded over a longer period, expectations develop in a certain way and define the psychological contract. Changes may lead to (the experience of) a breach of that contract and the underlying expectancies, and hence disappointment, frustration, resistance to change and a lack of commitment to the change and organization. Expectancy theory is a very straightforward concept. However, for practitioners it is very important to be aware of the contingencies and specific conditions involved, in particular when we talk about the effects of extrinsic motivation (like financial incentives) on the one hand and intrinsic motivation on the other hand. Other research shows that intrinsic motivation is a better predictor for quality of performance, whereas financial incentives are a better predictor for quantity of performance (Cerasoli, Nicklin, & Ford, 2014) (Level B). In addition, research by Weibel, Rost, and Osterloh (2009) shows that financial incentives increase performance of non-interesting tasks but decrease performance of interesting tasks.

Social Cognitive Theory

People learn by observing others.

What Is Social Cognitive Theory?

Social cognitive theory was developed by Bandura (1986) and is a learning theory with the central idea that people learn by observing others. The assumption is that each witnessed behaviour of others (social) has the potential to change a person's way of thinking (cognition). More fundamentally: "*Social cognitive theory*—the *social* portion of the title acknowledges the social origins of much human thought and action; the *cognitive* portion recognizes the influential contribution of cognitive processes to human motivation, affect and action" (Van Lange, Kruglanski, & Higgins, 2012a, p. 350). In Chapter 4, on the second social motive, understanding, we discussed Bandura's social learning theory (1977). With that theory and the related experiments ('the Bobo doll experiments' in 1961 and 1963) Bandura already demonstrated the relevance of learning from others, social learning, the value of modelling for acquiring new or additional behaviours. With the social cognitive theory Bandura (1986) elaborates and renames social learning theory. Social cognition further contributes to the insight in the social core motive of understanding. It does so by emphasizing the importance of cognition in encoding and performing behaviours. Social cognition theory defines behaviour as a result of personal, behavioural and contextual or environmental influences. However, social cognitive theory also sheds further light on the social motive of controlling (as Bandura's social learning theory also does, in fact, with its emphasis on a person's perceived self-efficacy and behavioural change). The idea relates to the need for perceived contingency between behaviour and outcomes. By observing others, and others in specific contexts, people are able not only to learn and understand causal relationships between behaviours and effects or outcomes, but also to develop a repertoire to control their environment and be in control in social situations. Conversely, the models, leaders, parents, institutions and societies (can) also use social cognitive theory as a way to influence others. Modelling can be executed in various ways, by interpersonal imitation but also by using (mass) media sources.

Leaders may 'lead by example'; parents raise their children by being a role model. Organizations design introduction programmes to socialize new members. Societies may deliberately diffuse certain behaviours by using psychosocial factors that influence and govern behavioural change, for example by using symbolic communication to influence the human thought, affect and action referred to earlier (Bandura, 2009). Social learning and social cognition theory provide an alternative to the dominant psychological view that emphasizes learning through the rewarding and punishing effects that behaviours produce. This alternative way of learning is more positive and efficient; direct experience, based on response consequences, is often the 'hard way'; errors can be highly costly and wrong actions can be fatal. Before one gets in control, one may be bankrupt, disqualified or 'dead'. Social cognitive theory shows the way to an abbreviated, more efficient and human way of acquiring mores, routines, social practices, skills and content. It does so by emphasizing the relationship between learning and the observation of models. It shows how cultural patterns, modelling and socialization can be used for control, survival and effective human development. Social cognitive theory puts the social context in a central position, but does not see human beings as static or passive. Neither are they seen as the product of simple stimulus-response mechanisms or solely shaped by their environment as in behaviourism. Nor are they seen as the product of inner forces, a mix of rational and irrational, conscious and unconscious drives and forces like in the psychodynamic perspective. Instead, they are seen as human agents that have their own will and ability, being self-reflecting, proactive, self-developing and self-regulating (Bandura, 1986). The perspective that social cognitive theory takes on individuals is illustrated by the four core properties of human agency: intentionality, forethought, self-reactiveness and self-reflectiveness. These properties can be described as follows: "*Intentionality* refers to the creation of and engagement in plans and strategies by which people realize pre-determined intentions to act. *Forethought* is the property whereby people set goals and anticipate future events: 'they foresee likely outcomes of prospective actions to guide and motivate their efforts anticipatorily' (Bandura, 2009, p. 8). *Self-reactiveness* is about the translation of plans into successful courses of action and the processes of self-management and self-motivation, necessary to do this. Finally, through *self-reflectiveness*, people reflect on their capabilities, the soundness of their thoughts and actions, and the meaning of their pursuits" (Pajares, Prestin, Chen, & Nabi, 2009, p. 285). With regard to human thought, affect and action, social cognitive theory has broadened the scope of modelling influences and the functions it serves (Bandura, 1986). Bandura states: "In addition to cultivating cognitive and behavioural competencies, modelling influences were shown to alter motivation, create and modify emotional proclivities, serve as social prompts that activate, channel and support given styles of behaviour, and shape images of reality" (Van Lange, Kruglanski, & Higgins, 2012a, p. 351).5.2.2 What Is the Relevance of Social Cognitive Theory for Organization and Change?

The social cognitive theory states that the acquisition of an individual's knowledge can be directly related to observing others in a social context. When an individual observes the behaviour of others (e.g. giving a presentation) and see the consequences of that behaviour (e.g. reaction of the crowd), the individual learns from that experience, as he or she remembers the steps taken by the observed individual. The theory states that people do not learn solely by performing certain actions (trial and error) but rather by replicating the actions of other human beings. Central in the social cognitive theory is self-efficacy. Self-efficacy can be defined as "beliefs about one's ability to successfully perform particular behaviours or courses of action" (Lent, Lopez, Jr., Lopez, & Sheu, 2008, p. 53). Self-efficacy is the confidence one has to achieve the desired result. It overlaps with self-esteem; people need to feel confident enough to perform certain actions. Observing behaviour of others increases individuals' knowledge, which in turn is beneficial for their performance, as they learn from observing others. In combination with self-efficacy, this might also increase job satisfaction and overall happiness. From an organizational and managerial perspective, social cognitive career theory (SCCT) is relevant. As the name implies, SCCT builds on the social cognitive theory and applies it to people's careers. "SCCT posits that individuals are more likely to pursue and be successful in occupations for which they have high self-efficacy" (Diegelman & Subich, 2001, p. 394). Chang and Edwards (2015) state: "SCCT posits that links between social cognitive variables (e.g. self-efficacy), person input (e.g. personality), goal-related behaviours and contextual factors all contribute to job outcomes (e.g. satisfaction; Lent, Brown, & Hackett, 1994; Lent & Brown, 2006, 2008) and can be considered as an integrative model of job satisfaction that consists of all theoretically relevant constructs" (p. 36). Social cognitive theory may also add to a better understanding of change and organizational topics like leadership ('lead by example'), team development (the role of 'relevant others'), change capacity and culture. Sinek's (2014) first two leadership lessons are 'so goes the culture, so goes the company' and 'so goes the leader, so goes the culture'. Leadership, 'model learning' and socialization are important factors in developing organizational culture, understanding organizational behaviour and facilitating and frustrating change. Self-efficacy is probably an important element of change capacity. Connor (2006) states: "People can only change when they have the capacity to do so. Ability means having the necessary skills and knowing how to use them. Willingness is the motivation to apply those skills to a particular situation. If you lack either ability or willingness, it is unlikely that you will successfully adapt to a change" (p. 129). Kriegel and Brandt (1996) advise: "Emphasizing strengths builds esteem and encourages people to do better in everything, including those things that give them trouble. When you're introducing change, remind people of their competence. Show them how the skills they already have will help them to excel in the new task" (p. 209).

Search Strategy

Relevant databases were searched using the terms 'social', 'cognitive', 'theory', 'proxy', 'agency', 'collective' and 'individual' in combination with 'meta-analysis' and 'systematic review'. The search yielded more than 200 articles. After screening the title and abstracts for relevance, eleven studies met the inclusion criteria. After thorough examination, another six studies were excluded. The five included studies had a low level of evidence ranging from C to D-. Given the central role of self-efficacy in social cognitive theory, an additional quick scan was carried out on that concept. We included two meta-analyses (level B-) and three case studies (level D-).

Main Findings

1. *Both self-efficacy and outcome expectations accounted for significant variance in predicting interest and pursuit intentions, generally supporting the social cognitive career theory (Diegelman & Subich, 2001; Level C).*
2. *Self-efficacy has a positive effect on performance (Level B-).*

   A meta-analytical study found a positive effect between self-efficacy and work-related performance (Stajkovic & Fred, 1998).

3. *Entrepreneurial self-efficacy (ESE) has a positive effect on firm performance (Level B-).*

   A meta-analytical study found a positive effect between ESE and firm performance (Miao, Qian, & Ma, 2016).

4. *(Leadership) Self-efficacy has a positive effect on organizational commitment, self-esteem, job satisfaction and managers' job autonomy (Level D-).*

   Researchers found that leadership self-efficacy has positive effects on multiple factors, including organizational commitment, performance and managers' job autonomy (Paglis & Green, 2002). Another study found that self-efficacy was positively correlated with organizational performance (Jacobsen & Andersen, 2017).

5. *Self-efficacy has an effect that leads to fewer turnover intentions (Level D-).*

   Increasing self-efficacy among employees results in fewer turnover intentions. This can be useful in keeping employees inside the organization (Lai & Chen, 2012).

What Is the Conclusion?

McCormick (2001 states that: "Social cognitive theory is a conceptual framework of human functioning that is well supported by a large body of empirical research" (p. 30). However, our search provided us with limited evidence regarding the social cognitive theory as such. Therefore, we searched in addition for both self-efficacy (as an essential part of social cognitive theory) and social cognitive *career* theory. This generated stronger evidence, including two high-level meta-analyses. The evidence not only supports the social cognitive career theory but also shows that self-efficacy is crucial, as it is positively related to multiple important factors for organizations, employees and change practitioners.

Practical Reflections

Social cognitive theory, but in particular the concept of self-efficacy, is a highly relevant concept for the understanding of organizational behaviour and change processes. Self-efficacy, or 'action control', can be an important basis for creating the right conditions and context for change. Providing supervisory support and constructive feedback can increase employees' self-efficacy. Other interventions are celebrating achievements, giving sincere compliments and treating colleagues with respect. Therefore, Kouzes and Posner emphasize that a leader must "invest in strengthening the capacity and the resolve of everyone in the organization" (p. 256), especially in situations of change. Exemplary leaders strive to create conditions in which people perform effortlessly and expertly despite the challenging or even difficult situation. Kriegel and Brandt (1996) advise: "Emphasizing strengths builds esteem and encourages people to do better in everything, including those things that give them trouble. When you're introducing change, remind people of their competence. Show them how the skills they already have will help them to excel in the new task" (p. 209).

Stress Appraisal Theory

Peoples' emotions are extracted from their evaluations of events. These appraisals or estimates will lead to individual variances of emotional reactions to the same stimulus or event.

What Is Stress Appraisal Theory?

The core idea of appraisal theory is that people's emotions are extracted from their evaluations of events (Lazarus, 2000). These appraisals or estimates will lead to individual variances of emotional reactions to the same stimulus or event (Smith & Lazarus, 1990). Stress appraisal theory refers to the evaluation process by which individuals evaluate stressful events and cope with them (e.g. Lazarus, 1966, 1974). Coping can be defined as 'the cognitive and behavioural efforts made to master, tolerate or reduce external and internal demands and conflicts among them' (Folkman & Lazarus, 1980, p. 223). Individuals differ in the evaluation of what is happening (to them), how they perceive the circumstances and how they react to and cope with circumstances (Lazarus & Folkman, 1984). The social nature of stress appraisal is related to two precursory conditions that affect the process of evaluation, environmental and personal variables. Environmental variables are outside the person and related to rules of behaviour that are governed by societal norms. These variables include demands, constraints, opportunity and culture. Personal variables are inside the person and include the person's goals and goal hierarchies, beliefs about self and context, and personal resources. In personality psychology, emotions are a function of personality or character; in neuropsychology they are a function of the chemical processes in the brain and in social psychology (within the context of appraisal theory) they are a function of the appraisal of and cognitive response to a situation. According to Lazarus, stress appraisal comes in two forms and two stages, a primary and a secondary stage. At the stage of primary appraisal one decides whether an event is stressful and relevant. Based on the appraisal an event can be associated with a threat, harm or loss, or a challenge. Consequently, stress can be related to negative (harm) and positive (challenge) types of stress. Harm appraisals are about past losses. Threat and challenge are about the future, about possible losses and gains. These appraisals provide insight into employees' expectations and concerns about potential consequences (Fugate, 2013). At the stage of secondary appraisal the central question is how to cope with a stressful, relevant event and which coping options are available. The decision on which available option to choose can be supported by a reference framework based on prior experience of exposure to similar situations. In dealing with stress, individuals constantly evaluate coping options in order to deal with stress in the context of personal goals and resources and environmental constraints. Primary appraisal is grounded in three components: goal relevance, goal congruence and type of ego involvement. Goal relevance refers to the extent to which an event refers to issues about which the person cares. Goal congruence describes the extent to which the developments and goals related to an event are in accordance with personal goals. The type of ego-involvement concerns aspects of personal commitment related to the event; to what extent are self-esteem, ego-identity, moral values and ego-ideal related or at stake. Secondary appraisal is defined by the components of blame or credit, coping potential and future expectations. Blame or credit results from an individual's evaluation of who is responsible, to blame or to credit for a certain event. According to Lazarus, coping potential can be defined as 'a person's evaluation of the prospects for generating certain behavioural or cognitive operations that will positively influence a personally relevant encounter' (Krohne, 2001, p. 4). Future expectations are the result of the appraisal of the further course or consequences of an encounter with respect to goal (in)congruence.

What Is the Relevance of Stress Appraisal Theory for Organization and Change?

The perspective that stress appraisal provides is highly relevant for organizations and organizational behaviour in general and change management and change processes in particular. It is related to subjects like change vision, change capacity, leadership, communication, performance management and resistance and commitment. Fugate (2013) illustrates this in his article 'Capturing the positive experience of change: antecedents, processes, and consequences'. Building on the insights of Oreg (2003), he states: "For any given change in a particular organization, some employees react negatively and suffer tremendous stress and negative health consequences . . . while others react positively and view change as an opportunity for development and advancement" (p. 15). Central are the causes of differences in individuals' reactions to change. Stress appraisal theory provides the basics for doing this. Like the theory, Fugate focuses on employees' cognitive appraisals of change by making use of the 'antecedent→process→outcome perspective', partly based on systems theory and systems management. The premise is that control over inputs and premises is a means of managing outcomes. Fugate states: "A person's cognitive appraisal of organizational change is important because it represents an evaluation of a person-situation transaction in terms of its meaning for social well-being (see Dewe, 1991)" (p. 16). Appraisals give meaning to (change) experiences and are predictors of affective, behavioural and other responses to organizational change (Fugate, 2013). The stress appraisal theory in general and Fugate's perspective of change appraisals in particular provide a relevant and helpful perspective for change management. Fugate defines personal and situation antecedents of employee appraisal of organizational change. Personal antecedents are: positive change orientation, positive psychological capital and employability. Situation antecedents are: change-related fairness, trust in management and perceived organizational support. The appraisal perspective helps to understand why and how people react to change visions and a concept like sense urgency (Kotter, 2008). In the change management literature these concepts sometimes seem to be undisputed. Ibarra, for example, emphasizes the importance of having a clear and inspiring vision. She states that "across studies and research traditions, vision has been found to be a defining feature of leadership" (p. 41). Bridges (1991) emphasizes the importance of clarifying the purpose: What is the idea behind what you're doing? People need a picture of how the outcome will look; participation asks for imagination. Kotter (2012) is very outspoken: "By far the biggest mistake people make when trying to change organizations is to plunge ahead without establishing a high enough sense of urgency in fellow managers and employees" (p. 4). Kriegel (1996) considers urgency as one of the four keys to lighting a firestorm in your organization (the other three are inspiration, ownership and rewards and recognition). Conner (2006) states that the urgency of burning-platform situations provides motivation for major change. Urgency can be generated by the high price of unresolved problems or the high cost of missed opportunities. Heath and Heath (2010) are more nuanced and provide an alternative. There is a cliché that "the bar must be raised" to motivate people to perform and to change. But they emphasize that you need to lower the bar and 'shrink the change' to motivate reluctant people. Bridges (1991) is very clear; he emphasizes the importance of conveying the problem and the necessity of change: people don't act if they do not see, acknowledge and understand the problem. Lazarus and Folkman (1984) teach that 'visions' and a 'sense of urgency' are not 'givens' from the perspective of the people involved. Depending on the person and the situation, a vision or sense of urgency can be associated with a threat, harm or loss, or a challenge. Thus the (change) appraisal perspective may also help to understand why resistance or commitments develop. In addition, it sheds light on the role and position in the change process of factors such as fairness and trust.

Search Strategy

We started to search relevant databases using the terms 'stress appraisal theory', 'appraisal theory' and 'model of appraisal'. The search yielded 315 articles. After screening the title and abstracts for relevance, no studies met the inclusion criteria. In addition, we focused on Fugate's change appraisal. Relevant databases were searched using the term 'change apprais*'. The search yielded ten articles. After screening the title and abstracts for relevance, five studies met the inclusion criteria. The included studies have evidence levels B-, C- and D-.

Main Findings

1. *The relationship between appraisal of organizational change and subsequent withdrawal behaviour is completely mediated (Level B-).*

   - Structural equation model results showed that coping with organizational change is a completely mediated process best represented by the stimulus-response theoretical structure, whereby negative appraisal is associated with reduced control and increased escape coping, which are positively related to positive and negative emotions, respectively. Negative emotions predicted sick time used and intentions to quit, which then predicted voluntary turnover (Fugate, Kinicki & Prussia, 2008).

- Results indicate that the stimulus-response model is the most accurate structural representation of how employees cope with organizational change. This finding aligns with arguments that emotions are a consequence of the appraisal-coping relationship and reinforces propositions derived from behavioural psychology. In addition, it supports research in which coping was found to mediate the appraisal-emotion relationship (e.g. Folkman & Lazarus, 1988) (Fugate, Kinicki & Prussia, 2008).

- Our findings also cast doubt on the benefits of simply "emphasizing the positive" when attempting to manage organizational change. This study therefore shows a disconnect between the form and function of affect in the context of organizational change, and it seems to support the contention of Cacioppo et al. (1999) that "it is useful to think of the affect system as an entity intimately related to yet distinguishable from the cognitive system" (p. 840) (Fugate, Kinicki & Prussia, 2008).

2. *Managers' engagement was associated with followers' appraisal of change (Level B-).*

- Transformational and transactional leadership styles were positively related to the engagement of managers. Managers' engagement was associated with followers' appraisal of change. The two leadership styles also had a direct, long-term effect on followers' change appraisal; positive for transformational leadership and negative for transactional leadership (Holten, 2015).

- The findings of our study support the contingency approach to leadership behaviour (Fiedler, 1967) and the theory of situational leadership (Vroom and Jago, 2007), suggesting that there may be a "right style for the right situation" (Holten, 2015).

- Transformational leadership may be an effective approach to enhance followers' positive appraisal of change. As this leadership style reveals both long-term and short-term positive effects, directly and indirectly, strategically increasing managers' transformational potential may well benefit the entire process of change. During the last stages of change, managers' direct engagement in change is associated with followers' change appraisal (Holten, 2015).

3. *Employees' change history in an organization is a key antecedent of their appraisals about organizational change (Level C-).*

- Change appraisals (challenge and harm appraisals) are associated with psychological contract violation, which in turn is associated with intentions to leave the organization, and, ultimately, with voluntary employee turnover.

- When employees report that previous change efforts in that company have not been successful and have been poorly managed, they are less likely to report that current changes present an opportunity for growth (Rafferty & Restubog, 2017).

4. *Top Management Team (TMT) and supervisory leaders play distinctly different, but both important, roles in driving employees' adjustment to change (Level C-).*

- Overall, results suggested that TMT and supervisory leaders play distinctly different roles in driving employees' adjustment to change. TMT transformational leadership displayed indirectly reduced psychological contract violation at Time 2 (T2) by increasing openness toward change at Time 1 (T1). In addition, TMT transformational leadership was also directly associated with affective commitment to the organization at T2. By contrast, supervisory leaders indirectly reduced psychological contract violation at T2 by reducing cynicism about change at T1 (Rafferty & Restubog, 2009).
- Results provided support for both direct and indirect relationships among leadership and employee adjustment. Of theoretical interest is the failure of psychological uncertainty about change to emerge as an important mediator of relationships in this study. Rather, TMT and supervisory transformational leadership influenced change outcomes through change attitudes (Rafferty & Restubog, 2009).
- Strategic uncertainty about change T1 displayed an indirect positive relationship with psychological contract violation T2 by increasing cynicism about change T1. Contrary to our expectations, however, while TMT transformational relationship was negatively correlated with strategic uncertainty, the indirect relationships between TMT leadership, strategic uncertainty, and cynicism about change were not significant. As such, in this particular study, it seems that factors other than the TMT were driving strategic uncertainty about change (Rafferty & Restubog, 2009).
- Contrary to expectations, job-related uncertainty was not significantly associated with any of the substantive constructs in the model (Rafferty & Restubog, 2009).
- There is considerable benefit to be gained by incorporating a range of conflicting employee attitudes when examining the processes that influence employees' adjustment to change (Rafferty & Restubog, 2009).

5. *Appraisal is central to coping with social change (Level D-).*

- Transformational leadership was related positively to the perception of change as a challenge and controllable, and negatively to threat and loss, but not to coping, although there was an association with positive affect (Ben-Zur, Yagil, & Oz, 2005).

- Challenge/controllability appraisals will be related positively to problem-focused coping and positive affect, whereas threat/loss appraisals will be related to emotion-focused coping and negative affect (Ben-Zur et al., 2005).
- The results support the cognitive model developed by Lazarus and Folkman (1984), which posits that appraisals of stress in terms of threat, loss or challenge affect coping strategies that in turn lead to emotional outcomes of the stressful encounter (Ben-Zur et al., 2005).
- Problem-focused coping was related to positive affect, while emotion-focused coping was related to negative affect (Ben-Zur et al., 2005).

What Is the Conclusion?

Stress appraisal as such and its sibling the concept of change appraisal are highly relevant and informative for the practice of management and change. The findings show that the appraisal of change is a key factor in change processes and the way people involved react to change, commit or resist. The concept underscores the important role of change history in change processes and the influence it has on the people involved. This appraisal is strongly related to the way people adjust to and cope with times of change.

Practical Reflections

For organizational and change practitioners the concept of change appraisals and its evidence has a set of lessons to learn and guidelines to provide. To start, employee experience is critically important because employees are ultimately responsible for executing change initiatives, and change succeeds or fails depending on employee behaviour (Armenakis & Bedeian, 1999). This study shows that negative appraisals influence employee withdrawal via a mediated process involving coping and emotions. The degree of such withdrawal (sick time used versus quitting) has serious implications for change effectiveness and organizational competitiveness (cf. Spreitzer & Mishra, 2002). Notably, a lack of employee commitment and engagement (e.g. withdrawal) erodes the competitive advantages that presumably motivated the changes. This is especially salient in knowledge-based organizations and industries. Voluntary turnover of key personnel not only costs an employer organizational knowledge, skills and abilities, but also their competitive position is further eroded if such employees then join competitors (Fugate, Kinicki, & Prussia, 2008). In addition, past change failures, whether they are real or perceived only in the minds of employees, continue to affect organizational change implementation success far into the future of a company (Rafferty, 2017). And: change management practitioners should consider whether there are groups within an organization that have especially negative perceptions of their change management history (Rafferty, 2017). By increasing the followers' confidence in their ability to achieve desirable outcomes, and by enhancing the perceived importance of communal values, transformational leaders have the ability to motivate followers in times of crisis to promote the necessary changes (Ben-Zur et al., 2005). Another lesson: transformational leadership may be considered an external coping resource, similar to social support, and may affect the stressful encounter processes in much the same way as other substantial resources, such as economic status. The perception by the individual that the leader can be relied on, can help during a crisis, and can implement change is one facet of the ability of transformational leadership to facilitate positive appraisal of change. Moreover, transformational leaders, through their vision, their ability to link their followers' self-concept to the collective mission, and their inspirational appeals, can present social change as both necessary and challenging and motivate their followers to play a role in it (Ben-Zur, 2005). And: appraisal, coping and personal well-being are likely to affect one another, so that the appraisal of the situation both affects and is affected by coping with it and the emotional reactions to it (Ben-Zur, 2005). Awareness of managers' role in communicating important information, interpreting the individual consequences and working actively and positively toward the change may be an area of positive investment for organizations in change (Holten, 2015). While transformational leadership is "trainable" (Kelloway & Barling, 2000), our findings suggest taking a training, sensibilizing approach to developing managers' change leadership skills (Holten, 2015). And finally, there is a need to provide training and development opportunities for leaders at all hierarchical levels regarding the demands and requirements of leading change. Such leadership development needs to recognize that presenting a vision and inspiring followers entails slightly different issues at different hierarchical levels. In the TMT, vision and inspirational leadership are directed toward organization-wide issues and concerns. In contrast, at the supervisory level, leader vision and inspiration involve translating organizational-level issues into a team-level change vision that addresses day-to-day issues and problems when implementing and managing change efforts (Rafferty & Restubog, 2009).

Self-Perception Theory

Individuals come to 'know' their own attitudes, emotions and other internal states partially by inferring them from observations of their own overt behaviour and/or the circumstances in which this behaviour occurs.

What Is Self-Perception Theory?

Self-perception theory was developed by Bem (1967, 1972) and concerns attitude formation, presented as an alternative (like self-affirmation theory) to dissonance theory (with its 'negative drive state'). The theory argued that 'attitudes were inferences stemming from observation from one's behaviour' (Fazio, 1987, p. 129). The assumption is that we observe our behaviour, and as a result reach conclusions about who we are. This is noteworthy, because conventional wisdom is that attitudes determine behaviours. Self-perception is sometimes described as being counterintuitive in nature. The simplicity of this theory is part of its elegance. Bem summarizes his own theory very simply: "Individuals come to 'know' their own attitudes, emotions and other internal states partially by inferring them from observations of their own overt behaviour and/ or the circumstances in which this behaviour occurs" (1972, p. 2). One's attitude could be directly detected from the overt behaviour by means of an implicit selection rule: "What must be my attitude if I am willing to behave in this fashion in this situation?" The theory emphasizes the critical role of behaviour, suggesting a partial equivalence between self and interpersonal perception: "To the extent that internal cues are weak, ambiguous or uninterpretable, the individual is in the same position as an outside observer, an observer who must necessarily rely upon those same external cues to infer the individual's inner states" (Bem, 1972, p. 2). Attitudes are induced directly and rationally, without internal cognition and mood states and in the same way people attempt to explain the behaviour of others (Robak, Ward, & Ostolaza, 2005). Fazio (1987) points to research (see: Fazio & Cooper, 1983) that has shown that self-perception is no longer an adequate alternative to dissonance theory. However, much evidence that is beyond the domain of dissonance theory, in particular concerning social influence phenomena, supports the theory. Fazio (1987) points to the fact that self-perception processes are central to the interpretation of foot-in-the-door phenomena: "People are more likely to comply with a large request, when that request has been preceded by a less demanding act of compliance" (p. 130). Another contribution of the theory is related to the over-justification effect. This effect is described as "the undermining of intrinsic interest in an activity that stems from the perception that one has engaged in the activity only as a means of reaching some desirable end" (Fazio, 1987, p. 130).

　Self-perception theory and its mechanisms can be further illustrated by the way they are applied in therapies. The starting point of a lot of traditional therapies is the assumption that psychological problems come from the inner part of the patient. The focus is on the (inner) problems. Self-perception theory, conversely, starts from the assumption that people derive attitudes, feelings and abilities from their external behaviours (Bem, 1972; Fazio, 1987). Here the focus is on external behaviours.

Therapies are focused on guiding patients to first change their behaviours. Haemmerlie and Montgomery (1982, 1984) describe the application of self-perception theory to 'heterosocial anxiety': "A treatment for heterosocial anxiety based on D. J. Bem's (1972) self-perception theory, involving use of prearranged, purposefully biased interactions with members of the opposite sex, was compared with an imaginal therapy technique and a no-treatment control group. . . . The biased interaction technique, unaffected by expectancy, caused significant changes in all three modes of responding and for both expectancy conditions. Results suggest that the biased interaction treatment, whereby the focus was on the observation of one's own successful performance in an area in which difficulty is normally encountered, was more effective for reducing anxiety than an imaginal technique in which the focus was on a client's internal states" (Haemmerlie and Montgomery, 1984[1]).

What Is the Relevance of Self-Perception for Organization and Change?

Self-perception theory provides relevant insights related to organizational and change subjects like change capacity, resistance, commitment and leadership. The central idea is that individuals will first show behaviour and as a result that behaviour will determine their attitude toward that kind of (social) behaviour. In accordance with self-perception theory and translating it into an organizational setting, employees who show a certain kind of behaviour will form their attitudes based on that behaviour. Helping people to behave out of their comfort zone, and positively reinforce this behaviour, may positively change their attitude. In this way, certain desirable behaviour that may benefit organizational change can be endorsed and reinforced.

The following example of the possible effect of self-perception is illustrative: "The self-perception effect might also carry over to later behaviour. For example, imagine that ordinarily you are shy at parties but have recently decided that you want to make new friends. You have decided that at the next party you will make an effort to be especially talkative to meet new people and it goes well. This behaviour influences your attitude toward social behaviour and leads you to perceive a greater outgoingness in yourself. The next time you are at a party you exhibit outgoing social behaviour without nearly as much effort. Act as if you are outgoing and you might become more so".[2] The perspective of self-perception may be helpful in the learning and adoption of new behaviours and teaches leaders about the conditions and possibilities they have to offer their people in order to change and adapt. It shows that experience as a result of external behaviours may be more effective than trying to change problems by confronting them with 'a sense of urgency' or vision and focusing on the inner problems these create for the people involved. The theory also explains foot-in-the-door phenomena (Fazio, 1987). These phenomena may lead managers to start their change process with small changes and interventions instead of large, transformational initiatives. Another contribution of the theory, related to the over-justification effect, warns against interventions that undermine the intrinsic interest in change as a result of being too focused on or driven by extrinsic motivators.

Search Strategy

Relevant databases were searched using the term 'self-perception', and 'self-perception' in combination with 'organization', 'employee', 'meta-analysis' or 'systematic review'. The search yielded more than 250 articles. After screening the title and abstracts for relevance, three studies met the inclusion criteria.

Main Findings

1. *More effective leaders have a greater level of self-perception accuracy (Level D-).*

   Managers tend to be overly optimistic about their own abilities and traits, which undermines the effectiveness of the manager. Self-perception accuracy is seen as a crucial ingredient for authentic leaders and in making a shared purpose, thus increasing the leaders' effectiveness (Herbst & Conradie, 2011).

2. *Leaders perceived as more authentic by themselves and employees are better at fostering higher follower job satisfaction (Level D-).*

   When leaders themselves and followers perceive them as being more authentic, leaders are better at fostering high follower job satisfaction (Černe, Dimovski, Marič, Penger, & Škerlavaj, 2014).

3. *Followers who see themselves as possessing both follower and leader qualities are prime candidates for leader emergence (Level E).*

   When followers have the self-perception of having both follower and leader qualities, they are prime candidates for leadership functions. Trust in the leader plays a vital role: "Findings about trust suggest that when followers work to build trust with their leader, they shore up their own potential and see themselves as having transformational behaviours" (Baker, Mathis, Stites-Doe, & Javadian, 2016, p. 223).

What Is the Conclusion?

Bem conducted multiple experiments to test his theory. These resulted in important insights and evidence. Building on these experiments, numerous studies have been conducted, providing evidence for the self-perception theory. In social psychology, self-perception theory is one of the "blockbuster theories" in terms of popularity, impact and scientific evidence. Even today, there are numerous studies that support the self-perception theory, making the theory valuable for social psychologists. The relevance and potential of the theory for organizations, management and change are clear. The specific evidence is limited but illustrative. The relevant studies focus in particular on leaders, followers and the interaction between them.

Practical Reflections

Self-perception theory as such, its evidence and results and also the specific evidence in the context of leadership and organization, encourage a continued search for interventions and applications to help people to change and develop.

Self-Determination Theory

People are not only moulded by their social contexts, but are inherently active, intrinsically motivated and oriented toward developing naturally through integrative processes.

What Is Self-Determination Theory?

Self-determination theory is an empirically derived, macro theory of human motivation and personality in social contexts that differentiates motivation in terms of being autonomous and controlled (Ryan & Deci, 2011). Ryan & Deci (2011) point to the dominant so-called standard social science model, characterized by "a relatively plastic human nature, moulded by its social contexts" (p. 416). Learning, being the acquisition of attitudes, values, motivations and behaviours, is primarily viewed as the product of social environments. These environments 'teach' individuals and define their values, needs, attitudes and behaviours. This perspective is manifest in social learning theory, with modelling and reinforcement as the most important behavioural and learning mechanisms. Self-determination theory (SDT) also focuses on social environments and their impact. However, it views human beings as "inherently active, intrinsically motivated and oriented toward developing naturally through integrative processes" (Deci & Ryan, 2011, p. 417). These qualities are inherent in human nature, develop over time, are essential to learning and impacted by social environments. The research findings of Ryan and Deci (2000) have led to insight that there are at least three innate psychological needs—competence, autonomy and relatedness—which when satisfied yield enhanced self-motivation and mental health and when thwarted lead to diminished motivation and well-being. These three basic needs are implicated across development (Ryan, Grant, Tigbe, & Granat, 2006). It thus rejects Maslow's (1971) hierarchy of needs. Theories like Maslow's do not address the interaction between inherent needs and social conditions that support functioning. SDT instead is about linking environmental factors to fundamental human needs (in order to explain and predict the impact of the social environment on intrinsic motivation) and emphasizes the conditions under which developmental processes like effective therapeutic change and prosocial behaviour will function most effectively: "Specifically, it will function effectively to the degree that the needs for competence, autonomy and relatedness are satisfied" (Deci & Ryan, 2012, p. 429). SDT is defined by three essential elements: (1) humans are inherently proactive with their potential and mastering their inner forces, like drives and emotions; (2) humans have an inherent tendency toward growth, development and integrated functioning; and (3) optimal development and actions are inherent in humans, but do not happen automatically; the inherent potential needs to be nurtured by the social environment (Deci & Vansteenkiste, 2004). The level and quality of functioning, development and growth is dependent on the satisfaction of the three innate psychological needs. Competence is about controlling the outcome and experiencing mastery. Autonomy is about the universal urge to be a causal agent of one's own life and to act in harmony with one's integrated self. Relatedness is about the universal psychological need to interact with others, to be connected and to care and to be taken care of. The needs are universal, but their relative importance and the way they are expressed will depend on factors like culture, experience and specific context. SDT is the basis for a variety of research projects and predictions. It evolved out of the research of Deci (1971) on the effects of extrinsic rewards on intrinsic motivation. More than 100 similar studies confirm the controversial idea that rewards do not always motivate persistent desired behaviour, and may even undermine intrinsic motivation. Further research puts the three basic needs in a central position. For example, research confirmed the prediction that feedback and choice would enhance experiences of competence and self-determination, fostering greater intrinsic motivation (Deci, Koestner, & Ryan, 1999a; Zuckerman, Porac, Lathin, & Deci, 1978).

What Is the Relevance of Self-Determination for Organization and Change?

The underlying mechanism of self-determination is fairly simple: when employees can fulfil their innate needs, it will allow them to function optimally and make personal growth possible. This will in turn have a positive effect on their job performance and probably more relevant factors for organizational functioning and change initiatives. It helps to see the human perspective on organization and change. It puts a set of psychological needs in the centre: competence, autonomy and relatedness. By doing this, it provides a framework and coordinates the development of change programmes, processes and interventions. As a result, the concept of self-determination is relevant and has potential for change management subjects like leadership, change capacity, cultural change, resistance and commitment. In addition, it is relevant in deciding on the way to motivate people for change and for the design of structures, (reward and appraisal) systems, goal-setting and feedback and hence performance management. Self-determination can be illustrated with popular change management ideas about commitment and autonomous teams. In sport the importance of commitment is undisputed. The legendary athlete Haile Gebrselassie teaches: "You need three things to win: discipline, hard work and, before everything maybe, commitment. No one will make it without those three. Sport teaches you that". And the world champion racing driver Mario Andretti states: "Desire is the key to motivation, but it's determination and commitment to an unrelenting pursuit of your goal—a commitment to excellence—that will enable you to attain the success you seek". Employee commitment to change objectives is often considered a prerequisite for successful change. Conner (1992) is very clear: "Successful change is rooted in commitment. Unless key participants in a transition are committed to both attaining the goals of the change and paying the price those goals entail, the project will ultimately fail. In fact, most change failures can be traced back to this lack of commitment, with obvious symptoms like sponsors terminating projects and more subtle signs such as target apathy as leading indicators" (p. 147). And: "Given that committed people will devote the time, money, endurance, persistence, loyalty and ingenuity necessary, it is easy to see why commitment is critical for successful change. It is the glue that provides the vital bond between people and change goals. It is the source of energy that propels resilient people and organizations through the process at the fastest, most effective pace possible—the optimum speed of change" (p. 148). With regard to the three psychological needs put forward by self-determination theory, that is, competence, autonomy and relatedness, Laloux's ideas with regard to teams are illustrative. Laloux (2014) provides us with 'A Guide to Creating Organizations Inspired by the Next Stage of Human Consciousness' and considers self-management (structures) and self-managing teams as defining elements. A team-based organization (TBO) is often described in very positive, attractive terms. An example can be found in the 'Business Dictionary'[3]: "non-traditional, innovative work environment relying on teams to achieve its objectives. TBOs' major characteristics include (1) mutual trust; (2) employee empowerment in planning, organization and goal-setting; (3) shared responsibility for self-management; (4) shared accountability for performance and (5) shared leadership".

Search Strategy

Relevant databases were searched using the term 'self-determination', and 'self-determination' in combination with 'meta-analysis' or 'systematic review'. The search yielded more than 400 articles. After screening the title and abstracts for relevance, six studies met the inclusion criteria.

After critically appraising the studies, one study was excluded because of serious methodological flaws.

Main Findings

1. *Perceived self-determination is positively related to multiple relevant factors for organizations (Level D-).*

   Perceived self-determination is positively related to perceived organizational support, mood and job performance of employees (Eisenberger, Rhoades, & Cameron, 1999). Eisenberger et al. (1999) state: "The stronger the desire for control, the greater was the observed relationship between performance reward expectancy and intrinsic motivation" (p. 1036). And: "Employees who were most concerned with self-determination took the greatest interest in their work activities when those activities were associated with expectations of reward for high performance" (p. 1036).

2. *Self-determination predicts organizational citizenship behaviour (Level D-).*

   Organizational citizenship behaviour (OCB) is behaviour that is not formally written down in a contract. Employees who engage in OCB are beneficial to organizations, as they do extra work on top of their formal contract. Self-determination predicts this kind of beneficial behaviour (Zhang & Chen, 2013).

3. *Turnover intentions are directly influenced by the degree of autonomy (Level D-).*

   The more autonomy the volunteers had in this cross-sectional study, the lower their intentions to quit were (Haivas, Hofmans, & Pepermans, 2013).

What Is the Conclusion?

The self-perception theory is a well-researched one. Based on its insights and 'track record' it may be concluded that it is highly relevant and useful for the field of change and organization. The specific evidence provides helpful insights with regard to the way in which beneficial behaviour for the organization and the positive functioning of employees can be stimulated and facilitated.

Practical Reflections

The evidence points in the direction that self-determination is positively related to multiple factors that contribute to more effective, but also more 'human' change. Self-determination theory addresses the psychological needs of the people involved in the change. The evidence shows that there are positive effects of self-determination on relevant factors like organizational citizenship behaviour (OCB). This underlines the relevance of the theory for practitioners in change processes. The three innate needs are coordinates for the design and development of change capacity, structures (like a team structure) and leadership (styles) that facilitate or enable 'better' and more effective change.

Social Dominance Theory

People are part of group-based social hierarchies in which concepts like stereotyping and group oppression are instrumental to the maintenance and stability of those hierarchies.

What Is Social Dominance Theory?

Social dominance theory (SDT) is a theory of intergroup relations and social hierarchy. The theory focuses on the maintenance and stability of group-based social hierarchies. It provides coherent and comprehensive theory that integrates insights into the nature of dynamics of intergroup conflict, stereotyping and group oppression (Sidanius & Pratto, 1999). Important sources for the theory include Blumer's group positions theory, social identity theory (SIT) and evolutionary psychology. SDT is influenced by personality psychology, social psychology and political sociology. Sidanius and Pratto characterize their theory as 'an attempt to connect the worlds of individual personality and attitudes with the domains of institutional behaviour and social structure' (1999, p. 31). The purpose of SDT is to identify the various intrapersonal, interpersonal, intergroup and institutional mechanisms that produce and maintain the group-based social hierarchy and how these mechanisms interact. SDT starts with the basic observation 'that all human societies tend to be structured as systems of *group-based social hierarchies*' (Sidanius & Pratto, 1999, p. 31). Hierarchies consist of a small number of dominant groups at the top combined with subordinate groups at the bottom. The dominant group is characterized by the possession of a disproportionately large share of the positive social value. Social value can be symbolic or material; examples are social status, wealth, and authority and power. If there is group-based inequality with regard to social value, according to SDT this will be maintained through three mechanisms or primary intergroup behaviours. The three mechanisms are aggregated individual discrimination, aggregated institutional discrimination and behavioural asymmetry. Widely shared cultural ideologies, like so-called legitimizing myths, provide the moral and intellectual justification for these behaviours (Sidanius & Pratto, 2011).

The social hierarchy can be further understood with the aid of stratification systems. Sidanius and Prato (1999) mention an age system, a gender system and an arbitrary-set system. In the first system it is adults and middle-aged people (versus children and younger adults) and males (versus females) who have disproportionate social and political power. The third system comprises socially constructed and highly salient groups. The groups are based on characteristics such as clan, caste, social class or religious sect. Sidanius and Pratto (1999, p. 38) formulate three primary assumptions on which SDT is based:

1. While age- and gender-based hierarchies will tend to exist within all social systems, arbitrary-set systems of social hierarchy will invariably emerge within social systems, producing a sustainable economic surplus.
2. Most forms of group conflict and oppression (e.g. racism, ethnocentrism, sexism, nationalism, classism, regionalism) can be regarded as different manifestations of the same basic human predisposition to form group-based social hierarchies.
3. Human social systems are subject to the counterbalancing influences of hierarchy-enhancing (HE) forces, producing and maintaining ever-higher levels of group-based social inequality, and hierarchy-attenuating (HA) forces, producing greater levels of group-based social equality.

The three mechanisms or proximal processes mentioned earlier drive group-based social hierarchy (Sidanius & Pratto, 1999). Aggregated individual discrimination consists of 'simple, daily and sometimes quite inconspicuous individual acts of discrimination of one individual against another' (pp. 39–41). Aggregated institutional discrimination is discrimination by the rules, procedures and actions of social institutions. Institutions also support the stability of the social hierarchy by the use of systematic terror. That is, 'the use of violence or threats of violence disproportionately directed against subordinates' (p. 41). This terror is likely to be the most ferocious if subordinates directly challenge and confront the hegemony of the dominant group. Systematic terror has three basic forms: official, semi-official and unofficial, and behavioural asymmetry. The first is the public and legally sanctioned violence and threat by organs of the state. Semi-official terror is carried out by officials of the state, but not overtly, not formally sanctioned by the state. Private individuals from dominant groups carry out unofficial terror. The third proximal process is that of behavioural asymmetry. This asymmetry has two forms: ideological asymmetry and asymmetrical in-group bias (Sidanius, Levin, Federico, & Pratto, 2001). The hierarchy-enhancing mechanism of behavioural asymmetry suggests "that dominants will behave in a more group-interested fashion than subordinates due to the consensual endorsement of hierarchy-enhancing legitimizing ideologies. Moreover, under certain circumstances, not only will subordinates not behave in as group-interested a fashion as dominants, but they will actually work *against* their own group's interests" (Sidanius et al., 2001, p. 318). That is to say that subordinates are not only passive victims; they may also actively participate in their own oppression. This can be defined as a form of group treason; the rationale may be that by doing this the current structure is stabilized and not replaced by one that is possibly worse.

Legitimizing myths drive the three proximal processes. Social dominance theory focuses on the roles beliefs play in the maintenance of group-based social inequality. The myths are therefore not only hegemonic, but also counter-hegemonic beliefs. The two functional types of legitimizing myths are hierarchy enhancing and attenuating. The first kind of ideology (like racism or meritocracy) provides support for group-based inequality; the second (like anarchism or feminism) provides support for group-based equality. People will endorse one of the two ideologies, depending on their social dominance orientation (SDO); people with higher SDO endorse the enhancing ideology; people with lower SDO endorse the attenuating ideology. With regard to ideologies, SDT draws a conceptual and empirical distinction between consensual and dissensual legitimizing ideology (Sidanius, Levin, & Pratto, 1996). Consensual ideology can be defined as 'that portion of the ideological space which does not separate groups and where different groups agree' (Sidanius et al., 2001, p. 328). Dissensual ideology, by contrast, separates socially constructed groups. To operationalize social dominance, researchers often use social dominance orientation (SDO), which is a personality trait. To measure SDO, the fourteen-item social dominance orientation scale was developed.

What Is the Relevance of Social Dominance for Organization and Change?

Social dominance is about hierarchy between groups in both society and organizational settings. This hierarchy creates difference in the allocation of resources. Social dominance can be used to 'protect' the already established hierarchy or to create inequality and therefore increase the differences in resource allocation for high- and low-status social groups. In the context of organization and change, social dominance is relevant for subjects like organizational culture (and subcultures), cultural change, leadership, teams, cooperation, communication, commitment and resistance to change. The social dominance orientation helps to understand why people are in favour of or against change. Consensual and dissensual legitimizing ideologies contribute to the understanding of different, formal and informal, groups or teams involved in organizational change and their change appraisal or orientation. The perspective of social dominance can help to develop a more precise, nuanced or realistic view of the way people react to a sense of urgency or (change) vision communicated by the leaders of an organization. In *Guiding Change Journeys*,

Chan Allen (2002) describes the achievement of a change vision as a new emergence or discovery that is a necessary, essential part of the change journey. She notes that a key job in guiding change is to help a system clarify its change intention, including goals and purpose: "Change intention shapes the course and quality of a change journey. Intention is like the needle of a compass. It points you in the right direction no matter what the circumstances" (p. 67). Zaffron and Logan (2009) talk about the creation of a new game by declaring that something is important. By using future-based language, you invite others to commit to the game. Watkins (2013) pleads for an inspiring vision, built on a foundation of intrinsic motivators, making people part of the story and containing evocative language in order to inspire and motivate people. However, the appraisal of such a vision (like a sense of urgency) may be influenced by the position of the people and groups involved in the hierarchy. The social dominance orientation will probably influence how people appreciate the change that is embedded in or a consequence of the vision or sense of urgency communicated. Hesselbein and Johnston (2002) consider a compelling aspiration as a *conditio sine qua non* in change; without it you will not overcome the many sources of resistance. Lippitt (in: Holman and Devan) (1999) considers a vision even as a necessary part of the 'change equation': $C = D \times V \times F > R$, Change + Dissatisfaction × Vision × First step > Resistance. With the perspective of social dominance, the change equation can be better understood; not only because of the vision as a factor, but also given 'dissatisfaction' as a factor.

Search Strategy

Relevant databases were searched using the terms 'social dominance', and 'social dominance' in combination with 'meta-analysis' or 'systematic review'. The search yielded more than 300 articles. After screening the titles and abstracts for relevance, sixteen studies met the inclusion criteria. After thorough examination, another five studies were excluded. Four studies were randomized, controlled, before-after studies with a high evidence level (around A).

Main Findings

1. *People with higher SDO (regardless of their own background) react negatively to members of low-status groups (Level A-).*

   Organizations often place individuals from traditionally low-status groups in certain leadership roles or staffing committees to enhance diversity. However, results from a randomized, controlled, before-after study show that individuals with high SDO will react negatively to individuals in low-status groups, even if they belong to this group themselves. A more effective strategy for organizations to overcome this problem would be to ensure that individuals with lower levels of SDO are involved in staffing decisions (Umphress et al., 2008).

2. *High-SDO individuals care more about voice and procedural fairness than individuals with low SDO (Level A).*

Individuals who score high in terms of SDO "care most about procedural fairness in group settings because it may help them to control the social environment (e.g. by maintaining social inequality)" (De Cremer, Cornelis, & Van Hiel, 2008, p. 72). Paradoxically, procedural fairness can be used to maintain the current 'unfair' social status difference and therefore protect individuals that are in a high social group. When engaging in procedural fairness, transparency and communication are required. Using your 'voice' for this matter can serve to maintain the difference in social status.

3. *Engaging in service learning has a positive effect on empathy and a negative effect on SDO (Level A-).*

Students who engage in service learning scored higher for empathy and lower for SDO compared with students who did not engage in a helping experience. Service learning is an effective way to reduce SDO and increase empathy (Brown, 2011).

4. *Employees who are part of a low-status group can be denied a leadership position when SDO is high within the organization (Level A).*

It is important to note that our findings are unfortunate because the most qualified person may potentially be overlooked for reasons not related to job performance. An organization, therefore, could be damaged because the most qualified individual, who is likely to contribute at a higher level, is denied the position (Simmons & Umphress, 2015, p. 1221).

5. *Intergroup contact can reduce SDO levels and prejudice (Level C).*

Making use of intergroup contact can be beneficial for the organization as it lowers the levels of SDO and prejudice (Dhont, Van Hiel, & Hewstone, 2014).

6. *Men are more social dominance–oriented than women (Pratto, Sidanius, Stallworth, & Malle, 1994, Level D-).*

What Is the Conclusion?

Social dominance is a well-researched concept, including in the organizational context. The evidence shows that a social dominance orientation can be detrimental to organizations because it increases negative attitudes toward individuals in lower social groups, decreases empathy and can hinder the promotion of employees who perform outstandingly but that are part of lower social groups. This hindering of promotion can undermine the performance of organizations, because the best skilled/ suited employees are not in the 'right' hierarchical place. These findings are also relevant to organizational change practitioners. Having the right people in the right place can be the difference between change success or total failure. The evidence also contributes to the understanding of the reason why people, from different informal or formal groups, do or do not cooperate and develop resistance or commitment with regard to a change initiative. The perspective of social dominance also helps to understand differences in orientation of groups during change, for example with regard to important concepts like voice and fairness. Procedural fairness is seen as beneficial for organizational change, as it has a positive effect on multiple factors such as work performance, change commitment and the acceptance of organizational changes. However, procedural fairness can also be used by employees who score highly in terms of SDO for their own position or benefit. They can use their voice (opinion) to influence and even control the social environment, further increasing the social inequality and ultimately creating more unfairness.

Practical Reflections

For the practice of organization and change, several implications of the concept (and its evidence) can be used to prevent or limit social dominance within organizations. First, to compete optimally with competition, organizations should select the most qualified candidate for a certain position, even if this candidate is considered part of a low-status group. In addition, employers should select individuals with low levels of SDO and involve them in staffing decisions, no matter what their own demographic background is. Also, be aware that procedural fairness can be used to maintain or even increase social inequality as individuals with high SDO can use this fairness to express their own voice and therefore control the social environment. Letting all involved employees express their voice in an equal manner can be used to decrease social inequality. In addition, promote intergroup contact to reduce both SDO levels and prejudice among employees. Finally, make use of service learning to decrease SDO and increase empathy. This might only be relevant in a school setting, as (community) service learning focusses on this particular group. However, organizations can reap the rewards of service learning later on, when the students become employees with increased empathy and lower levels of SDO.

Theory of Planned Behaviour

A person's attitude toward behaviour, subjective norms and perceived behavioural control in combination shape that person's behavioural intentions and behaviours.

What Is the Theory of Planned Behaviour?

The central idea of the theory of planned behaviour (TPB) is that a person's attitude toward behaviour, subjective norms and perceived behavioural control in combination shape that person's behavioural intentions and behaviours (Ajzen, 1985). Ajzen proposed TPB in order to further develop and improve the predictive power of a former theory, that of the reasoned action (Ajzen, 2005). The theory of reasoned action (TRA) (Fishbein, 1967; Fishbein & Ajzen, 1975; Ajzen & Fishbein, 1980) focuses on a person's basic motivation to perform an action. The theory posits 'that behavioural intentions are a function of salient information or beliefs about the likelihood that performing a particular behaviour will lead to a specific outcome' (Madden, Scholder Ellen, & Ajzen, 1992, p. 3). In other words, if the suggested behaviour is evaluated positively (attitude) and the perception is that significant others want the person to perform it (subjective norm), then this results in a higher intention (motivation) and a higher probability that the behaviour will be performed. TPB is a very influential theory: "The theory of planned behaviour (TPB; Ajzen, 1991) is perhaps the most influential theory for the prediction of social and health behaviours" (Rivis, Sheeran, & Armitage, 2009, p. 2985). Alok, Raveendran, and Prasuna (2014) add: "Ajzen's (1991) well-established Theory of Planned Behaviour (TPB) is a very robust model which explicitly captures the motivational factors driving behaviour. It attempts to explain the relationship between attitudes and social influences on intentions and behaviour. Behavioural Intention (BI), in turn, is determined by an individual's attitude towards the behaviour, the Subjective Norms (SN) concerning the behaviour and Perceived Behavioural Control (PBC)" (p. 118).

Based on a meta-analysis (Sheppard, Hartwick, & Warshaw, 1988), we may conclude that the model of reasoned actions proves to 'predict behavioural intentions quite well and is useful for identifying where and how to target strategies for changing behaviour' (p. 3). TPB is an extension of the theory of reasoned action. The core remains the same: general attitudes, beliefs and preferences related to behaviour predict intentions; intentions predict behaviour (Barber, 2011). But TPB also incorporates perceived behavioural control as an antecedent to behavioural intentions. Perceived behavioural control is based on Bandura's concept of self-efficacy (1977) in which two types of expectations are central. Self-efficacy is the conviction that one can successfully execute the behaviour required to perform and can cope with the situation. Outcome expectancy refers to the estimation of the extent to which behaviour will lead to a certain outcome. Bandura considers self-efficacy to be the most important precondition for behavioural change. The importance and contribution of self-efficacy or perceived behavioural control (Fishbein & Cappella, 2006) is illustrated by research in which TRA and TPB were compared. TPB proves to be superior for the prediction of target behaviour and explained more variation in behavioural interventions (Madden et al., 1992). This supports the inclusion and underlines the relevance of perceived behavioural control.

What Is the Relevance of the Theory of Planned Behaviour for Organization and Change?

The theory of planned behaviour states that attitude, subjective norms and perceived behavioural control influence the intentions of a person's behaviour. The intentions are the motivational factors that predict performance and influence the performance of the behaviour. Some scholars criticize the theory, because it is based on cognitive processing and does not include an emotional component. Clearly, many behaviours are influenced by emotions. These can influence the beliefs and other constructs of planned behaviour. The theory with the important concept of perceived behavioural control is relevant to change-related subjects such as change capacity, change vision, performance management, communication, resistance, commitment and cooperation. Perceived behavioural control is key to change capacity, for example. For this reason, we again refer to the statement of Connor (2006): "People can only change when they have the capacity to do so. Ability means having the necessary skills and knowing how to use them. Willingness is the motivation to apply those skills to a particular situation. If you lack either ability or willingness, it is unlikely that you will successfully adapt to a change" (p. 129).

Search Strategy

Relevant databases were searched using the terms 'planned behaviour' and 'theory' in combination with 'meta-analysis' or 'systematic review'. The search yielded more than 450 articles. After screening the titles and abstracts for relevance, eleven studies were included. After thorough examination, another three studies were excluded. Of the total of eight studies included, two used a meta-analytical approach.

Main Findings

1. *Increasing moral norms/anticipated regret can influence behaviour (Level B-).*

    "Increasing the salience of moral norms/anticipated regret may be particularly useful in strengthening intentions to engage in health-promoting behaviours (e.g. Abraham & Sheeran, 2004, Study 2) and weakening intentions to engage in health-risk behaviours. For example, asking people to focus on their feelings after engaging in a risky behaviour should reduce people's intentions to engage in the behaviour and, subsequently, should reduce risk-taking behaviour" (Rivis et al., 2009, p. 3009).

2. *Self-identity is an important predictor of intentions and behaviour and should be incorporated in the theory of planned behaviour (Level C).*

"Multiple regression analyses showed that self-identity explained an increment of 6% of the variance in intention after controlling for the TPB components, and explained an increment of 9% of the variance when past behaviour and the TPB components were controlled. The influence of self-identity on behaviour was largely mediated by the strength of behavioural intentions" (Rise, Sheeran, & Hukkelberg, 2010, p. 1085). Self-identity relates to aspects of one's self-perception (e.g. I see myself as a 'social person').

3. *Attitude and subjective norm (as part of the theory of planned behaviour) are predictors of behavioural intention (Level D-).*

Attitude was found to be the strongest predictor of intention and the theory of planned behaviour was most effective for smaller and easier-to-implement decisions than bigger and harder-to-implement decisions (Arnold et al., 2006).

4. *In a relationship conflict setting, the theory of planned behaviour can be used to understand intention and predict behaviour accurately before it occurs (Level D-).*

"The findings support TPB as a model for understanding the type of style adopted in case of a relationship conflict. Understanding intention means that behaviour can, in effect, be accurately predicted before it occurs, thus offering organizations a timeframe for intervention" (Alok, Raveendran, & Prasuna, 2014, p. 129).

5. *During organizational relocation, attitude, subjective norm and perceived behavioural control all predicted intentions to support the change (Level E).*

"The TPB also contributed to our understanding of the relationship between two specific change management strategies (communication and participation) and intentions to behaviourally support change" (Jimmieson, Peach, & White, 2008, p. 28).

6. *Theory of planned behaviour was found to be a better predictor of unethical behaviour than the theory of reasoned action (Level E).*

Results from a low-level, cross-sectional study show that the theory of planned behaviour can be used successfully to predict the intention to perform unethical behaviour and that TPB is a better predictor of unethical behaviour than the theory of reasoned action (Chang, 1998).

What Is the Conclusion?

The theory of planned behaviour proves to be important for predicting behavioural intentions. By predicting intentions, TPB influences behaviour. Evidence illustrates that this may also be the case in an organizational change setting (relocation). The possible implications of the perspective of TPB for change management practitioners can be illustrated as follows: "TPB is a useful framework for pre-implementation assessments of readiness for change as it can provide organizations with an early indication of employee beliefs and determinants of their intentions prior to the change event" (Jimmieson et al., 2008, p. 28). Including self-identity in the TPB model seems to make TPB even more effective in predicting intentions and behaviour.

Practical Reflections

The evidence shows that the theory of planned behaviour (TPB) probably contributes to a better understanding and execution of change. An important question is how to effectively use TPB to optimally benefit from it. Some initial answers can be given based on the evidence. With regard to communication, an initial practical guideline focuses on consistency and alignment: "Norms will be more effective when there is consistency between the message of descriptive and injunctive norms. When we are trying to change behaviour or promote new behaviour, these messages need to be aligned. A normative message from managers and peers enhances the effectiveness of the message. The important referent should be the role model for the behavioural change. Moreover, if group members observe a referent performing obliging style, they are likely to view such behaviour as typical and appropriate and in turn exhibit such behaviours" (Alok et al., 2014, pp. 129–130). In addition to communication, training can also contribute: "Longitudinal research has shown that training can increase people's confidence to accept a more proactive and interpersonal role within the workplace (Axtell & Parker, 2003). Regular meetings at which employees are coached to handle situations they find 'difficult' can prove to be effective. The change agent can design self-statements to examine the specific ways in which he/she talks to them before, during and after confrontations. These self-statements will be helpful to trainees in effectively assessing the results of their own behaviour, in anger management, in reflective thinking, in active listening and in handling conflict in different situations. Organizations should also consider these skills to be an important criterion for selection" (Alok et al., 2014, p. 130).

Minority Influence Theory

A strongly held and consistently expressed minority view can have extensive influence on the majority, as most majority members just follow the rest and lack strongly held views.

What Is Minority Influence?

Minority influence is a form of social influence where a minority position in a group has a certain amount of influence on the majority to accept the minority's beliefs and/or behaviour. To have disproportionate influence as a minority, a strongly held view is required. As most people in the majority do not hold strong views, they are vulnerable to influence from strongly held minority views. This may sound negative, but minority influence can be beneficial for groups, as it fosters divergent thinking and reduces conformity pressures (Ng & Van Dyne, 2001). Most of the research conducted into minority influence focuses on how the majority influenced the minority, because the general idea was that the minority had little influence on the majority. In the 1960s, Serge Moscovici had a different vision. The Romanian psychologist believed it was possible for a minority to influence the majority. In 1969, he investigated behavioural styles in minority influence in his studies. He found that a consistent minority was more successful in changing the views of the majority than an inconsistent minority (McLeod, 2007).

What Is the Relevance of Minority Influence for Organization and Change?

The perspective of minority influence shows that a strongly held and consistently expressed minority view can have extensive influence on the majority, because most majority members just follow the rest and lack strongly held views. In the context of organization and change, minority influence is relevant to subjects like change vision and change capacity, (overcoming) resistance and (building) commitment, communication, cooperation and performance management. Minority influence can be important for groups, because it is positively linked to effectiveness and performance. For example, looking at alternatives minorities propose in a group can be beneficial for the quality of the final decision made. Minority influence can also be linked to Kotter's concept of the guiding coalition (or 'Gideon gang'). The guiding coalition can be seen as a minority with a strongly held view or belief that is the 'avant-garde' in a change process. By being passionate and consistent in their vision or view, they kick-start the change and influence the majority. Starting with the minority instead of focusing (immediately) on the majority can also be seen as an alternative change strategy. Hesselbein (2002) states that change starts with the passionate few. He introduces a more 'organic', strong, meritocratic variant of the guiding coalition: "Leaders (and teachers) spend too much time trying to remediate weaknesses and too little building on strengths. Remember Georg Solti, conductor of the Chicago Symphony, who found twenty musicians who had passion to do something new: rather than trying to push the entire organization forward, he focused on the top performers. It's an atypical strategy, but it's the most effective one" (p. 27).

Search Strategy

Relevant databases were searched using the terms 'minority' and 'influence' in combination with 'organization', 'employee', 'change', 'work', 'meta-analysis' and 'systematic review'. The search yielded close to 250 articles. After screening the titles and abstracts for relevance, one meta-analysis and five studies met the inclusion criteria. After thorough examination, two more studies were excluded.

Main Findings

1. *Individuals who avoid conflict and strive for harmony within the group are less likely to benefit from minority influence (Level A).*

    Individuals who prefer harmony, therefore avoiding conflict, will increase the chance of ignoring possible better alternatives in group decision-making (Ng & Van Dyne, 2001).

2. *Individuals exposed to a minority influence agent who held a leadership position in the group were more likely to improve the quality of their decisions (Level A).*

    Furthermore, the "results suggest that being in a leadership role might provide minority influence agents with a sense of legitimacy so that they feel more empowered and less uncomfortable voicing a different opinion" (Ng & Van Dyne, 2001, p. 220).

3. *Minority influence on the public is higher when minorities do not expect future interaction with the same group members and majorities do (Level A).*

    "Minorities were more likely to express dissent when they expected future interaction with different group members, whereas majorities were more open toward divergent information when they expected future interaction with the same members" (San Martin, Swaab, Sinaceur, & Vasiljevic, 2015, p. 10). This led to an increase in systematic information processing by the group, increasing group effectiveness. Another study (Level D-) shows that "remote and argument-consistent minority opinion holders caused more majority change and improvement in majority and group correctness compared to a collocated argument-consistent minority" (Bazarova, Walther, & McLeod, 2012, p. 310).

4. *Minorities judged by targets to be especially consistent wielded greater influence than less consistent-appearing sources (Level B-).*

    Being consistent seems important for group members that form a minority, as it increases their influence on the majority (Wood, Lundgren, Ouellette, Busceme, & Blackstone, 1994).

What Is the Conclusion?

The evidence on minority influence provides relevant and helpful insights to groups, individual members and their leaders. They can help to develop better decision-making, and better team or organizational development and have the potential to contribute to more effective change. Minority influence is very important for the effectiveness and quality of (group) decision-making: "Making sure that minority arguments get heard in group discussions can be critical for the quality of decision-making" (San Martin et al., 2015, p. 11). Looking properly at ideas and alternatives that minorities suggest can positively affect the quality of decision-making and ultimately decisions. To improve minority influence, minorities need to be consistent in their communication, as it increases their influence on the majority. Furthermore, minorities in leadership positions are more likely to improve the quality of group decisions. A possible threat for minority influence is a group that strives for harmony and avoids conflict. This is in line with a social psychological phenomenon called 'groupthink', which can be potentially harmful for organizations.

Practical Reflections

Decisions and their quality, decision-making and the decision-making process, and the involvement of different relevant groups and the dynamics within and between these groups are essential for change initiatives and change processes. Poor or suboptimal decision-making can have severe and even damaging effects on organizations and groups and individuals within these organizations. Minority influence proves to have the potential to positively impact the quality and effectiveness of the decisions and the underlying decision-making processes. The concept and its perspective are therefore very relevant and potentially helpful in designing and managing change. To illustrate in a practical way how the concept can be translated for the practice of organizations and change, some guidelines can be formulated. Begin by reinforcing group and organizational norms to encourage consideration of (minority) ideas and alternatives. Then give change agents legitimacy and authority to enhance their confidence in expressing divergent options. In addition, adopt computer-mediated group decision-making systems to reduce conformity pressure associated with face-to-face interaction. Another helpful guideline: assign a person in the group to be the devil's advocate. This stimulates constructive conflict, improving group decision-making. "Giving authority to or appointing high-status individuals as change agents also sends strong cues to others that the organization encourages and rewards speaking up" (Ng & Van Dyne, 2001, p. 221). This also counteracts the threat of groupthink.

Motivation Crowding Theory

External motivators may undermine the intrinsic motivation of individuals.

What Is Motivation Crowding Theory?

The motivation crowding theory states that external motivators (like monetary incentives or punishments) may undermine the intrinsic motivation of individuals. The underlying mechanism is simple: when extrinsic motivators such as monetary incentives are given, this can undermine intrinsic motivation because of a 'crowd out' effect. An individual is intrinsically motivated to perform a certain activity when the person receives no apparent reward from the activity other than the activity itself. When adding extrinsic motivators, this intrinsic motivation is undermined, because there is an additional reward besides the activity itself. The motivational crowding theory emanates from two different scientific perspectives and is used in both (labour) economics and (social) psychology (see: Frey & Jegen, 1999). One of the first to write about this theory was Richard Titmuss in 1970 in his book *The Gift Relationship: From Human Blood to Social Policy* (1970). Titmuss wrote that financially compensating blood donors has a negative effect on the willingness of people to donate blood. The second perspective is that of psychology, in particular that of cognitive social psychology (see: Deci & Ryan, 1985; Deci, Koestner, & Ryan, 1999a, 1999b; Pittman & Heller, 1987; Lane, 1991). In this area, it first appeared in 1971 when it was introduced by Deci in an article about 'the effects of externally mediated rewards on intrinsic motivation'. Psychologists "have identified that under particular conditions monetary (external) rewards undermine intrinsic motivation. The application of rewards for undertaking an activity thus has indirect negative consequences, provided intrinsic motivation is considered to be beneficial" (Frey & Jegen, 1999, p. 2). Frey and Jegen (1999) mention several terms that have been used to describe this effect: 'the hidden cost of reward', 'overjustification hypothesis' and 'corruption effect'. The idea is also coined as 'Cognitive Evaluation Theory' (Deci, Koestner, & Ryan, 1999a). Frey and Jegen call Timuss's idea a 'mere hunch' and point to the many experiments that support the described motivational effect: "the evidence for a detrimental effect comes from a wide variety of works in which a large number of subjects and methodological parameters have been varied" (McGraw, 1978, pp. 55–58). In 2001 Deci, Koestner and Ryan stated that the finding that extrinsic rewards can undermine intrinsic motivation has been highly controversial since it first appeared in 1971. To illustrate, in 1988 Rummel and Feinberg employed a meta-analysis focused on the question of whether the supposed detrimental effects of extrinsic rewards on intrinsic motivation exist. The analysis showed that the phenomenon defined by Deci exists within strictly defined parameters. But in 1994 Cameron and Pierce, for example, published a meta-analysis and concluded that the undermining effect was minimal and largely inconsequential for educational policy. Based on this meta-analysis, Cameron and Pierce advocated abandoning the cognitive evaluation theory of Deci and Ryan (1980). However, in 1999 a meta-analysis was published by Deci, Koestner and Ryan that not only showed that the 1994 meta-analysis was seriously flawed from a methodological perspective and that its conclusions were incorrect, but also provided strong support for cognitive evaluation theory (Deci & Porac, 1978; Deci & Ryan, 1980; Ryan, 1982).

What Is the Relevance of Motivation Crowding for Organization and Change?

The motivation crowding theory is relevant and helpful with regard to the context of organization and change, in particular behavioural change. It can be related to change-related topics such as leadership, culture and cultural change, change capacity, commitment, cooperation and compliance, and, last but not least, performance management. Focusing on cultural change, change capacity and performance management, one of the central questions is which behaviour has to be or can be stimulated or reinforced in what way. An answer calls for choices with regard to the stimuli, interventions, 'reward and appraisal'. The concept of motivation crowding helps to understand what kind of interventions and rewards facilitate or possibly frustrate change and performance, as well as a factor such as job satisfaction. With regard to cooperation, commitment and compliance, Frey and Jegen (1999) provide research and insights into government rules and civic virtues (e.g. Schultz & Weingast, 1994). From the perspective of organizational citizenship behaviour (OCB, see: 5.5) and change, one could see an analogy that can be helpful in the context of organization and change. Frey and Jegen (1999) point to a body of research indicating that "people's perceptions of how they are treated by the authorities strongly affect their evaluation of authorities and laws, and their willingness to cooperate with them. . . . Citizens who consider the constitution and its laws, and the authorities acting on the basis of them, to be fair and treating them respectfully tend to be more compliant than those with more negative perceptions of government" (p. 18).

These insights relate (at least in an analogical way) to essential topics in the area of change and organization such as trust (or confidence) in leaders, participation and fair process. Kriegel (1996), for example, emphasizes that resistance to change increases as trust in an organization's leader decreases. Trustworthiness and believability are seen as the foundations of leadership. Watkins (2013) emphasizes the importance of credibility and trust in demanding situations: "As people come to trust your judgment, your ability to learn accelerates, and you equip yourself to make sound calls on tougher issues" (p. 8). Kouzes and Posner (2012) state that exemplary leaders create a climate of trust. Without trust you cannot accomplish extraordinary things. They state: "Trust is a strong, significant predictor of employee satisfaction, the quality of communication, honest sharing of information, acceptance of change, acceptance of the leader's influence, and team and organizational performance" (pp. 219–220). Maurer (2010) states: "Trust can make or break a change. But sadly, many who lead change seem to ignore this critically important ingredient. They seem to believe that a good idea will win the day. It won't" (p. 14). With regard to participation, an important element of the way people are treated (whether it is by 'government', leaders or change agents), Watkins (2013) points to the use of consultation to gain commitment: "Be clear on which elements of your vision are non-negotiable, but beyond these, be flexible enough to consider the ideas of others and allow them to have input and to influence the shared vision. In that way, they share ownership" (p. 187). Kriegel (1996) advocates a fair change process: "The way you introduce change makes a world of difference in how people feel about it" (pp. 218–219). He explains that if major changes are implemented, employees will be less resistant when they understand the decision in context and feel that they are being treated honestly. However, in practice a fair process is often lacking and employees experience major changes as if a bombshell has been dropped. According to Kriegel: "Many companies simply announce a downsizing scheme like it was a new health plan or accounting procedure. No input. No Q&A. No dialogue. It's not just the bad news, but the form of delivery that bends employees out of shape. No wonder people feel victimized and disrespected. The rumour mills start racing and the resistance starts rising" (p. 219). He emphasizes the importance of providing a structure for employees to express their natural disappointment and sense of loss. This is not the same as involving people in the creation of change, but helps them move to acceptance. In addition, a reputed author and consultant states on his website: "How you lead the change—not what you are changing—is the key to raising the success rate of change projects to 8 out of 10 . . . rather than 3 out of 10 that 30 years of research indicates is the average success rate". Bo Vestergaard explains both the concept and its effects in a very clear way: "What is Fair Process? Simply put, fair process is honest communication about 1) What is already decided, 2) What your employees can influence (or decide for themselves) and 3) By what criteria their input to your decisions will be judged. Effects of fair process: The most common effect of fair process is building employees' trust in you as a manager and a rise in employee engagement and inner motivation to develop solutions and implement decisions. The tangible results are quicker and better implementation".

Search Strategy

Relevant databases were searched using the terms 'motivational crowding', 'crowding' and 'effect', also in combination with 'meta-analysis' or 'systematic review'. The search yielded close to 250 articles. After screening the titles and abstracts for relevance, one meta-analysis and 10 studies met the inclusion criteria. After thorough examination, five studies were excluded. Using the snowball technique, we found another relevant meta-analysis. In total, we included two meta-analyses and five studies.

Main Findings

1. *Psychological needs play a central role in performance contexts (Level B-).*

   "Addressing psychological need satisfaction, as we show here, can have performance benefits to organizations for employees, students and even athletes. But beyond this, there are many indirect benefits as well. Organizations seeking to be better corporate citizens can boost engagement, intrinsic motivation and psychological well-being by instituting policies and programmes that help employees meet their need for autonomy, competence and relatedness. In turn, an extensive body of work has shown that improved engagement (Christian, Garza, & Slaughter, 2011), intrinsic motivation (Cerasoli et al., 2014) and psychological well-being (Ford et al., 2011) are associated with higher performance" (Cerasoli, Nicklin, & Nassrelgrgawi, 2016, p. 805). In another study with a low level of evidence (E), it was found that intrinsic motivation plays an important role in improving employees' work engagement and that intrinsic motivation did not diminish when extrinsic motivation entered (Putra, Cho, & Liu, 2017).

2. *Intrinsic motivation has a positive effect on quality of performance; extrinsic motivation has a positive effect on quantity of performance (Level B).*

   This meta-analysis found that both intrinsic and extrinsic motivation have a positive effect, but on a different factor. Intrinsic motivation is better for the quality of the performance and extrinsic for the quantity of performance (Cerasoli et al., 2016). However, in a 2017 study with a low level of evidence (E), this distinction is disconfirmed, as only intrinsic motivation has a positive effect on employees' vigour, dedication and absorption when both extrinsic and intrinsic motivation are measured together (Putra et al., 2017).

3. *'Hard' enforcement actions have a detrimental effect on intrinsic motivation, whereas 'soft' enforcement actions do not (Level D-).*

   'Hard' enforcement actions (based on the use of directives, monitoring and threats of punishment) have a negative effect on the intrinsic motivation of employees, whereas 'soft enforcement actions' (based on dialogue and suggestions) do not. A combination of both forms is also detrimental for intrinsic motivation (Mikkelsen, Jacobsen, & Andersen, 2017).

4. *Monetary incentives may have a positive effect on job satisfaction, as long as they are large enough (Level D).*

    Extrinsic incentives like a bonus can have a positive effect on job satisfaction. However, if an employee gets a small bonus, this can lead to negative effects on job satisfaction. Managers should therefore pay enough, or not pay at all (Pouliakas, 2010).

What Is the Conclusion?

The evidence is very clear: there is little doubt about the positive effects of intrinsic motivation on both job satisfaction and (organizational) performance. Creating and maintaining intrinsic motivation of employees is very important. Given the positive effects on the people involved, their organizations and their performance, it should be central in the way people and organizations are motivated, managed and led. However, the often mentioned negative effect of extrinsic motivators needs to be nuanced. Extrinsic motivators like money can be helpful and effective in changing and managing organizational behaviour, if *properly* used. For example, evidence shows that the *quantity* of performance can be improved by monetary incentives. Intrinsic motivation, on the other hand, is important in positively influencing the quality of work. Furthermore, there is some evidence that indicates that extrinsic motivation does not undermine intrinsic motivation, if intrinsic motivation already exists. The evidence also shows that when using monetary incentives they have to be large or significant enough, as small incentives can have a negative effect on job satisfaction.

Our earlier research (REAs) (ten Have et al., 2017) focused on the question of whether financial incentives are an effective way to encourage change and improve performance. A first and important finding (based on a Level-A evidence) was that there is strong evidence that, overall, financial incentives have a moderate positive effect on performance (e.g. Cerasoli et al., 2014; Weibel et al., 2009). This positive effect is often referred to as the *price effect*: the financial incentive increases the intention to perform well because of the monetary benefit. However, this effect differs among forms of incentives, types of motivation and performance outcomes.[4] The specific findings with regard to the motivation crowding theory in the organizational context contribute to the insights into when and how the effect differs. The (final) conclusion of the earlier research (ten Have et al., 2017) already indicated this: "The scientific research literature strongly supports the claim that financial incentives are an effective way to encourage behavioural change and improve performance.

However, the opposition of the price effect and crowding-out effect, which can occur under certain circumstances, requires a thoughtful approach as outcomes can vary widely when financial incentives are used" (p. 165).

Practical Reflections

For the practice of organization and change the scientific research and insights are helpful, if not necessary. This applies to the specific research on the motivation crowding theory and financial incentives as an instrument in general. Several management gurus write about and emphasize the importance of financial incentives and the related principles and underlying mechanisms. The scientific research and insights help to assess and nuance the more popular statements and help to operationalize the necessary differentiation. To illustrate the more popular perspectives, with regard to financial incentives and reward as a way to reinforce commitment to change, Heller (1998) advises very clearly: "Be willing to pay generously for achievement. People may change their behaviour radically for significant pay rewards" (p. 51). He explains: "People want to feel that their reward will match their efforts; if it does, this will reinforce their commitment to the new ways" (p. 51). Kriegel and Brandt (1996) are also very straightforward: "The most obvious way to motivate employees to get excited about your plans is through rewards" (p. 260). But he is also more specific: "There are two kinds of rewards: extrinsic incentives, like the corner office, money, gifts and titles, and intrinsic rewards, which appeal to more abstract personal needs. People do things not just to get an object or the cash to buy it. They're also motivated by such intangibles as recognition, fairness, flexibility, creativity, meaningfulness and freedom. These internal factors have more impact on readiness for change than traditional extrinsic rewards do" (p. 261). Connor (2006) states: "A lack of willingness stems from a shortage of motivation and should be addressed through consequence management (the combination of rewards and punishments)" (p. 129). An international consultant states: "Employees are going to inevitably repeat behaviours for which they are rewarded. For example, if an employee is rewarded for his or her productivity, he or she is going to focus on productive behaviours and, as a result, this will help to drive productivity". Watkins (2013) talks about 'aligning incentives' and a 'baseline question': "how best to incentivize team members to achieve desired goals. What mix of monetary and non-monetary rewards will you employ?" (p. 183). In addition, for practice it is important to emphasize that extrinsic motivation factors, when used properly, do not necessarily lead to a crowding-out effect. It is important to make sure that the incentives are large and significant enough. If aimed at improving the quantity of work, they can be very effective. Managers and other practitioners have to be aware of the important and essential role of intrinsic motivation in organizations and for people.

This is particularly important when one considers extrinsic motivation as an instrument or intervention in order to improve performance or implement change. One has to be very sensitive to the possible detrimental effects of extrinsic motivational factors on intrinsic motivation. It is noted again that in particular the use of 'hard' enforcement actions (e.g. monitoring and threats of punishment) likely have a negative effect on intrinsic motivation. For that reason, one should prefer 'soft' enforcement actions like dialogues, coaching and consultation.

Notes

1. Haemmerlie and Montgomery, 1984, Abstract, http://psycnet.apa.org/record/1985-12587-001
2. http://psychology.iresearchnet.com/social-psychology/social-psychology-theories/self-perception-theory/
3. www.businessdictionary.com/definition/leadership.html
4. Adapted from: Ten Have et al., 2017, p. 163

6 Trusting, Organizational Behaviour and Change

A First Short Story of Trusting and Change

> Trust is an individual's willingness to be vulnerable to others. Trustworthiness reduces employee uncertainty related to change. Formed relationships and enduring bonds with others have implications for both the physical and psychological well-being of the individual. Procedural justice reflects the perceived fairness of decision-making processes and the degree to which they are consistent, accurate, unbiased and open to voice and input. People feel most comfortable when they are getting exactly what they deserve from their relationships—no more and certainly no less. Antisocial or inhumane conduct can put pressure on trust and trustworthiness. Moral disengagement is about mechanisms that prevent us feeling bad when doing bad things. Group trust and strong emotion can also be (or become) counterproductive. Groupthink occurs when a group of people make faulty decisions because of the desire to maintain harmony and conformity in the group.

Trusting is core social motive number four. It is one of the two (relatively) affective motives (the other is self-enhancing). Trusting is the need to view others as basically benign, seeing the world as a benevolent place (Fiske, 2004). Trust involves "confidence or faith that some other, upon whom we must depend, will not act in ways that occasion us painful consequences" (Boon, 1995, p. 656). People have a predisposition to trust others. This can make them vulnerable, but also facilitates interactions with others. People differ and some of them are relatively paranoid instead of trusting, although most people are biased toward seeing the best in other people and do expect fairly good outcomes from the interaction with other people (Fiske, 2004). Trust facilitates group cohesion and provides a relatively efficient mechanism for group functioning. Trust is 'materialized' in attachments: enduring emotional bonds between people in family, group and organizational settings that reduce stress and provide security, safety and comfort. Attachment is positively related to trustworthiness. Trust is protected by and developed through the phenomenon of fair process. People typically trust others to behave in a prosocial way, but are sensitive to antisocial behaviour and inequity. People have their strategies to deal with own behaviour that puts trust (in the social context and in themselves) at stake, for example by the cognitive restructuring of inhumane conduct into benign or worthy conduct by moral justification. Trusting is related to change and management topics such as compliance, cooperation, structure and systems, and resistance to change.

In this chapter the following theories and concepts are presented and assessed:

Trust
Attachment theory
Fair process: Justice theory and procedural justice
Equity theory
Moral disengagement
Groupthink

Trust[1]

Trust is an individual's willingness to be vulnerable to others. Trustworthiness reduces employee uncertainty related to change.

What Is Trust?

Trust can be described as an individual's willingness to be vulnerable to others (Lewis & Weigert, 1985). Mayer, Davis, and Schoorman (1995) define trust as "the willingness of a party to be vulnerable to the actions of another party . . . irrespective of the ability to monitor or control that other party" (p. 712). There are numerous other definitions of trust that sometimes overlap or even imply very different things. For example, Colquitt, Scott, and LePine (2007), in their review of the trust literature, note that trust is sometimes viewed by scholars as a behavioural intention, a cognitive action, a personality trait or a synonym for a variety of concepts such as trustworthiness, cooperation or risk taking. Mayer et al. (1995) define trust as "the willingness of a trustor to be vulnerable to the actions of a trustee, based on the expectation that the trustee will perform a particular action" (Colquitt et al., 2007, p. 909). Colquitt et al. point out that trust therefore has two primary components: the acceptance of vulnerability and positive expectations. Conceptually, trust is distinguished from the supposed antecedents of trust, namely trustworthiness and trust propensity. Trustworthiness focuses on certain characteristics of the trustee, as perceived by the trustor. Mayer et al. (1995) identify ability, benevolence and integrity as characteristics with a unique impact on trust. Ability is the assumed knowledge and skills of the trustee to perform expected behaviour. Benevolence is the assumed intention of the trustee to do good toward the trustor. And integrity is the extent to which the trustee is believed to be fair and to adhere to moral and ethical principles. Ability and integrity are considered to be cognition-based sources of trust, implying rational decision-making, and benevolence is considered to be more an affect-based source of trust, implying care and supportiveness. Trust propensity focuses on the trustor. It is considered to be a stable characteristic or personality trait that also influences how someone interprets the environment and makes sense of events and what triggers are paid attention to. In other words, people who score higher on trust propensity are more readily inclined to trust and interpret cues about someone's trustworthiness more positively. What is implied by trust, Colquitt et al. (2007) point out, has consequences for how the construct is operationalized and measured. Some questionnaires focus more on the vulnerability component, whereas others refer to the positive expectation component. They also distinguish direct measures that simply ask respondents to rate the extent to which they trust someone (e.g. their CEO, supervisor or co-worker, organization or board) (ten Have, ten Have, Huijsmans, & Otto, 2016). Several researchers have come up with models (and have empirically tested them) for the underlying mechanisms by which trust influences organizational outcomes. In line with the proposed definition and the corresponding antecedents of trust, the mechanism in place can be depicted graphically (see Figure 6.1). Trust can have different referents, such as leadership or co-workers. Organizational outcome can also refer to a wide variety of variables, such as job

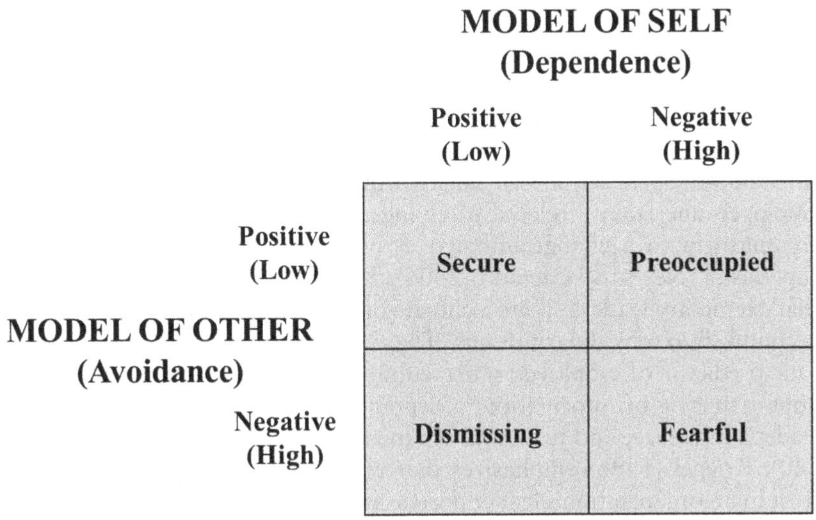

Figure 6.1 Attachment Styles
(Adapted from: Bartholomew, 1990)

satisfaction, task performance, organizational citizenship behaviour and so on. This model is very basic, and there are many ways in which trust and its effects can be conceptualized. However, the model captures most of these ways in an integrative manner.

What Is the Relevance of Trust for Organization and Change?

What is implied by trust, Colquitt et al. (2007) point out, has consequences for how the construct is operationalized and measured. Some questionnaires focus more on the vulnerability component, whereas others refer to the positive expectation component. They also distinguish direct measures that simply ask respondents to rate the extent to which they trust someone (e.g. their CEO, supervisor or co-worker, organization or board) (ten Have et al., 2016). Several researchers have come up with models (and have empirically tested them) for the underlying mechanisms by which trust influences organizational outcomes. In line with the proposed definition and the corresponding antecedents of trust, the mechanism in place can be depicted graphically (Figure 6.1).

Trust can have different referents, such as leadership or co-workers. Organizational outcome can also refer to a wide variety of variables, such as job satisfaction, task performance, organizational citizenship behaviour and so on. This model is very basic, and there are many ways in which trust and its effects can be conceptualized. However, the model captures most of these ways in an integrative manner. In the area of organization and change, trust relates to subjects like leadership, cooperation, culture, commitment, communication, resistance and change capacity. In the context of organization and change, trust in leadership or management represents the belief that managers will act in their people's best interests (Fugate, 2013). Trust in management has four dimensions: (1) concern for employees' interests; (2) management's strategic competence, (3) management reliability and (4) openness and honesty (Mishra and Spreitzer, 1998). Trustworthiness in each dimension reduces employee uncertainty related to change. Research shows that affective commitment to a change initiative is positively related to trust in the supervisor (Neves & Caetano, 2006). Kouzes and Posner (2012) state that exemplary leaders create a climate of trust. Without trust you cannot accomplish extraordinary things. They state: "Trust is a strong, significant predictor of employee satisfaction, the quality of communication, honest sharing of information, acceptance of change, acceptance of the leader's influence, and team and organizational performance" (pp. 219–220). Kriegel (1996) emphasizes that resistance to change increases as trust in an organization's leader decreases. Trust also relates to communication and change. Jimmieson, Rafferty, and Allen (2013) explain that in change processes communication can be seen as a form of treatment that promotes (procedural) justice, which has been shown to have implications for trust (e.g. Brockner, 1996; Konovsky & Pugh, 1994). With regard to organizational culture, Caldwell (2013) states that "strong cultures may also include employee cynicism about change (Wanous, Reichers, & Austin, 2000), which results in employees' low trust in the motives and competency of management to successfully construct and implement change" (p. 267). The earlier-mentioned relationship between change, fairness and trust is also visible in the work of Armenakis and Harris (2009). They point to change readiness strategies that include a justice climate to enhance voice and perceived control and reduce uncertainty. It is probable that as a result the strategies build trust and reduce resistance to change and increase commitment.

Search Strategy

The specific focus is on finding scientific evidence for the effect of trust in leadership during organizational change. In addition, the focus is on other organizational outcomes that might be directly or indirectly related to the success of an organizational change initiative. Examples are organizational citizenship behaviour or performance. Relevant databases were searched by combining the key word 'trust'—and possible related key words such as 'confidence' and 'faith'—with key words related to leadership, such as 'supervisor', 'CEO', 'board', 'management' and 'leader' (ten Have et al., 2016). The initial search yielded a total of 122 studies. After screening the abstracts for relevance, 112 studies were excluded. Full-text screening of the articles resulted in the exclusion of another three studies. Finally, after critical appraisal of the remaining seven articles, a total of four meta-analyses—representing results from more than 428 single studies—were included. All four meta-analyses, which have a level of evidence of B, were published between 2007 and 2013. Especially insightful and relevant to our assumption was the thorough meta-analysis by Colquitt et al. (2007), which builds on, refines and complements Dirks and Ferrin's (2002) earlier work on the effects of trust in leadership and the model of organizational trust of Mayer et al. (1995).

Main Findings

1. *Dispositional trust (trust propensity) and positive expectations have a positive effect on cooperation (Level B).*

   "Overall, dispositional trust (trust propensity, see Figure 6.1) had a small effect on cooperation. However, positive expectations of the trustee's behaviour toward the trustor had a strong effect on cooperation. It is also found that trust has a stronger relationship with cooperation during situations with stronger conflicts of interests. In other words, when the stakes are higher, trust matters more" (Balliet & Van Lange, 2013); (ten Have et al., 2016, p. 85).

2. *Trust has medium positive (and beneficial) effects on process and outcome-related variables of negotiations (Level B).*

"Trust has medium positive effects on integrative behaviours (enlarging the pie or creating a win-win situation), the trustor's outcome, the joint outcome and outcome satisfaction during and following negotiations" (Kong, Dirks, & Ferrin, 2014); (ten Have et al., 2016, p. 86).

3. *Trust in leadership as well as organizational trust in general have small to medium beneficial effects on a wide variety of organizational outcomes (Level B).*

"These two findings are based on meta-analyses that focus on studies on the role of trust in the resolution of conflicts and negotiations, respectively. More relevant to our assumption are the results found by Dirks and Ferrin (2002), who specifically focus on the effect of trust in leadership on a wide variety of outcome variables such as job satisfaction, organizational commitment, intent to quit, belief in information, decision commitment, organizational citizenship behaviour and job performance. The effects were small to medium, and they were all in a beneficial direction. Colquitt et al. (2007) found that trust, with both leadership and co-workers as referents, was moderately related to organizational outcomes such as risk-taking, task performance, organizational citizenship behaviour and counterproductive behaviour. Again, all effects were in a beneficial direction, implying that counterproductive behaviour was negatively related and organizational citizenship behaviour positively related to trust" (ten Have et al., 2016, p. 86).

4. *Several variables with small to medium effects on trust (so-called antecedents of trust) have been identified (Level B).*

"Transformational leadership, transactional leadership, interactional justice, procedural justice, distributive justice, participative decision making and perceived organizational support all have small to medium positive effects on trust. Unfulfilled expectations have a medium negative effect on trust (Dirks & Ferrin, 2002). Ability, benevolence, integrity and trust propensity all have small to medium positive effects on trust" (Colquitt et al., 2007); (ten Have et al., 2016, p. 86).

What Is the Conclusion?

The theory and evidence show that trust, as such and in leadership, is a key factor in organizations and change processes. It has positive effects on organizational behaviours and a factor such as cooperation. It can play an important role in creating readiness for change, creating commitment and reducing resistance to change. Trust in leadership proves to be an important factor in organizations as such and change processes in particular. The right leadership style and fair process and (procedural) justice provide ways to develop and stimulate trust during times of change.

Practical Reflections

Fostering trust has many benefits. Maurer (2010) states: "Trust can make or break a change. But sadly, many who lead change seem to ignore this critically important ingredient. They seem to believe that a good idea will win the day. It won't" (p. 14). Trust in a leader has an effect on attitudinal, behavioural and performance outcomes. Trust in general, also among employees, is a vital component of effective working relations. In change processes, organizations and their leaders must be aware of the potential effect of trust or a lack of trust. The model of organizational trust proposed by Mayer et al. (1995) identifies some levers that enable leaders to increase trust. Because the propensity to trust is mostly considered to be a stable personality trait of the trustor, this will be hard for the leader to influence. This indicates that it is very important to select the 'right' leaders, in particular during times of change. Although trust is not a one-way process, leaders do have considerable influence on the characteristics of trustworthiness, the other antecedent of trust, as these are the characteristics that leaders display to their followers. Leaders, or more general change agents, have to be authentic and consistent in displaying integrity. In addition, they have to be honest about their abilities and capabilities, and have to show a genuine interest in employees. As a result, trust is likely to increase. Consequently, trust will result in better overall performance and a more pleasant working environment.[2]

Attachment Theory

Formed relationships and enduring bonds with others have implications for both the physical and psychological well-being of the individual.

What Is Attachment Theory?

Attachment theory is a theory of social and interpersonal behaviour of individuals. The attachment theory was developed by the British psychiatrist Bowlby (1907–1990). Shaver and Mikulincer (2013) explain the origins, related to "Bowlby's experiences as a family therapist at the Tavistock Clinic in London, where social and family relationships were considered alongside individual psychodynamics as causes of psychological and social disorders" (p. 161). The theory describes the formation and quality of interpersonal relationships. A central idea in attachment theory is that humans have the innate tendency to form relationships and enduring bonds with others (Bowlby, 1969, 1973). These strong bonds ensure support for the individual and form a protective shield in times of uncertainty and stressful situations. De Wachter (2011) endorses the theory as follows: "Man always wants to attach. That's because we are so desperately helpless when we are born. Put a child in the grass, a few hours later it is dead. An earthworm is born and is immediately an 'earthworm'". Attachment theory has a specific focus, namely on how human beings respond within relationships when hurt, separated from loved ones or perceiving a threat (Waters, Corcoran, & Anafarta, 2005). The theory is not designed and formulated as a general theory of relationships. Cole and Cole define attachment as: "An enduring emotional bond that infants form with specific people, usually beginning with their mothers, sometime between the ages of seven and nine months. Children are said to be attached to someone when they seek to be near that person, are distressed when they are separated from that person, are happy when they are reunited with the person, and orient their actions to the person even in the person's absence" (p. 618). When an infant is separated from its parent, the infant goes through three stages of emotional reactions. The first stage is protest; the infant cries and refuses to be consoled by others. The second is despair; in this stage the infant is sad and passive. The third stage is detachment; the infant actively disregards and avoids the parent if the parent returns (Hazan & Shaver, 1987). The idea of attachment is also applied to categories other than infants. Attachment theory provides not only a framework for understanding emotional reactions in infants, but also provides a way to understand, for example, love, resistance, fear, avoidance, loneliness and grief in adults. In fact, attachment was first studied in non-human animals, then in human infants and later in human adults. Attachment styles are ways of dealing with attachment, separation and loss in close personal relationships. Bartholomew (1990) defines four attachment styles, based on the combination of models of 'self' and 'others': secure, preoccupied, dismissing and fearful (Figure 6.2).

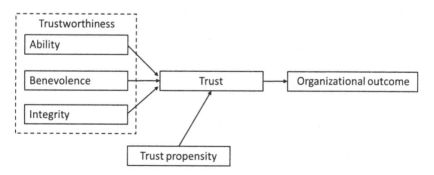

Figure 6.2 A Simplified Version of the Model of Organizational Trust, Based on Mayer et al. (1995)

Mikulincer and Florian (1998), for example, studied the relationship between adult attachment styles and emotional and cognitive reactions to stressful events. They focused on the ways adult attachment styles seem to affect one's coping and emotional reactions to the terror of personal death, military and war-related stressors, interpersonal losses, personal failure, parenthood-related stressors and chronic pain. Mikulincer, Florian, and Weller (1993) describe three attachment styles: secure, avoidant and ambivalent. Based on their research on traumas (focusing on the way people reacted to the Iraqi missile attack on Israel during the Gulf War), they described coping strategies. They learned that secure people used relatively more support-seeking strategies in coping with the trauma, ambivalent people used more emotion-focused strategies and avoidant people used more distancing strategies. In addition, their research showed that ambivalent people reported more distress than secure people. Avoidant persons reported higher levels of somatization, hostility and trauma-related avoidance than secure persons.

What Is the Relevance of Attachment for Organization and Change?

With regard to human infants, the fundamental assumption in attachment research on humans is that sensitive responding by the parent to the infant's needs results in an infant who demonstrates secure attachment. A lack of such sensitive responding results in insecure attachment (Lamb, Thompson, Gardner, Charnov, & Estes, 1984). Ainsworth, Blehar, Waters, and Wall (1978) developed a taxonomy of secure, avoidant and resistant attachment as a way of classifying infant behaviour in the 'strange situation'. The 'strange situation' is originally a procedure in which the child is observed playing for twenty-one minutes while caregivers and strangers enter and leave the room. In this way, researchers recreate the flow of the familiar and unfamiliar presence in most children's lives. The situation varies in stressfulness.

Analogical, organizational changes can be seen as, or as creating, 'strange situations'. One can imagine that people in organizations may also react with differing attachment styles. Someone with a secure style may embrace change, while another person with a different style may display avoidance or resistance. From the perspective of organization and change, attachment can be related to subjects such as leadership, in particular the relationship and interaction between leaders and followers, change capacity, organizational structure, resistance and cooperation. Shaver and Mikulincer (2013) mention a wealth of applications of attachment theory and research. First of all, they mention a number of laudable prosocial effects which can be seen as relevant to situations of organizational change: for example, reducing dogmatism, intolerance of ambiguity and intergroup hostility, and increasing participation in community activities. They also explicitly mention leadership development, group dynamics and organizational functioning (Mikulincer & Shaver, 2007). As has been said, attachment theory was initially developed to describe the mother-infant relationship. But as Shaver and Mikulincer (2013) make clear, it has been enhanced for both interpersonal relations of adults in everyday life and relationships in an organizational setting. Tziner, Ben-David, Oren, and Sharoni (2014) add: "On this basis, a large body of research attests to the importance of individual differences in adult attachment styles as a predictor of attitudes, feelings, behaviours and interpersonal relationships at work" (p. 556). The assumption is that the formed relationships and enduring bonds with others have implications for both the physical and psychological well-being of the individual. It is also suggested that the relationships are beneficial for organizations and employees, as it may increase factors such as work performance and job satisfaction.

Search Strategy

Relevant databases were searched using the term 'attachment theory' and 'attachment' in combination with 'work', 'organization', 'employee', 'change', 'meta-analysis' or 'systematic review'. The search yielded more than 150 articles. After screening the titles and abstracts for relevance, seventeen studies met the inclusion criteria. After thorough examination, another eight studies were excluded. Nine were included (level of evidence D- to E).

Main Findings

1. *Attachment is positively related to trustworthiness (Level D-).*

   Findings in a study indicate that attachment has a positive effect on the level of trustworthiness in professional and emotional relationships (Frazier, Gooty, Little, & Nelson, 2015). In addition to this, trustworthiness has a positive effect on various important factors for both organizations and employees, including job performance, organizational citizen behaviour (OCB), organizational commitment and job satisfaction (Veldsman & Coetzee, 2014; Level D-). Another study found that if an employee is more emotionally attached to his/her employer and/or the company, the employee tends to be more loyal to the company (Gemmel & Verleye, 2010; Level D-).

2. *Attachment affects both psychological and physical well-being (Level D-).*

   One study indicated that when a person has a secure attachment style, it increases his/her vigour in terms of emotional energy, cognitive liveliness and physical strength (Little, Nelson, Wallace, &

Johnson, 2011). "Bowlby (1988) described secure attachment as the capacity to connect well and securely in relationships with others while also having the capacity for autonomous action as situationally appropriate" (Little et al., 2011, p. 466). However, another study shows there are also forms of attachment (attachment avoidance and attachment anxiety) that have negative effects on psychological well-being (Landen & Wang, 2010; Level D-). Attachment anxiety is defined as: a state of mind in which a person is insecure about close relationships, while still maintaining these close relationships. Attachment avoidance is defined as: a situation/state of mind in which a person literally avoids relationships, and when he or she does commit the relationship remains distant and cold.

3. *The style of attachment influences the turnover intention of employees (Level E).*

   People with avoidant and anxious attachment styles have more turnover intentions, whereas people with secure attachment styles have fewer turnover intentions (Tziner et al., 2014).

What Is the Conclusion?

Attachment theory is a well-researched one, with a lot of evidence and a wealth of applications: "More than a half-century's worth of research supports the idea of attachment as crucial for optimal human functioning" (Hudson, 2013, p. 157). The evidence illustrates the relevance and importance of attachment for organizational settings and change. It has a positive effect on trustworthiness, which influences relevant organizational factors such as OCB, commitment and job satisfaction. Theory and research teach an important lesson to leaders, their followers and change agents; the attachment style is crucial. When an employee has a secure attachment style, it is beneficial for both his psychological and physical well-being, increases trust and loyalty and decreases turnover intention. When the attachment style is anxious or avoidant, it has detrimental effects on psychological and physical well-being, and increases the turnover rate. The positive effects on trust and loyalty with these two styles are at least questionable. In studies in organizational settings, attachment is often described as 'commitment'. In our earlier research on 'evidence-based change management' (ten Have et al., 2017), commitment was an important topic. A high level meta-analysis showed that affective commitment has a positive but small effect on performance (Riketta, 2002). This effect even becomes negative when organizational trust and organizational identification are taken into account (Ng, 2015). These findings indicate that both trust and identification are more important in explaining performance than commitment. However, if attachment (commitment) increases trustworthiness and loyalty, it becomes important again. The potential contribution of attachment in the context of organizations and change management is clearly illustrated by Veldsman and Coetzee (2014): "Managers and organization development practitioners could identify the overall level of psychological work immersion of employees and the people performance enablers that may potentially contribute to high or low levels of psychological attachment. Strengthening the managerial practices and behaviours that underpin the people performance enablers and that contribute to the psychological attachment of employees may potentially contribute to the overall business performance of the business" (p. 10).

Practical Reflections

The included studies provide a set of practical guidelines which 'operationalize' the idea of attachments. First of all, in the case of secure attached individuals, managers should encourage and reward indications or signs of this style. An example is rewarding the individuals for acting independently when needed, but also asking for help at the right moment (Little et al., 2011). A different approach is needed for insecure attached individuals. Managers should recognize employees who lack the secure attachment that is needed. Consequently, the manager should know that the relationship between him/her and the individual is of critical importance, because this employee likely has few other physical, emotional and cognitive resources to draw upon to remain productive (Little et al., 2011). Little and colleagues (2011) also state: "Training managers to use security priming techniques with insecure followers could be quite effective in terms of increasing vigour at work and organizational citizenship behaviour while decreasing deviance" (pp. 478–479). In addition, managers can try to improve the work centrality (job-skill fit) and recruit people who have a secure attachment style. This could all be done through modifying recruiting and selection procedures (Tziner et al., 2014). Tziner adds: "Interestingly, previous studies have suggested that supervisors can function as attachment figures (e.g. Davidovitz, Shaver, Mikulinces, & Popper, 2007) by acknowledging the negative effects of insecure attachment relationships and trying to provide 'an island of security' for their insecure employees, by being responsive to employees' needs for security and protection" (Tziner et al., 2014, p. 562). Finally, when talking to or counselling people with highly dangerous or stressful jobs, it might be useful to explore their attachment history (Landen & Wang, 2010).

Fair Process: Justice Theory and Procedural Justice[3]

Procedural justice reflects the perceived fairness of decision-making processes and the degree to which they are consistent, accurate, unbiased and open to voice and input.

What Is Fair Process?

Fairness or justice is a fundamental concept that takes many forms in different disciplines, such as theology, philosophy, law and psychology. Greenberg (1987) introduced the construct of organizational justice in psychology. This construct does not refer to a universal or absolute form of justice; rather, it is about the fairness as perceived by employees—a subjective experience. Organizational justice can be divided into three elements: distributive justice (outcomes), procedural justice (process) and interactional justice (interaction). Fair process is essentially a synonym for procedural justice and defined as the following: "Procedural justice reflects the perceived fairness of decision-making processes and the degree to which they are consistent, accurate, unbiased and open to voice and input" (Colquitt et al., 2013, p. 200). Various researchers have applied different standards that vary in terms of their operationalization of procedural justice as a construct. Leventhal's (1980) six criteria of procedural justice, for example, are well known and often used to determine the fairness of procedures: (a) the consistency rule, stating that allocation procedures should be consistent across persons and over time; (b) the bias-suppression rule, stating that personal self-interests of decision-makers should be prevented from operating during the allocation process; (c) the accuracy rule, referring to the goodness of the information used in the allocation process; (d) the correctability rule, dealing with the existence of opportunities to change an unfair decision; (e) the representativeness rule, stating that the needs, values and outlooks of all the parties affected by the allocation process should be represented in the process; and (f) the ethicality rule, according to which the allocation process must be compatible with fundamental moral and ethical values of the perceiver (Leventhal, 1980, in Cohen-Charash & Spector, 2001, p. 280). To understand the underlying mechanism of why the perception of a fair process may help to increase acceptance of the outcome, it is interesting to consider the first empirical research on procedural justice that was conducted in a judicial setting (Thibaut & Walker, 1975). The researchers compared the inquisitorial system of continental Europe with the Anglo-Saxon adversarial system of justice. It turned out that, irrespective of the final verdict, the Anglo-Saxon adversarial system was perceived to be fairer. In continental Europe, judges control both decision and process. Under the Anglo-Saxon judicial system, however, those affected by the decision can exert more influence on the judicial proceedings. As Thibaut and Walker indicated, this influence on the process makes the outcome more acceptable, even when these outcomes may be disadvantageous in terms of self-interest. Later empirical research replicated the finding that when procedures are perceived as fair, reactions are favourable, largely irrespective of the outcome. However, when procedures are perceived to be unfair, the importance of the fairness of the outcome increases; that is, distributive justice. This interaction effect is called the *fair process effect* and has been shown empirically in several studies in different contexts (for a review, see Brockner & Wiesenfeld, 1996).

What Is the Relevance of Fair Process for Organization and Change?

In the context of organization and change, fair process is related to subjects like participation, resistance and commitment, leadership and culture, and change capacity. Ibarra (2015) points to the importance of engaging people in the change by developing supportive processes: "Naïve leaders act as if the idea itself is the ultimate selling point. Experienced leaders, on the other hand, understand that the process is just as important, if not more so" (p. 45). Brockner (in HBR EI) (2015, 2006) builds the 'business case for fair process'; fair process makes great 'business sense'. He states: "From minimizing costs to strengthening performance, process fairness pays enormous dividends in a wide variety of organizational and people-related challenges" (p. 44). According to Brockner, process fairness has three drivers: (1) how much input employees believe they have in the decision-making process; (2) how employees believe decisions are made and, (3) implementation (e.g. consistent, accurate, transparent, not biased). He states that change will go more smoothly if process fairness is in place. Leaders have to express authentic interest to create a trusting environment in which people feel that they can safely voice their anxieties, objections and worries regarding the change at hand. Brockner not only builds the business case for fair process, but he also advocates that there is a moral imperative for companies to practise process fairness as the right thing to do. Collins (2001) also emphasizes the importance of processes that guarantee that people will be heard in the right way. His 'good-to-great leaders' lead with questions (not answers), engage in dialogue and debate (not coercion) and build 'red flag' mechanisms: "red flag mechanisms give you a practical and useful tool for turning information into information that cannot be ignored and for creating a climate where the truth is heard" (p. 80).

Search Strategy

To gain an overview of the relevant literature on fair process in general, relevant databases were searched using the key words 'organizational justice', 'procedural justice' and 'fair process'. In a second search, these key words were combined with 'organizational change' to identify studies in which fair process was applied in the context of organizational change. Initially, the general search that focused on fair process in general resulted in more than 2,000 articles. Filtering for meta-analyses and systematic reviews, our search yielded thirty-seven results. After screening the abstracts for relevance, twenty-seven studies were excluded. Full-text screening and critical appraisal of the remaining ten articles did not result in additional exclusions. All the meta-analyses included were of moderate quality (Level B). The second search, in which the key term 'organizational change' was added to narrow down the results to the context of change management, resulted in forty-three studies. After screening the abstracts for relevance, twenty-nine studies were excluded. Full-text screening of the articles resulted in the exclusion of another five studies. Critical appraisal of the remaining nine articles did not lead to more exclusions. One of the nine studies was a non-controlled, before-after study. The other eight studies had a cross-sectional study design.

Main Findings

1. *Fair process has a medium to large positive effect on organizational outcomes (Level A).*

   "The results showed relationships between the dimensions of justice and certain organizational outcomes, such as performance, productivity, organizational citizenship behaviour, satisfaction and commitment" (Cohen-Charash & Spector, 2001; Viswesvaran & Ones, 2002). More specifically, the meta-analyses clearly illustrated the importance of procedural justice (fair process) in relation to organizational outcomes. Compared with the other types of justice (i.e. distributive justice and interactional justice), procedural justice is the best predictor of work performance, counterproductive work behaviour and affective commitment (Cohen-Charash & Spector, 2001). Viswesvaran and Ones (2002) found similar results: "Organizational commitment, organizational citizenship behaviour and productivity were more associated with procedural justice than distributive justice. The effects that have been found were medium to large. Because the results were consistent throughout all the meta-analyses, evidence Level A was assigned" (ten Have et al., 2016, p. 128).

2. *Fair process has a medium positive effect on the affective commitment of both survivors and victims of a downsizing operation (Level B).*

   "Van Dierendonck and Jacobs (2002) presented an overview of the impact of fairness on organizational commitment on both survivors and victims after a downsizing operation. This specific type of organizational change often increases the level of insecurity among employees and triggers sense-making processes. One of their results revealed that procedural justice mattered more to survivors of the downsizing operation than distributive justice. 'Employees who felt that they were given a full and fair explanation of why and how people were dismissed are more likely to accept the layoff process and to remain more positive about the organization' (p. 105). Van Dierendonck and Jacobs also found that fairness in general mattered more when mass layoffs were instigated for profit maximization reasons. These results indicate that attention to fairness in a downsizing process is a vital driver of commitment in the critical time period following a downsizing operation" (ten Have et al., 2016, p. 128).

3. *Fair process has a low to medium positive effect on the acceptance of organizational changes (Level D).*

    "The findings of one study indicated that if leaders act in a procedurally fair way, employees are more likely to accept organizational changes (Tyler & De Cremer, 2005). In addition, Saruhan (2014) indicated that effective communication and perceptions of justice are crucial factors in reducing employee resistance and increasing favourable behaviour toward change, thereby increasing the possibility that the change process will be successfully implemented. Although the effect sizes of both studies were small to medium, these studies provided the best available evidence on this subject, which makes them relevant for both researchers and practitioners" (ten Have et al., 2016, p. 129).

4. *Fair process has a large positive effect on change commitment (Level D).*

    "One study indicated procedural justice as, in fact, a predictor of change commitment (Bernerth, Armenakis, Field, & Walker, 2007). Procedural justice was found to be strongly positively related to affective change commitment and moderately negatively related to organizational cynicism" (ten Have et al., 2016, p. 129).

5. *An unfair process has a small to medium negative effect on employee behaviour further to a breach of the psychological contract (Level D).*

    "Kickul, Lester, and Finkl (2002) found that procedural justice was an important determinant of behaviour following breaches of external outcomes (e.g. pay) in terms of the psychological contract between the employer and the employee. When procedural justice was perceived to be low, employees showed less organizational change behaviour, satisfaction and in-role job performance. These employees were also more likely to leave the organization. Although this study showed small to medium effect sizes, the findings may be relevant to the field of organizational change, where psychological contracts play an important role" (ten Have et al., 2016, p. 129).

What Is the Conclusion?

Fair process in the organizational and change context is a well-researched phenomenon. It has positive effects on organizational outcomes like commitment, performance, organizational citizenship behaviour and satisfaction. In addition, fair process has a positive effect on the acceptance of changes and change commitment.

Practical Reflections

The fair process effect in organizations is observed when change leaders increase the degree to which the decision-making process is consistent, accurate, unbiased and open to employee input. When procedural justice is not taken into account, employees may feel treated unfairly, and dissatisfaction may increase. To actively design a fair change process, the six classic criteria for procedural justice named by Leventhal (1980)—which are still used by many researchers—may serve as a useful checklist. These criteria can be turned into practical guidelines for organizational change as follows: (1) the change approach needs to be consistently applied to all employees at all times; (2) it needs to be impartial, meaning that prejudice or stereotyping are eliminated; (3) the information on which decisions are based needs to be accurate; (4) if the situation demands it, opportunities should be provided to correct or change plans or processes; (5) those responsible for the organizational change (the change managers or executives responsible) need to represent the interests of all those affected by the change; and (6) the ethical standards and values of those involved should never be disregarded. Although this all sounds logical and righteous, in practice it is not always possible to fully apply all guidelines. Sometimes, change leaders simply do not have enough time or resources to apply all of these criteria. Sometimes—for example, in times of conflict within a multiparty organization—it is impossible to represent all of the interests of all stakeholders, given the complexity of those involved and their stakes in possible outcomes. In such cases, it seems prudent only to deviate from the criteria for fair process intentionally and transparently, which, for example, means explaining the choices that have been made, as these can reduce the overall fairness of the change process.

Equity Theory

People feel most comfortable when they are getting exactly what they deserve from their relationships—no more and certainly not less.

What Is Equity Theory?

Equity theory was introduced by workplace and behavioural psychologist John Adams in 1965. Since then, equity theory has become one of the biggest theories in social psychology. The theory covers a range of areas such as justice, fairness, (social) exchange and expectancy. Equity theory explains how people appraise the remuneration for their work. What is considered as fair is set against the income-outcome ratio of peers. Getting rewarded too little compared with one's peers, either in money, influence or prestige, may result in frustration or anger. Getting rewarded too much, on the other hand, may result in feelings of guilt. This nagging sense may cause the employee to invest less rather than more to restore the balance. Explaining the appropriate allocation norms beforehand and striking the right balance, with an emphasis on outcomes, is referred to as *distributive justice*. In sum, "According to equity theory, people feel most comfortable when they are getting exactly what they deserve from their relationships—no more and certainly not less" (Van Lange, Kruglanski, & Higgins, 2012a, p. 200). Equity theory is relatively straightforward. It consists of four propositions: "proposition 1: Men and women are 'hardwired' to try to maximize pleasure and minimize pain; proposition 2: Society, however, has a vested interest in persuading people to behave fairly and equitably. Groups will generally reward members who treat others equitably and punish those who treat others inequitably; proposition 3: Given societal pressures, people are most comfortable when they perceive that they are getting roughly what they deserve from life and love. If people feel over-benefited, they may experience pity, guilt and shame. If they feel under-benefited, they may experience anger, sadness and resentment; proposition 4: People in inequitable relationships will attempt to reduce their distress through a variety of techniques—by restoring psychological equity, actual equity or leaving the relationships" (Van Lange, Kruglanski, & Higgins 2012b, p. 202). An important concept is *equity sensitivity*. Equity sensitivity focuses on the differences between people regarding social exchange (input versus output, giving versus receiving) and how 'fair' this distribution is. Equity sensitivity describes three different kinds of people: (1) benevolents: people who are 'givers' and like to give more than they receive; (2) entitleds: people who are 'getters' and like to receive more than they give; (3) sensitives: people who prefer equality between giving and receiving.

What Is the Relevance of Equity Theory for Organization and Change?

Equity theory can be related to organizational and change topics such as leadership, performance managements, organizational systems (in particular reward systems), commitment, resistance and cooperation. In organizational settings, equity theory focuses especially on the balance between what employees give (input) to an organization and what they receive from that organization (output). The input, or what an employee gives to the organization, can be metrics such as time, skill, trust, effort and loyalty. The output, or what an employee receives from the organization, can be salary, benefits (car, phone, tickets for a concert, etc.) and job security. Outputs can also be praise, good reputation and a sense of achievement. According to equity theory, this balance has implications for the satisfaction of employees. In addition, the perception of balance of other colleagues is important, as this can also influence the satisfaction. For example, when colleagues perform less but receive more, you might feel dissatisfied (why don't I get more salary?) and your input might decline (why should I work harder than my colleague, while he gets more salary and praise?). The basic assumption here is that when employees perceive balance between their inputs and outputs, this will positively affect their organizational commitment, job satisfaction and performance and lower factors such as the turnover rate and absenteeism. When this balance is distorted, it will have negative consequences for both employee and organization. Equity theory proposes that both high input—low output and low input—high output are detrimental.

Search Strategy

Relevant databases were searched using the term 'equity', and 'equity' in combination with 'theory', 'work', 'motivation', 'employee', 'change', 'meta-analysis' or 'systematic review'. The search yielded more than 600(!) articles. After screening the titles and abstracts for relevance, seventy-two studies met the inclusion criteria. After thorough examination, another forty-nine were excluded. No included studies were meta-analyses or systematic reviews.

Main Findings

1. *Equity sensitivity is a better predictor of non-behavioural outcomes than behavioural ones (Level A).*

    In a controlled, before-after measurement study, the researchers found that equity sensitivity failed to moderate reactions to distributive justice. Equity sensitivity did not affect organizational citizenship behaviour (extra-role performance), which was also found in another study (Allen, Evans, & White, 2011; level C-). Furthermore, equity sensitivity did not have an effect on psychological contract breach. These results, combined with other studies, suggest that equity sensitivity is a better predictor of non-behavioural outcomes (like job satisfaction) than behavioural outcomes (like organizational citizenship behaviour) (Scott & Colquitt, 2007).

2. *Benevolent individuals have the highest pay satisfaction, perceived pay fairness and lowest turnover intentions compared with entitleds and equity sensitives (Level C).*

    The researchers also found that "Entitled individuals did not report lower overall pay satisfaction, perceived pay fairness or higher turnover intentions than Equity Sensitive individuals. All three equity sensitivity groups preferred being over-rewarded to being equitably rewarded, and were relatively distressed when under-rewarded" (Shore, 2004, p. 722).

3. *Being over-rewarded had a positive effect on pay satisfaction, but this effect is small (Level C).*

"However, being over-rewarded resulted in a relatively small increase in reported pay satisfaction, and a small decrease in the intention to change jobs beyond what resulted from being equitably rewarded. Although over-rewarding individuals is likely to produce certain favourable outcomes, some over-rewarded individuals may experience feelings of guilt and engender resentment among under-rewarded individuals" (Shore, 2004, p. 727).

4. *Both random and merit layoffs are perceived as more unfair to colleagues than to individuals themselves and these layoffs aroused guilt and remorse. Still, the performance of merit layoffs 'survivors' is higher than that of the 'survivors' of random layoffs (Level C).*

Both random layoffs and merit layoffs (based on the performance of the individuals) increase the guilt and remorse of individuals. During random layoffs, individuals increase the quantity of their output. However, the best performance gain is from merit layoffs, as the 'survivors' perform better in relation to their random layoff counterpart (Brockner et al., 1986).

5. *Firms that use equity-based compensation (EBC) perform better compared with companies that do not use EBC (Level D).*

When EBC increases, so does the firm performance. "As firms become more human capital intensive, compensation plans for employees become more important to attracting and retaining highly skilled employees" (Frye, 2004, p. 52). In another study, equity compensation is a positive predictor of both sales and employee growth, but not of firm growth (Arbaugh, Cox, & Camp, 2004; Level D-).

6. *Equity sensitivity is positively related to job performance, organizational citizenship behaviour and organizational commitment (Level D-).*

Contrary to earlier-mentioned findings, this study finds a positive relationship between equity sensitivity and job performance. "Individual differences in equity sensitivity significantly predicted job performance in both Studies 1 and 2, such that as benevolence increased there was a corresponding increase in job performance" (Bing & Burroughs, 2001, p. 286). The limitation of this study is its low level of evidence, as it is only cross-sectional. Another low-quality study finds that equity sensitivity is positively related to organizational citizenship behaviour (Akan, Allen, & White, 2008). Other research-ers find a positive effect of equity sensitivity on higher levels of organizational commitment when individuals perceive the organi-zation as high performing. When individuals perceive the organiza-tion as low performing, individuals who are equity-sensitive tend to exhibit lower levels of organization commitment (Vella, Caruana, & Pitt, 2012).

7. *Procedural equity is the most important determinant of employee pay satisfaction, compared with three other forms of equity (Level D-).*

   The study compared four forms of equity (individual, procedural, external and internal equity). Of these forms, procedural equity had the most positive effect on pay satisfaction, with individual equity being the second most important. Third was external equity and fourth, internal equity. Still, all four forms are important, as "dis-satisfaction with pay may lead to significant organizational prob-lems, including decreased motivation and performance and increased absenteeism and turnover" (Terpstra & Honoree, 2003, p. 72).

8. *Perceptions of internal equity are more important than perceptions of external equity in predicting job satisfaction and organizational commitment, but both have a positive effect (Level D).*

   In two separate cross-sectional studies, the researchers found that internal equity is more important than external equity in predicting perceived job satisfaction (Khalifa, 2011) and each of the compo-nents of organizational commitment (Khalifa & Trong, 2011).

9. *Equity theory is best applicable in situations with a high level of per-ceived certainty (Level D).*

   "In other situations, where information concerning the tasks and its characteristics is quite unpredictable and less certain, the assessment of the reward system as equitable or inequitable can be a very dif-ficult task and persons tend to use maximization as the operating norm" (Neumann, 1980, p. 153).

What Is the Conclusion?

Equity theory is a strong and well-researched theory. In the domain of organization and change there are multiple studies from the perspective of equity theory. The evidence provides some interesting findings. Firms that make use of equity seem to perform better than firms that do not. When using equity, procedural equity seems most important, but other forms must not be neglected. Equity sensitivity has a positive effect on job satisfaction. The positive effect of equity sensitivity on performance, organizational citizenship behaviour and organizational commitment is found in some studies. This remains unclear and needs additional research, but it might be beneficial and will not do any harm. Benevolent individuals ('givers') have the highest pay satisfaction and perceived pay fairness and the lowest turnover intentions compared with the entitled ones and equity sensitives. Being over-rewarded seems to have a positive effect on pay satisfaction, but this effect is small and might lead to negative consequences like feelings of guilt and resentment. Internal equity (inside the organization) seems more important than external equity (comparing with another organization) for factors like job satisfaction and commitment.

Practical Reflections

From the equity perspective, a set of practical guidelines and insights can be given for the practice of management and change. The first is that when using equity-based compensation, employees prefer non-retirement forms of EBC such as shares, stock options and purchase gains. In addition, managers should promote fairness in the organization by implementing procedures to allocate fair rewards (ensuring that rewards are appropriate for the amount of work) and promote interactions between employees that are based on respect and dignity. When employees raise concerns about fairness, managers should be open to alleviate those concerns. Managers should always ensure that employees perceive fair treatment when they compare themselves with colleagues. And managers should focus on internal equity by "achieving and communicating internal salaries equity, internal fringe benefits equity, internal promotion opportunities equity and internal status equity" (Khalifa, 2011, p. 141). Furthermore, HR should develop strategies that foster an equitable working environment, which can sustain employees' organizational commitment. Alternatively, promoting team-building activities can do this. Entitled employees are highly sensitive to equity issues, and managers should develop strategies to deal with these types of employees.

Moral Disengagement

What Is Moral Disengagement?

Moral disengagement is about mechanisms that prevent us feeling bad when doing bad things.

Moral disengagement is a social psychological term proposing mechanisms that do not make us feel bad when doing bad things. We justify our behaviour when it is not consistent with our norms and values. Albert Bandura, who also developed the social-cognitive theory, coined moral disengagement in 1999. The moral disengagement may centre on: the cognitive restructuring of inhumane conduct into a benign or worthy one by moral justification, sanitizing language and advantageous comparison; disavowal of a sense of personal agency by diffusion or displacement of responsibility; disregarding or minimizing the injurious effects of one's actions; and attribution of blame to and dehumanization of those who are victimized (Bandura, 1999). Many inhumanities operate through a supportive network of legitimate enterprises run by otherwise considerate people who contribute to destructive activities by disconnected subdivision of functions and diffusion of responsibility. Given the many mechanisms for disengaging moral control, civilized life requires, in addition to humane personal standards, safeguards built into social systems that uphold compassionate behaviour and renounce cruelty (Bandura, 1999). Moral disengagement is the process of convincing the self that ethical standards do not apply to oneself in a particular context. This is done by separating moral reactions from inhumane conduct and disabling the mechanism of self-condemnation. Moral disengagement involves a process of cognitive re-framing of destructive behaviour as morally acceptable without changing the behaviour or the moral standards. Figure 6.3 shows the points in the process of internal control at which moral self-censure can be disengaged from reprehensible conduct:

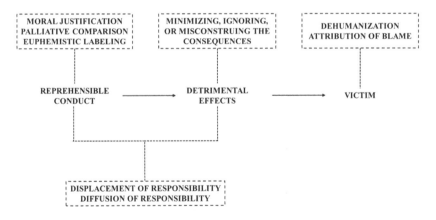

Figure 6.3 The Process of Disengagement

(Source: from *Social Foundations of Thought and Action: A Social Cognitive Theory* (p. 376), by A. Bandura, 1986, Englewood Cliffs, NJ: Prentice Hall.)

The moral disengagement may centre on: (1) the reconstrual of the conduct itself so it is not viewed as immoral; (2) the operation of the agency of action so that the perpetrators can minimize their role in causing harm; (3) the consequences that flow from actions; or (4) how the victims of maltreatment are regarded by devaluing them as human beings and blaming them for what is being done to them.

(1) Reconstrual of the conduct itself so it is not viewed as immoral can have different forms: moral justification, palliative or advantageous comparison, and euphemistic labelling. Moral justification is detrimental conduct that is made personally and socially acceptable by portraying it as serving socially worthy or moral purposes. Palliative or advantageous comparison means that the way we view behaviour is coloured by what it is compared against. In the case of euphemistic labelling, language shapes thought patterns on which actions are based. Activities can take on very different appearances depending on what they are called. Euphemistic language is widely used to make harmful conduct respectable and to reduce personal responsibility for it. (2) The operation of the agency of action so that the perpetrators can minimize their role in causing harm can have the form of displacement of responsibility: people do not feel personally responsible for the actions. Because they are not the actual agent of their actions, they are spared self-condemning reactions. A second form is that of diffusion of responsibility: after activities become routinized into detached subfunctions, people shift their attention from the morality of what they are doing to the operational details and efficiency of their specific job. Group decision-making is another common practice that gets otherwise considerate people to behave inhumanely. When everyone is responsible, no one really feels responsible. (3) When moral disengagement centres on the consequences that flow from actions, it is about the disregard or distortion of consequences. This is the case when people pursue activities that are harmful to others for reasons of personal gain or social pressure, when they avoid facing the harm they cause or when they minimize it. If minimization does not work, the evidence of harm can be discredited. As long as the harmful results of one's conduct are ignored, minimized, distorted or disbelieved, there is little reason for self-censure to be activated. (4) The final set of disengagement practices operates on the recipients of detrimental acts. The forms are dehumanization and attribution of blame. Dehumanization means that the strength of moral self-censure depends partly on how the perpetrators view the people they mistreat. In the process called 'attribution of blame', people view themselves as faultless victims driven to injurious conduct by forcible provocation. The cognitive mechanisms do not operate independently. They are interrelated in the sociostructural, or 'organizational', context to promote incorrect or inhumane (organizational) behaviours in daily practice (see: Bandura, 1999).

What Is the Relevance of Moral Disengagement for Organization and Change?

In the area of organization and change, moral disengagement can be related to (bad) leadership and organizational cultures, resistance to change and (a lack of) cooperation and commitment. It helps to see, define or name problematic behaviours and to treat or change them. For example, the repeated use of euphemistic labelling, diffusion of responsibility or distortion of consequences can be strong indicators that the culture or a change process is or is becoming problematic. If this is the case, resistance will grow, commitment will decrease and cooperation will become more and more difficult. Leaders can and have to act on this; they have to lead by example, take the necessary measures and develop an organizational climate in which disengagement can turn into engagement as a basis for change and performance. Moore et al. (2012) illustrate the relevance of moral disengagement for the organizational context. They demonstrate that the propensity to morally disengage predicts several relevant outcomes that are relevant in the organizational context, for example self-reported unethical behaviour, a decision to commit fraud and supervisor- and co-worker-reported unethical work behaviours. Barsky (2011) studied the effects of moral disengagement and participation on organizational or work behaviour. His research shows a significant relationship between moral disengagement and people's likelihood of unethical decision-making. He also found that participation in goal-setting is positively related to deceptive behaviour. In addition, moral justifications tended to increase in reported incidences of unethical behaviour only when employees did not feel that they had the opportunity to participate in setting their performance goals at work (Barsky, 2008). Eckes (2001), in his book *Creating the Six Sigma Culture*, identifies 'maladaptive behaviours' such as 'No Follow Through' (not completing action items) and the 'Interrupter'. He emphasizes that the importance of facilitative skills needs to change these behaviours. Kouzes and Posner (2012) emphasize the importance of supervisory support focused on creating a climate in which people are fully engaged and feel in control of their own lives. "In a climate of competence and confidence, people don't hesitate to hold themselves personally accountable for results, and they feel profound ownership for their achievements" (p. 243). Kouzes and Posner emphasize that a leader must "invest in strengthening the capacity and the resolve of everyone in the organization" (p. 256), especially in situations of change. Exemplary leaders strive to create conditions in which people perform effortlessly and expertly despite the challenging or even difficult situation.

Search Strategy

Relevant databases were searched using the terms 'moral disengagement', 'change' and 'organization'. The search yielded thirty articles. After screening the titles and abstracts for relevance, nine studies met the inclusion criteria. Some included studies were papers that were conceptual in nature while others were more empirically research-oriented. Ultimately, three included studies had a level of evidence: A-, D- and D-.

Main Findings

1. *People can switch their ethicality on or off in various ways (Level A-).*

   The authors find that morality, to a certain extent, is derived from the situation one finds oneself in; people respond to the permissiveness of their environments and seize the opportunity to behave unethically. On the one hand, the results provide further evidence of the pervasive dishonesty of ordinary people. On the other hand, they show that an intervention as simple as exposure to a moral code reduces dishonest behaviour—and, furthermore, that signing a moral code can completely eliminate dishonesty. . . . If a situation permits dishonesty, then one should expect to observe dishonesty. At the same time, a simple intervention, such as merely reminding actors about established moral codes, could counteract the effect of a permissible situation (Shu, Gino, & Bazerman, 2009).

2. *Job insecurity increases workplace deviance and intentions to leave by encouraging employees to morally disengage (Level D-).*

   Job insecurity is positively related to interpersonal deviance (1a), organizational deviance (1b) and intention to leave (1c). And moral disengagement mediates the positive association between job insecurity and those three issues (Huang, Ashford, Wellman, Lee, & Wang, 2017).

3. *Individual differences in moral disengagement directly predicted unethical behaviour and functioned as a mediator of the relationship between authenticity and unethical behaviour (Level D-).*

   The authors applied the Situational Strength Hypothesis to examine unethical behaviour in the business context which they argue takes the form of a moral grey zone—situations that are morally ambiguous and in which leaders and followers together engage in practices that potentially harm others, yet might benefit the organization, the follower or the leader (Knoll, Lord, Petersen, & Weigelt, 2016).

What Is the Conclusion?

Moore, Detert, Klebe Treviño, Baker, and Mayer (2012) are very clear; they conclude that scholars and practitioners seeking to understand a broad range of undesirable workplace behaviours can benefit from taking an individual's propensity to morally disengage into account. The studies included show that and how interventions like signing a moral code work. Moral disengagement can be fostered by job insecurity, not seldom inherent to change initiatives like organizational restructuring and cost-reduction programmes. Moral disengagement directly predicts unethical behaviour in organizations.

Practical Reflections

The concept of moral engagement is relevant and insightful for the practice of management and change. Research shows that moral disengagement is situationally dependent. Circumstances will influence the moral disengagement of the people involved. Based on the articles assessed, one can see the analogy for the organizational context, for example that a restructuring (a certain kind of organizational change) will lead to job insecurity which could increase workplace deviance and intentions to leave by making employees become morally disengaged.

The research shows that everyone can be 'morally disengaged' from time to time and be guilty of one or more mechanisms. Individual differences in moral disengagement directly predicted unethical behaviour and functioned as a mediator of the relationship between authenticity and unethical behaviour. In conclusion, the evidence also shows that exposure to a moral code or signing one can reduce dishonest behaviour. Fiske (2004) explains that moral disengagement reduces self-censure and eases aggression (Bandura, Barbaranelli, Caprara, & Pastorelli, 1996). She emphasizes that moral disengagement but also moral exemption, moral hypocrisy, socially induced evil and socially sanctioned violence "all name forms of violence that seem prosocial to the perpetrators but aggressive from the perspective of victims or observers" (p. 378). Building on that, Fiske concludes that perceived moral mandates can lead people to excuse any means to reach their valued goals. It is not difficult to imagine how a robust change initiative and the leaders, believers and change agents involved here fit in. Fiske's observations do contain an important warning with regard to the boundaries and ethics of change management and organizational behaviour.

Groupthink

Groupthink occurs when a group of people make faulty decisions because of the desire to maintain harmony and conformity in the group.

What Is Groupthink?

Groupthink is a psychological phenomenon that occurs when a group of people make faulty decisions because of the desire to maintain harmony and conformity in the group. It thus illustrates the failure of groups to consider all available and relevant information in decision-making (Janis, 1972). Groupthink can result in irrational or dysfunctional decision-making outcomes that can have serious consequences. This is a result of aiming for too much cohesiveness. Groupthink can be defined as: "group members' effort to collectively reduce the potential damage from threat and to ward off negative images of the group that produces" . . . "the genuine sharing of illusory beliefs" (Turner, Pratnakis, Probasco, & Leve, 1992, p. 795). Janis, the founding father of groupthink, made a groupthink model incorporating twenty-four variables. He defined four categories of variables: (1) the antecedent conditions of groupthink; (2) symptoms of groupthink; (3) symptoms of defective decision-making; and (4) outcomes. The idea is that antecedent conditions within a group influence the group to become a victim of groupthink. Once a group becomes a victim of the groupthink phenomenon, symptoms of defective decision-making appear, with decisions of poor quality as a result (Won-Woo, 2000). Janis considered group cohesion the most important antecedent of groupthink (Janis, 1972). Festinger (1950) defined group cohesion as: "the resultant of all the forces acting on the members to remain in the group" (p. 274). Festinger elaborated on this and stated: "these forces may depend on the attractiveness or unattractiveness of either the prestige of the group, members in the group or the activities in which the group engages" (p. 274). Two more recent studies also showed that group cohesion includes both socially cohesive and task-cohesive elements (Bernthal & Insko, 1993; Chang & Bordia, 2001). Since 1971 groupthink has been researched and discussed intensively. It has been a research topic and discussion subject in a variety of disciplines, including psychology, business, politics, communication and many more. Most of the research dates back to the '80s and '90s. Relevant studies conducted in 2009, 2010 and 2015 illustrate that groupthink is still seen as relevant. However, Fiske (2004) is critical and clear: "Although an appealing theory that deserves to be true, and although evidence from descriptive studies seemed supportive, nonetheless groupthink experiments failed to pin it down clearly. . . . General models of group problem-solving currently seem more useful" (p. 496).

What Is the Relevance of Groupthink for Organization and Change?

Notwithstanding the clear and critical reflection of Fiske (2004), groupthink is a very popular concept in organizational contexts and part of the vocabulary of a lot of managers and consultants. The problem it aims to describe and address is related to subjects like change vision, change capacity, leadership, team development (group dynamics, group problem-solving and decision-making), communication, organizational culture and communication. Popular belief is that groupthink can occur when certain preconditions are met, for example when the group is highly cohesive, has no access to contrary options and is ruled by a directive leader. This can lead to negative outcomes such as having only a few alternatives for a problem and the favoured solution never being critically examined. In other words, expert opinion is not sought and the group only selects information that is positive for their "well-founded solution". Beliefs and insights like this, which are around in practice, combined with the popularity of the concept as such and its links with relevant topics from the organizational context, make it worth further analysing groupthink and its evidence.

Search Strategy

Relevant databases were searched using the term 'groupthink', and 'groupthink' in combination with 'meta-analysis' or 'systematic review'. The search yielded more than 300 articles. After screening the title and abstracts for relevance, one meta-analysis and nine studies were included. After critically appraising the studies, two studies were excluded because of serious methodological flaws.

Main Findings

1. *High social groups have the highest perception of groupthink and high task-cohesive groups the lowest perception of groupthink (Bernthal & Insko, 1993; Level B).*

2. *When task cohesion is high, social-emotional cohesion does not necessarily lead to groupthink (Level B).*

   When both task cohesion and social cohesion within groups are high, groupthink will not necessarily increase as long as the reasons for forming the group are clear and the group follows procedures designed to counteract the possibility of groupthink (Bernthal & Insko, 1993; Mullen, 1994).

3. *Groups with dominant individuals produce higher-quality decisions and are less likely to be affected by groupthink compared with groups without dominant individuals (Level B).*

   Highly dominant groups make more statements of agreement and disagreement and use more time to make a decision compared with low dominant groups (Callaway, Marriott, & Esser, 1984).

4. *Groupthink is a stress-reduction process (Level B).*

   A controlled, before-after study found evidence for the idea proposed by Janis (1972) that groupthink is essentially a stress-reduction process (Callaway et al., 1984).

5. *High group confidence in the early stages of a group assignment leads to fewer conflicts; high group confidence near the end of the deadline leads to less conflict and increases group performance (Level B).*

   In the early stages of a group project, (too much) confidence can result in fewer conflicts. If there are not enough conflicts early on, there is an increased chance of groupthink. Near the end of a deadline, a high level of trust decreases conflicts and increases performance, because fewer conflicts are needed at the end of project (Goncalo, Polman, & Maslach, 2010).

6. *Concurrence Seeking Behaviour (GTB) as part of groupthink has negative effects on Business Process Reengineering (BPR)* (Riccobono, Bruccoleri, & Größler, 2015) *(Level B).*

What Is the Conclusion?

Fiske (2004) points to the groupthink experiments that failed and the possibly more useful general models of group problem-solving. Having said that, we see a set of studies in the organizational context that resulted in a collection of evidence and relevant insights. The evidence provides insights with regard to the perception of groupthink and the relationship between task and social-emotional cohesion. The evidence also provides insights with regard to the kind of group members and the effect on the quality of decision-making. In addition, the research provides insights with regard to conflicts, group confidence and performance, and the conceptualization of groupthink as a stress-reduction process.

Practical Reflections

Assuming that groupthink can threaten the effectiveness of groups and has the potential to undermine their performance and change programmes, the following counteractive guidelines can be helpful. These guidelines are based on and inspired by the evidence presented. For example, the first part is based on the research of Bernthal and Insko (1993). They state: "As long as the reasons for forming the group are clear and the group follows procedures designed to counteract the possibility of groupthink, high levels of social-emotional cohesion should not present a problem" (p. 85). As a guideline: be clear on the reasons for forming the group and set clear group goals. Assign the role of devil's advocate in a group (on a rotating basis) and use a critical reviewer when making important group decisions. Do not allow individuals to express their preferences in advance and plan open sessions to reconsider alternatives. Stimulate honest consideration of all alternatives before making a final decision. Form subgroups to allow a more detailed discussion and discuss group ideas with people outside the group. Invite experts to regularly and actively join group meetings. It must be noted that having high group cohesion does not necessarily mean that groupthink lurks around every corner. The research indicates that particularly when the task cohesion is low and the social cohesion is high, groupthink can become a dangerous force to be reckoned with.

Notes

1. This text is based on and partly earlier published in 'Reconsidering Change Management: Applying Evidence-Based Insights in Change Management Practice' (2016).
2. This text is based on and partly earlier published in 'Reconsidering Change Management: Applying Evidence-Based Insights in Change Management Practice' (2016, p. 87).
3. This text and the REA were published previously in Ten Have et al., 2016, p. 125–131. The research was conducted by L. Millenaar MSc.

7 Self-Enhancing, Organizational Behaviour and Change

A First Short Story of Understanding and Change

Human beings strive for internal consistency in order to function mentally in the real world. Cognitive dissonance is a form of mental discomfort or psychological stress that is experienced by a human being who simultaneously holds two or more contradictory beliefs, ideas, convictions or values. The discomfort or stress that results from the internal inconsistency motivates people to reduce the cognitive dissonance. By fulfilling the need to protect self-integrity in the face of threat, self-affirmations can enable people to deal with threatening events and information without resorting to defensive biases. People seek to maintain views of their social systems—and their attendant norms, rules and social structures—as relatively legitimate, even when confronted with information suggesting the opposite. To enhance self, people may interpret, distort or ignore the information coming from social comparison in order to see themselves more positively. Self-guides like the actual, ought and ideal self guide behaviour and may lead to experienced discrepancies. People can have prevention or promotion focus; analysing this helps to understand or predict what people avoid or approach. 'Present others' may cause an increase in the likelihood of highly accessible responses of people and a decrease in the likelihood of less accessible responses. Positive interpersonal stimuli like praise, a compliment, a smile, touch or even attention can reinforce behaviour, as a positive reaction followed the behaviour. People desire to view themselves in a positive light. As a result, self-esteem is often the result of, or the compromise between, self-evaluation and self-enhancement. Human beings seek confirmation of their self-concept, whether it is positive or negative. This may lead to a clash between delusion and truth, belief and fact; between the affective goal and related need to self-enhance and the cognitive goal and need to have an accurate self-view.

Self-enhancing, the need for viewing self as basically worthy or improvable, is the fifth core social motive and one of the two (relatively) affective motives (the other is trusting). Self-enhancement "involves either maintaining self-esteem or being motivated by the possibility of self-improvement . . ., people like to feel good about themselves. . . . People feel instantly good when they receive positive feedback about themselves", says Fiske (2004, p. 22). Also, self-enhancement helps to maintain the group and the group has the potential to enhance self. Social exclusion makes people feel bad and can lead to social and self-destructive behaviours; social inclusion will stimulate the opposite. Organizational and change contexts have to facilitate self-enhancement to increase effectiveness. Leaders, managers and change agents have to be aware of the need and potential of self-enhancement. Self-enhancing is related to change and management topics like change vision, change capacity, commitment and resistance to change, cooperation, leadership and culture.

In this chapter the following theories and concepts are presented and assessed:

Cognitive dissonance—
Self-affirmation—
System justification—
Social comparison theory—
Self-discrepancy—
Social facilitation—
Social reinforcement theory—
Self-esteem—
Self-verification theory

Cognitive Dissonance Theory

What Is Cognitive Dissonance?

The inventor of cognitive dissonance theory, Leon Festinger (1957), proposed that human beings strive for internal consistency in order to function mentally in the real world: "Cognitive dissonance can be seen as an antecedent condition which leads to activity oriented toward dissonance reduction just as hunger leads to activity oriented toward hunger reduction. It is a very different motivation from what psychologists are used to dealing with but, as we shall see, nonetheless powerful" (p. 3). Cognitions can be relevant or irrelevant. Relevant cognitions can be consonant or dissonant. Cognitive dissonance is a form of mental discomfort or psychological stress that is experienced by a human being who simultaneously holds two or more contradictory beliefs, ideas, convictions or values. The discomfort or stress that results from the internal inconsistency motivates people to reduce the cognitive dissonance. Dissonance is a twofold concept: "Dissonance describes both the perceived incongruity and the discomfort predicted to result: people feel tense, aroused and uneasy from salient, self-involving incongruities. This state of dissonance comes from the ratio of dissonant to consonant cognitions" (Fiske, 2004, p. 232).

Strategies to reduce the cognitive dissonance are: change the behaviour or the cognition, justify the behaviour or the cognition by adding new cognitions, and ignore or deny information that conflicts with existing beliefs. Festinger's 'consistent psychology' as a necessary condition to function is also visible in the tendency of people to categorize other people in terms of, for example, social background, gender and race to manage their social interactions (see: Duckitt, 1992). Elliot and Devine (1994) state that most empirical research investigating the motivational properties of cognitive dissonance has focused on the arousal component of dissonance rather than on the psychological component explicitly delineated by Festinger. The results of their two experiments support Festinger's conceptualization of cognitive dissonance as a fundamentally motivational state. It is shown that positive social behaviours can be promoted by using cognitive dissonance. In an experimental setting, Stone, Aronson, Crain, Winslow, and Fried (1994) applied cognitive dissonance theory to the problem of AIDS prevention among sexually active young adults: "Dissonance was created after a pro-attitudinal advocacy by inducing hypocrisy-having subjects publicly advocate the importance of safe sex and then systematically making the subjects mindful of their own past failures to use condoms. It was predicted that the induction of hypocrisy would motivate subjects to reduce dissonance by purchasing condoms at the completion of the experiment. The results showed that more subjects in the hypocrisy condition bought condoms and also bought more condoms, on average, than subjects in the control conditions" (p. 116). Cognitive dissonance shows that actions can affect attitudes: making a choice or undertaking an action can lead a person to develop an increased preference over time for the chosen alternative. In summary, cognitive dissonance theory is based on three fundamental assumptions: (1) humans are sensitive to inconsistencies between actions and beliefs; (2) recognition of this inconsistency will cause dissonance, and will motivate an individual to resolve the dissonance; and (3) dissonance will be resolved in one of three basic ways: change beliefs, change actions and change perceptions of action.

What Is the Relevance of Cognitive Dissonance for Organization and Change?

Human beings strive for internal psychological consistency, in order to function mentally in the real world. A person's own actions or the confrontation with new information may lead to mental discomfort when these contradict that person's personal beliefs, values, ideals and convictions. Experienced internal inconsistency and the resulting discomfort, being psychologically uncomfortable, may motivate a person to deploy a defensive strategy in order to reduce cognitive dissonance. People make change to justify their stressful behaviour; they have the ambition to interpret the past and present in a way congenial to its desires and needs

(Greenwald, 1980). The concept of cognitive dissonance is relevant and helpful in the context of organization and change. Cognitive dissonance may be an explanation for resistance to change, as the reduction of dissonance can be a solution to resistance.

The reduction of cognitive dissonance can be an element of a change strategy and may enhance change capacity. The reduction can be helpful if not conditional for the development of teams, cooperation and commitment. The concept provides leaders with useful guidelines for the way they design their change vision and communicate about the change.

Search Strategy

Relevant databases were searched using the terms 'cognitive' and 'dissonance', also in combination with 'meta-analysis' or 'systematic review'. The search yielded more than 400 articles. After screening the titles and abstracts for relevance, seventeen studies met the inclusion criteria. After thorough examination, three studies were excluded.

Main Findings

1. *Emotional dissonance has a negative effect on job satisfaction, organizational citizenship behaviour, organizational commitment and organizational identification (Level D-).*

    Multiple cross-sectional studies show that emotional dissonance has negative effects on multiple factors that have detrimental effects on organizations and presumably on organizational change. These factors are job satisfaction (Abraham, 1999b; Lewig & Dollard, 2003), organizational citizenship behaviour (Cheung & Cheung, 2013), organizational commitment (Abraham, 1999b) and organizational identification (Mishra & Bhatnagar, 2010).

2. *Emotional dissonance has a positive effect on burnout rate, (emotional) exhaustion and turnover intention (Level D-).*

    Several studies show that emotional dissonance has positive effects on multiple factors that have detrimental effects for both employee and employer as well as organizational change. These factors are burnout rate (Baker & Heuven, 2006; Carrasco, Martínez-Tur, Moliner, Pieró, & Ramis, 2014; Cheung & Tang, 2007; Cheung & Cheung, 2013; Diestel & Schmidt, 2010; Heuven & Bakker, 2003; Karatepe, 2011), (emotional) exhaustion (Abraham, 1999a; Bakker & Heuven, 2006; Cheung & Cheung, 2013; Heuven & Bakker, 2003; Karatepe, 2011; Lewig & Dollard, 2003; Mishra & Kumar, 2016) and turnover intention (Abraham, 1999b; Mishra & Bhatnagar, 2010; Mishra & Kumar, 2016).

What Is the Conclusion?

Emotional dissonance, a part of cognitive dissonance, has many negative effects for employees, employers, everyday running of the organization and organizational change. The evidence points in the same direction: (emotional) dissonance of employees can be detrimental; dealing with it in the right way is critical.

Practical Reflections

Based on the studies, a set of guidelines for practitioners can be formulated. Several included studies give multiple guidelines on how to deal with (emotional) dissonance: reduce emotional dissonance at work by exceeding organizational requirements and letting employees act in a manner that conforms to their own experienced emotions. Provide training for employees in which techniques are taught to facilitate the use of genuine emotions in the workplace. Use deep acting to achieve this. Training on how to cope with emotionally demanding jobs or interactions is also very useful. Provide training for supervisors to learn how to provide assistance to employees coping with emotional dissonance and disengagement. Strengthen the available resources on the shop floor by the use of appropriate rewards and benefits, career opportunities, lifetime employment and job security. Intrinsic job rewards such as compliments for certain achievements are also important. Create social networks and encourage employees to take part in more (team) activities or gatherings to enhance the overall morale. Finally, make use of periodic staff opinion surveys to understand problems employees may have.

Self-Affirmation

By fulfilling the need to protect self-integrity in the face of threat, self-affirmations can enable people to deal with threatening events and information without resorting to defensive biases.

What Is Self-Affirmation?

The fifth core social motive is self-enhancing. Fiske (2010) describes this motive as 'the need for viewing self as basically worthy or improvable'. When people are faced with setbacks and disappointments of daily life, with changes or with failure, sustaining self-integrity often is a major undertaking (Sherman & Cohen, 2006). In those situations, the view of oneself as worthy comes under pressure. A lot of research suggests that people have a 'psychological immune system' to cope with this pressure (Gilbert, Pinel, Wilson, Blumberg, & Wheatley, 1998). This system is based on cognitive strategies and even distortions focused on altering the meaning of an event in such a way that the conclusion is that their beliefs or actions were misguided. An example of such a defensive adaptation is provided by the theory of cognitive dissonance (Festinger, 1957, 1962). Some of these defensive responses indeed directly reduce the threat to self-integrity and are adaptive. However, they come with a price; they may forestall learning from important experiences and they may threaten the integrity of their relationships with others (e.g. Murray, Holmes, MacDonald, & Ellsworth, 1998). An alternative way that reduces or even eliminates the dependence on defensive adaptations can be found in the process of self-affirmation (Sherman & Cohen, 2006). Interventions based on this alternative perspective typically bring about a more expansive view of the self and its resources, weakening the implications of a threat for personal integrity (Cohen & Sherman, 2014). Steele (1988) first proposed the theory of self-affirmation: "It asserts that the overall goal of the self-system is to protect an image of self-integrity, of its moral and adaptive adequacy. When this image of self-integrity is threatened, people respond in such a way as to restore self-worth . . . one way that this is accomplished is through defensive responses that directly reduce the threat. But another way is through the affirmation of alternative sources of self-integrity. Such 'self-affirmations', by fulfilling the need to protect self-integrity in the face of threat, can enable people to deal with threatening events and information without resorting to defensive biases" (Sherman & Cohen, 2006, p. 185). An important premise of self-affirmation theory is that people are motivated to maintain self-integrity (Sherman & Cohen, 2002). When confronted with a threat, people can choose to accommodate to that threat or to deploy a defensive strategy (e.g. denying or avoiding the threat). Self-affirmation provides an alternative and the third way. Whereas defensive strategies are direct psychological adaptations, self-affirmation uses the indirect psychological adaptation of affirming self-resources unrelated to the provoking threat (Sherman & Cohen, 2006). Steele (1988) teaches that although people try to maintain specific self-images (like being a good mother or team member), that is not their primary motivation. Above all, individuals prove to be motivated to maintain *global* self-integrity, a global perception of their goodness, virtue and efficacy. An important point is that there is some fungibility or exchangeability in the sources of self-integrity. Self-affirmation, with its interventions, builds on that. A relative positive feeling in one domain may make people more willing and able to tolerate a threat to their self-integrity in another domain. Interventions or self-affirmations include "reflecting on important aspects of one's life irrelevant to the threat, or engaging in an activity that makes salient important values unconnected to the threatening event" (Sherman & Cohen, 2006, p. 186). The theory provides a basis to reinterpret classic research findings in cognitive dissonance. Seen from the perspective of cognitive dissonance, people have a basic motivation for psychological consistency. This leads them in the case of inconsistency to change attitudes in order to align them with past behaviour. They do this by using forms of rationalization and self-justification. However, Steele (1988) demonstrated that when people are provided with the alternative of self-affirmation, being able to affirm their self-integrity in an alternative domain, the rationalization effect disappears: "For example, when people were given the opportunity to express the importance of a cherished personal value (e.g. when science students were allowed to don a white lab coat, or when people who valued aesthetics were allowed to assert their love of art), these individuals did not defensively change their attitudes to make them concordant with their behaviour" (Cohen et al., 2007, p. 788). Self-affirmation has four basic tenets (Sherman & Cohen, 2006, pp. 187–189): (1) people are motivated to protect the perceived integrity and worth of self, (2) motivations to protect self-integrity can result in defensive responses, (3) the self-system is flexible and (4) people can be affirmed by engaging in activities that remind them of 'who they are' (and doing so reduces the implications for self-integrity of threatening events).

What Is the Relevance of Self-Affirmation for Organization and Change?

Change may put the view of oneself as worthy under pressure. It is suggested that people have a 'psychological immune system' to cope with this pressure. Demetriades and Walter (2016) state: "When faced with information that challenges a person's integrity or self-worth—highlighting discrepancies between desired and actual behaviour, identifying contradictions in beliefs or emphasizing ignorance—the self-system is activated to diminish the threat. Often this occurs through maladaptive biases that rationalize, skew or reject the perception of the threat so that it appears less relevant or severe" (p. 1132). Self-affirmation provides a more positive and constructive alternative. Compared with more defensive strategies, it does not threaten the integrity of social relations and reduces the risk that one does not learn under pressure or in situations of change. Because it enables people to deal with threatening events and information in a more positive way, it relates to change factors such as commitment, cooperation, change capacity, culture and resistance. The strategy of self-affirmation may help change leaders and agents in designing and developing a stimulating organizational climate and a leadership style that is more constructive and sensitive. To emphasize the importance of this, Kriegel and Brandt (1996) states: "Offer respect, understanding and acknowledgement and you'll foster incredible loyalty, enough to propel you through incremental or transformative organizational change" (p. 185).

Search Strategy

Relevant databases were searched using the term 'self-affirmation'. The search yielded more than 489 articles. After screening the titles and abstracts for relevance, only four studies met the inclusion criteria (A-, A-, B, E).

Main Findings

1. *Self-affirmation is effective in increasing knowledge through information-seeking and interpersonal discussion (Level B).*

   "Self-affirmation induces a motivation to seek information and engage in interpersonal discussion with others". "Interpersonal discussion and information-seeking facilitate enhanced issue-relevant knowledge". (Demetriades & Walter, 2016; Level B).

2. *Providing employees with opportunities to affirm themselves in a positive manner will help eliminate negative outcomes which accompany layoffs (Level A).*

   "The present findings suggest that the negative effects of unfairness were reduced when individuals engaged in self-reaffirmation. Self-reaffirmation did not alter the perceived level of fairness, but it apparently influenced the implications of individuals' fairness perceptions for their self-integrity" (Wiesenfeld, Brockner, & Martin, 1999, Level A).

   "There is a clear indication that maintaining an open dialogue with employees and providing them with opportunities to affirm themselves in a positive manner will help to eliminate some of the negative outcomes which accompany layoffs" (Petzall, Parker, & Stoeberl, 2000, p. 601; Level E).

   "Organizing the survivors into work teams, where they can develop new loyalty bonds to the other members of their team, is one approach to weather the turbulent period. Another approach would be to design jobs that are inherently challenging, thereby enriching the individual workers and rewarding superior performance" (Petzall et al., 2000, p. 601; Level E).

3. *Self-affirmation has a positive effect on de-escalation of commitment (Level A).*

   "Self-affirmations can be a practical psychological vehicle to help prevent escalation of commitment to failing courses of action" (Sivanathan, Molden, Galinsky, & Ku, 2008, p. 13; Level A).

   "If properly implemented, self-affirmation mechanisms could provide an important avenue in mitigating the grave costs to individuals and organizations that result from throwing good time and money after bad" (Sivanathan et al., 2008, p. 13; Level A).

What Is the Conclusion?

The evidence shows that self-affirmation is not only a relevant alternative strategy (for the more defensive ones) with potential, as such and in the context of management and change, but it also stimulates information-seeking and interpersonal discussion and thereby the increase of relevant knowledge. It also helps to prevent escalation of commitment to failing courses of action. Last but not least, self-affirmation opportunities for employees contribute to the elimination of negative consequences of layoffs. When organizations implement layoffs, "they should do so in ways that are minimally disruptive to the employees who remain. One way is by ensuring that the layoffs are perceived as fair" (Weisenfeld, Brockner, & Martin, 1999, p. 457).

Practical Reflections

One could say that self-affirmation theory states the obvious regarding organizational change. It claims that communication, transparency and trust are important factors, given their potential to reduce the threats or disruptiveness that often accompany change. But in daily practice these factors are easily overlooked. Self-affirmation shows that there is an alternative for defensive strategies to changes and threats.

System Justification

People seek to maintain views of their social systems—and their attendant norms, rules and social structures—as relatively legitimate, even when confronted with information suggesting the opposite.

What Is System-Justification Theory?

System-justification theory, like social dominance theory, grew out of a critique of social identity theory (the critique related more to deficiencies in the social identity research than to deficiencies in the theory itself) (Rubin & Hewstone, 2004). Fifteen years after the introduction of the theory (Jost & Banaji, 1994), Kay and Friesen (2011) concluded that research from the perspective of system-justification theory has demonstrated that people engage in motivated psychological processes that bolster and support the status quo. They state: "Humans are a deeply social and interdependent species. Virtually everyone is embedded within social systems—from companies, community organizations and universities to broader societies such as one's city or country. Although many of these systems may function quite well, it is unlikely any are perfect. Recent theory and research under the umbrella of system-justification theory (Jost & Banaji, 1994), however, suggest that people seek to maintain views of their social systems—and their attendant norms, rules and social structures—as relatively legitimate, even when confronted with information suggesting the opposite" (p. 360). Jost and Banaji proposed that stereotypes operate to serve system justification; the psychology of legitimizing current social arrangements, even at personal and group cost (Fiske, 2004). Depending on the status of a group, these costs will vary. Fiske (2004) teaches: "For high-status groups, supporting the self (ego justification), the group (group justification) and the system all are compatible processes. But for low-status groups, system justification operates at the expense of the other two" (p. 446). Kay and Friesen (2011) consider the motivated psychological processes that bolster and support the status quo to be highly contextual. Groups and individuals do not justify their social systems at all times but are more likely to do so under certain circumstances. Kay and Friesen distinguish four categories of 'circumstances' or contexts in which groups and individuals are prone to engage in system-justifying processes: system threat, system dependence, system inescapability and low personal control. In these contexts, leaders and change agents who wish to promote social change might expect resistance.

Jost, Banaji, and Nosek (2004) point out that most theories in social psychology stress topics such as self-interest, intergroup conflict, in-group bias, out-group antipathy, dominance and resistance. System-justification theory is influenced by these theories, including the social identity and social dominance theories mentioned previously, but it departs from them in several respects. They explain: "Advocates of system justification theory argue that (a) there is a general ideological motive to justify the existing social order, (b) this motive is at least partially responsible for the internalization of inferiority among members of disadvantaged groups, (c) it is observed most readily at an implicit, non-conscious level of awareness and (d) paradoxically, it is sometimes strongest among those who are most harmed by the status quo" (p. 881). System-justification theory also draws on the logic of cognitive dissonance. This logic is the basis for the strongest form of the theory's hypothesis that people are motivated to preserve the belief that existing social arrangements are fair, legitimate, justifiable and necessary (Jost, Pelham, Sheldon, & Ni Sullivan, 2003). This is described as follows: "people who are most disadvantaged by the status quo would have the greatest psychological need to reduce ideological dissonance and would therefore be most likely to support, defend and justify existing social systems, authorities and outcomes" (p. 13). Jost et al. (2003) note the following with regard to the research related to the hypothesis: "Taken together, these findings are consistent with the dissonance-based argument that people who suffer the most from a given state of affairs are paradoxically the least likely to question, challenge, reject or change it. Implications for theories of system justification, cognitive dissonance and social change are also discussed" (p. 13). Jost and Hunyady (2003) also point to the possible palliative function as a reason for people to engage in system justification. They propose that system-justifying ideologies, in particular in the case of conflicts with other interest and motives, "serve a palliative function in that they reduce anxiety, guilt, dissonance, discomfort and uncertainty for those who are advantaged and disadvantaged" (p. 111). By defining specific hypotheses, Jost and Hunyady relate system justification to, among other things, the rationalization of the status quo, the internalization of inequality (out-group favouritism and depressed entitlement), and relationships among ego, group and system-justification motives, including consequences for attitudinal ambivalence, self-esteem and psychological well-being. System justification can also be related to the concept of shared reality. Jost, Ledgerwood, and Hardin (2008) integrate system justification and shared reality theories "to propose that ideologies may function as prepackaged units of interpretation that spread because of basic human motives to understand the world, avoid existential threat and maintain valued interpersonal relationships" (p. 171). Based on the evidence, Jost et al. suggest that affiliative motives may influence ideological beliefs to align with the progressive or conservative views shared within a given relationship or group. System-justification theory provides a perspective which helps to understand social arrangements, hierarchies and differences in status within and between groups, and their justification. Related to this, Fiske (2004) points to society's status beliefs (Ridgeway, 2001) as a way to understand and organize cooperation across unequal groups (e.g. traditional gender roles). Related to this is the social dominance orientation (SDO), one's degree of preference for inequality among social groups. Research into social dominance shows that high-SDO people seek hierarchy-enhancing professional roles and low-SDO people seek hierarchy-attenuating roles. In addition, it was shown that SDO was related to beliefs in a large number of social and political ideologies that support group-based hierarchy and to support for policies that have implications for intergroup relations (Pratto, Sidanius, & Stallworth, 1994). Related to SDO are 'legitimating myths', ideologies that intellectually and morally justify the superiority of high-status groups in the existing social structure (Sidanius, Levin, Federico, & Pratto, 2001).

What Is the Relevance of System Justification for Organization and Change?

System-justification theory provides a very insightful perspective that helps to understand organizational behaviour and change in organizations. It contributes to the understanding of motives and dynamics in and between groups. From the perspective of organization and change, it is particularly relevant for topics like resistance to change, commitment, cooperation, communication, organizational culture(s) and change vision. The palliative function of system justification not only helps to further understand the reasons for resistance, but it is also insightful for the ones who have to lead the change.

Search Strategy

Relevant databases were searched using the terms 'justification theory' and 'justification' in combination with 'organization', 'employees' and 'theory'. The search yielded more than 200 articles. After screening the titles and abstracts for relevance, two studies were included. A literature search technique called 'snowballing' was used to strengthen the research, identifying two additional studies.

Main Findings

1. *System-justification hinders organizational change when communicating a sense of organizational crisis (Level C-).*

   "Stemming from the basic idea that people have a desire to defend and legitimize the current state of affairs, research emerging from SJT demonstrates that, generally, because deviations from the status quo are psychologically threatening, they are unlikely to be supported, especially in contexts where people's system justification motive is heightened, such as when their system is faced with external threats to its legitimacy" (Proudfoot & Kay, 2014, p. 176).

2. *System-justification motives are capable of overriding ego—and group justification motives (Level C-).*

   The motives for system justification can be so strong that they override the ego and group justification motives which are associated with the protection of both individual and collective interests and esteem (Jost, Banaji, & Nosek, 2004).

3. *System justification is a significant barrier in achieving equal opportunity in an organizational context (e.g. race, colour, religion, sex, age and sexual orientation) (Level C-).*

   System justification fosters resistance to policies that attenuate hierarchy and organizations that put such policies into practice. Furthermore, the people who strongly believe the system is fair are also likely to resist progressive action that actually is beneficial for the world they believe in (Phelan & Rudman, 2011).

What Is the Conclusion?

Based on the research with regard to system justification and social change, it can be concluded that the theory is very relevant and useful for the field of management and change. More specific evidence adds to this conclusion. The research shows that system justification may hinder organizational change and helps to explain resistance to change and how motives on the system, group and individual level interact with one another in social contexts.

Practical Reflections

In managing change, leaders and change agents have to be aware of the phenomenon of system justification and the underlying mechanisms and its possible consequences. Understanding the concept may motivate leaders and change agents not to take reactions to change initiatives at face value, particularly when those reactions come from people lower in the hierarchy. System justification helps to understand why and how, and by whom, the dynamics of change are sometimes thwarted by the stability in insights, hierarchy and positions desired by individuals and groups involved.

Social Comparison Theory

To enhance self, people may interpret, distort or ignore the information coming from social comparison in order to see themselves more positively.

What Is Social Comparison Theory?

Social comparison is about the comparison of self with others. Leon Festinger (1954) was the one who coined the term *social comparison* and the one who proposed a systematic theory. Suls and Wheeler (2013) point to the fact that the concept has been in circulation since we have had social philosophers and social scientists. With regard to self-understanding stemming from comparison, Aristotle was already concerned with comparisons among people, as were Bentham, Rousseau and Kant. Marx was also aware of the power of social comparisons: "A house may be large or small. As long as the surrounding houses are equally small, it satisfies all social demands for a dwelling. But let a palace reside beside the little house, and it shrinks from a little house to a hut" (quoted by Useem, 1975, p. 53). Festinger's very first research dealt with social factors affecting levels of aspiration (Hertzman & Festinger; 1940; Festinger, 1942). This research showed that: "subjects would lower their aspirations if they found themselves above group average and raise their aspirations if they scored below the group average. Moreover, the status of the group made a difference. The undergraduate participants raised their level of aspiration the most when they had scored below high school students, and they lowered their level of aspiration the most when they had scored above graduate students" (Suls & Wheeler, 2013, p. 4). The following research culminated in an earlier theory of Festinger (1950), that of informal social communication. This theory posited that: "people in groups desire to attain uniformity of opinion either because group consensus provides confidence in one's own opinion or because agreement was needed to coordinate group goals" (Suls & Wheeler, 2013, p. 4). In 1954 Festinger's new theory of social comparison followed. In the theory of informal social communication, the emphasis was on the power of the group over the individual. The theory of social comparison focused on the way individuals use groups to fulfil the information needed to evaluate their abilities and opinion. So, this theory is not only about whether opinions are correct, but also about what people's abilities allow them to do (Suls & Wheeler, 2012). Social comparison leads to pressures toward uniformity: in the case of opinions, because agreement with others makes us feel more confident with regard to our own opinions; in the case of abilities, the comparison with others with similar abilities gives sight of our possibilities for action in a certain context. Suls and Wheeler (2012) emphasize the 'unidirectional drive upward for abilities', which does not exist for opinions; complete opinion agreement will satisfy everyone, whereas completely equal abilities within a group will satisfy no one. As Festinger states: "The pressures cease acting on a person if he is just slightly better than the others. It is obvious that not everyone in a group can be slightly better than everyone else. The implication is that, with respect to the evaluation of abilities, a state of social quiescence is never reached" (1954, p. 125). Thornton and Arrowood (1966) described two different motivations that may operate in the process of social comparison: self-evaluation and self-enhancement. Self-evaluation leads people to choose a comparison target that is quite similar to them; they compare with someone who exemplifies the trait ('a positive instance') (Wood, 1989; Suls & Wheeler, 2012). When the purpose of social comparison is self-enhancement instead, people may not choose a comparison target that is similar to them. They address this motivation by asking: "How far am I from the best-off person?" To enhance self, people may interpret, distort or ignore the information coming from social comparison in order to see themselves more positively. For example, if a chosen comparison target proves to outperform someone, one may downplay the similarity between target and oneself. This relates to Festinger's theory of cognitive dissonance (1957). Further theoretical developments identified four self-evaluation motives, self-enhancement being one of them together with self-assessment, self-verification and self-improvement (Taylor, Neter, & Wayment, 1995). Social comparison further developed with the concept of downward comparison described by Wills (1981) in an integrative theory paper. Suls and Wheeler (2012) point out that this "undoubtedly caused a shift from accurate self-evaluation to concerns about self-enhancement" (p. 9). Downward comparison is seen as a way of coping, thereby relating social comparison not only to the core social motive of self-enhancing, but also to the motive of controlling.

Downward comparison is present when people look at or are exposed to others they consider to be worse off than themselves and as a result of the comparison feel better about themselves or their own situations. Wood, Taylor, and Lichtman (1985) showed that when cancer patients were interviewed, they voiced spontaneous comparisons and that a large majority of the comparisons were with patients who were less fortunate. The study also identified the coping function of social comparison. The counterpart of downward comparison is upward comparison. Whereas the first can elevate self-regard and subjective well-being, the second may lead to lower self-regard. However, this is not always the case. People may compare upward in order to improve their self-image or to create a more positive perception of their personal reality (Collins, 1996). In the case of upward comparison, people may associate with similarities of an elite or higher-positioned group. In the case of a downward comparison, people will focus on disassociating from similarities of the comparison group (Suls, Marin, & Wheeler, 2002). In the case of the cancer patients, we see passive downward comparison. In the case of active downward comparison, people derogate the comparison target or cause harm to the target. In this way, a situation is generated in which the target is worse off and a chance to make a downward comparison is created. Regarding the role of similarity in social comparison, Goethals and Darley (1977) provide additional insights. If the goal is to increase confidence for value judgments, people prefer to compare with others who are similar in terms of opinions, characteristics or abilities. However, if the goal is to validate one's beliefs, people prefer to compare with people who are dissimilar.

What Is the Relevance of Social Comparison for Organization and Change?

In the organizational context, social comparison is strongly related to team development, cooperation, culture and commitment. Bartel (2001) is very clear: "Social comparisons are an important means through which people come to understand their identities as organization members" (p. 379). There is extensive and varied research on the effects of social comparison, in the context of management and organization with regard to, for example, performance, organizational citizenship behaviour and job satisfaction. Greenberg, Ashton-James, and Ashkanasy (2007) state that social comparison processes are embedded in most social interaction. For the organizational (psychological) context they identify six particular topics of interest: organizational justice, performance appraisal, virtual work environments, affective behaviour in the workplace, stress and leadership. Greenberg et al. (2007) say: "Our assertion that fully understanding human behaviour in the workplace requires appreciating social comparison is far from hyperbole" (p. 38). They note that the role of social comparison is clear (explicitly or implicitly in the relevant studies) with regard to organizational practices such as performance appraisal and fundamental psychological processes in organizations such as perceiving fairness and experiencing affect. Greenberg et al. (2007) also point out that for a topic like leadership, social comparison processes have largely gone unacknowledged.

Search Strategy

Relevant databases were searched using the term 'social comparison', and 'social comparison' in combination with 'work', 'change', 'employee' and 'organization'. In total, we found more than 300 studies. After reading the abstracts, nineteen studies were included. After critically appraising these studies, another eight were excluded. Of the included studies, one used a randomized, controlled, before-after measurement method (Level A).

Main Findings

1. *Social comparison feedback is more effective than objective feedback for high performers, but objective feedback is more effective than social comparison for low performers (Level A).*

   Individuals who perform well can further increase their performance when making use of social comparison feedback. For individuals who perform poorly, objective feedback is more helpful to increase their performance. This might be explained by the punishing effect social comparison can have when performing poorly and the social comparison is upward. Social comparison can even be harmful, as in some cases it had a negative effect on the performance of the low performers. The high performers all benefitted from social comparison (Moon, Lee, Lee, & Oah, 2017).

2. *Upward social comparison is negatively related to job satisfaction and affective (organizational) commitment, but downward social comparison is positively related to job satisfaction and affective (organizational) commitment (Level C).*

   In this interrupted time series study, downward social comparison seems to be more effective as it may increase job satisfaction and affective commitment. Upward social comparison, on the other hand, is negatively related to job satisfaction and affective commitment (Brown, Ferris, Heller, & Keeping, 2007).

3. *Upward social comparison positively affected organizational commitment, whereas downward social comparison positively impacted job satisfaction (Level D-).*

   This study found the opposite effect of commitment in comparison with the foregoing study, because upward social comparison has a positive effect on organizational commitment. Downward social comparison has a positive effect on job satisfaction (Foley, Ngo, & Loi, 2016).

4. *Downward comparison decreases levels of burnout, whereas upward comparison increased levels of burnout (Level D-).*

   Upward social comparison seems to give more stress, emotional exhaustion and cynicism, therefore increasing the levels of burnout. Downward comparison, on the other hand, lowers these variables, decreasing the levels of burnout (Halbesleben & Buckley, 2006).

5. *Individuals have more positive affect after downward comparison and more negative affect after upward comparison (Level E).*

   In these studies in a hospital setting, nurses had a more positive affect after downward comparison. Furthermore, they tend to feel happy when seeing colleagues perform in an outstanding manner, and tend to feel worried when seeing colleagues perform poorly (Buunk, Zurriaga, & Peiró, 2010). However, when individuals perceive the social climate as cooperative, they have more positive affect after upward comparison and more negative affect after downward comparison (Buunk et al., 2005).

6. *Downward social comparison has a positive effect on OCB, while upward social comparison has a negative effect on OCB (Level E).*

   OCB, or organizational citizenship behaviour, is extra-role performance. This can be increased by downward social comparison. Upward social comparison decreases this behaviour (Spence, Brown, & Heller, 2011).

7. *A focal firm enjoys a greater increase in sales compared with a more reputable firm and avoids comparison with a less reputable firm (Level E).*

   This finding shows that upward comparison can lead to more sales when firms compare themselves with a more reputable firm, even when consumers have a different opinion about which is the more reputable firm (Kim & Tsai, 2012).

What Is the Conclusion?

Social comparison is a well-researched concept with clear relevance for the organizational context and change. There is clear specific evidence with regard to social comparison and organizational behaviour; multiple studies report effects relating to social comparison. First, there is a difference between upward and downward comparison, and the effects of these two types of comparison. All studies that reported effects of downward comparison are beneficial for the organization. Downward comparison has a positive effect on commitment, job satisfaction, positive affect and

OCB. Furthermore, downward comparison decreases the burnout rate of employees. The effects of upward social comparisons are more ambiguous. Multiple studies report negative correlations between upward social comparison and factors such as job satisfaction, commitment and negative affect. Upward social comparison also increases the burnout rate of employees. However, one study (with a low level of evidence) reported a positive relationship between upward social comparison and commitment. The question remains whether upward social comparison is beneficial for the organization. At this point, it seems likely that upward social comparison does more harm than good for both employees and the organization as a whole. Greenberg et al. (2007) underscore the relevance and potential as well as the evidence of social comparison in the context of organizational practices and psychological processes in organizations. They make clear that, given the importance of social comparison in organizations and the unleashed potential, further research should be stimulated.

Practical Reflections

Social comparison can be beneficial for organizations, but it is important to use it properly. Most studies found that downward social comparison is beneficial for both employees and organizations, but upward social comparison can be harmful. Furthermore, social comparison tends to be more effective for high performers, while low performers are better off with objective comparison. When comparing the organization with competitors, upward social comparison can be beneficial, as it can increase the sales of local firms. Within organizations, downward social comparison is preferable; between organizations upward social comparison is likely to be the better choice. Managers should be aware that employees use both upward and downward social comparison, and that these forms of comparison have implications for their job satisfaction, commitment, organizational citizenship behaviour, burnout rate and affect. The focus should be on using downward social comparison within an organization, as this is the most beneficial. It is important that managers stimulate and reinforce downward comparison. Foley et al. (2016) state: "Managers who are striving to understand how employees' perceptions of the work environment are related to positive work attitudes can now look to social comparisons to provide some additional insights. For example, when attempting to get to know their subordinates better, managers can ask: 'How do you rate your career progress?' and listen for cues indicating USC* or DSC**" (p. 157).

  * Upward social comparison
 ** Downward social comparison

Self-Discrepancy Theory

Self-guides like the actual, ought and ideal, self guide behaviour and may lead to experienced discrepancies. People can have prevention or promotion focus; analysing this helps to understand or predict what people avoid or approach.

What Is Self-Discrepancy?

Self-discrepancy theory (Higgins, 1987) builds on the notion that people who hold conflicting or incompatible beliefs are likely to experience discomfort. This notion has a long history in (social) psychology and is central in, for example, the theory of cognitive dissonance (Festinger, 1957). The development of the theory was guided by three specific aims: "(a) to distinguish among different kinds of discomfort that people holding incompatible beliefs may experience, (b) to relate different kinds of emotional vulnerabilities systematically to different types of discrepancies that people may possess among their self-beliefs, and (c) to consider the role of both the availability and the accessibility of different discrepancies people may possess in determining the kind of discomfort they are most likely to suffer" (Higgins, 1987, p. 319). The theory is seen as one of the major theories in the social psychology of the self and emotion (Fiske, 2004). Self-discrepancy theory focuses on the impact of self-knowledge on how people feel and behave, and this knowledge is used to fit social standards and adapt to group life. Self-guides are self-state representations, mechanisms that regulate behaviour; they can be described as 'self-directive standards' or 'acquired guides for being'. Three self-guides are the actual self, the ought self and the ideal self. The first is the result of self-perception. The ought self is who people morally should be, following themselves or 'significant others'. Responsibilities are key, if one meets these safeness and security results; if not, then 'punishment' follows. The ideal self represents who you want to be or who others want you to be. Desires, wishes and aspirations are key—if these are met, a feeling of accomplishment and reward results; if not, sadness and disappointment are the results. A prevention focus, avoiding negative consequences, is characteristic for the ought self; a promotion focus, obtaining positive consequences, is characteristic for the ideal self. The theory "proposes that people differ as to which self-guide they are especially motivated to meet. Not everyone is expected to possess all of the self-guides—some may possess only ought self-guides, whereas others may possess only ideal self-guides" (Higgins, 1987, p. 321). Research on self-discrepancy theory shows emotional vulnerabilities as a function of self-knowledge (Higgins, Bond, Klein, & Strauman, 1986). According to the theory, people are motivated to reduce the gap in order to remove inequality in self-guides.

Prevention focus and promotion focus lead to different behavioural patterns for goal achievement (e.g. Shah & Higgins, 1997, 2001). People with a promotion focus are driven to minimize the actual-ideal discrepancy and work on attaining their ideals. Characteristic among others is that they generate many hypotheses and keep them all open, are open to change, may be distracted by competing temptations, and feel more pleasure over gains and less pain over losses. People with a prevention focus are motivated to minimize the actual-ought discrepancy and work to maintain safety and security. These people generate fewer hypotheses and commit to one, prefer stability, resist distraction, and feel more pain over losses and less pleasure over gains (Fiske, 2004). Which of the two regulatory focuses works best is context-dependent or 'contingent'; the one—promotion or prevention—that matches the task means and incentives will be the most effective (Shah, Higgins, & Friedman, 1998). Lee, Aker, and Gardner (2000) learn that independent people, cultures and situations encourage a promotion focus, with ideal self-guides as the dominant factor; their counterparts encourage a prevention focus with ought self-guides as the dominant factor.

What Is the Relevance of Self-Discrepancy for Organization and Change?

Self-discrepancy helps to understand why people struggle with themselves in social contexts and situation, for example in organizations and during organizational change. In times of change, people may experience that the change vision and ambition lead to extra demands and expectations that influence the self-views, in particular the ought self (extra responsibilities) and the ideal self (extra desires and aspirations). This may lead to increased discrepancy and dissonance. This is relevant for both the 'producers' and the 'co-producers' or 'consumers' of change initiatives. Depending on the dynamics of their self-views and their focus (prevention or promotion), people will react in different ways on change and should be approached in different ways. Self-discrepancy relates to change management topics like the already-mentioned change vision, and change capacity, resistance to change, communication, leadership, organizational culture and performance management.

Search Strategy

Relevant databases were searched using the term 'self-discrepancy' and 'self-guides'. The searched yielded 346 articles. After screening the title and abstracts for relevance, six studies met the inclusion criteria; finally, two studies were included.

Main Findings

1. *People who realize their calling experience congruence between their actual self and their ideal self (Level D-).*

   - Results showed that the realization of one's calling in the world of employment affects not only a person's current life satisfaction but also his or her life satisfaction measured sixteen weeks later (Hagmaier & Abele, 2014).
   - The relation between calling and life satisfaction was mediated by self-congruence and engagement orientation (Hagmaier & Abele, 2014).
   - People who have realized their calling appear to experience outer congruence, with reality coming very close to their ideals and inner congruence as well as an engagement orientation playing an important mediating role in the calling—life satisfaction relation (Hagmaier & Abele, 2014).

2. *Self-discrepancies are associated with specific affective states (Level D-).*

   - Self-discrepancies are associated with specific affective states, with the ideal-own self-discrepancy emerging as the most consistent predictor of specific affective states (Barnett, 2017).
   - Sadness was positively associated with the ideal-own self-discrepancy; and joviality, self-assurance, and surprise were negatively associated with the ideal-own self-discrepancy (Barnett, 2017).
   - Serenity was negatively associated with the ideal-other self-discrepancy (Barnett, 2017).
   - Guilt was positively associated with the should-other self-discrepancy, and attentiveness was negatively associated with both the ideal-own and should-own self-discrepancies (Barnett, 2017).

What Is the Conclusion?

Self-discrepancy theory provided additional language to describe, and concepts to understand the way people may react to change, how they can be or are motivated and how resistance to change can be moderated or reduced. Self-views provide a fruitful perspective for management and change. The concepts of prevention focus and promotion focus contribute to the understanding of the way people (may) react to demand and expectations related to change and performance in organizations. The specific evidence provides insightful learnings with regard to affective states and experienced congruence of people in organizational settings.

Practical Reflections

The evidence on self-discrepancy provides a set of possible practical guidelines for leaders and (other) (change) management practitioners. These guidelines for the leader-follower relationship are based on insights provided by research with regard to the counsellor-client relationship. To start, counsellors are encouraged to help identify and foster a client's calling because the realization of this calling will enable the person to experience outer congruence (the fit between a person and his/her environment) and have a positive influence on the person's life satisfaction (Hagmaier & Abele, 2014). In addition, if someone is unable to realize his or her calling, coaches might advise the person to "craft" his or her work to reduce the gap between the ideal and reality, thereby increasing his or her satisfaction (Hagmaier & Abele, 2014). And, counsellors should be aware of a person's inner congruence to achieve longer-lasting life satisfaction (Hagmaier & Abele, 2014). To overcome the gap between knowing one's calling and realizing one's calling, an engagement orientation to happiness might also be a key feature and starting point in counselling interventions (Hagmaier & Abele, 2014; see also Elangovan, Pinder, & Mclean, 2010). The evidence also suggests that attentiveness is related to an individual being closer to who they wish to be and feel obligated to be—that is, related to the own standpoint of self (Barnett, 2017). And, self-focused attention increases critical awareness between real and behavioural standards (Barnett, 2017).

Social Facilitation

'Present others' may cause an increase in the likelihood of highly accessible responses of people and a decrease in the likelihood of less accessible responses.

What Is Social Facilitation?

Social facilitation is about changes in responses of individuals, as a result of the presence of others. The theory of social facilitation helps to understand why we are motivated to do certain tasks and less motivated for others. According to this theory, this presence may cause an increase in the likelihood of highly accessible responses and a decrease in the likelihood of less accessible responses (Smith, Mackie, & Claypool, 2014). A central insight underlying the concept of social facilitation is that of interdependence. The degree of interaction and interdependence will vary depending on the group. Interdependence means that each group member will influence other group members by his or her thoughts, emotions and behaviours (Kelley et al., 1983). Even in the case of minimal interdependence, his or her mere presence can produce arousal. Zajonc (1965) describes this as 'the present other'. Social facilitation can occur as a result of both passive and active 'present others'. The first is called the 'audience effect' (e.g. Dashiell, 1935) and the second the 'co-action effect' (Triplett, 1898; Chen, 1937). The co-action effect can be described as improved task performance as a result of the presence of others doing the same task. Zajonc (1965) developed the stern activation theory. Arousal improves performance of easy, well-learned behaviours (e.g. Aiello & Douthitt, 2001). However, in the case of difficult, novel or more complex tasks, the presence of others may lead to declining performance (e.g. Guerin, 1986). This is called 'social inhibition'. Zajonc (1965) gives an explanation for the apparently contradictory effects related to social facilitation. Key concepts in the explanation he proposes are accessibility, dominant responses and non-dominant responses. Smith et al. (2014) explain accessibility as follows: "Accessible thoughts and feelings are more likely to come to mind than are less accessible ones; similarly, accessible behaviours are more likely to be performed than are less accessible ones" (p. 398). The accessible ones are simple, well learned and highly practised, and were coined by Zajonc as dominant responses. The non-dominant responses are complex or new. Motivation is high when performing an easy task that others observe. Individuals are likely to get positive feedback as a result. Motivation is lower for more difficult tasks because individuals fear making mistakes. Individuals may receive unfavourable feedback from others. Zajonc's idea, his drive hypothesis for social facilitation, that arousal positively influences simple tasks and negatively influences difficult tasks was confirmed by the subsequent research of, among others, the already mentioned Guerin and Aiello and Douthitt. The arousal itself is explained by the concepts of evaluation apprehension and distraction (Geen, 1991; Nijstad, 2013). Evaluation apprehension develops as a result of the presence of others who are in a position to judge us; when we focus on what other people may think of us, arousal is created (Rosenberg, Rosenthal, & Rosnow, 1969). The concept of social facilitation helps to appreciate that the motivation for doing a task is also influenced by how good we *perceive* ourselves to be at the task and whether others are evaluating us.

Distraction is the result of the presence of others that causes us to monitor them, to think about them and to react to them. Distraction is produced by the conflict between a focus on a task and the attention paid or the reaction to others. This may be 'solved' by splitting attention (Baron, 1986). A study by Markus (1978) with regard to the effect of mere presence on social facilitation generated results that are entirely consistent with the so-called drive-construct. Zajonc (1972) states that the presence of others generates arousal because it is a social stimulus that, in contrast to physical stimuli, exerts an influence on the individual that is 'less regular, less systematic, less redundant and therefore much less predictable'.[1] Zajonc (1972) elaborates: "In the presence of others, some degree of alertness or preparedness for the unexpected is generated, not because there is the anticipation of positive or negative incentives, or threat of evaluation, but simply because one never knows what sort of responses—perhaps even novel and unique—might be required for the individual" (p. 16). Markus (1978) emphasizes that the drive theory of social facilitation stands in sharp contrast to many other explanations of social behaviour. These other explanations put cognitive processes in a central position; social behaviour is defined as the result of the type and amount of information available to the individual and his ability to assimilate and operate upon that information. Markus acknowledges that many, in particular complex, forms of social behaviour involve inferences, attributions, judgments, and decisions. However, probably there is also an important part of social behaviour that can be described as occurring at a more fundamental and unmonitored level (Markus, 1978). The effects of social facilitation and the 'present other' of Zajonc can be seen as examples of this.

In addition to Zajonc's activation theory and his drive hypothesis for social facilitation, other activation theories and hypotheses were developed. The evaluation apprehension hypothesis (Henchy & Glass, 1968) was already mentioned; another example is the learned drive hypothesis. This activation hypothesis states that activation only increases when actors feel that the audience, the present other(s), is capable of evaluating their performance (Cottrell, Wack, Sekerak, & Rittle, 1968). With the hypothesis concerning the 'distraction conflict' mentioned earlier and, among other things, 'overload' and the 'feedback loop', explanations shifted from activation to attention (Strauss, 2002). The overload hypothesis builds on the distraction-conflict hypothesis. The explanation focuses on cognitive overload caused by distractors. This overload, instead of arousal, leads to a worse performance of complex tasks and a better performance of simple tasks. The feedback loop hypothesis states that as a result of being observed, being given attention by others, people focus attention on themselves. By doing this, people create self-awareness and evaluate the gap between their actual and anticipated behaviour, which may be the basis for improving performance. Following this feedback loop hypothesis, social facilitation occurs through evaluation. The other perspective is that of mere presence. Based on research, Markus (1978) sees mere presence as 'one of the variables' contributing to social facilitation and influencing people's performance (Markus, 1978). Bond and Titus (1983) performed a meta-analysis of 241 studies of the effects of the presence of others on human task performance and physiology. Bond and Titus concluded that the presence of others heightens an individual's physiological arousal only if the individual is performing a complex task and the presence of others increases the speed of simple task performance and decreases the speed of complex task performance. In addition, they concluded that the presence of others impairs complex performance accuracy and slightly facilitates simple performance accuracy, although the facilitation is vulnerable to the "file drawer problem" of unreported null results, and social facilitation effects are surprisingly unrelated to the performer's evaluation apprehension.

What Is the Relevance of Social Facilitation for Organization and Change?

Social facilitation is a well-researched concept. It considers the presence of others as an influential factor in human (and organizational) behaviour. It helps to understand why we are motivated to do certain tasks and less motivated for others. In the context of organizations and change, social facilitation can be related to, for example, team development, change capacity, performance management, organizational culture and cooperation.

Search Strategy

Relevant databases were searched using the terms 'social facilitation' and 'audience effect'. The search yielded more than 100 articles. After screening the titles and abstracts for relevance, nine studies met the inclusion criteria. After thorough examination, another six studies were excluded. Two of the included studies were meta-analyses.

Main Findings

1. *In a laboratory study, the effect of social facilitation was confirmed: "The pattern of results suggested the operation of a social facilitation effect, as highly skilled, monitored participants keyed more entries than highly skilled, non-monitored participants. The opposite pattern was detected among low-skilled participants. No signs of social loafing were detected among group-monitored participants. Non-monitored workers and members of cohesive groups felt the least stressed" (Aiello & Kolb, 1995, p. 339; Level A-).*

2. A meta-analysis of 241 studies concluded that "(a) the presence of others heightens an individual's physiological arousal only if the individual is performing a complex task; (b) the presence of others increases the speed of simple task performance and decreases the speed of complex task performance; (c) the presence of others impairs complex performance accuracy and slightly facilitates simple performance accuracy, though the facilitation is vulnerable to the 'file drawer problem' of unreported null results; and (d) social facilitation effects are surprisingly unrelated to the performer's evaluation apprehension" (Bond & Titus, 1983, p. 265, Level B-).

3. *A more recent meta-analysis concludes that social presence of others decreases performance of individuals who are negatively oriented,*

and improves performance for individuals who are positively oriented. Furthermore, the researchers found that personality is a more substantial factor than task complexity (Uziel, 2007; Level B-).

What Is the Conclusion?

Social facilitation theory is a strong one, based on evidence at a high level. The specific evidence provides a set of relevant and helpful insights with regard to organizations, organizational behaviour and change. A first example: highly skilled individuals will perform better than low-skilled individuals when monitored. With simple tasks, the presence of others has a positive effect on the speed, but it decreases the speed of complex tasks. In addition, a surprising finding is that Uziel (2007) claims that personality is a more substantial factor than task complexity. When people have positive orientation (extraversion and high self-esteem), they perform better when monitored. People with a negative orientation (neuroticism and low self-esteem) perform worse. Uziel (2007) states: "As hypothesized, positive orientation predisposed individuals to improve their performance under social presence, whereas negative orientation predisposed individuals to experience performance impairment under social presence" (p. 594).

Practical Reflections

For the practice of management and change, being aware that the presence of others has certain effects on performance is important knowledge for managers. Furthermore, the presence of others does not have to be physical. Digital presence is also presence. In these times of rapid digitalization, digital presence will become more dominant. Training employees is always important, but it is essential when they work in groups or there is a presence of others. This not only enhances their skills, but also increases self-esteem, which seems to be more important than the task complexity.

Social Reinforcement Theory

Positive interpersonal stimuli like praise, a compliment, a smile, touch or even attention can reinforce behaviour, as a positive reaction followed the behaviour.

What Is Social Reinforcement?

Social reinforcement, or socially mediated reinforcement (direct reinforcement), involves the delivery of reinforcement that requires the behaviour of another organism. If another person is involved with the function of the behaviour, this would be defined as "social reinforcement", or socially mediated reinforcement. In the case of negative reinforcement, another person or group removes the aversive stimulus (Cooper et al., 2007). Social reinforcement is a form of positive psychology in which a positive interpersonal stimulus is given like praise, a compliment, a smile, touch or even attention. In this way, certain behaviour is reinforced, as a positive reaction followed the behaviour. Within organizations, leadership can be described as a process through which the supervisor structures reinforcement contingencies that modify the behaviour of the subordinates (Sims, 1977). For example, when an employee finishes a project that is beneficial for the organization, his/her manager can use a compliment or praise to reinforce the good behaviour of the individual. Instead, or in combination with (formal) leaders or managers, informal leaders and other 'relevant others' may socially reinforce behaviour. Manz and Sims (1987) note "that a work environment entails many important contingencies that the supervisor does not directly control" (p. 361). They mention the capability of the subordinate to exercise self-management and define this as a substitute for leadership. So, besides social reinforcement from an outside source, the reinforcement can also come from within. Self-reinforcement is closely related to social reinforcement and involves giving yourself positive approval of certain behaviour. A reinforcement contingency is an environmental cue that precedes employee behaviour and also a reward that subsequently reinforces employee behaviour (Manz & Sims, 1987). Fiske (2004) points to the relationship between attraction phenomena and the language and concepts of social learning. Fiske (2004) explains: "In reward theories of attraction, people feel rewarded by people who like them but also by people who make them feel good, agree with them and look good. Indeed, besides the reward power of good looks, liking and agreement, we like people who are merely present when we are rewarded in other ways" (p. 272). For the human being as a social animal, social reinforcement is essential and vital. To function in a healthy and productive way, social beings need recognition in some form. Social reinforcement is crucial for mental and physical health, functioning and performance. Without social reinforcement, people can become depressed or unhealthy, which is detrimental to our everyday functioning and (job) performance. Self-reinforcement can help people to a certain level, but in the end almost everybody needs social reinforcement to fulfil social needs.

What Is the Relevance of Social Reinforcement for Organization and Change?

Social reinforcement provides a way to stimulate (job) performance and to change organizational behaviour. In the context of organization and change, social reinforcement is related to topics such as leadership and organizational culture, teams, commitment and resistance, change capacity, cooperation and communication. It is probably one of the most important instruments of leaders and 'relevant others' in social and organizational contexts. Mourier and Smith (2001) underline the importance of positive, and if necessary other, feedback: "Provide positive recognition when expectations are met and negative consequences when expectations aren't met" (p. 32). Kouznes and Posner (2012) emphasize the importance of appraisal: "People need to know if they're making progress toward the goal or simply marking time. Their motivation to perform a task increases only when they have a challenging goal and receive feedback on their progress" (p. 282).

Search Strategy

Relevant databases were searched using the terms 'social reinforcement' and 'attention', both in combination with 'organization', 'employee', 'work', 'change', 'meta-analysis' or 'systematic review'. The search yielded more than 200 articles. After screening the titles and abstracts for relevance, seventeen studies met the inclusion criteria. After thorough examination, eleven studies were excluded, mostly because of serious methodological flaws. From the perspective of social reinforcement and attention, five relevant studies were selected. Earlier research (ten Have, ten Have, Huijsmans, & Otto, 2016) showed that in the context of organization and change, social reinforcement is strongly related to the concept of 'supervisory support'. Supervisory support is a way to socially reinforce employees because perceived supervisory support is often defined as: "employees' beliefs concerning the extent to which the supervisor values their contribution and cares about their well-being" (Edmondson & Boyer, 2013, p. 2187). The main findings of our earlier research are added.

Main Findings Concerning Social Reinforcement

1. *Positive (social) reinforcement has a positive impact on the quality of the performance of employees (Level B).*

    Researchers found that giving positive (social) reinforcement to service employees increases the quality of their performance (Welsh, Bernstein, & Luthans, 1992).

2. *When job stressors increase, punishment-sensitive individuals will have a stronger increase in stress than individuals who are not punishment-sensitive (Level B-).*

    This stronger increase in stress can be detrimental to both employees and employers (Van der Linden, Beckers, & Taris, 2007). Social reinforcement might help to decrease this stress because of its positive impact on employees.

The main findings with regard to 'supervisory support' (ten Have et al., 2016) are:

1. Perceived supervisory support has a moderate positive effect on performance, a strong positive effect on job satisfaction and organizational commitment and a negative effect on turnover intentions (Level A: Edmondson & Boyer, 2013; Luchman & González-Morales, 2013; Mor Barak, Travis, Pyun, & Xie, 2009; Ng & Sorensen, 2008).
2. Perceived supervisory support has a positive effect on commitment to change, increases positive change evaluations and lowers psychological stress in the context of organizational change (Level D: Chauvin et al., 2014; Fuchs & Prouska, 2014; Neves, 2011).

What Is the Conclusion?

Positive reinforcement is a relevant and effective concept in the context of management and change. The evidence shows that positive reinforcements such as supervisory support are crucial for the functioning of both organization and employees. Positive reinforcements increase the quality of employees' work and performance. Supervisory support has multiple positive effects. The evidence shows that supervisory support as a form of social reinforcement increases job satisfaction and organizational commitment and decreases employees' turnover intentions. Findings also indicate that punishment-sensitive individuals react more strongly to increasing job stressors, which lead to higher levels of stress. Increased supervisory support might help these employees. In relation to organizational change, supervisory support proves to be beneficial. Studies found that supervisory support has a positive effect on the commitment to change, increases positive change evaluations and lowers psychological stress in organizational change contexts.

Practical Reflections

With regard to the practice of management, Kouzes and Posner (2012) emphasize the importance of supervisory support. It has to be focused on creating a climate in which people are fully engaged and feel in control of their own lives. "In a climate of competence and confidence, people don't hesitate to hold themselves personally accountable for results, and they feel profound ownership for their achievements" (p. 243). Based on the findings, several guidelines for practitioners can be given. First, be sincere, be specific and give employees concrete and constructive feedback. Reward even small increases in performance and development. Show appreciation and reward good effort, and show genuine appreciation. Schedule time to listen to employees and value and implement their suggestions. Empathize with employee needs.

Self-Esteem (and Self-Enhancement)

People desire to view themselves in a positive light. As a result, self-esteem is often the result of, or the compromise between, self-evaluation and self-enhancement.

What Is Self-Esteem?

Self-esteem is a social psychological construct that can be defined as "an individual's positive or negative evaluation of himself or herself" (Jones, 1990, in: Smith et al., 2015, p. 107). It is related to the self-concept: "The self-concept is what we think about the self; self-esteem is the positive or negative evaluations of the self, as in how we feel about it" (Smith et al., 2014, p. 107). Self-esteem is dependent on many factors, such as how well we view our own performance and appearance, and how satisfied we are with our social relations (Tafarodi & Swann, 1995). Feelings of mastery (Baumeister, Campbell, Krueger, & Vohs, 2003) and connectedness to others (Leary, Tambor, Terdal, & Downs, 1995) are crucial for the level of self-esteem. The feelings of the self are reflected in an individual's agreement or disagreement with statements like "I feel inferior to others at this moment" and "I feel as smart as others" (Heatherton & Polivy, 1991). If mastery and connectedness are high, if people perform well and are included by others, their self-esteem is high. Self-esteem encompasses beliefs about oneself and emotional states like pride and shame (Hewitt, 2009). Self-esteem can be seen as a measure of how well people are using their self-knowledge to navigate the social world (Smith et al., 2015). People desire to view themselves in a positive light. As a result, self-esteem is often the result of, or the compromise between, self-evaluation and self-enhancement. Self-enhancing biases are instrumental in the process that has to 'produce' certain self-esteem for an individual. A self-enhancing bias can be defined as "any tendency to gather or interpret information concerning the self in a way that leads to overly positive evaluations" (Smith et al., 2014, p. 109). Individuals 'use' selective memory and selective perception in order to remember or see those things that have the most positive implications for their self-esteem. As a result, people think that their sense of humour and honesty are above average, distort memories of performances (e.g. matches, exams) and believe that they can control the event that they will experience to a greater extent than they really can (Crocker & Park, 2004). Baumeister et al. (2003) reviewed the research on self-esteem in order to determine whether having high self-esteem was as helpful as many people seem to think. Based on their findings, we can conclude that self-esteem seems to be a valuable resource; people with high self-esteem are in many ways better able to deal or to cope with their environment, more active and happier. However, these people may also delude themselves and engage in various negative behaviours (Baumeister, Smart, & Boden, 1996). But Baumeister (1993) also sees self-esteem as 'the likeliest candidate for a social vaccine', self-esteem as an 'all purpose social vaccine' that protects people against vulnerability to a wide range of social vulnerabilities (Mercy & Peter, 2014).

Self-enhancement may contribute to a higher self-esteem, but also has the potential to create negative consequences for people, for example by creating self-delusion that leads to setting unrealistic goals which may create failure and disappointment (Shaver, 2015). Therefore, the affective goal of having a high self-esteem has to be balanced with the cognitive goal of having an accurate self-view (e.g. Kirkpatrick & Ellis, 2004). Ellis (2001, 2006) criticizes the concept of self-esteem; he qualifies it as self-defeating and ultimately self- and socially destructive. Self-esteem increases initiative, probably based on confidence, and feels good; it operates like a bank of positive emotions. People with high self-esteem are among other things more willing to approach others and to risk new undertakings (Baumeister & Tierney, 2012). However, it may also make people overconfident, unadvisable, incautious, ineffective, defensive and vulnerable. The critique of Ellis (2001) is fundamental and is summarized by Mercy and Peter (2014): "The scholar claimed that self-esteem is based on arbitrary definitional premises, and over-generalized, perfectionistic and grandiose thinking. He argued that people with high self-esteem are more likely to minimize the consequences of risky behaviour, rationalizing risky behaviour and convincing themselves that the behaviour will not cause harm to themselves or others, which may contribute to behaviours like drinking, taking drugs and engaging in early sexual intercourse as well as other risk taking behaviours" (p. 168). Ellis (2005) therefore proposes a 'healthier' alternative: unconditional self-acceptance and unconditional other-acceptance.

What Is the Relevance of Self-Esteem for Organization and Change?

For people to function in an effective and healthy way, self-esteem is important, particularly in organizations and in times of change. Change, but also daily challenges may put pressure on people's self-esteem. As said, Baumeister (1993) described self-esteem as a social vaccine; it plays a significant role in people's ability to cope with their environments. In the organizational and change context, self-esteem is related to topics such as leadership, change capacity, commitment and resistance to change. Maurer (2010) states: "progress without resistance is impossible. People will always have doubts and questions. Even when you are the champion of change, you will still have doubts. Will this really work? Have I given the idea sufficient thought? Resistance is a natural part of any change" (p. 35).

Search Strategy

Relevant databases were searched using the term 'self-esteem' in combination with 'meta-analysis' or 'systematic review'. The search yielded more than fifty meta-analyses/systematic reviews. After screening the titles and abstracts for relevance, nine articles were included. After thorough examination, one additional article was excluded.

Main Findings

1. *Self-esteem is positively related to job performance and job satisfaction (Level B-).*

   Multiple included meta-analyses found that self-esteem is positively related to job performance (Bowling, Eschleman, Wang, Kirkendall, & Alarcon, 2010; Chang, Ferris, Johnson, Rosen, and Tan, 2012; Judge, Erez, & Bono, 1998; Judge & Bono, 2001) and that self-esteem is positively related to job satisfaction (Bowling et al., 2010; Judge & Bono, 2001).

2. *Self-esteem has a negative effect on depressions and anxiety (Level A-).*

   Individuals with high self-esteem generally have a reduced likelihood of depressions and lower levels of anxiety compared with individuals with low self-esteem (Sowislo & Orth, 2013).

3. *Individuals with high self-esteem show more in-group bias than individuals with low self-esteem (Level B-).*

   Individuals with high self-esteem tend to favour their own group more than other groups, compared with individuals with low self-esteem (Aberson, Healy, & Romero, 2000). In-group bias can lead to negative treatment of members of out-groups, which is something an organization might want to avoid when working with multiple groups such as project groups.

4. *Self-esteem is negatively related to counterproductive work behaviour (Level B-).*

   In an organizational setting, researchers found that self-esteem lowers counterproductive work behaviour (Whelpley & McDaniel, 2016).

What Is the Conclusion?

The findings show that self-esteem plays a very important role in organizations and is related to various positive effects. It contributes in a positive way to job performance and job satisfaction and also reduces the chances of depression. Self-esteem also lowers levels of anxiety and decreases counterproductive work behaviour. The findings also show an increased in-group bias as a result of higher self-esteem. This can be a cause for concern, and attention should be paid to this bias, as it can negatively affect both the running and changing of organizations. Increasing the overall self-esteem of employees and nurturing this self-esteem seem to be critical for the long-term success of the organization.

Practical Reflections

Given the importance of self-esteem, organizations should find ways to increase it. The included meta-analyses and systematic reviews give no clear indications of how organizations can increase this self-esteem. However, some interventions like increasing supervisory support, giving constructive feedback, celebrating achievements/improvements, giving compliments when employees deserve them and treating people with respect are likely to increase the employee's self-esteem.

Self-Verification Theory

People seek confirmation of their self-concept, whether it is positive or negative. This may lead to a clash between delusion and truth, belief and fact; between the affective goal and related need to self-enhance and the cognitive goal and need to have an accurate self-view.

What Is Self-Verification?

The assumption in self-verification theory is that people want to be known and understood by others according to their self-views, including self-concepts and self-esteem. The concept of self-verification focuses on the tendency of people to seek confirmation of their self-concept, whether it is positive or negative (Swann & Ely, 1984). This tendency may lead to a clash between delusion and truth, belief and fact; between the affective goal and related need to self-enhance and the cognitive goal and need to have an accurate self-view (Shaver, 2015). The outcome will vary, for example with the kind of relationship. Close relationships are more often formed with people who contribute to self-verification. In the case of distant relationships, people often tend to prefer self-enhancing feedback. In general, enhancement more often prevails over verification (Shaver, 2015). Self-enhancement theory, the drive for positive evaluations, is seen as a competing theory to or an even stronger theory than self-verification. Some theorists contend that the desire for self-enhancement is prepotent and more powerful than rival motives such as self-verification. If this is true, it could be stated that even people with negative self-views will embrace positive evaluations. A meta-analytic review of the relevant literature resulted in ample evidence of self-enhancement strivings but little evidence of its prepotency. Instead, the evidence suggested that motives related to self-verification and motives related to self-enhancement are both influential but control different response classes. Kwang and Swann (2010) add: "In addition, other motives may sometimes come into play. For example, when rejection risk is high, people seem to abandon self-verification strivings, apparently in an effort to gratify their desire for communion. However, when rejection risk is low, as is the case in many secure marital relationships, people prefer self-verifying evaluations" (p. 263). Efficient and effective behaviours probably benefit from the balance between, and reconciliation of, enhancement and verification. With that balance people will become able to accept their shortcomings and weaknesses and to improve themselves. Prescott Lecky (1892–1941) was the first to articulate the underlying idea of self-verification theory, posthumously published in 1945 as *Self-Consistency: A Theory of Personality* (Lecky, 1945). Lecky proposed "that chronic self-views give people a strong sense of coherence and they are thus motivated to maintain them" (Swann, 2012, p. 25). Related ideas are visible in so-called self-consistency models such as that of cognitive dissonance (Festinger, 1957). But people like Festinger transformed Lecky's idea in a fundamental way. They abandoned the emphasis on the role of chronic self-views in consistency strivings. Self-verification theory reinstates the central role of self-views. Swann (2012) explains: "Dissonance theory (Aronson, 1968; Festinger, 1957), for example, emphasized the ways in which people found consistency by bringing their transient self-images into accord with their factual behaviours. Self-verification theory (Swann, 1983) reversed this trend by reinstating Lecky's belief that stable self-views organize people's efforts to maximize consistency. Therefore, rather than changing self-views willy nilly to match behaviour, self-verification theory holds that people are motivated to maximize the extent to which their experiences confirm and reinforce their self-views" (p. 26). From this perspective "stable self-views act like the rudder of a ship, giving people a sense of continuity and coherence. . . . From a pragmatic perspective, people sense that being understood eases social interaction and being misunderstood creates turbulence" (Swann, Milton, & Polzer, 2000, p. 239). People use several self-verification strategies to create self-verifying worlds (Swann, 2012). The first is based on the construction of self-verifying "opportunity structures", social environments that satisfy their needs (McCall & Simmons, 1966). A second strategy involves the systematic communication of self-views to others. People display identity cues, for example by the clothes they wear. A variant of this second self-verification strategy is communicating one's identity to others through one's actions. Swann (2012) gives the example of depressed college students who were more likely to solicit unfavourable feedback from their roommates than were non-depressed students. Such efforts resulted in negative evaluations, and thus self-verification (Swann, Wenzlaff, Krull, & Pelham, 1992). If people think that others do not see them in a way that confirms their self-views, they will redouble their actions. Swann (2012) also explains what happens if these strategies fail.

In that case they might deploy the third strategy of self-verification: 'seeing' non-existent evidence. We categorize self-verification under the core social motive of 'enhancing self', central in this chapter. However, Fiske (2004) does relate self-verification (also) to the core social motive of understanding; it serves social survival needs. Fiske (2004) states: "People do seem to strive for self-verification, which indeed is accuracy, in the sense of consensus about the person's self-views. This serves the core social motive of understanding, in that the socially shared view affirms the self-concept. In general, the social world works better if people's self-views essentially agree with other people's views of them" (p. 187). It is for that reason that Fiske says that self-verification greases the social wheels and reduces conflict in interaction. Consistent with this, research shows that self-verifications improved connections to the group and fostered harmony and productivity in diverse workgroups (Swann, Kwan, Polzer, & Milton, 2003).

What Is the Relevance of Self-Verification for Organization and Change?

The relevance of self-verification in organizational settings is illustrated by the research of Swann et al. (2003); it fosters harmony and productivity in workgroups. In organizational and change processes, it greases the social wheels and reduces conflict. One can imagine that significant or radical changes in organizations put pressure on the self-views of people involved. Self-verification theory sheds light on the possible consequences and helps managers and change agents, for example, to understand the thoughts and behaviours of those people and provide a behavioural repertoire for them. Self-verification is related to management and change topics such as leadership, cooperation and resistance to change.

Search Strategy

Relevant databases were searched using the terms 'self-verification' and 'self-view' in combination with 'meta-analysis' or 'systematic review'. The search yielded more than 250 articles. After screening the titles and abstracts for relevance, four studies and one meta-analysis met the inclusion criteria. Two included studies have a high level of evidence (level B and B-).

Main Findings

1. *Self-verification contributes to productivity in group projects that require creativity (Level B-).*

   Self-verification has a positive effect on the feeling of connection to the project group and improved project grades of MBA students on creative tasks (tasks that benefit from divergent perspectives). Thus, project groups tend to be more effective when self-verification is high (Swann, Milton, & Polzer, 2000).

2. *Neither the desire for self-verification nor the desire for self-enhancement is dominant or more important (Levels B-, C).*

In general, it is believed that self-enhancement theory is more dominant and important compared with the self-verification theory. However, a meta-analysis and a good-quality study both state that there is no evidence that one of the theories is dominant or more important (Anseel & Lievens, 2006; Kwang & Swann, 2010). It is even stated that "the robustness of self-verification strivings in our results throws into question the proper interpretation of dozens of studies that are widely assumed to represent evidence for self-enhancement theory: studies that were not included in our meta-analyses because the investigators failed to include measures of self-views" (Kwang & Swann, 2010, p. 275).

3. *Core self-evaluations enhance job satisfaction (Level B) and positively affect ethical leadership (Level D-).*

Based on the self-verification theory, people with high core self-evaluations (CSE^2) tend to seek positive feedback to reinforce how they see themselves. Having high core self-evaluations has a positive effect on job satisfaction and promotes ethical leadership, which are both beneficial for the organization (Ahn, Lee, & Yun, 2016; Wu, 2012).

What Is the Conclusion?

The findings show positive relationships between self-verification and factors like job satisfaction, group productivity and connection (identification) within groups. Three of the five studies included, of which one is a meta-analytical study, have a high evidence level. The positive effects found are fairly robust. The insights they provide can be useful when implementing change and, for example, using workgroups to achieve this change (as self-verification has a positive effect on in-group connection and productivity). Through CSE, self-verification also increases job satisfaction and positively affects ethical leadership. Given the specific positive effects on multiple relevant factors (in the context of management and change), self-verification has significant potential to contribute to effective interventions and actions in the area of organization and change.

Practical Reflections

If the relevance of and the specific evidence with regard to the concept of self-verification are compared with its position in the practice of management and change, we may conclude that there is a serious unleashed potential. The concept contributes to leadership development, productivity and creativity in organizations. In addition, it has positive effects on the connectivity or identification in groups. It may help organizational and change practitioners to better understand people in organizations and as a result organizational behaviour such as resistance to change and commitment.

Notes

1. in: Markus (1978), p. 395.
2. CSE refers to "fundamental premises that individuals hold about themselves and their functioning in the world" (Judge et al., 1998, p. 161) and comprises "the overlap of four well-established traits: self-esteem, self-efficacy, emotional stability and locus of control" (Ahn et al., 2016, p. 2).

8 The Social Psychology of Change Management

Introduction

Social psychology is essential for the effectiveness and development of the field of change management. Social psychology is necessary to understand people in change processes. People are social animals and change in organizations is a social process. Social psychology is necessary to understand people in change processes; it teaches us that meaning is key during change and intervention. Social psychology makes change management comprehensible to people and allows them to consider their actions in groups and the organization on their merits. These were the leading notions in the first chapter. They may seem obvious and self-evident, but practice and science, as well as the popular change management literature, show that it is not. The essential basis of each profession and each science exists in its 'body of knowledge', the systematic and validated formal knowledge (Greenwood, 1957; Barber, 1963; Freidson, 1973; Abbott, 1988). Systematic and formal knowledge in particular defines professional work (Wilensky, 1964). Professional effect and contribution are defined by the quality of knowledge and the quality of its application. But however excellent the process of application may be, without the right knowledge it will probably not fly. Sometimes the required knowledge does not exist or is not available. Then, practitioners are forced to experiment, to prototype, to work according to trial and error—which can also be done in an evidence-based way. But when the knowledge does exist and when knowledge can be made available, not using it is, from a professional perspective, unforgiveable. It was for these reasons that we started our process to make social psychological knowledge available for the science and practice of management in general and change management in particular. The popular change management literature shows that subjects such as cooperation, leadership, vision and mission, communication, resistance to change, participation, structure and culture are important, if not essential, for the discipline and its organizational context. Almost without exception, social psychology is a discipline—if not *the* discipline—that provides the insights, knowledge and behavioural repertoire that is helpful or necessary to tackle these subjects. Remember that "social psychology is the scientific attempt to understand and explain how the thoughts, feelings and behaviours of individuals are influenced by the actual, imagined or implied presence of other human beings" (Allport & Lindzey, 1954, p. 5). The same popular literature also shows, however, that social psychology is underutilized, if not absent, in the more than fifty most popular, bestselling books on change management that have been analysed. The fact that there is a relatively small, high-quality collection of more scholarly books that do address change management topics and issues by using social psychological theories, concepts, insights and evidence (e.g. Boje et al., 2012; Oreg et al., 2013) does not make the underutilization or absence mentioned previously any less noteworthy. The same applies to the fact that a lot of change management practitioners and probably a subset of the managers 'know' the founding fathers and great thinkers like Lewin, Schein, Weick and Argyris. Managers and other practitioners probably buy and read the popular books and are influenced by their approach and the gurus and 'management thinkers' who write them. To illustrate this, as stated in the first chapter, our analysis showed that some of the popular books still mention Albert Bandura (e.g. Bandura, 1963) and his social-cognitive learning theory. 'Groupthink' and group dynamics are referred to frequently (e.g. Janis, 1982). The notion of 'social proof' is visible in opinions about model behaviour, 'significant others' and the dissemination of ideas (e.g. Sherif, 1935; Cialdini et al., 1999). But that is about it. The process we started was focused on collecting, analysing and presenting or making available social psychological knowledge relevant to change management in an encyclopaedic, coherent and evidence-based way. We therefore selected approximately forty of the most relevant social psychological theories and concepts, categorized and connected these by using Fiske's five core social motives and assessed the evidence that was relevant (to change management). After the beginning of this book with the introductory and methodological chapters, we presented five chapters with the results of our research process. In this final chapter, we reflect on the process and its results and present some additional thoughts and notions with regard to a social psychology of change management and its conceptualization. In addition, we show that the five categories and the related theories are not only fruitful and helpful in themselves, but also through their combinations. We will reflect briefly on the methodology and possible consequences for additional research and give some pointers for a future agenda for science and practice.

A Social Psychological Perspective on Change Management

The second step after the conclusion that unleashing the potential of social psychology for change management is logical, necessary and helpful was selecting the most promising and relevant theories. This led to a selection of more than forty social psychological theories and concepts, categorized by five core social motives: belonging, understanding, controlling, trusting and self-enhancing.

Based on the definitions and conceptualizations, five (first) short stories of belonging, understanding etc. of change were presented. Taken together, they make up an initial social psychological story of change:

Belonging. Being social animals, people have a desire to form and maintain social bonds. Social connectedness unifies and is stimulated by shared common goals and interests. Perceived cohesion influences the behaviour of the individual and the group. It has two dimensions: a sense of belonging and feelings of morale. Conformity is the convergence of individuals' thoughts, feelings or behaviour toward a social or group norm. Corporate visions and missions, shared senses of urgency or core values are instrumental in developing such kinds of consensus or agreement. An individual's self-concept is partly derived from his knowledge of his membership in a social group (or groups) and the value or emotional significance attached to that membership. People have a personal identity and a social identity; psychological depersonalization of the self produces 'group behaviour' and emergent group processes such as influence, cooperation and cohesiveness. Belonging to a group stimulates prosocial behaviour toward the in-group. People function securely if they believe that they are contributing to a meaningful change or mission. Standards and goals have to be inviting and inclusive, including for minority groups within the organization. Negative stimuli such as threats and urgency can be effective in change, but positive ambitions, mirroring positive emotions and feelings, create more self-efficacy or action control in dealing with changes and challenges.

Understanding. Understanding is about understanding as the social need for shared meaning and prediction. A social representation is the ensemble of thoughts and feelings being expressed in verbal and overt behaviour of actors that constitutes an object for a social group. Social representations frame objects or issues in socially recognizable ways, in socially shared schemas. People are motivated to explain and understand the causes of events and behaviours. As a form of sense-making they assign causes to behaviour of themselves and others. Judgments are grounded in and based on people's attitudes; to understand or to make sense, people will compare the position advocated by an idea with their own position regarding that idea. Most of the behaviours that people display are the result of social learning, either deliberately or inadvertently, through modelling, the influence of example. The presence of others causes social impact, an influence that can be real or perceived, direct or indirect (implied), experienced or imagined. How group members believe their goals are related impacts their dynamics and performance significantly. Social contexts are 'forums of transaction' with social exchange as the market mechanism. Individuals voluntarily act in favour of another person or an organization, motivated by individuals' expectations of reciprocity.

Controlling. Individuals will act in a certain way based on the expectation that the act will be followed by a given outcome. People learn by observing others. People's emotions are extracted from their evaluations of events. These appraisals or estimates will lead to individual variances of emotional reactions to the same stimulus or event. Individuals come to 'know' their own attitudes, emotions and other internal states partially by inferring them from observations of their own overt behaviour and/or the circumstances in which this behaviour occurs. People are not only moulded by their social contexts, but they are also inherently active, intrinsically motivated and oriented toward developing naturally through integrative processes. People are part of group-based social hierarchies in which concepts like stereotyping and group oppression are instrumental to the maintenance and stability of those hierarchies. A person's attitude toward behaviour, subjective norms and perceived behavioural control in combination shape that person's behavioural intentions and behaviours. A strongly held and consistently expressed minority view can have extensive influence on the majority, as most majority members just follow the rest and lack strongly held views. External motivators may undermine the intrinsic motivation of individuals.

Trusting. Trust is an individual's willingness to be vulnerable to others. Trustworthiness reduces employee uncertainty related to change. Formed relationships and enduring bonds with others have implications for both the physical and psychological well-being of the individual. Procedural justice reflects the perceived fairness of decision-making processes and the degree to which they are consistent, accurate, unbiased and open to voice and input. People feel most comfortable when they are getting exactly what they deserve from their relationships—no more and certainly no less. Antisocial or inhumane conduct can put pressure on trust and trustworthiness. Moral disengagement is about mechanisms that prevent us feeling bad when doing bad things. Group trust and strong emotion can also be or become counterproductive. Groupthink occurs when a group of people make faulty decisions because of the desire to maintain harmony and conformity in the group.

Self-enhancing. Human beings strive for internal consistency in order to function mentally in the real world. Cognitive dissonance is a form of mental discomfort or psychological stress that is experienced by a human being who simultaneously holds two or more contradictory beliefs, ideas, convictions or values. The discomfort or stress that results from the internal inconsistency motivates people to reduce the cognitive dissonance. By fulfilling the need to protect self-integrity in the face of threat, self-affirmations can enable people to deal with threatening events and information without resorting to defensive biases. People seek to maintain views of their social systems—and their attendant norms, rules and social structures—as relatively legitimate, even when confronted with information suggesting the opposite. To enhance self, people may interpret, distort or ignore the information coming from social comparison in order to see themselves more positively. Self-guides such as the actual, ought and ideal self guide behaviour and may lead to experienced discrepancies. People can have prevention or promotion focus; analysing this helps to understand or predict what people avoid or approach. 'Present others' may cause an increase in the likelihood of highly accessible responses of people and a decrease in the likelihood of less accessible responses. Positive interpersonal stimuli such as praise, a compliment, a smile, touch or even attention can reinforce behaviour, as a positive reaction followed the behaviour. People desire to view themselves in a positive light. As a result, self-esteem is often the result of, or the compromise between, self-evaluation and self-enhancement. People seek confirmation of their self-concept, whether it is positive or negative. This may lead to a clash between delusion and truth, belief and fact; between the affective goal and related need to self-enhance and the cognitive goal and the need to have an accurate self-view.

An Evidence-Based Social Psychology of Change Management

In addition to the theoretical and conceptual or more deductive contribution of social psychology to change management, specific evidence was gathered. This was done to feed change management from the inductive or empirical perspective with evidence that resulted from the application of social psychological theories and ideas in the organizational context or related to change management topics and issues. The evidence-based methodology, more specifically the 'rapid evidence assessment' ('REA'), was used for this. The results and insights are the core of Chapters 3 through 7.

Table 8.1 Change Management Topics

Mission, vision, strategy	Performance management	Resistance
Leadership	Change capacity	Commitment
Culture	Change vision	Cooperation
Structure	Teams/team development	Participation
Systems	Communication	

Reflecting from the perspective of organization and change, the question for each theory was what the specific relevance could be (paragraph 2 of the REA format—see Chapter 2). The perspective was operationalized by using a set of 'change management topics', resulting from earlier evidence-based research and a team analysis. The topics are displayed in Table 8.1.

These topics were also used in describing the conclusion and/or practical reflections with regard to each theory and change management (paragraphs 5 and 6 of the REA format). In this final chapter, we give five illustrations or examples, one per core social motive, by presenting an exemplary theory and a summary of the specific evidence.

Belonging—Social Cohesion

To start with, as a theory related to the core social motive of belonging, social cohesion provided a set of relevant insights based on evidence specific to the organizational context, in addition to its basic notion. It is relevant for topics such as performance (management), cooperation, communication, commitment and team development. The basic notion is that perceived cohesion influences the behaviour of the individual and the group. It has two dimensions: a sense of belonging and feelings of morale. The evidence shows that group cohesion has a moderate to large effect on performance and that cohesive groups are more productive than non-cohesive groups. In addition, the nature of the task has a substantial influence on the cohesion-performance relationship and group cohesion is positively related to multiple factors that are beneficial for both organizations and change. Both task cohesion and social cohesion also have a positive effect on perceived subordinate performance, with task cohesion having the strongest effect. Finally, task and group interdependence strengthen group cohesion, further leading to employees' willingness to engage in more organizational citizenship behaviour.

Understanding—Cooperation/Competition (Social Interdependence Theory)

The theory on cooperation/competition, or the social interdependence theory, is related to the motive of understanding. Its basic notion is that the way in which group members believe their goals are related impacts their dynamics and performance significantly. The theory is relevant for teams and team development, goal-setting and feedback, leadership and culture, change capacity and, of course, cooperation and commitment. The specific evidence shows that intragroup cooperation outperforms intragroup competition. In teams, cooperative rewards promote accuracy and competitive rewards promote speed. In addition, a combination of cooperation and competition is the most effective. Individual competition leads to a decrease in the willingness of individuals to cooperate, and intergroup competition itself does not increase within group cooperation.

Controlling—Stress Appraisal Theory/Change Appraisals

The stress appraisal theory, and its sibling the concept of 'change appraisal', is related to the social motive of controlling. The basic notion of the theory is that people's emotions are extracted from their evaluations of events. These appraisals or estimates will lead to individual variances of emotional reactions to the same stimulus or event. The concept of change appraisals is relevant to change management topics such as change vision, change capacity, leadership, communication, performance management and resistance and commitment. First, the evidence shows that appraisal is central to coping with social change. Further specific evidence on change appraisal casts doubt on the benefits of simply "emphasizing the positive" when attempting to manage organizational change. The evidence shows a disconnect between the form and function of affect in the context of organizational change, and it seems to support the contention of Cacioppo and Gardner (1999) that "it is useful to think of the affect system as an entity intimately related to yet distinguishable from the cognitive system" (Fugate, 2008, p. 840). In addition, managers' engagement was associated with followers' appraisal of change. The evidence also shows that employees' change history in an organization is a key antecedent of their appraisals about organizational change. Finally, the Top Management Team (TMT) and supervisory leaders play distinctly different, but both important, roles in driving employees' adjustment to change.

Trusting—Fair Process and Procedural Justice

Related to the core social motive of trusting are the concepts of fair process and procedural justice. The basic notion is that procedural justice reflects the perceived fairness of decision-making processes and the degree to which they are consistent, accurate, unbiased and open to voice and input. In the organizational context, these concepts are related to topics such as participation, resistance and commitment, leadership and culture, and change capacity. The evidence shows that fair process has a medium to large positive effect on organizational outcomes. In addition, it has a medium positive effect on the affective commitment of both survivors and victims of a downsizing operation. Fair process has a positive effect on the acceptance of organizational changes and a large positive effect on change commitment. Finally, an unfair process has a small to medium negative effect on employee behaviour following a breach of the psychological contract.

Self-Enhancing—Social Reinforcement
(and a Specific Form: Supervisory Support)

Social reinforcement—including a specific form of it in the organizational and change context, namely 'supervisory support'—is related to the core social motive of self-enhancing. The basic notion of social reinforcement as a form of positive psychology is that positive interpersonal stimuli such as praise, a compliment, a smile, touch or even attention, when given, reinforce certain behaviour (because a positive reaction followed that behaviour). In the context of management and change, social reinforcement (and supervisory support) is relevant for topics such as leadership and organizational culture, teams, commitment and resistance, change capacity, cooperation and communication. The evidence shows that positive (social) reinforcement has a positive impact on the quality of employees' performance. In addition, when job stressors increase, punishment-sensitive individuals will have a stronger increase in stress than individuals who are not punishment-sensitive. Specifically with regard to supervisory support as a form of social reinforcement, the evidence shows that perceived supervisory support has a moderate positive effect on performance, a strong positive effect on job satisfaction and organizational commitment and a negative effect on turnover intentions. Perceived supervisory support also has a positive effect on commitment to change, increases positive change evaluations and lowers psychological stress in the context of organizational change.

Developing the Social Psychological
Change Management Framework

The categorization based on Fiske's core social motives provides an initial model that helps to structure, relate and integrate the numerous findings that resulted from the more than forty REAs with the purpose of (further) developing a social psychology of change management. From the perspective of education, science and practice, there are at least three reasons for continuing to 'model' or conceptualize the social psychology of change management. The first was already introduced in Chapter 2; research (Gage & Berliner, 1992) shows that students who study models before a lecture may recall as much as 57% more on questions concerning conceptual information, compared with students who receive instruction without the advantage of seeing and discussing models. The second is inspired by Bower (2000), who states: "It is one thing to recognize that a corporation is a complex non-linear system interacting with a very rich and changing environment. It is another to provide a map of that system that permits managers to act in an intentionally rational fashion" (p. 84). From the change management perspective an initial version of such a map has already been developed (ten Have et al., 2015). The map or model of change competence and the purposive change ('what it should be, and how it should be accomplished'; the combination of 'change vision' and 'change capacity') of Bower (2000) has already been introduced in Chapter 2. The perspective of social psychology with the five core social models visualized (in the same way as the change competence model, with the two 'lemniscates' (see Chapter 2) and the related theories and the specific evidence (in the organizational context) provide a new 'layer' for the original model and the opportunity to develop a deeper understanding of why change (management) does or does not 'work'. The third reason is related to the first two reasons, and in particular the second, and has to do with the interrelatedness (including dependencies, causal relationships, positive and negative synergies) between the social psychological element of factors for change management, that is to say between the five core social motives, the related theories and concepts, and the 'change management topics'. In this section, we focus on the second reason and its consequences and thus, in parallel, serve the first reason mentioned. The third reason is further addressed in the next section 'Social Motives, Organization and Change: More Than the Sum of Parts) '.

The change topics mentioned earlier can be 'positioned' in the change competence model (see Figure 8.1) (ten Have et al., 2015). Most topics are specifically related to a 'category', one of the five parts of the model or a combination of these. The parts are: connection plus rationale and effect (together with connection making up the 'change vision'), and focus and energy (together with connection making up the change capacity). Mission, for example, is 'located' in the field of the rationale; commitment is related to energy and structure to focus. Resistance can be caused by a variety of reasons, spread over the five fields of the model. Change vision and capacity are, as described, related to two sets of three factors. Communication is comparable with resistance to change in this perspective. Performance management is strongly related to the combination of focus and effect, and energy (resources, motivation) also has its role. In this final chapter, we illustrate how concepts such as mission, change capacity and resistance, but also the (five) change competent factors, including focus, energy and connection, can be better understood by using social psychological theories and evidence and providing a limited but illustrative set of examples. They are first described and structured in Table 8.2 (being 'positioned' in the change competence model; Figure 8.1).

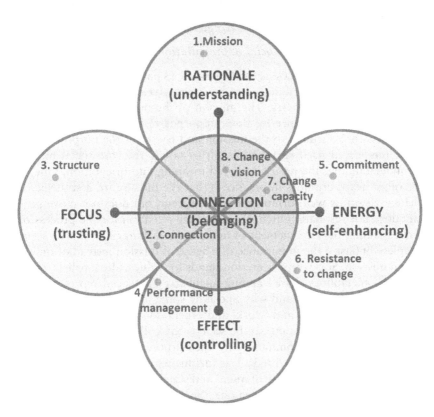

Figure 8.1 The Change Competence Model Enriched With Examples of Social Psychological Insights

Table 8.2 Change Management Topics, Social Motives and Social Psychological Theories and Concepts Illustrated

Change Management Topic/Factor	Core Social Motive(s)	Social Psychological Theory (Illustration, Example)
1. Mission	Understanding	Social representation theory
2. Connection	Belonging	Self-categorization theory (Organizational identification)
3. Structure	Trusting and belonging	Attachment theory
4. Performance management	Trusting and controlling	Expectancy theory
5. Commitment	Self-enhancing	Self-discrepancy theory
6. Resistance to change	Controlling and self-enhancing	Stress appraisal theory (Change appraisals)
7. Change capacity	Trusting and self-enhancing (and belonging)	Attachment theory (see 4.) and social reinforcement
8. Change vision	Understanding and controlling (and belonging)	Social representation (see 1.) and stress appraisal theory

Example 1: Mission and Social Representation Theory

In starting a change process, a clear rationale as part of the 'what it should be' question of Bower (2000) and his 'purposive change' is helpful and important, if not necessary. The mission of the organization provides a relevant point of reference for Bower's purposive change, which by definition has to contribute to the mission and has to fit the purpose. Having a mission in itself is not sufficient to satisfy the core social motive of understanding, the need for shared meaning and orientation. One of the often-heard critiques in practice is that the mission (or a strategic or change vision) is well formulated and coherent, but does not move people, does not resonate. Often, the necessary attention for the process of sense-making, the management of meaning, is lacking. This is why some people emphasize the importance of a sense of mission instead of only a sound mission. Social representation stands for values, ideas, beliefs, practices and metaphors shared among members. The social representation theory helps to understand why and how some ideas, like missions and values, become shared and 'work' and others do not. The theory shows that a social representation can be seen as the collective elaboration "of a social object by the community for the purpose of behaving and communicating" (Moscovici, 1963). It is for this reason that Rijsman (1997) introduces a '*social* ontology of mind' and states that without intersubjective co-ordination there is no meaning: "meaning is referential reality that follows from the co-ordinated activity between subjects" (p. 146).

Example 2: Connection and Self-Categorization Theory (Organizational Identification)

Numerous practitioners, managers and consultants, for example, emphasize the importance of connection, in organizations as such and in times of change in particular. One may fear that in many cases the connection called for remains something superficial, trivial, an empty vessel. Connection becomes less trivial and instead essential when we understand that it is deeply related to the most fundamental core social motive: that of belonging. The need for strong, stable relationships is a—if not *the*—defining characteristic of the social or 'organizational' animal. For the organizational context, from a social psychological perspective, self-categorization theory and its sibling organizational identification help to understand how and why connection works. The theory explains how and when people will define themselves as individual and group entities and the impact of this variability in self-perception ('I' to 'we'). Evidence indicates that both workgroup and organizational identification are associated with individuals' experience of reduced strain and burnout as well as greater health and well-being. Illustrating the importance and nature of belonging in the organizational context, the evidence suggests that social identifications in organizations are important for individuals' health and well-being and for their productivity and performance (Steffens, Haslam, Schuh, Jetten, & van Dick, 2017).

Example 3: Structure and Attachment Theory

Structure, not to be confused with something like organizational schemes or organograms, is strongly related to the core social motives of connection and trusting. Structure in social settings is about relationships and trust. Attachment theory helps to understand how and why secure or insecure relationships between organizational members, for example leaders or 'relevant others' and followers, form and develop. It also helps to understand why structure and systems are important in social contexts and in the change competence factor parts of both focus and connection. Shaver and Mikulincer (2013) mention a wealth of applications of attachment theory and research. First of all, they mention a number of laudable prosocial effects which can be seen as relevant to situations of organizational change: for example, reducing dogmatism, intolerance of ambiguity and intergroup hostility, and increasing participation in community activities. They also explicitly mention leadership development, group dynamics and organizational functioning (Mikulincer & Shaver, 2007).

Example 4: Performance Management and Expectancy Theory

Related to both the running and changing of organizations is performance management. From a social psychological perspective, performance management is strongly related to the social motives of controlling and trusting. People have a need for perceived contingency between behaviour and outcomes (Fiske, 2004). To function, people need to have sufficient trust in the social environments, in the systems and people that provide the context for their performance and the way it is evaluated. Expectancy theory helps to understand how focus and effect, through trusting and controlling, work in organizational and change contexts. It deepens the insights into change and behaviour by shedding light on an important behavioural mechanism. The theory "predicts that an individual will act in a certain way based on the expectation that the act will be followed by a given outcome. . . . Simply put, the theory states that the actions of an individual are driven by expected consequences" (Renko, Kroeck, & Bullough, 2012, pp. 668–669).

Example 5: Commitment and Self-Discrepancy Theory

Like connection, commitment is also a broadly and 'easily' used term in the context of management and organization, risking becoming an empty vessel. Commitment is related to change capacity and hence in particular with the change competence factors of focus and energy. But the core social motives of trusting and self-enhancing and the related social psychological theories have the potential to deepen the insights into commitment (and change capacity). Here we elaborate on self-enhancing and the self-discrepancy theory. This theory helps to understand why people are motivated and committed to change, or not. Self-discrepancy shows that in times of change, people may find that the change vision and ambition lead to extra demands and expectations that influence the self-views, in particular the ought self (extra responsibilities) and the ideal self (extra desires and aspirations). This may lead to increased discrepancy and dissonance. This is relevant for both the 'producers' and the 'co-producers' or 'consumers' of change initiatives. Depending on the dynamics of their self-views and their focus (prevention or promotion), people will react to change in different ways and should be approached in different ways.

Example 6: Resistance to Change and Stress Appraisal Theory (Change Appraisals)

Resistance to change has many causes and can take different forms. It can be related to all five change competence factors as well as all five core social needs. A weak rationale for change will not help the development of shared understanding. If a change process does not satisfy the need for self-enhancement, energy will leak away. Here we focus on the combination of energy and effect, self-enhancing and controlling. A theory that helps to understand these in the context of change is stress appraisal theory and more specifically the concept of change appraisals. Stress appraisal theory refers to the evaluation process by which individuals evaluate stressful events and cope with them (e.g. Lazarus, 1966, 1974). Coping can be defined as 'the cognitive and behavioural efforts made to master, tolerate or reduce external and internal demands and conflicts among them' (Folkman and Lazarus, 1980, p. 223). Individuals differ in the evaluation of what is happening (to them), how they perceive the circumstances and how they react to and cope with circumstances (Lazarus & Folkman, 1984). Fugate (2013) states: "A person's cognitive appraisal of organizational change is important because it represents an evaluation of a person-situation transaction in terms of its meaning for social well-being (see Dewe, 1991)" (p. 16). Following the theory, effects of change can be perceived or experienced in terms of a threat, harm or loss, or a challenge. Consequently, stress can be related to negative (harm) and positive (challenge) types of stress.

Example 7: Change Capacity and Social Reinforcement Theory Plus Attachment Theory

Following the change competence model, change capacity is based on the combination of focus and energy plus connection. From the social psychological perspective, trusting and self-enhancing plus belonging are relevant in order to understand change capacity. We addressed the combination of belonging and trusting, and the deepening of insight into focus and connection as such and as important parts of change capacity, in example 3, together with the attachment theory. Building on this, the social psychological insight into change capacity can be further developed by adding the theory of social reinforcement. If trust and belongingness are at an adequate level as a result of the process of attachment, change capacity can be further developed by stimulating self-enhancement. Social reinforcement theory provides a way and a mechanism for doing this. To function in a healthy and productive way, social beings need recognition in some form. Social reinforcement is crucial for mental and physical health, functioning and performance. Without social reinforcement, people can become depressed or unhealthy, which is detrimental to our everyday functioning and (job) performance. Self-reinforcement can help people to a certain level, but in the end almost everybody needs social reinforcement to fulfil social needs. This shows that change capacity is not only about delivering change and performance; it is also about healthy organizations and healthy people.

Example 8: Change Vision and Social Representation Theory Plus Stress Appraisal Theory

Like change capacity, change vision is also an assemblage of three leading factors: rationale and effect plus (or in) connection. From a social psychological perspective, it relates to understanding and controlling plus belonging. For a change process to work, a shared understanding is necessary, as we can learn from social representation theory (example 1). This is necessary, but not sufficient, because it is an important part, but only one part, of the change vision. People are not only guided by the 'larger' story of change, the rationale. They will also evaluate a change initiative, and perhaps even primarily or ultimately, on the 'smaller' story, its perceived effect and personal consequences: 'what's in it for me'. Therefore, a change vision has to satisfy not only the motive of understanding, but at least also the motive of controlling. A change vision that works is based on rationale and effect, and understanding and controlling that are sufficiently aligned or related.

Social Motives, Organization and Change: More Than the Sum of Parts

According to Fiske (2004), the underlying principle of the model based on the core social motives is oriented toward the (better) survival of 'the social animal'. Fiske (2004) said: "All five motives orient toward making people fit better into groups, thus increasing their chances for survival" (p. 16). From this perspective, chance of survival or chance of change (in order to adapt to changing circumstances, contexts, conditions or demands) could be defined as the sum of its parts. The parts are the five social core motives: belonging, understanding, controlling, trusting and enhancing self. However, one can also see it as more (or even less) than the sum of its parts. The motives can be seen as interrelated, in positive or negative ways, in terms of synergies or trade-offs, as protagonists and antagonists. To illustrate this, one can imagine that there is a synergy between understanding and controlling, that a lack of trust can hamper a feeling of belongingness and that there could be a trade-off between controlling and trusting. In the model, the overlap between the five parts and the tangents or intersections between them, visualize these 'meetings', confrontations or interrelations—directly or indirectly where trusting and self-enhancing, understanding and controlling are related to one another by belonging. Based on the interrelatedness and combinations of the core social motives, Fiske provides a variety of insights. These insights further deepen the understanding of change management and validate or explain insights that had already been developed using the change competence model (ten Have, ten Have, Huijsmans, & Van der Eng, 2015). To illustrate this we give four examples where we relate and 'mirror' combinations of the change competence model factors (connection, rationale, effect, focus, energy) with matching combinations of the core social motives (belonging, understanding, controlling, trusting, self-enhancing). Change competence can be hampered or weakened by dysfunctions; these can be 'local' (e.g., a dysfunctional rationale as a result of strategic withholding or an inaccurate mission). Dysfunctions can also relate to combinations and be more 'integral' (Table 8.3).

Example 1. Selfishness and 'Enlightened Self-interest': Energy and Effect, Self-Enhancing and Controlling

The first of the four examples relates to the dysfunction called 'selfishness' that results when the combination of energy and effect becomes separated and has a life of its own. This dysfunction may appear, for

Table 8.3 Dysfunctions, Theories, Factors and Motives

Change Management Topic/Dysfunction	Social Psychological Theory or Concept	Change Competence Factors	Core Social Motives
1. Selfishness	Social learning	Energy and effect	Self-enhancing and controlling
2. Collective fantasy	Similarity	Rationale and energy	Understanding and self-enhancing
3. Ivory tower	Schemas	Focus and rationale	Understanding and trusting
4. Organizational culture	Social norms	Connection and rationale	Belonging and understanding

example, when professionals confronted with a drastic restructuring of their service firm or with fierce internal politics seek refuge on the outside with a client, get their energy there and measure effect there. Sooner or later this will undermine the collectivity, be detrimental to organizational identification and put pressure on organization citizenship behaviour (OCB). Fiske (2004) explicitly links egoism to the combination of self-enhancing and controlling. In the case of egoism, 'what's-in-it-for-me' constitutes the primary motive. Building on this from the social psychological perspective, that of social learning in particular, she explains how this motive works by using, for example, the concepts of reciprocity and social rewards and also equity and exchange. Based on this, Fiske points to the idea of 'enlightened self-interest', showing that selfish behaviour pays off in the short term but not the long term. These insights validate, help to further understand and deepen the organizational change phenomenon of selfishness.

Example 2. Collective Fantasy and Similarity: Rationale and Energy, Understanding and Self-Enhancing

The second example focuses on the collective fantasy dysfunction, the negative side of the combination of rationale and energy in the change competence model. This dysfunction is characterized by major visions, delusions of grandeur, a disturbed self-image and unbridled energy in the wrong direction. While dysfunction is one possible outcome, it is important to remember that the combination of rationale and effect can also be (very) functional or effective; if the proportions are correct, we have a missionary organization with a dream and a drive that makes change happen. Fiske (2004) introduces the concept of similarity ('liking those who like us'), for example, shared interests, personality, social or professional background, and based on the combination of being understandable and enhancing. She points to the balance theory that predicts "that people like to agree with their friends and to befriend those who agree with them" (Fiske, 2004, p. 264). The social psychological insights and concepts related to similarity help to further understand and predict or estimate the risk of developing a collective fantasy. The perspective of similarity helps to explain why the phenomenon of collective fantasy is often observed in closed professional communities where people mostly stay for a very long period and are very engaged and missionary.

Example 3. Ivory Tower and Schemas: Rationale and Focus, Understanding and Trusting

The third example concerns a function that is the result of the combination of the change competence factors of rationale and focus, the reason for change and the change direction. This combination provides guidance, clarity, a clear context, rules and priorities in a change process and hence a sound basis for leading changes in an effective way. The how and why of this can be further understood by the concept of schemas and expectations. With regard to these social psychological concepts, Fiske says: "People understand and trust the familiar" (2004, p. 142). Fiske defines a schema as "a cognitive structure containing the attributes of a concept or type of stimulus and the relationships among the attributes" (p. 143). If leaders or other change agents can provide the right framing, a change road map and new or adapted cognitive schemas that are fit for purpose, change will be more effective. In most cases this is not easy given the nature of schemas and the nature of change. So, the concept of schemas, as a 'product' of understanding and trusting, also helps to understand why change is often so difficult. Fiske (2004) states: "If thinking is for the pragmatic purpose of doing, people must have such workable structures to organize and anticipate the data they experience. Expectations and various schemas provide the scaffolding on which we build our impressions of others from the information available. People use workable, habitual structures for social cognition: we understand new information by reference to old, familiar schemas and expectations" (p. 143). The dysfunction located at the intersection of rationale and focus is the 'ivory tower'; leadership designs and formulates a reason and direction but is not able to bridge the gap between, on the one hand, the specifications and schemas related to the change and, on the other hand, the old, habitual, familiar schemas and expectations of the other people in the organization.

Example 4. Organizational Culture and Social Norms: Rationale and Connection, Understanding and Belonging

The fourth and final example relates to the combination of rationale and connection in the change competence model. For a change process to be effective, these factors have to be well developed *and* related. A rationale without connection is an empty vessel and connection without a rationale is—in the organizational context at least—like 'l'art pour l'art'. The relevance and interaction of rationale and connection can be better understood as the concept of social norms. From the perspective of organization and change, these norms are strongly related to organizational culture and cultural change. Fiske (2004) relates social norms to the combination of the core social motives belonging and understanding. Fiske states: "People need shared norms—such as equity and exchange systems, communal norms or other relational models—to understand what rules apply to different relationships. In order to belong to groups, people want to understand the shared ground rules about different kinds of relationships" (2004, p. 309). The rationale for change, the mission and the purpose have to be considered as the most important beacons for people in the context of organizational change. Change brings a new order that will influence the shared norms or ground rules. Cultural change calls for a redefinition or transformation of the set of social norms in an organization. The concept of social norms and the combined perspectives of understanding and belonging help to understand how and why people have to adjust their social rules and why this is sometimes so difficult.

Methodological Reflections: Some Notions and Thoughts

An important objective of our research and book was to enrich and deepen the body of knowledge of change management by 'mining' social psychology. The book presents social psychological knowledge relevant to change management in an encyclopaedic, coherent and evidence-based way. We experienced our earlier project focus on developing change management in an evidence-based way of working, *Reconsidering Change Management* (ten Have et al., 2016), as a journey. That was seen as a 'stopping place' and 'starting point' for the next stages of the journey toward effective change management to make better organizations that 'work' and contribute. The way to accomplish this in the case of that project was by collecting, analysing and presenting the scientific research and insights available, focusing on more, better, relevant and useful or helpful evidence for practice (and science). The project presented in this book, *The Social Psychology of Change Management*, had the same focus. It can be seen as one of the next stages of the journey described in our earlier book. With *The Social Psychology of Change Management* we have reached the next 'inn' where we tell our story and share our experiences, the insights and the evidence gathered with other 'travellers', so they are possibly better prepared for the next stages of their scientific or practical journey. With regard to the next stages, the question from a research and methodological perspective could be 'what's next'? The short answer is: making more, better, relevant and useful evidence available for the science and practice related to change management; that is, additional evidence in terms of quantity, level (of evidence), specificity and fitness for purpose. Reflecting on the results of our research focused on social psychological contributions to change management, we can formulate some thoughts and notions that may be helpful for the way forward.

To begin with, related to the field of change management, we have the conceptual and empirical insights of approximately forty social psychological theories and concepts, as theories and concepts in their own right and in the form of specific evidence (illustrated in 8.3). This 'result' can be further exploited and developed in several ways. First of all, the evidence with regard to the theories in themselves (i.e. not specifically related to management and change) will develop further. This will provide further insights that may be relevant to change management. Second, hopefully and probably there will be more research with a focus on the specific relationship between these social psychological theories and concepts and the context of organization, management and change. Our project showed that there is a way to go and probably a large potential. We found a serious amount of specific evidence. However, the quality and quantity showed a lot of differences between the theories and concepts researched, ranging from limited evidence, relatively low levels and with limited specificity to serious and specific evidence. In some cases, the results improved greatly when a 'translation' of the initial theory to a more context-specific concept was found, for example in the case of self-categorization theory and organizational identification. Therefore, third, another way to further develop the body of knowledge from a social psychological perspective can be the further development of such more context-specific theories and concepts based on the pure or classic social psychological ones. Another example of this is the 'translation' of stress appraisal theory into the concept of 'change appraisals'. As Fugate (e.g. 2008) illustrates, such 'translations' can form the basis for better and more specific evidence, related to change management that is 'fit for purpose'. It is noteworthy that this approach has a tradition at the intersection of the classic social sciences and the field of organization, management and change. An illustrative point in this regard is the way in which Argyris and Schon (e.g. Argyris, 1990) developed the concept of organizational learning and Schein (1985) his concept of organizational culture. These three 'ways' in particular will contribute further to an encyclopaedic and evidence-based social psychological knowledge base for change management. A fourth way is by designing or developing models or conceptualizations that connect the concepts and language of change management and social psychology. We did this, for example, by linking the core social motives of Fiske (2004) and the change competence model (ten Have et al., 2015) and by making use of the same concept or visualization. This provided a frame of reference and an integrative way to look at the social psychology of change management. A fifth way is by further 'modelling' and conceptualizing, and thus connecting and integrating, change management (topics) and the insights and language of social psychology (directly or in the translated form, or 'middleware' as in the concept of 'change appraisal'). We did this by relating change management topics (e.g. change capacity, leadership and resistance to change) and factors (e.g. rationale, energy) with Fiske's categorization of the core social motives to social psychological theories. This was illustrated in 8.4 and 8.5 with (only) eight plus four examples. Those examples show just a small part of the possibilities but give an illustrative indication of the potential (contribution) of social psychological insights for the field of change management. A sixth way is the path from 'pure' practice to science and evidence. Controlled environments and scientific experiments were and are important for the development of social psychology.

However, practice may be less 'controlled'; it is or becomes 'real' (in the process between 'subjects') and 'integral' by definition and therefore relevant and a rich source of knowledge, for both practitioners and scientists. Experience of practitioners as such is an important source of evidence. Through reflection by practitioners and with the help of scientists, this evidence can be made available to feed other practitioners and the body of knowledge. The last three points will also contribute to making the body of knowledge or evidence more encyclopaedic and evidence-based, but will in particular contribute to making this more coherent and integral and thus may help to create 'meaning'. If there is such a thing as a destination, then those six 'methodological' signposts may be helpful in following the road.

Final Remarks

In summary, the purpose of our research and this book is threefold.

The first aim is to further unlock the potential contribution of social psychology as a source for change management as a discipline and practice in a comprehensive, systematic and structured way ('encyclopaedic'). The second aim is to assess the available social psychological theories, concepts and research and fuel change management with the evidence and insights found (evidence-based, scientific). The third aim is to present, categorize and integrate the theories and findings by using a framework based on five core social motives (Fiske, 2004) and our change management methodology (ten Have et al., 2015) (cohesive, systemic, practical).

The overarching goal, however, inspired by the ideas and perspective of leading thinkers like Kurt Lewin, James Q. Wilson and Susan T. Fiske, is to make the world a better place. Social psychologists (being social scientists) study practical social issues, in our case issues related to change management, and application to real-world problems is a key goal.

Changes usually concern issues with a great organizational, emotional, economic and social impact. Therefore, this book goes beyond the domain of organizational sciences.

Change is promised by presidential candidates. Advocated by world leading organizations and asked for by ordinary people. How wide or small, how private or public, how long term or short term. Changes are rarely accomplished by individuals. Changes are social processes which have to be organized. Therefore, knowledge of social psychology is fundamental for change initiatives and neglecting that is professional irresponsible behaviour.

We hope that this book will provide—in the words of Noam Chomsky—'a course of intellectual self-defence'.

Appendix A
Overview of Authors and Researchers

Authors

Steven ten Have, PhD, is a full professor of strategy and change at the Vrije Universiteit Amsterdam, the Netherlands; chair of the Foundation for Evidence-Based Management; and partner at TEN HAVE Change Management.

John Rijsman, PhD, is a full professor of social psychology at Tilburg University, the Netherlands. He obtained his PhD in experimental social psychology from the University of Louvain in 1970, and, after a short stay at the University of Southern Illinois, was asked in 1972 to become chair of social psychology at the new faculty of psychology in Tilburg, where he has stayed ever since. The first part of his career was devoted entirely to experimental social psychology, but over the years he became more and more interested in the tacit knowledge of experienced practitioners in complex professional domains, leading to more and more PhD research with advanced reflective practitioners in these domains, more than sixty of which have obtained faculty positions at various universities in the world, or otherwise important positions in society. The basic aim of that endeavour, as also exemplified in this book, was and is to better understand and better act in a complex societal world by combining fundamental insight with highly developed practical experience. Rijsman was Editor in Chief of the *European Journal of Social Psychology*, Associate Editor of the *European Journal of Psychology of Education*, member of the review board of many other national and international journals, and often asked by the Dutch Royal Academy of Sciences to act as a reviewer of grant applications for fundamental research. His own work, apart from the work with his PhD students, is published in several articles or chapters of books, and is mostly about the social construction of meaning by coordinated interaction with other subjects, and especially the social construction of the meaning of Self in comparison with that of Others, and all its consequences (see also this book).

Wouter ten Have, PhD, is a full professor of organization and change at the Vrije Universiteit Amsterdam, the Netherlands; visiting university lecturer of change management (MBA health-care management) at the Amsterdam Business School, the Netherlands; and partner at TEN HAVE Change Management.

Joris Westhof, MSc, is a business consultant at Zestgroup, the Netherlands.

Lead Researcher

Hans van Emmerik, MSc, is a former consultant of TEN HAVE Change Management.

Researchers

Ruben ten Have, student of Philosophy, Politics and Economics (PPE) at the Vrije Universiteit Amsterdam, the Netherlands and research-assistant at TEN HAVE Change Management.

Lianne Ossenkoppele, MSc, is a former consultant of TEN HAVE Change Management.

Cornell Vernooij, MSc, is a consultant of TEN HAVE Change Management.

Appendix B
Examples of Matrix for Each Core Social Motive

1. Belonging

Social Identity Theory

Author and Year	Design	Sector/ Population	Moderator/ Mediator	Effect Size	Main Findings	Limitations	Level
Amiot (2012)	Non-controlled, before-after study N = 149	Hospital employees	Mediators: perceived similarities and perceived identity threat	High	In accord with social identity theory and past merger research (Tajfel & Turner, 1986; Terry, 2003; Terry et al., 2001) and supporting H1, the negative effects of the merger were most marked for employees of the low-status organization throughout the merger: These employees reported higher identity threat, lower identification with the new merged organization, and lower perceptions of a common in-group identity. Members of the lower-status premerger organization also perceived fewer similarities between the two premerger organizations. Increased perceived identity threat was associated with reduced identification with the new merged organization and a lesser perception that there was a common in-group identity. These findings suggest that both perceived similarity and perceptions of identity threat are important mechanisms for the establishment of a new identity during times of organizational mergers.	More than 20% dropout of participants Unclear if all measurement methods used were reliable and valid	D

(Continued)

Social Identity Theory (Continued)

Author and Year	Design	Sector/Population	Moderator/Mediator	Effect Size	Main Findings	Limitations	Level
Avanzi et al. (2014).	Cross-sectional study N = 195	Italian food industry firm	Moderator: Organizational identification	Medium	Organizational identification is a key variable. It first relates to turnover intentions by helping employees to perceive stronger support that helps them cope with stress (indirect effect via organizational support and emotional exhaustion). At the same time, it helps those who do not feel optimally supported to maintain the relationship with their organization (moderation of the effect of support on turnover intentions that is not mediated by emotional exhaustion). Results supported our hypotheses: social identification increased the perception of organizational support which in turn reduced emotional exhaustion which was finally related to turnover intentions. Furthermore, social identification moderated the relation between organizational support and turnover intentions.	Participants not randomly selected Sample size not large enough	E
Bergami & Bagozzi (2000)	Cross-sectional study Italy N = 409 Korea N = 283	Italian food service company Electronics division of Samsung Corporation in Korea	Mediator: social identity	Medium	The results show that affective commitment and self-esteem are the primary motivators of citizenship behaviours. Moreover, cognitive identification performs as a central mediator between prestige and stereotypes on the one hand, and affective commitment and self-esteem on the other. Identification is thus an indirect determinant of citizenship behaviours.	Participants not randomly selected	D
Boen, Vanbeselaere & Cool (2006)	Cross-sectional N = 234	Producing company	NA	Medium	Consistent with our first hypothesis, post-merger status was positively related to post-merger identification among employees of the low-status premerger organization, and this correlation was higher than among employees of the high-status premerger organization. In addition to what was predicted, post-merger status and post-merger identification were not significantly related among employees of the high-status premerger group. That is, employees who already belonged to a high-status organization before the merger or acquisition were not at all influenced by post-merger status in their organizational identification. By contrast, employees who belonged to a low-status organization before the merger or acquisition were strongly influenced by the perceived status of the new organization in their identification with this organization. This result suggests that managers can enhance the post-merger identification of employees of the low-status premerger organization by providing or emphasizing	No information on random selection of participants Unclear if all measurement methods used were reliable and valid	E

			Moderator	Effect size	Findings		
Dokko, Kane, & Tortoriello (2014)	Cross-sectional study N = 87	R&D division in a multinational high-tech company	Moderator: tie strength	No effect size	information that makes the newly merged organization compare favourably with rival companies. Conversely, they should be discrete in communicating information that would make it clear that the new organization compares rather negatively with relevant comparison organizations. Found is that social identity influences the creative generativity of boundary-spanning ties. Specifically, stronger team identity renders interactions with colleagues on other work teams less generative of creative ideas, while identification with an overarching, superordinate group (e.g., a division) enhances creative generativity. We also hypothesize and find that tie strength attenuates the negative effect of team identity. The strong and consistent support we find for our hypotheses suggests that social identity plays an important role in the innovative performance of individuals at work. The findings from our study suggest that the extent to which organizational members attach their own identity to these groups has important implications for their creativity.	Participants not randomly selected Sample size not large enough	E
Huang (2013)	Non-controlled, posttest-only study N = 1501	Employees of R&D departments at Taiwanese IT firms	NA	Small—medium	We found that as employees perceived more TFL at Time 1, they were more likely to show increases in social identification development behaviours over time. Further, increases in social identification development behaviours demonstrate their positive relationship with task performance and organizational citizenship development behaviours over time. My empirical model confirms all of my proposed hypotheses, and these findings highlight that the potential dynamic consequences of organization behaviours can lead to employee career development. Within social psychology, Tajfel's (1978) social identity has become central to the discipline, as well as in conceptual and empirical work in anthropology and cultural studies (e.g. Eriksen, 2001; Holland, 1997), wherein it has pushed the concept of identity to the forefront of contemporary academic discussions. We have therefore attempted to rectify this by investigating the multi-dimension of social identity (e.g. Bergami & Bagozzi, 2000; Ellemers et al., 1999) with due consideration of the underlying nature by including the three distinct aspects of social identity from the changes in organization development behaviours.	NA	D

(Continued)

Social Identity Theory (Continued)

Author and Year	Design	Sector/ Population	Moderator/ Mediator	Effect Size	Main Findings	Limitations	Level
					Moreover, I am the first to draw social identity into the perspective of development behaviours in order to explain how individuals' behaviours are sculpted. That is, individuals' social identity development behaviours could indeed be influenced by the perception of TFL at Time 1, and this impact subsequently could foster job performance development behaviours. The results of this study suggest that through a leader's TFL behaviours, internal organizational management may transform followers into identification outcomes. First, my results suggest that social identification can enhance job performance and that these improvements in job performance are likely to take the form of both task performance and OCB. Second, my results also suggest that a good job performance by an employee may be achieved when TFL behaviours are accompanied by the enforcement of social identification development behaviours. The results of this study suggest that the the three different aspects of social identification serve as meaningful constructs that have several different avenues of unexplored content.		D
Loi, Chan, & Lam (2014)	Non-controlled, posttest-only study N = 306	Employees of two garment-manufacturing companies in the southern part of China	Moderator: Job security Mediator: Organizational identification	Medium	Social identity theory maintains that people tend to classify themselves and others into various social groups according to the prototypical characteristics ascribed to or abstracted from the members of the groups (Tajfel & Turner, 1979, 1986). Classification is relational and comparative, which means the definition of oneself is relative to other people being classified in other comparable categories (Ashforth & Mael, 1989). For instance, the category of 'female' becomes meaningful in relation to the category of 'male'. Such process of classification provides individuals with a systematic means of defining self and others, which generates their social identification (i.e. the perception of belonging-ness) to a particular group category. Within the organization, employees may have different levels or foci of identification (such as workgroups, leaders, co-workers; Ashforth et al., 2008; Riketta & van Dick, 2005). In this study, we focus on organizational identification, which is a specific form of social identification where individuals define themselves in terms of their membership in a particular organization (Mael & Ashforth, 1992).	–	

According to Hogg and Terry (2000), organizational identification is motivated by two independent and fundamental human needs: uncertainty reduction and self-enhancement. The uncertainty reduction motive has been cited by researchers (Pratt, 1998; Weick, 1995) as one of the basic human needs that individuals want to satisfy. It reflects an individual's need of order in the social world and addresses how a person constructs his or her self-concept in order to answer the question 'Who am I?' By identifying to a social category, one becomes more certain in how to behave and what to expect from the physical and social environment within which one finds oneself (Hogg & Terry, 2000). On the other hand, the self-enhancement motive refers to an individual's attempt to think of his or her social identity in a positive manner such that his or her self-esteem can be ultimately enhanced. Through the process of identification, an individual strives to promote the perception that he or she is a worthwhile person (Ashforth et al., 2008). This logic explains why people tend to identify with prestigious or well-performing organizations (Dutton, Dukerich, & Harquail, 1994).

Given that the uncertainty reduction and self-enhancement motives govern people's cognitive system, any identity cue within the social context that can draw individuals' attention to these two motives should facilitate the identification process. Current literature has suggested that, under the organizational context, identity cues such as distinctiveness of organizational values, prestige of an organization, opportunities for career advancement, and salience of interorganizational competition (Ashforth & Mael, 1989; Ashforth et al., 2008; Brown, 1969; Dutton et al., 1994; Mael & Ashforth, 1992) can facilitate the development of organizational identification. LMX (leader-member exchange), on the other hand, signifies the quality of exchange relationship within the supervisor—subordinate dyad. Because employees usually seek information from their immediate supervisor regarding their organizational membership (Loi, Lai, & Lam, 2012), the quality of LMX should also deliver important identity cues to the employees.

Results of this research highlight the importance of developing organizational identification from the quality of leader–follower dyadic relationship.

Social Identity Theory (Continued)

Author and Year	Design	Sector/ Population	Moderator/ Mediator	Effect Size	Main Findings	Limitations	Level
					Building on the social identity perspective, our findings evidenced that organizational identification is an underlying mechanism linking LMX and job satisfaction.		
					Building on the social identity perspective, this study examines the effects of LMX on organizational identification and job satisfaction. As predicted, we found that the quality of LMX had a positive relationship with employee organizational identification, and organizational identification acted as the mediator between LMX and job satisfaction. Furthermore, both the positive relationship between LMX and organizational identification and the indirect effect of LMX on job satisfaction through organizational identification were found to be strong and significant when employees possessed low levels of job security. Our findings provide important implications to both theory and managerial practices.		
					The findings of this study also provide implications for management practitioners. As LMX has a direct effect on organizational identification and an indirect effect on job satisfaction, a high-quality supervisor–subordinate relationship is the crucial success factor for cultivating employees' strong identification to the organization and positive feelings about their jobs.		
Topa, Morales, & Moriano (2009)	Non-controlled, before-after measurement Time 1 N = 566 Time 2 N = 153	Spanish army soldiers	Mediator: Social identity	Medium—high	The general tenet that the social identity approach is useful to understand organizational behaviour is supported. Social identity does mediate the relation between the features of the organizational context and people's behaviour in those contexts. In addition, its impact is a long-lasting one, as shown by the fact that, even two years after entry in the organization, social identity is still exerting its influence, though to a lesser degree, on job satisfaction and OCB. Thus, the prediction that social identity would mediate the relations between the PCB and employees' attitudes and behaviours was supported by the adjustment of the structural equations model to the data. Social identity T1—OCB (r = .27) Social identity T2—OCB (r = .41)	More than 20% dropout rate	C-

2. Understanding

Social Exchange Theory

Author and Year	Design	Sector/ Population	Moderator/ Mediator	Effect Size	Main Findings	Limitations	Level
Bal Chiaburu, & Jansen (2010)	Cross-sectional N = 266	Service organization situated in the Mid-Atlantic region of the USA	Moderator: Social exchange relationships	Medium–high	It was found that the negative relationship between psychological contract breach and work performance was moderated by social exchanges, such that the relationship was stronger for employees with high social exchange relationship, perceived organizational support and trust. All in all, both task and contextual performance are higher when employees have strong social exchanges and perceive low contract breach. For organizations, it is advantageous to invest in trust among employees as well as a sound psychological contract with employees. Social exchange relationships—Trust in the organization (r = .56) Social exchange relationships—Psychological contract breach (r = −.45) Social exchange relationships—Perceived organizational support (r = .57) Social exchange relationships—OCB (r = .18)	No information on random selection of participants	D-
Byrne, Pitts, Chiaburu, & Steiner (2011)	Cross-sectional N = 119	Full-time employees from a variety of occupations at a single organization	Mediator: Social exchange	Medium–large	This paper finds that managerial trustworthiness was positively related to job performance and organizational commitment via perceptions of organizational support (POS) and social exchange with the organization; and that POS was related to organizational commitment through social exchange with the organization. Further, according to our hypothesized model, social exchange appears necessary for POS to relate to outcomes, and more generally, that social exchange with the organization serves as mediator between key attitudes toward the organization and employee outcomes. Though the directionality of relationships cannot be determined, the results support what we hypothesized based on theory. The implications of our findings are that relationships built on social exchange, which requires reciprocation (Gouldner, 1960), are central to how employees connect with their organization. Organizations should pay attention to nurturing and protecting these relationships.	Response rate to low	D-

(Continued)

Social Exchange Theory (Continued)

Author and Year	Design	Sector/Population	Moderator/Mediator	Effect Size	Main Findings	Limitations	Level
					Social exchange with the organization fully mediated the relationship between trustworthiness of the manager and both organizational commitment (indirect path = 0.56, p < 0:05, direct path = 0.18, ns) and job performance (indirect path = 0.22, p < 0:05, direct path = 0.07, ns). Social exchange—Organizational commitment (r = .70) Social exchange—Perceived organizational support (r = .58)		
Jayawardana (2010)	Non-controlled, before-after study N = 110	Sri Lankan garment factory	NA	No effect size given	"The study also demonstrates that employees experiencing social exchange relationships are also likely to exhibit high organizational commitment and demonstrate increased levels of citizenship behaviours. The study suggests that a social exchange process can be created between employees and their organization when employees perceive that they are being provided with higher organizational support, in this case opportunities for job enrichment, skill acquisition and workplace decision-making, leading to positive outcomes for the organization in the form of improved performance and quality levels".	NA	C
Kamdar & Van Dyne (2007)	Cross-sectional N = 230	One division of a multinational conglomerate	NA	Medium	"When employees have high-quality work relationships, this proximal influence neutralizes the role of personality. This suggests that high-quality social exchange relationships can compensate for potentially negative consequences of problematic personality traits such as low conscientiousness or low agreeableness". "results show significant relationships for specific predictors of task performance. Helping supervisors, and helping coworkers—based on consonant conceptualizations in which predictors are matched to targets of behaviour. Conscientiousness, but not agreeableness, and LMX, but not TMX, predicted task performance". "Results have important practical implications. As demonstrated by past research, organizations can enhance task performance by recruiting employees who are high in conscientiousness and by encouraging supervisors to develop close, supportive relationships with subordinates. Moving beyond past research, results also demonstrate that high-quality social exchange relationships can compensate for less-desirable personality characteristics. This has important practical implications because managers often inherit employees and do not have the opportunity to select on the basis of personality".	No information on random selection of participants	D-

Study	Design	Setting	Variable	Sample size	Findings	Limitations
Kim, Aryee, Loi, & Kim (2013)	Cross-sectional (N = 320)	Manufacturing company in the southern part of South Korea	Moderator: Social exchange with organization was moderated by leader—member exchange (LMX) quality	High	"In view of the recognition of a social exchange-based employment relationship as a source of competitive advantage, our finding relating P—O fit to perceived social exchange with organization has implications for organizations. Specifically, organizations can foster a social exchange-based employment relationship through the careful selection of employees in terms of their P—O fit. The moderating influence of high-quality LMX suggests that building supportive leadership not only enhances perceived social exchange with organization among high P—O fit employees but also mitigates the potentially less than positive work experience of low P—O fit employees, leading such employees to perceive a social exchange-based employment relationship. Thus, leadership training that highlights sensitivity to the needs of employees and developmental opportunities for subordinates may complement selection practices to foster perceived social exchange with organization". Organizational social exchange—P-O fit (r = .46) Organizational social exchange—LMX-subordinate (r = .66) LMX-subordinate—Job satisfaction (r = .39) LMX-subordinate—Organizational commitment (r = .40)	D- No information on random selection of participants
Yigit (2016)	Cross-sectional N = 270	Kocaeli University (Turkey)	NA	Medium—large	"According to the second hypothesis of the research, it is accepted that some levels of dependent variable of social exchange have positive effect on the independent variable organizational commitment. According to this result, it is possible to say that when the level of organizational commitment increases, social exchange level of Kocaeli University employees also increases. In order to increase patient and employee satisfaction, employees equipped with the best skills should be chosen; socialization process of employees should be supported and it should be understood that organizations are a means of social exchange for employees. Therefore, social exchange, organizational socialization and organizational commitment processes established between the parties must be managed effectively".	E No information on random selection of participants Sample size not large enough

3. Controlling

Theory of Planned Behaviour

Author and Year	Design	Sector/ Population	Moderator/ Mediator	Effect Size	Main Findings	Limitations	Level
Rise, Sheeran, & Hukkelberg (2010)	Meta-analysis N = 40 independent tests, 11,607 respondents	NA	Mediator: intention	Medium– high	Multiple regression analyses showed that self-identity explained an increment of 6% of the variance in intention after controlling for the TPB components, and explained an increment of 9% of the variance when past behaviour and the TPB components were controlled. The influence of self-identity on behaviour was largely mediated by the strength of behavioural intentions. Mediation analysis suggests that the influence of self-identity on behaviour was largely, and perhaps entirely, mediated by the strength of behavioural intention. In our view, these findings warrant the conclusion that self-identity is a vital predictor of intentions and behaviour and should be incorporated into the dominant model of attitude—behaviour relations; that is, the theory of planned behaviour.	Unclear if most included studies used a control group, random assignment and/ or before-after measurements Process to select studies not clearly defined and reproducible Methodological quality of each study was not assessed	C
Rivis, Sheeran, & Armitage (2009)	Meta-analysis N = 73 articles (79 tests)	NA	Mediator: Intention	Medium– high	The main aims of the present study were to quantify the strength of the anticipated affect/intention and moral norm/ intention relationships, and to determine the predictive validity of anticipated affect and moral norms in the theory of planned behaviour. The finding that anticipated affect and moral norms contributed an additional 5% and 3%, respectively, to the variance explained in intentions, after attitudes and other TPB variables had been taken into account, provides strong evidence to support the argument that measures of anticipated affect and moral norms should be included in the TPB. At a practical level, the findings also possess important implications for interventions designed to reduce risky behaviours and increase healthy behaviours. Increasing the salience of moral norms/ anticipated regret may be particularly useful in strengthening intentions to engage in health-promoting behaviours (e.g. Abraham & Sheeran, 2004, Study 2) and	Unclear if most included studies used a control group, random assignment and/ or before-after measurements Methodological quality of each study was not assessed	B-

(Continued)

| Alok, Raveen-dran, & Prasuna (2014) | Cross-sectional N = 133 | Indian IT services companies and MNC having significant India-centric delivery capabilities | NA | Medium | The purpose of this paper is to test the efficacy of TPB in relationship conflict among software employees. The five variables of the TPB comprising attitude, Injunctive Subjective Norms (ISN), Descriptive Subjective Norms (DSN), Conflict Efficacy (CE) and Structural Assurance (SA) have been studied in relation to obliging and dominating style. By developing relationship vignettes, salient beliefs toward conflicts were elicited and a questionnaire was designed. SEM for 133 responses has been used for testing path suitability and significance. Overall, TPB explained about 38% and 42% of the variance in behavioural intention to opt for obliging and dominating style, respectively.

The findings support TPB as a model for understanding the type of style adopted in case of a relationship conflict. Understanding intention means that behaviour can, in effect, be accurately predicted before it occurs, thus offering organizations a timeframe for intervention. Some of the interventions that can be implied by the change agents would be:
• **Communication:** Norms will be more effective, when there is consistency between message of descriptive and injunctive norms. When we are trying to change behaviour or promote new behaviour, these messages need to be aligned. Normative message from managers and peers enhances the effectiveness of the message. The important referent should be the role model for the behavioural change. Moreover, if group members observe referent performing obliging style, they are likely to view such behaviour as typical and appropriate and in turn exhibit such behaviours.
• **Training:** Longitudinal research has shown that training can increase people's confidence to accept a more proactive and interpersonal role within the workplace. | Unclear if participants were randomly selected | D- |

weakening intentions to engage in health-risk behaviours. For example, asking people to focus on their feelings after engaging in a risky behaviour should reduce people's intentions to engage in the behaviour and, subsequently, should reduce risk-taking behaviour.

Theory of Planned Behaviour (Continued)

Author and Year	Design	Sector/ Population	Moderator/ Mediator	Effect Size	Main Findings	Limitations	Level
Arnold et al. (2006)	Cross-sectional N = 1,175	UK's National Health Service	NA	Only z values given	We examined the capacity of the extended TPB to predict intention to work for the UK's National Health Service (NHS) as a nurse, physiotherapist or radiographer among three groups: those not professionally qualified, those in training and those qualified but not currently working for the NHS. We found strong support for attitude and subjective norm as predictors of behavioural intention, with or without controlling for alternative career intentions. There was some support for perceived behavioural control as a predictor of intention, but less for moral obligation and identity. As hypothesized, attitude was a stronger predictor of intention among the qualified respondents than the other two groups. We conclude that the TPB is less effective for the bigger and harder-to-implement decisions in life than for smaller and easier-to-implement ones. Also, the absolute and relative importance of some TPB variables varies with personal circumstances. Our findings suggest that assessing intention net of alternative intention leaves the capacity of attitude and subjective norm to account for intention unscathed, or even strengthened. We interpret this as strong evidence for the importance of attitude and SN, which are both core TPB constructs.	Unclear if participants were randomly selected	D-
Chang (1998)	Cross-sectional N = 181	Hong Kong Universities	NA	Medium–high	The principal objective of this study was to assess the applicability of two social psychological theories, theory of reasoned action and theory of planned behaviour, to the predicting of unethical behaviour. Theory of planned behaviour was found to be better than the theory of reasoned action in predicting unethical behaviour. The results indicated that perceived behavioural control is a better predictor of behavioural intention then attitude. The direct effect of subjective norm on behavioural intention was not significant, but the indirect effect through attitude was highly significant	Unclear if participants were randomly selected Unclear if all measurement methods used were reliable and valid	E

Study	Design	Sample	Mediator	Effect size	Findings	Limitations
					Our results show that perceived behavioural control is the most important predictor of intention to use illegal software copies. The usefulness of perceived behavioural control in predicting (un)ethical behaviour has been substantiated by our results and is consistent with most situations involving decisions of performing unethical behaviour. As mentioned previously, the performers of unethical behaviour do not have total control in most situations. Opportunities and resources must exist before they can be performed. Results from the present study show that theory of planned behaviour can be used quite successfully to predict the intention to perform unethical behaviour. As such, it provides a solid theoretical basis for the study of unethical behaviour, and it is better than the theory of reasoned action, which does not take the resources and opportunity into account, in predicting unethical behaviour. However, the attitude and subjective norm components are not as independent as the theory predicts, which has been supported by previous studies.	
Jimmieson, Peach, & White (2008)	Cross-sectional N = 149	Employees undergoing the first phase of a building relocation	Partial mediator: Subjective norm and perceived behavioural control	Small—medium	Utilizing the Theory of Planned Behaviour (TPB) as a framework for understanding employee intentions to support organizational change, this study examined the extent to which attitude, subjective norm, and perceived behavioural control (PBC), as well as the interactive effect of group norm and in-group identification, predicted intentions to carry out change-supportive activities. Attitude, subjective norm and PBC each predicted intentions. A significant interaction emerged, with group norm predicting intentions only for employees who identified strongly with their reference group. Employees who perceived sufficient information about the relocation reported stronger intentions, an effect that was partially mediated via subjective norm and PBC. Similarly, participation predicted intentions via subjective norm.	E Unclear if participants were randomly selected Unclear if all measurement methods used were reliable and valid

(*Continued*)

Theory of Planned Behaviour (Continued)

Author and Year	Design	Sector/ Population	Moderator/ Mediator	Effect Size	Main Findings	Limitations	Level
					The inclusion of group norm and in-group identification contributed to the power of the model to explain intentions, suggesting that interventions designed to foster favourable group norms and strengthen social identity may be key to maximizing change receptiveness. The TPB also contributed to our understanding of the relationship between two specific change management strategies (communication and participation) and intentions to behaviourally support change. From an applied point of view, the TPB is a useful framework for pre-implementation assessments of readiness for change as it can provide organizations with an early indication of employee beliefs and determinants of their intentions before the change event. Indeed, one of the major advantages of the TPB approach, inherent in its belief basis, is its ability to identify the underlying beliefs that distinguish between intenders and non-intenders for the specific behaviour under investigation.		
					The identification of beliefs that underlie attitude, subjective norm and perceived behavioural control may help change managers to develop a greater understanding of the psychological factors that distinguish between those employees who support the change and those who do not. Such assessments should help change agents to make targeted choices about strategies and tactics that are needed to help foster employee enthusiasm for change. The TPB also might be used as a process model of change management by progressively measuring intentions (and its determinants) across successive stages of a change program.		

4. Trusting

Groupthink

Author and Year	Design	Sector/ Population	Moderator/ Mediator	Effect Size	Main Findings	Limitations	Level
Berntal & Insko (1993)	Non-randomized, controlled, before-after study N = 138 (females)	Undergraduate students (psychology), University of North Carolina	NA	Only F values given	Low social—high task-oriented groups have the lowest perception of groupthink. High social groups have the highest perception of groupthink. Conditions preventing groupthink can be instituted by providing a task-oriented focus within the decision-making group. This research, however, shows that social-emotional cohesion does not have to be sacrificed if task-oriented cohesion has a strong presence in the group. As long as the reasons for forming the group are clear and the group follows procedures designed to counteract the possibility of groupthink, high levels of social-emotional cohesion should not present a problem. Janis (1982) presents ten techniques for counteracting the tendency toward groupthink. For example, group organizers could assign the role of devil's advocate on a rotating basis to each of the group members. From the outset, groups and group leaders should develop a policy of detailed criticism and evaluation for any course of action and the means for incorporating criticism to avoid stalemates. Another possibility is to allow group members to take group decisions or policies to independent outside groups for evaluation and discussion. Similarly, outside experts should be invited on a regular basis to attend group meetings and provide impartial evaluation of group actions. Finally, groups should be sure to form subgroups to allow more detailed discussion and promote a less threatening atmosphere for alternative viewpoints. Interestingly, many of the preventive measures discussed previously not only make groupthink more unlikely, but they also promote task-oriented cohesion within the group. By following all these procedures, goals and goal-path clarity become much more evident for group members, and the purposes of their meetings become very structured and task focused.	Unclear if control group was similar to the intervention group at the start of the study	B-

(Continued)

Groupthink (Continued)

Author and Year	Design	Sector/ Population	Moderator/ Mediator	Effect Size	Main Findings	Limitations	Level
Callaway, Marriott, & Esser (1984)	Non-randomized, controlled, before-after study N = 112	Psychology students	NA	Only F values given	The results of this study provide support for a stress-reduction explanation of groupthink with respect to groups composed of either high- or low-dominance individuals. There was a tendency for groups composed of individuals scoring above the median on dominance to report more attempted and actual influence by the group, make more statements of agreement and disagreement, and use more time to make a decision than there was for low-dominance groups. High-dominance groups reported lower levels of state anxiety and produced higher-quality decisions than low-dominance groups. Despite the support for a stress-reduction explanation of groupthink with respect to dominance, the manipulation of decision-making procedures affected only decision time. The decision procedures instructions reduced the time required to reach a decision, presumably by orienting the group to the decision task. However, the manipulation of decision-making procedures affected neither decision quality nor the process variables assumed to mediate groupthink. In groups of low-dominance individuals, perhaps the assignment of the roles of critical evaluator and devil's advocate (prescribed by Janis, 1972, to counteract groupthink) must involve personal accountability in order to overcome the natural reticence of such individuals.	Unclear if control group was similar to the intervention group at the start of the study	B-
Goncalo, Polman, & Maslach (2010)	Interrupted time series N = 262 (main study)	Undergraduate students	Mediator: Process conflict	Medium	Existing research has shown that collective efficacy can reduce decision-making vigilance when it reaches levels that are excessive or exceed actual capability (Tasa & Whyte, 2005), but our research calls attention to the timing of when collective efficacy emerges. Confidence that comes too soon is problematic, while confidence near a task deadline may facilitate group performance.	NA	B

We found that early collective efficacy reduces early process conflict in particular, possibly because such conflicts require foresight about how a group should go about completing its tasks (Vancouver & Kendall, 2006; Audia, Locke, & Smith 2001). Overconfident groups may put off those discussions because they are reluctant to devote too much time and effort to tasks they feel almost assured of completing successfully (Moore & Healy, 2008). The motivation to consider alternative strategies may be higher in groups that do not feel quite so certain about their probability of success. We do not, however, think that it would be advisable to lower a group's confidence to counteract this problem. Instead, it may be more effective to encourage debate around issues relating to the process of getting work done using techniques such as dialectical inquiry (Schweiger, Sandberg, & Ragan, 1986) or by encouraging conflict either by instructions (Nemeth, Personnaz, Personnaz, & Goncalo, 2004) or by building shared norms that permit the expression of alternative viewpoints (Postmes, Spears, & Cihangir, 2001; Goncalo & Staw, 2006). We found that early process conflict was positively associated with group performance, while process conflict near the task deadline was negatively associated with group performance. One reason for the discrepancy between our findings and those reported by Jehn and Mannix (2001) may simply be due to differences in our analytical approach; we controlled for process conflict at the middle and at the end of the groups' interaction and we also measured performance as a continuous variable as opposed to conducting a median split.

Of the many antecedent factors that contribute to the rise of groupthink (i.e. lack of methodical procedures for search and appraisal; directive leadership), Janis (1972) emphasized group cohesiveness above all others.

First and foremost, the results of these analyses reveal that quality of group decision-making is not a simple effect of group cohesiveness.

Mullen (1994)	Meta-analysis N = 9	NA	NA	Medium	B- Unclear if most studies included used a control group, random assignment or before-and-after measurement

(Continued)

253

Groupthink (Continued)

Author and Year	Design	Sector/ Population	Moderator/ Mediator	Effect Size	Main Findings	Limitations	Level
					Interpersonal attraction may contribute to groupthink, whereas commitment to task may thwart groupthink. In a sense, cohesiveness in terms of commitment to task may actively thwart groupthink by undoing one of the antecedents conditions for groupthink, namely the lack of methodical procedures for search and appraisal of decision alternatives. Group size: Cohesiveness tends to impair decision quality as group size increased.	Methodological quality of each study not assessed	
Riccobono, Bruccoleri, & Größler (2015)	Interrupted time series N = 71	First-year MBA students (large Italian university)	Moderators: Level of previous relationships Level of interpersonal evaluation	Small—medium	The main contribution of this study is twofold. First, we explicitly consider and measure the core construct of groupthink phenomenon; that is, GTB. Existing organizational behaviour literature has, contrarily, considered only its causes, symptoms, and outcomes. Second, we show evidence that GTB does have a negative impact on group performance in BPR project settings. Accordingly, managers in charge of BPR projects should consider the following practices suggested by Janis (1972) as remedies for this negative behaviour: usage of a critical reviewer when making important group decisions; not allowing individuals to express their preferences in advance; consideration of all alternatives before making the final decisions and open sessions to reconsider alternatives; discussion of ideas with people outside of the group; invitation of experts to group meetings. Moreover, our research adds to these remedies some useful suggestions about how to set and/or incentivize personal traits and interpersonal ties that weaken the negative effect of GTB. From one side, a manager should encourage individuals' understanding that they control (perceived control) and are responsible (conscientiousness) for project tasks and performance. This could be achieved, for example, by clearly sharing with the group the BPR project's work breakdown structure, indicating responsibilities and roles. Furthermore,	Criteria used to select subjects not clearly defined	B-

					managers should frame the members' perception of a debate with their peers as something pleasant, useful and effective in making decisions and/or in solving problems related to the project. In other words, they are asked to increase the group members' interpersonal evaluation. From the other side, managers should inhibit individual feelings that one member is more capable than others (overconfidence) and they should be well informed about past private and professional experiences of each individual with the others members (previous relationships). However, it is important to take into account that these two last characteristics might have a positive direct impact on overall project performance. Accordingly, we suggest the manager evaluate, case by case, the possibility to adopt the appropriate remedies suggested by Janis to directly reduce GTB instead of just compensating its negative effect.		
Turner, Pratnakis, Probasco, & Leve (1992) Experiment 1	Randomized, controlled, before-after study N = 180	Undergraduate students	NA	Medium—large	Experiment 1 produced the poor decision quality associated with groupthink by manipulating group cohesion (using group labels) and threat to group members' self-esteem. Self-reports of some groupthink and defective decision-making symptoms were independently, but not interactively, affected by cohesion and threat. Experiment 2 confirmed the success of the cohesion manipulation. Experiment 3 replicated the poor-quality decision-making observed in Experiment 1 and provided support for a social identity maintenance perspective on groupthink: Groups that operated under groupthink conditions but who were given an	Unclear if all measurement methods used were reliable and valid	A-
Turner, Pratnakis, Probasco, & Leve (1992) Experiment 2	Randomized, controlled, before-after study N = 180	College students	NA	Medium—large		NA	A
Turner, Pratnakis, Probasco, & Leve (1992) Experiment 3	Randomized, controlled, before-after study N = 123	College students	NA	Medium—large	excuse for potential poor performance produced significantly higher-quality decisions than groups who worked under groupthink conditions alone. The results are used to interpret the groupthink phenomenon as a collective effort directed at warding off potentially negative views of the group.	Unclear if all measurement methods used were reliable and valid	A-

(Continued)

Groupthink (Continued)

Author and Year	Design	Sector/ Population	Moderator/ Mediator	Effect Size	Main Findings	Limitations	Level
					Results obtained in Experiments 1 and 3 reinforce the view of groupthink as a process in which group members attempt to maintain a shared, positive view of the functioning of the group in the face of a collective threat (Janis, 1982). This approach is predicated on the induction of a group social identity—an attribute characteristic of many groups in the original case studies. This identity is important in two respects. First, it ensures that members categorize and perceive themselves as a group and develop a positive view of the group they are motivated to maintain. Second, it provides the basis on which the shared threat can operate. The current research reinforces one interpretation (among possible others) that might be useful in facilitating this research: The view of groupthink as group members' effort to collectively reduce the potential damage from threat and to ward off negative images of the group that produces, as Janis (1982, p. 167) termed it, "the genuine sharing of illusory beliefs".		

5. Self-Enhancing

Self-verification theory

Author and Year	Design	Sector/ Population	Moderator/ Mediator	Effect Size	Main Findings	Limitations	Level
Ahn, Lee, & Yun (2016)	Cross-sectional N = 253 (sub-ordinates) and 254 supervisors	Various organi-zations in South Korea	Mediator: Ethical leader-ship	Small—medium	Our study has practical and managerial implications as well. First of all, we found that ethical leadership exerted positive effects on follower job performance. In today's fast-paced economy, sometimes leaders' moral responsibility is pushed back on the priority list. As our results suggest, however, ethical leadership is beneficial to the organization, as it can induce followers to exert more effort in contributing to the organization. Thus, organizations need to encourage managers to display ethical leadership. In addition, focusing on individual characteristics among supervisors, the present study demonstrated that leaders who have an overall positive self-view (i.e. high CSE) are more likely to engage in ethical leadership. This result suggests that ethical leadership can be promoted not only by activating leaders' positive self-image, but as Chang, Ferris, Johnson, Rosen, and Tan (2012) suggested, CSE scores can be taken into account when making personnel decisions. It may be prudent for organizational human resource management teams to keep this in mind before making leadership appointments.	Respondents not randomly selected	D-
Anseel (2006)	Non-controlled, before-after study N = 389	Employees	NA	Small—medium	Both feedback scores and self-ratings predicted feedback satisfaction in opposite directions. This seems to be in line with predictions of self-verification theory. However, self-verification theory also predicts that both effects will be equally strong. This was not the case. Feedback scores were stronger in predicting feedback satisfaction, indicating that self-enhancement strivings are more dominant than self-verification strivings in guiding feedback satisfaction. This finding is consistent with recent research on self-evaluation in social psychology which has demonstrated that people often try to simultaneously satisfy self-enhancement and self-verification motives when processing feedback.	Criteria used to select subjects not clearly defined	C-

(Continued)

Self-verification theory (Continued)

Author and Year	Design	Sector/ Population	Moderator/ Mediator	Effect Size	Main Findings	Limitations	Level
					In general, little evidence was found for self-verification as the dominant motive underlying feedback reactions. Instead, the results seem to corroborate self-enhancement theory, which predicts that people are motivated to view themselves as favourably as possible. Furthermore, it seems that certainty does not play a key role as a moderator of feedback reactions and, thus, does not strengthen the self-verification motive.		
Kwang & Swan (2010)	Meta-analysis N = 38 (studies)	NA	NA	Medium	The results of our meta-analysis confirm earlier evidence that self-enhancement strivings influence affective responses but self-verification strivings shape cognitive reactions. At the very least, the findings from the meta-analysis reported here refute the contention that the desire for self-enhancement routinely overrides the desire for self-verification. More interestingly, the robustness of self-verification strivings in our results throws into question the proper interpretation of dozens of studies that are widely assumed to represent evidence for self-enhancement theory: studies that were not included in our meta-analyses because the investigators failed to include measures of self-views.	Unclear if most studies included used a control group, random assignment or before-and-after measurement. Methodological quality of each study not assessed	B-
Swann, Milton, & Polzer (2000)	Interrupted time series N = 423	MBA students University of Texas	NA	Medium	Self-verification processes contributed to productivity on projects that required creativity. These data thus extend previous evidence linking self-verification to relationship intimacy and satisfaction. We should emphasize, however, that even if self-verification effects are in some sense consequences rather than, or as well as, determinants of group processes, simply demonstrating that groups that are conducive to self-verification tend to be more effective is, of itself, important. Among other things, this finding identifies group processes that are associated with good performance on creative tasks. This finding may also provide a useful perspective on efforts to manage diversity in the workplace.	Criteria used to select subjects not clearly defined	B-

Appendix C
Bibliography

Abbot, A. (1988). *System of professions: Essay on the division of expert labour.* Chicago, IL: The University of Chicago Press.

Aberson, C. L., Healy, M., & Romero, V. (2000). Ingroup bias and self-esteem: A meta-analysis. *Personality and Social Psychology Review, 4*(2), 157–173.

Abraham, C., & Sheeran, P. (2004). Deciding to exercise: The role of anticipated regret. *British Journal of Health Psychology, 9*(2), 269–278.

Abraham, R. (1999a). Emotional dissonance in organizations: Conceptualizing the roles of self-esteem and job-induced tension. *Leadership & Organization Development Journal, 20*(1), 18–25.

Abraham, R. (1999b). The impact of emotional dissonance on organizational commitment and intention to turnover. *The Journal of Psychology, 133*(4), 441–455.

Ahn, J., Lee, S., & Yun, S. (2016). Leaders' core self-evaluation, ethical leadership, and employees' job performance: The moderating role of employees' exchange ideology. *Journal of Business Ethics*, 1–14.

Aiello, J. R., & Douthitt, E. A. (2001). Social facilitation from Triplett to electronic performance monitoring. *Group Dynamics: Theory, Research, and Practice, 5*(3), 163–180.

Aiello, J. R., & Kolb, K. J. (1995). Electronic performance monitoring and social context: Impact on productivity and stress. *Journal of Applied Psychology, 80*(3), 339–353.

Ainsworth, M. D. S., Blehar, M. C., Waters, E., & Wall, S. (1978). *Patterns of attachment: A psychological study of the strange situation.* Hillsdale, NJ: Erlbaum.

Ajzen, I. (1985). From intentions to actions: A theory of planned behavior. In: J. Kuhl & J. Beckmann (Eds.), *Action Control: From cognition to behavior* (pp. 11–39). Springer, GER: Heidelberg.

Ajzen, I. (1991). The theory of planned behavior. *Organizational Behavior and Human Decision Processes, 50*(2), 179–211.

Ajzen, I. (2005). *Attitudes, personality, and behavior* (2nd ed.). London: McGraw-Hill.

Ajzen, I., & Fishbein, M. (1980). *Understanding attitudes and predicting social behavior.* Englewood Cliffs, NJ: Prentice-Hall.

Akan, H., Allen, R. S., & White, C. S. (2008). Equity Sensitivity and organizational citizenship behavior in a team environment. *Small Group Research, 40*(1), 94–112.

Alderfer, C. (1972). *Existence, relatedness, & growth.* New York, NY: Free Press.

Alessandrini, K. L. (1981). Pictoral-verbal and analytic-holistic learning strategies in science learning. *Journal of Educational Psychology, 73*(3), 358–368.

Allen, R. A., Evans, W. R., & White, C. S. (2011). Affective organizational commitment and organizational citizenship behavior: Examining the relationship through the lens of equity sensitivity. *Organization Management Journal, 8*(4), 218–228.

Allen, V. L. (1965). Situational factors in conformity. *Advances in Experimental Social Psychology, 2*, 133–175.

Allport, G. W., & Lindzey, G. (1954). *Handbook of social psychology.* Cambridge, MA: Addison-Wesley.

Alok, S., Raveendran, J., & Prasuna, M. G. (2014). Predicting the conflict-style intention to manage relationship conflict: An exploratory extension of theory of planned behavior. *South Asian Journal of Management, 21*(1), 117–133.

Amiot, C. E., Terry, D. J., & McKimmie, B. M. (2012). Social identity change during an intergroup merger: The role of status, similarity, and identity threat. *Basic and Applied Social Psychology, 34*(5), 443–455.

Andrews, M. C., Kacmar, K. M., Blakely, G. L., & Bucklew, N. S. (2008). Group cohesion as an enhancement to the justice-affective commitment relationship. *Group & Organization Management, 33*(6), 736–755.

Anseel, F., & Lievens, F. (2006). Certainty as a moderator of feedback reactions? A test of the strength of the self-verification motive. *Journal of Occupational and Organizational Psychology, 79*, 533–551.

Antman, E. M. (1992). A comparison of results of meta-analyses of randomized controlled trials and recommendations of clinical experts. *Journal of the American Medical Association, 286*(2), 240–248.

Arbaugh, B., Cox, L. W., & Camp, S. M. (2004). Employee equity, incentive compensation, and Growth in entrepreneurial firms. *New England Journal of Entrepreneurship, 7*(1), 1–11.

Argyris, C. (1990). *Overcoming organizational defenses: Facilitating organizational learning.* Needham Heights, MA: Allyn & Bacon.

Aristotle (328 BC), *Politica* I, 1253a, 15–18.

Armenakis, A. A., & Bedeian, A. G. (1999). Organizational change: A review of theory and research in the 1990s. *Journal of Management, 25*(3), 293–315.

Armenakis, A. A., & Harris, S. G. (2009). Reflections: Our journey in organizational change research and practice. *Journal of Change Management, 9*(2), 127–142.

Arnold, J., Clark, J. L., Coombs, C., Wilkinson, A., Park, J., & Preston, D. (2006). How well can the theory of planned behavior account for occupational intentions? *Journal of Vocational Behavior, 69*(3), 374–390.

Aronson, E. (1968). *Theories of cognitive consistency: A sourcebook.* Chicago, IL: Rand McNally.

Aronson, E. (2016). *The social animal.* New York, NY: Worth Publishers.

Aronson, J. (1995). A pragmatic view of thematic analysis. *The Qualitative Report, 2*(1), 1–3.

Asch, S. E. (1951). Effects of group pressure upon the modification and distortion of judgments. In: H. Guetzkow (Ed.), *Groups, leadership and men; research in human relations* (pp. 177–190). Oxford: Carnegie Press.

Asch, S. E. (1955). Opinions and Social Pressure. *Scientific American, 193*(5), 31–35.

Ashforth, B. E., Harrison, S. H., & Corley, K. G. (2008). Identification in organizations: An examination of four fundamental questions. *Journal of Management, 34*(3), 325–374.

Ashforth, B., & Mael, F. A. (1989). Social identity theory and organization. *The Academy of Management Review, 14*(1), 20–39.

Atkinson, J. W. (1957). Motivational determinants of risk-taking behavior. *Psychological review, 64*(6), 359–372.

Audia, P. G., Locke, E. A., & Smith, K. G. (2001). The paradox of success: An archival and a laboratory study of strategic persistence following radical environmental change. *Academy of Management Journal, 43*(5), 837–853.

Avanzi, L., Fraccaroli, F., Sarchielli, G., Ullrich, J., & Van Dick, R. (2014). Staying or leaving: A combined social identity and social exchange approach to predicting employee turnover intentions. *International Journal of Productivity and Performance Management, 63*(3), 272–289.

Axtell, C. M., & Parker, S. K. (2003). Promoting role breadth self-efficacy through involvement, work redesign and training. *Human relations, 56*(1) 113–131.

Bailey, J. R., & Raelin, J. D. (2015). Organizations don't resist change, people do: Modeling individual reactions to organizational change through loss and terror management. *Organizational Management Journal, 12*(3), 125–138.

Baker, A. B., & Heuven, E. (2006). Emotional dissonance, burnout, and in-role performance among nurses and police officers. *International Journal of Stress Management, 13*(4), 423–440.

Baker, S. D., Mathis, C. J., Stites-Doe, S., & Javadian, G. (2016). The Role of trust and communication in fostering followers' self perceptions as leaders. *Journal of Managerial Issues, 28*(3–4), 210–230.

Bal, P. M., Chiaburu, D. S., & Jansen, P. G. W. (2010). Psychological contract breach and work performance. *Journal of Managerial Psychology, 25*(3), 252–273.

Balliet, D., & Van Lange, P. A. M. (2013). Trust, conflict, and cooperation: A meta-analysis. *Psychological Bulletin, 139*(5), 1090–1112.

Bandura, A. (1963). *Social learning and personality development*. New York, NY: Holt, Rinehart, and Winston.

Bandura, A. (1969). Social-learning theory of identificatory processes. In: D. A. Goslin (Ed.), *Handbook of socialization theory and research* (pp. 213–262). Chicago, IL: Rand McNally & Company.

Bandura, A. (1971). *Social learning theory*. Morristown, NJ: General Learning Press.

Bandura, A. (1972). *Socialization: Lexikon der Psychologie, Band III*. Freiburg im Breisgau, GR: Herder.

Bandura, A. (1977). *Social learning theory*. Englewood Cliffs, NJ: Prentice Hall.

Bandura, A. (1986). *Social foundations of thought and action: A social cognitive theory*. Englewood Cliffs, NJ: Prentice-Hall.

Bandura, A. (1999). Moral Disengagement in the Perpetration of Inhumanities. *Personality and Social Psychology Review, 3*(3), 193–209.

Bandura, A. (2009). Cultivate self-efficacy for personal and organizational effectiveness. In: E. A. Locke (Ed.), *Handbook of principles of organization behaviour* (pp. 179–200). Oxford, UK: Blackwell.

Bandura, A., Barbaranelli, C., Caprara, G. V., & Pastorelli, C. (1996). Mechanisms of moral disengagement in the exercise of moral agency. *Journal of Personality and Social Psychology, 71*(2), 364–374.

Baranik, L. E., & Eby, L. (2016). Organizational citizenship behaviors and employee depressed mood, burnout, and satisfaction with health and life: The mediating role of positive affect. *Personnel Review*, *45*(4), 626–642.

Barber, B. (1963). Some problems in the sociology of professions. *Daedalus*, *92*(4), 669–688.

Barber, J. S. (2011). The theory of planned behaviour: Considering drives, proximity and dynamics. *Vienna Yearbook of Population Research*, *9*, 31–35.

Barnett, M. D., Moore, J. M., & Harp, A. R. (2017). Who we are and how we feel: Self-discrepancy theory and specific affective states. *Personality and Individual Differences*, *111*(1), 232–237.

Barnett, S. A. (2017). *The Rat: A study in behavior*. New York, NY: Routledge.

Baron, R. M., & Kenny, D. A. (1986). The moderator—Mediator variable distinction in social psychological research: Conceptual, strategic, and statistical considerations. *Journal of Personality and Social Psychology*, *51*(6), 1173–1182.

Barsky, A. (2008). Understanding the ethical cost of organizational goal-setting: A review and theory development. *Journal of Business Ethics*, *81*, 63–81.

Barsky, A. (2011). Investigating the effects of moral disengagement and participation on unethical work behavior. *Journal of Business Ethics*, *104*(1), 59–75.

Bartel, C. A. (2001). Social comparisons in boundary-spanning work: Effects of community outreach on members' organizational identity and identification. *Administrative Science Quarterly*, *46*(3), 379–413.

Bartholomew, K. (1990). Avoidance of intimacy: An attachment perspective. *Journal of Social and Personal Relationships*, *7*(2), 147–178.

Baruch, Y., O'Creevy, M. F., Hind, P., & Vigoda-Gadot, E. (2004). Prosocial behavior and job performance: Does the need for control and the need for achievement make a difference? *Social Behavior and Personality*, *32*(4), 399–412.

Bauer, M. W., & Gaskell, G. (1999). Towards a paradigm for research on social representations. *Journal for the Theory of Social Behavior*, *29*(2), 163–186.

Baumeister, R. F. (1993). *Self-esteem: The puzzle of low self-regard*. New York, NY: Plenum Press.

Baumeister, R. F., Campbell, J. D., Krueger, J. L., & Vohs, K. D. (2003). Does high self-esteem cause better performance, interpersonal success, happiness, or healthier lifestyles? *Psychological Science in the Public Interest*, *4*(1), 1–44.

Baumeister, R. F., & Leary, M. R. (1995). The need to belong: Desire for interpersonal attachments as a fundamental human motivation. *Psychological Bulletin*, *117*(3), 497–529.

Baumeister, R. F., Smart, L., & Boden, J. M. (1996). Relation of threatened egotism to violence and aggression: The dark side of high self-esteem. *Psychological Review*, *103*(1), 5–33.

Baumeister, R. F., & Tierney, J. (2012). *Willpower: Rediscovering our greatest strength*. London: Penguin Books Ltd.

Bazarova, N. N., Walther, J. B., & McLeod, P. L. (2012). Minority influence in virtual groups: A comparison of four theories of minority influence. *Communication Research*, *39*(3), 295–316.

Becker, G. S. (1974). A theory of social interactions. *Journal of Political Economy*, *82*(6), 1063–1093.

Beersma, B., Hollenbeck, J. R., Humphrey, S. E., Moon, H., Conlon, D. E., & Ilgen, D. R. (2003). Cooperation, competition, and team performance: Toward a contingency approach. *Academy of Management Journal*, *46*(5), 572–590.

Belasco, J. A. (1990). *Teaching the elephant to dance. Empowering change in your organization*. New York, NY: Crown Publishers.

Bellemare, C., Lepage, P., & Shearer, B. S. (2009). Peer pressure, incentives, and gender: An experimental analysis of motivation in the workplace. *IZA Institute of Labor Economics*, 1–24.

Bem, D. J. (1967). Self-perception: An alternative interpretation of cognitive dissonance phenomena. *Psychological review*, 74(3), 183.

Bem, D. J. (1972). Self-perception theory. *Advances in Experimental Social Psychology*, 6(1), 1–62.

Ben-Zur, H., Yagil, D., & Oz, D. (2005). Coping strategies and leadership in the adaptation to social change: The Israeli Kibbutz. *Anxiety, Stress & Coping*, 18(2), 87–103.

Bergami, M., & Bagozzi, R. P. (2000). Self-categorization, affective commitment and group self-esteem as distinct aspects of social identity in the organization. *British Journal of Social Psychology*, 39(4), 555–577.

Bernerth, J. B., Armenakis, A. A., Field, H. S., & Walker, H. J. (2007). Justice, cynicism, and commitment: A study of important organizational change variables. *The Journal of Applied Behavioral Science*, 43(3), 303–326.

Berntal, P. R., & Insko, C. A. (1993). Cohesiveness without groupthink: The interactive effects of social and task cohesion. *Group & Organization Studies*, 18(1), 66–87.

Bertrams, J. (1999). *De kennisdelende organisatie*. Schiedam, NL: Scriptum.

Bing, M. N., & Burroughs, S. M. (2001). The predictive and interactive effects of equity sensitivity in teamwork-oriented organizations. *Journal of Organizational Behavior*, 22, 271–290.

Blau, P. (1986). *Exchange and power in social life* (2nd ed.). Wiley, New York, NY: Routledge.

Boen, F., Vanbeselaere, N., & Cool, M. (2006). Group status as a determinant of organizational identification after a takeover: A social identity perspective. *Group Processes & Intergroup Relations*, 9(4), 547–560.

Boje, D., Burnes, B., & Hassard, J. (2012). *The Routledge companion to organizational change*. New York, NY: Routledge.

Bollen, K. A., & Hoyle, R. H. (1990). Perceived cohesion: A conceptual and empirical examination. *Social Forces*, 69(2), 479–504.

Bond, C. F., Jr., & Titus, L. J. (1983). Social facilitation: A meta-analysis of 241 studies. *Psychological Bulletin*, 94(2), 265–292.

Boon, S. D. (1995). Trust. In: A. S. R. Manstead & M. Hewstone (Eds.), *Blackwell encyclopedia of social psychology* (pp. 656–657). Oxford: Blackwell.

Boorstin, D. J. (1998). *The seekers: The story of man's continuing quest to understand his world*. New York, NY: Random House.

Bots, R. T. M., & Jansen, W. (2013). *Organisatie en informatie*. Groningen, NL: Noordhoff Uitgevers.

Bottoni, G. (2016). A multilevel measurement model of social cohesion. *Social Indicators Research*, 129(3), 1–23.

Boulton, D. (1987). Learning: The central dynamic of a human being. Retrieved May 11, 2018, from www.implicity.org/centdyn.htm

Boundenghan, M., Desrumaux, P., Léoni, V., & Nicolas, C. V. (2012). Predicting prosocial behavior in the workplace: Links with organizational justice, commitment, affectivity, and personality. *Revue Internationale De Psychologie Sociale*, 3–4, 13–38.

Bower, J. L. (2000). The purpose of change: A commentary on Jensen and Senge. In: M. Beer & N. Nohria (Eds.), *Breaking the Code of Change* (pp. 83–95). Boston, MA: Harvard Business Review Press.

Bowlby, J. (1969). *Attachment and loss: Attachment* (Vol. I). New York, NY: Basic Books.

Bowlby, J. (1973). *Attachment and loss: Separation* (Vol. II). New York, NY: Basic Books.

Bowlby, J. (1988). Developmental psychiatry comes of age. *The American Journal of Psychiatry, 145*(1), 1–10.

Bowling, N., Eschleman, K., Wang, Q., Kirkendall, C., & Alarcon, G. (2010). Meta-analysis of the predictors and consequences of organization-based self-esteem. *Journal of Occupational and Organizational Psychology, 83*(3), 601–626.

Braaten, L. J. (1991). Group cohesion: A new multidimensional model. *Group, 15*(1), 39–55.

Bramesfeld, K. D., & Gasper, K. (2008). Happily putting the pieces together: A test of two explanations for the effects of mood on group-level information processing. *British Journal of Social Psychology, 47*, 285–309.

Brehmer, B. (1976). Social judgment theory and the analysis of interpersonal conflict. *Psychological bulletin, 83*(6), 985.

Brehmer, B. (1988). The development of social judgment theory. *Advances in Psychology, 54*, 13–40.

Bridges, W. (1991). *Managing transitions: Making the most of change*. Boston, MA: Addison-Wesley.

Brockner, J. (1996). Understanding the interaction between procedural and distributive justice: The role of trust. In: R. M. Kramer & T. R. Tyler (Eds.), *Trust in organizations: Frontiers of theory and research* (pp. 390–413). Thousand Oaks, CA: Sage Publications, Inc.

Brockner, J. (2006). Why it's so hard to be fair. *Harvard Business Review, 84*(3), 122–129.

Brockner, J., Greenberg, J., Brockner, A., Brotz, J., Davy, J., & Carter, C. (1986). Layoffs, Equity theory, and work performance: Further evidence of the impact of survivor guilt. *Academy of Management Journal, 29*(2), 373–384.

Brockner, J., & Wiesenfeld, B. M. (1996). An integrative framework for explaining reactions to decisions: The interactive effects of outcomes and procedures. *Psychological Bulletin, 120*(2), 189–208.

Brown, D. J., Ferris, D. L., Heller, D., & Keeping, L. M. (2007). Antecedents and consequences of the frequency of upward and downward social comparisons at work. *Organizational Behavior and Human Decision Processes, 102*(1), 59–75.

Brown, J. D. (1986). Evaluations of self and others: Self-enhancement biases in social judgments. *Social Cognition, 4*(4), 353–376.

Brown, M. (1969). Identification and some conditions of organizational involvement. *Administrative Science Quarterly, 14*(3), 346–355.

Brown, M. A. (2011). Learning from service: The effect of helping on helpers' social dominance orientation. *Journal of Applied Social Psychology, 41*(4), 850–871.

Bruhn, J. (2009). *The group effect: Social cohesion and health outcomes*. Boston, MA: Springer.

Burnes, B., & Cooke, B. (2012). Kurt Lewin's field theory: A review and re-evaluation. *International Journal of Management Reviews*, 15(4), 408–425.

Burns, J. M. (1978). *Leadership*. New York, NY: Harper & Row.

Bushman, B. J., & Wells, G. L. (2001). Narrative impressions of literature: The availability bias and the corrective properties of meta-analytic approaches. *Personality and Social Psychology Bulletin*, 27(9), 1123–1130.

Buunk, A. P., Zurriaga, R., & Peiró, J. M. (2010). Social comparison as a predictor of changes in burnout among nurses. *Anxiety, Stress, and Coping*, 23(2), 181–194.

Buunk, A. P., Zurriaga, R., Peiró, J. M., Nauta, A., & Gosalvez, I. (2005). Social comparisons at work as related to a cooperative social climate and to individual differences in social comparison orientation. *Applied Psychology*, 54(1), 61–80.

Byrne, Z., Pitts, V., Chiaburu, D., & Steiner, Z. (2011). Managerial trustworthiness and social exchange with the organization. *Journal of Managerial Psychology*, 26(2), 108–122.

Cacioppo, J. T., & Gardner, W. L. (1999). Emotion. *Annual Review of Psychology*, 50, 191–214.

Caldwell, S. (2013). Change and fit, fit and change. In: S. Oreg, A. Michel, & R. T. By (Eds.), *The psychology of organizational change: Viewing change from the employee's perspective*. Cambridge: Cambridge University Press.

Callaway, M. R., Marriott, R. G., & Esser, J. K. (1984). Effects of dominance on group decision making: Toward a stress-reduction explanation of groupthink. *Journal of Personality and Social Psychology*, 49(4), 949–952.

Cameron, J., & Pierce, W. D. (1994). Reinforcement, reward, and intrinsic motivation: A meta-analysis. *Review of Educational research*, 64(3), 363–423.

Campbell, A., & Nash, L. L. (1992). *A sense of mission: Defining direction for the large corporation*. Boston, MA: Addison-Wesley Longman.

Campbell, A., & Yeung, S. (1990). *Do you need a mission statement?* Special Report No. 1208. London: The Economist Publications Management Guides.

Campbell, D. T. (1982). Legal and primary-group social norms. *Journal of Social and Biological Structures*, 5(4), 431–438.

Canegallo, C., Ortona, G., Ottone, S., Ponzano, F., & Scacciati, F. (2008). Competition versus cooperation: Some experimental evidence. *The Journal of Socio-Economics*, 37(1), 18–30.

Cantril, H. (1941). *The psychology of social movements*. Piscataway, NJ: Transaction Publishers.

Carless, S. A., & De Paola, C. (2000). The measurement of cohesion in work teams. *Small Group Research*, 31(1), 71–88.

Carrasco, H., Martínez-Tur, V., Moliner, C., Peiró, J. M., & Ramis, C. (2014). Linking emotional dissonance and service climate to well-being at work: A cross-level analysis. *Universitas Psychologica*, 13(3), 947–960.

Carron, A. V., & Spink, K. S. (1995). The group size-cohesion relationship in minimal groups. *Small Group Research*, 26(1), 86–105.

Cerasoli, C. P., Nicklin, J. M., & Ford, M. T. (2014). Intrinsic motivation and extrinsic incentives jointly predict performance: A 40-year meta-analysis. *Psychological Bulletin*, 140(4), 980–1008.

Cerasoli, C. P., Nicklin, J. M., & Nassrelgrgawi, A. S. (2016). Performance, incentives, and needs for autonomy, competence, and relatedness: A meta-analysis. *Motivation and Emotion*, 40(6), 781–813.

Černe, M., Dimovski, V., Marič, M., Penger, S., & Škerlavaj, M. (2014). Congruence of leader self-perceptions and follower perceptions of authentic leadership: Understanding what authentic leadership is and how it enhances employees' job satisfaction. *Australian Journal of Management, 39*(3), 453–471.

Chalmers, I., Enkin, M., & Keirse, M. J. (1993). Preparing and updating systematic reviews of randomized controlled trials of health care. *The Milbank Quarterly, 71*(3), 411–437.

Chan Allen, R. (2002). *Guiding change journeys: A synergistic approach to organization transformation.* New York, NY: John Wiley & Sons.

Chan, J., To, H. P., & Chan, E. (2006). Reconsidering social cohesion: Developing a definition and analytical framework for empirical research. *Social Indicators Research, 75*(2), 273–302.

Chang, A., & Bordia, P. (2001). A multidimensional approach to the group cohesion-group performance relationship. *Small Group Research, 32*(4), 379–405.

Chang, C.-H., Ferris, D. L., Johnson, R. E., Rosen, C. C., & Tan, J. A. (2012). Core self-evaluations: A review and evaluation of the literature. *Journal of Management, 38*(1), 81–128.

Chang, M. K. (1998). Predicting unethical behavior: A comparison of the theory of reasoned action and the theory of planned behavior. *Journal of Business Ethics, 17*(16), 1825–1834.

Chang, Y., & Edwards, J. K. (2015). Examining the relationships among self-efficacy, coping, and job satisfaction using social career cognitive theory: An SEM analysis. *Journal of Career Assessment, 23*(1), 35–47.

Chauvin, B., Rohmer, O., Spitzenstetter, F., Raffin, D., Schimchowitsch, S., & Louvet, E. (2014). Assessment of job stress factors in a context of organizational change. *European Review of Applied Psychology, 64*(6), 299–306.

Chen, C. H. V., Tang, Y. Y., & Wang, S. J. (2009). Interdependence and organizational citizenship behavior: Exploring the mediating effect of group cohesion in multilevel analysis. *The Journal of Psychology, 143*(6), 625–640.

Chen, S. C. (1937). The leaders and followers among ants in nest-building. *Psychological Zoology, 10*(4), 437–455.

Cheung, F. Y.-L., & Cheung, R. Y.-H. (2013). Effect of emotional dissonance on organizational citizenship behavior: Testing the stressor-strain-outcome model. *The Journal of Psychology, 147*(1), 89–103.

Cheung, F. Y.-L., & Tang, C. S.-K. (2007). The influence of emotional dissonance and resources at work on job burnout among Chinese human service employees. *International Journal of Stress Management, 14*(1), 72–87.

Chiang, C.-F., & Jang, S. C. S. (2008). An expectancy theory model for hotel employee motivation. *International Journal of Hospitality Management, 27*, 313–322.

Chiang, C.-F., & Jang, S. C. S., Canter, D. D., & Prince, B. (2008). An expectancy theory model for hotel employee motivation: Examining the moderating role of communication satisfaction. *International Journal of Hospitality & Tourism Administration, 9*(4), 327–351.

Christian, M. S., Garza, A. S., & Slaughter, J. E. (2011). Work engagement: A quantitative review and test of its relations with task and contextual performance. *Personnel Psychology, 64*(1), 89–136.

Cialdini, R. B., & Goldstein, N. J. (2004). Social influence: Compliance and conformity. *Annual Reviews Psychology, 55*(1), 591–621.

Cialdini, R. B., Wosinska, W., Barett, D. W., & Gornik-Durose, M. (1999). Compliance with a request in two cultures: The differential influence of social proof and commitment/consistency on collectivists and individualists. *Personality and Social Psychology Bulletin, 25*(10), 1242–1253.

Claus, W. J. M. (1991). Veranderen van organisatieculturen. In: J. J. Swanink (Ed.), *Scoren met cultuurverandering. Inzichten en ervaringen van managers, wetenschappers en organisatieadviseur* (pp. 46–83). Schiedam, NL: Scriptum.

Cohen, G. L., & Sherman, D. K. (2014). The psychology of change: Self-affirmation and social psychological intervention. *Annual Review of Psychology, 65*, 333–371.

Cohen, G. L., Sherman, D. K., Bastardi, A., Hsu, L., McGoey, M., & Ross, L. (2007). Bringing the partisan divide: Self-affirmation reduces ideological closed-mindedness and inflexibility in negotiation. *Journal of Personality and Social Psychology, 93*(3), 415–430.

Cohen, J. (1988). *Statistical power analysis for the behavioral sciences* (2nd ed.). Mahwah, NJ: Lawrence Erlbaum Associates Inc.

Cohen-Charash, Y., & Spector, P. E. (2001). The role of justice in organizations: A meta-analysis. *Organizational Behavior and Human Decision Processes, 86*(2), 278–321.

Collins, J. C. (2001). *Good to great: Why some companies make the leap . . . and others don't*. New York, NY: HarperCollins Publishers.

Collins, J. C., & Porras, J. I. (1996). Building your company's vision. *Harvard Business Review, 74*(5), 65–77.

Colquitt, J. A., Scott, B. A., & LePine, J. A. (2007). Trust, trustworthiness, and trust propensity: A meta-analytic test of their unique relationships with risk taking and job performance. *Journal of Applied Psychology, 92*(4), 909–927.

Colquitt, J. A., Scott, B. A., Rodell, J. B., Long, D. M., Zapata, C. P., Conlon, D. E., & Wesson, M. J. (2013). Justice at the millennium, a decade later: A meta-analytic test of social exchange and affect-based perspectives. *Journal of Applied Psychology, 98*(2), 199–236.

Conner, D. R. (1992). *Managing at the speed of change: How resilient managers succeed and prosper where others fail*. New York, NY: Random House.

Conner, D. R. (2006). *Managing at the speed of change: How resilient managers succeed and prosper where others fail*. New York, NY: Random House.

Cooper, J. O., Heron, T. E., & Heward, W. L. (2007). Cooper, Heron, and Heward's applied behavior analysis (2nd ed.). *Journal of Applied Behavior Analysis, 43*(1), 161–174.

Cottrell, N. B., Wack, D. L., Sekerak, G. J., & Rittle, R. H. (1968). Social facilitation of dominant responses by the presence of an audience and the mere presence of others. *Journal of Personality and Social Psychology, 9*(3), 245–250.

Crocker, J., & Park, L. E. (2004). The costly pursuit of self-esteem. *Psychological Bulletin, 130*(3), 392–414.

Cropanzano, R., & Mitchell, M. S. (2005). Social exchange theory: An interdisciplinary review. *Journal of Management, 31*(6), 874–900.

Cummings, T. G., & Huse, E. F. (1989). *Organizational development and change*. New York, NY: West Publishing Company.

Dashiell, J. F. (1935). Experimental studies of the influence of social situations on the behavior of individual human adults. In: *A handbook of social psychology* (pp. 1097–1158). Worcester, MA: Clark University Press.

Davidovitz, R., Shaver, P. R., Mikulinces, M., & Popper, M. (2007). Leaders as attachment figures: Leaders' attachment orientations predict leadership-related mental representations and followers' performance and mental health. *Journal of Personality and Social Psychology*, 93(4), 632–650.

De Cremer, D., Cornelis, I., & Van Hiel, A. (2008). To whom does voice in groups matter? Effects of voice on affect and procedural fairness judgments as a function of social dominance orientation. *The Journal of Social Psychology*, 148(1), 61–76.

De Wachter, D. (2011). *Identiteit in borderline-times: Het einde van de normaliteit*. Houten, NL: Terra Lannoo.

Deci, E. L. (1971). Effects of externally mediated rewards on intrinsic motivation. *Journal of Personality and Social Psychology*, 18(1), 105.

Deci, E. L., Koestner, R., & Ryan, R. M. (1999a). A meta-analytic review of experiments examining the effects of extrinsic rewards on intrinsic motivation. *Psychological Bulletin*, 125(6), 692–700.

Deci, E. L., Koestner, R., & Ryan, R. M. (1999b). The undermining effect is a reality after all—Extrinsic rewards, task interest, and self-determination: Reply to Eisenberger, Pierce, and Cameron (1999) and Lepper, Henderlong, and Gingras (1999). *Psychological Bulletin*, 125(6), 692–700.

Deci, E. L., & Porac, J. (1978). Cognitive evaluation theory and the study of human motivation. *The Hidden Costs of Reward: New Perspectives on the Psychology of Human Motivation*, 149, 155–157.

Deci, E. L., & Ryan, R. M. (1980). Self-determination theory: When mind mediates behavior. *The Journal of Mind and Behavior*, 1(1), 33–43.

Deci, E. L., & Ryan, R. M. (1985). *Intrinsic motivation and self-determination in human behavior*. New York, NY: Plenium.

Deci, E. L., & Ryan, R. M. (2012). Self-determination theory. In: P. A. M. Van Lange, A. W. Kruglanski, & E. T. Higgins (Eds.), *Handbook of theories of social psychology: Vol. 1* (pp. 416–437). Thousand Oaks, CA: Sage Publications, Inc.

Deci, E. L., & Vansteenkiste, M. (2004). Self-determination theory and basic need satisfaction: Understanding human development in positive psychology. *Richerche di Psicologia*, 27, 23–40.

Demetriades, S. Z., & Walter, N. (2016). You should know better: Can self-affirmation facilitate information-seeking behavior and interpersonal discussion? *Journal of Health Communication*, 21(11), 1131–1140.

Den Hartog, D. N., De Hoogh, A. H. B., & Keegan, A. E. (2007). The interactive effects of belongingness and charisma on helping and compliance. *Journal of Applied Psychology*, 92(4), 1131–1139.

Deutsch, M. (2012). A theory of cooperation—Competition and beyond. In: P. A. Van Lange, A. W. Kruglanski, & E. T. Higgins (Eds.), *Handbook of theories of social psychology* (Vol. 2). Thousand Oaks, CA: Sage Publications, Inc.

Dewe, P. (1991). Primary appraisal, secondary appraisal and coping: Their role in stressful work encounters. *Journal of Occupational Psychology Banner*, 64(4), 331–351.

Dhont, K., Van Hiel, A., & Hewstone, M. (2014). Changing the ideological roots of prejudice: Longitudinal effects of ethnic intergroup contact on social dominance orientation. *Group Processes & Intergroup Relations*, 17(1), 27–44.

Diegelman, N. M., & Subich, L. M. (2001). Academic and vocational interests as a function of outcome expectancies in social cognitive career theory. *Journal of Vocational Behavior, 59*(3), 394–405.

Diestel, S., & Schmidt, K.-H. (2010). Interactive effects of emotional dissonance and self-control demands on burnout, anxiety, and absenteeism. *Journal of Vocational Behavior, 77*(3), 412–424.

Dirks, K. T., & Ferrin, D. L. (2002). Trust in leadership: Meta-analytic findings and implications for research and practice. *Journal of Applied Psychology, 87*(4), 611–628.

Dokko, G., Kane, A. A., & Tortoriello, M. (2014). One of us or one of my friends: How social identity and tie strength shape the creative generativity of boundary-spanning ties. *Organization Studies, 35*(5), 703–726.

Drzensky, F., & Van Dick, R. (2013). Organizational identification and organizational change. In: *The psychology of organizational change*. Cambridge: Cambridge University Press.

Duck, J. D. (1993). Managing change: The art of balancing. *Harvard Business Review, 71*(6).

Duckitt, J. H. (1992). *The social psychology of prejudice*. Westport, CT: Praeger Publishers.

Dulipovici, A., & Robey, D. (2013). Strategic alignment and misalignment of knowledge management systems: A social representation perspective. *Journal of Management Information Systems, 29*(4), 103–126.

Dutton, J. E., Dukerich, J. M., & Harquail, C. V. (1994). Organizational images and member identification. *Administrative Science Quarterly, 39*(2), 239–263.

Eberly, M. B., Holley, E. C., Johnson, M. D., & Mitchell, T. R. (2017). It's not me, it's not you, it's us! An empirical examination of relational attributions. *Journal of Applied Psychology*, 1–21.

Eckes, G. (2001). *Making Six Sigma last: Managing the balance between cultural and technical change*. New York, NY: John Wiley & Sons.

Edmondson, D. R., & Boyer, S. L. (2013). The moderating effect of the boundary spanning role on perceived supervisory support: A meta-analytic review. *Journal of Business Research, 66*(11), 2186–2192.

Eisenberger, R., Rhoades, L., & Cameron, J. (1999). Does pay for performance increase or decrease perceived self-determination and intrinsic motivation? *Journal of Personality and Social Psychology, 77*(5), 1026–1040.

Elangovan, A. R., Pinder, C. C., & Mclean, M. (2010). Callings and organizational behavior. *Journal of Vocational Behavior, 76*(3), 428–440.

Ellemers, N., Van Rijswijk, W., Roefs, M., Simons, C. (1997). Bias in intergroup perceptions; balancing group identity with social reality. *Personality and Social Psychology Bulletin, 23*(2), 186–198.

Elliot, A. J., & Devine, P. G. (1994). On the motivational nature of cognitive dissonance: Dissonance as psychological discomfort. *Journal of Personality and Social Psychology, 67*(3), 382.

Elliot, A. J., & Thrash, T. M. (2002). Approach-avoidance motivation in personality: Approach and avoidance temperaments and goals. *Journal of Personality and Social Psychology, 82*(5), 804–818.

Ellis, A. (2001). *Feeling better, getting better, staying better: Profound self-help therapy for your emotions*. Oakland, CA: Impact Publishers.

Ellis, A. (2005). Can rational-emotive behavior therapy (REBT) and acceptance and commitment therapy (act) resolve their differences and be integrated? *Journal of Rational-Emotive and Cognitive-Behavior Therapy, 23(2)*, 153–168.

Ellis, A. (2006). *The myth of self-esteem: How rational emotive behavior therapy can change your life forever.* Amherst, MA: Prometheus Books.

Emerson, R. M. (1976). Social exchange theory. *Annual Review of Sociology, 2(1)*, 335–362.

Eppink, D. J., & ten Have, S. (2008). Omgaan met tegenstellingen in de strategietheorie: en situatie-afhankelijke benadering. *Maandblad voor Accountancy en Bedrijfseconomie, 82(6)*, 301–311.

Eriksen, T. H. (2001). Ethnic identity, national identity, and intergroup conflict: The significance of personal experiences. In: R. D. Ashmore, L. Jussim, & D. Wilder (Eds.), *Social identity, intergroup conflict, and conflict reduction* (pp. 42–68). New York, NY: Oxford University Press.

Evans, C. R., & Dion, K. L. (1991). Group cohesion and performance: A meta-analysis. *Small Group Research, 43(6)*, 690–701.

Fazio, R. H. (1987). Self-perception theory: A current perspective. In: M. P. Zanna, J. M. Olson, & C. P. Herman (Eds.), *Social influence: The Ontario symposium* (Vol. 5, pp. 129–150). Hillsdale, N.J: Lawrence Erlbaum Associates Inc.

Fazio, R. H., & Cooper, J. (1983). Arousal in the dissonance process. In: J. T. Cacioppo & R. E. Petty (Eds.), *Social psychophysiology* (pp. 122–152). New York, NY: Guilford Press.

Ferris, K. R. (1977). A test of the expectancy theory of motivation in an accounting environment. *The Accounting Review, 52(3)*, 605–615.

Festinger, L. (1950). Informal social communication. *Psychological Review, 57*, 271–282.

Festinger, L. (1954). A theory of social comparison processes. *Human Relations, 7(2)*, 117–140.

Festinger, L. (1957). *A theory of cognitive dissonance.* Stanford, CA: Stanford University Press.

Festinger, L. (1962). *A theory of cognitive dissonance* (Vol. 2). Stanford, CA: Stanford University Press.

Fiedler, F. E. (1967). *A theory of leadership effectiveness.* New York, NY: McGraw-Hill.

Fink, A. (1998). *Conducting research literature reviews: From the Internet to paper.* London: Sage Publications, Inc.

Fishbein, M. (1967). Attitude and the prediction of behavior. In: M. Fishbein (Ed.), *Readings in attitudes theory and measurement.* New York, NY: Wiley.

Fishbein, M., & Ajzen, I. (1975). *Belief, attitude, intention, and behavior: An introduction to theory and research.* Reading, MA: Addison-Wesley.

Fishbein, M., & Cappella, J. N. (2006). The role of theory in developing effective health communication. *Journal of Communication, 56(s1)*, S1–S17.

Fiske, S. T. (2004). *Social beings: Core motives in social psychology.* Hoboken, NJ: Wiley.

Fiske, S. T. (2010). *Social beings: Core motives in social psychology* (2nd ed.). Hoboken, NJ: Wiley.

Fiske, S. T., Gilbert, D. T., & Lindzey, G. (2010). *The handbook of social psychology* (Vol. 1, 4th ed.). Oxford: Oxford University Press.

Fiske, S. T., & Taylor, S. E. (2013). *Social cognition: From brains to culture.* Thousand Oaks, CA: Sage Publications, Inc.

Foley, S., Ngo, H.-Y., & Loi, R. (2016). Antecedents and consequences of upward and downward social comparisons: An investigation of Chinese employees. *International Journal of Organizational Analysis*, 24(1), 145–161.

Folkman, S., & Lazarus, R. S. (1980). An analysis of coping in a middle-aged community sample. *Journal of Health and Social Behavior*, 21(3), 219–239.

Folkman, S., & Lazarus, R. S. (1988). *Manual for the ways of coping questionnaire: Research edition.* Palo Alto, CA: Consulting Psychologists Press.

Ford, P., De Ste Croix, M., Lloyd, R., Meyers, R., Moosavi, M., Oliver, J., . . . Williams, C. (2011). The long-term athlete development model: Physiological evidence and application. *Journal of Sport Sciences*, 29(4), 389–402.

Frazier, M. L., Gooty, J., Little, L. M., & Nelson, D. L. (2015). Employee attachment: Implications for supervisor trustworthiness and trust. *Journal of Business and Psychology*, 30(2), 373–386.

Fredrickson, B. L. (1998). Cultivated emotions: Parental socialization of positive emotions and self-conscious emotions. *Psychological Inquiry: An International Journal for the Advancement of Psychological Theory*, 9(4), 279–281.

Fredrickson, B. L. (2001). The role of positive emotions in positive psychology: The broaden-and-build theory of positive emotions. *American Psychologist*, 56(3), 218–226.

Fredrickson, B. L., & Branigan, C. (2005). Positive emotions broaden thought-action repertoires: Evidence for the broaden-and-build model. *Cognition and Emotion*, 19(3), 313–332.

Freidson, E. (1973). *The professions and their prospects.* Thousand Oaks, CA: Sage Publications, Inc.

Frey, B. S., & Jegen, R. (1999). Motivation crowding theory: A survey of empirical evidence. *Journal of Economic Surveys*, 15(5), 589–611.

Frye, M. B. (2004). Equity-based compensation for employees: Firm performance and determinants. *The Journal of Financial Research*, 27(1), 31–54.

Fuchs, S., & Prouska, R. (2014). Creating positive employee change evaluation: The role of different levels of organizational support and change participation. *Journal of Change Management*, 14(3), 361–383.

Fugate, M. (2013). Capturing the positive experience of change: Antecedents, processes, and consequences. In: S. Oreg, A. Michel, & R. T. By (Eds.), *The psychology of organizational change: Viewing change from the employee's perspective.* Cambridge: Cambridge University Press.

Fugate, M., Kinicki, A. J., & Prussia, G. E. (2008). Employee coping with organizational change: An examination of alternative theoretical perspectives and models. *Personnel Psychology*, 61, 1–36.

Futrell, C., Parasuraman, A., & Sager, J. (1983). Sales force evaluation with expectancy theory. *Industrial Marketing Management*, 12, 125–129.

Gage, N. L., & Berliner, D. C. (1992). *Educational psychology* (5th ed.). Boston, MA: Houghton Mifflin Company.

Gazzaniga, M. S., & Heatherton, T. (2006). *Psychological science: Mind, brain, and behavior* (2nd ed.). New York, NY: Norton & Company Inc.

Geen, R. G. (1991). Social motivation. *Annual Review of Psychology*, 42(1), 377–399.

Gemmel, P., & Verleye, K. (2010). Emotional attachment to a hospital: Bringing employees and customers into the engagement zone. *Journal of Applied Management and Entrepreneurship, 15*(3), 78–93.

George, J. M., & Bettenhausen, K. (1990). Understanding prosocial behavior, sales performance, and turnover: A group-level analysis in a service context. *Journal of Applied Psychology, 75*(6), 698–709.

Ghoshal, S., & Bartlett, C. A. (1996). Rebuilding a behavioral context: A blueprint for corporate renewal. *Sloan Management Review, 37(2),* 23–36.

Gilbert, D. T., Wilson, T. D., Pinel, E. C., & Blumberg, S. J. (1998). Immune neglect: A source of durability bias in affective forecasting. *Journal of Personality and Social Psychology, 75*(3), 617–638.

Glass, C. (2009). Exploring what works: Is SF the best way of harnessing the impact of positive psychology in the workplace. *The Journal of Solution Focus in Organisations, 1*(1), 26–41.

Goethals, G. R., & Darley, J. M. (1977). *Social comparison theory: An attributional approach.* Hoboken, NJ: John Wiley & Sons.

Goette, L., Huffman, D., & Meier, S. (2006). The impact of group membership on cooperation and norm enforcement: Evidence using random assignment to real social groups. *American Economics Review, 96*(2), 212–216.

Gok, K., Deshpande, S., Deshpande, A. P., & Hunter, G. (2012). Comparing promoter and employee attributions for the causes of firm failure: The case of an Indian petrochemical company. *The International Journal of Human Resource Management, 23*(12), 2576–2596.

Goncalo, J. A. & Staw, B. M. (2006). Individualism-collectivism and group creativity. *Organizational Behavior and Human Decision Processes, 100*(1), 96–109.

Goncalo, J., & Duguid, M. M. (2008). Hidden consequences of the group serving bias: Causal attributions and the quality of group decision making. *Cornell University ILR School,* 1–65.

Goncalo, J., Polman, E., & Maslach, C. (2010). Can confidence come too soon? Collective efficacy, conflict and group performance over time. *Organizational Behavior and Human Decision Processes, 113*(1), 13–24.

Gouldner, A. W. (1960). The norm of reciprocity: A preliminary statement. *American Sociological Review, 25*(2), 161–178.

Grant, A. M., & Gino, F. (2010). A little thanks goes a long way: Explaining why gratitude expressions motivate prosocial behavior. *Journal of Personality and Social Psychology, 98*(6), 946–955.

Greenberg, J. (1987). A Taxonomy of organizational justice theories. *Academy of Management Review, 12*(1), 9–22.

Greenberg, J., Ashton-James, C. E., & Ashkanasy, N. M. (2007). Social comparison processes in organizations. *Organizational Behaviour and Human Decision Processes, 102*(1), 22–41.

Greenberg, J., & Baron, R. A. (2008). *Behavior in organizations.* Upper Saddle River, NJ: Prentice Hall.

Greenberg, J., Solomon, S., & Pyszczynski, T. (1997). A terror management theory of social behavior: The psychological functions of self-esteem and cultural worldviews. *Advances in Experimental Social Psychology, 24,* 93–159.

Greenwald, A. G. (1980). The totalitarian ego: Fabrication and revision of personal history. *American Psychologist, 35*(7), 603–618.

Greenwood, E. (1957). Attributes of a profession. *Social Work, 2*(3), 44–55.

Grusec, J. E. (1992). Social learning theory and developmental psychology: The legacies of Robert Sears and Albert Bandura. *Developmental Psychology, 28*(5), 776–786.

Guerin, B. (1986). The effects of mere presence on a motor task. *The Journal of Social Psychology, 126*(3), 399–401.

Gully, S. M., Devine, D. J., & Whitney, D. J. (1995). A meta-analysis of cohesion and performance. *Small Group Research, 26*(4), 497–520.

Gurevich, G., Kliger, D., & Weiner, B. (2012). The role of attribution of causality in economic decision making. *The Journal of Socio-Economics, 41*(4), 439–444.

Hackman, J. R., & Porter, L. W. (1968). Expectancy theory predictions of work effectiveness. *Organizational Behavior and Human Performance, 3*, 417–426.

Haemmerlie, F. M., & Montgomery, R. L. (1982). Self-perception theory and unobtrusively biased interactions: A treatment for heterosocial anxiety. *Journal of Counseling Psychology, 29*(4), 362–370.

Haemmerlie, F. M., & Montgomery, R. L. (1984). Purposefully biased interactions: Reducing heterosocial anxiety through self-perception theory. *Journal of Personality and Social Psychology, 47*(4), 900–908.

Hagmaier, T., & Abele, A. E. (2014). When reality meets ideal: Investigating the relation between calling and life satisfaction. *Journal of Career Assessment,* 1–16.

Haivas, S., Hofmans, J., & Pepermans, R. (2013). Volunteer engagement and intention to quit from a self-determination theory perspective. *Journal of Applied Social Psychology, 43*, 1869–1880.

Halbesleben, J. R. B., & Buckley, M. R. (2006). Social comparison and burnout: The role of relative burnout and received social support. *Anxiety, Stress, and Coping, 19*(3), 259–278.

Hara, A., Tanaka, K., Ohkubo, T., Kondo, T., Kikuya, M., Metoki, H., . . . Imai, Y. (2012). Ambulatory versus home versus clinic blood pressure: The association with subclinical cerebrovascular diseases: The Ohasama Study. *Hypertension, 59*(1), 22–28.

Harvey, P., Madison, K., Martinko, M., Crook, T. R., & Crook, T. A. (2014). Attribution theory in the organizational sciences: The road traveled and the path ahead. *The Academy of Management Perspectives, 28*(2), 128–146.

Hawkley, L. C., Thisted, R. A., Masi, C. M., & Cacioppo, J. T. (2012). Loneliness predicts increased blood pressure: 5-year cross-lagged analyses in middle-aged and older adults. *Psychological Aging, 25*(1), 132–141.

Hazan, C., & Shaver, P. (1987). Romantic love conceptualized as an attachment process. *Journal of Personality and Social Psychology, 52*(3), 511–524.

Heath, C., & Heath, D. (2010). *Switch: How to change things when change is hard.* New York, NY: Broadway Books.

Heatherton, T. F., & Polivy, J. (1991). Development and validation of a scale for measuring state self-esteem. *Journal of Personality and Social Psychology, 60*(6), 895–910.

Heider, F. (1958). *The psychology of interpersonal relations.* New York, NY: Wiley.

Heifetz, R. A., Grashow, A., & Linsky, M. (2009). *The practice of adaptive leadership: Tools and tactics for changing your organization and the world.* Boston, MA: Harvard Business Review Press.

Heifetz, R. A. (2009). *The practice of adaptive leadership: Tools and tactics for changing your organization and the world.* Boston, MA: Harvard Business Review Press.

Heifetz, R. A., & Laurie, D. (2001). The work of leadership. *Harvard Business Review, 79*(12), 131–141.

Heller, J. (1998). *Essential managers: Managing change.* New York, NY: D. K. Publishing.

Henchy, T., & Glass, D. C. (1968). Evaluation apprehension and the social facilitation of dominant and subordinate responses. *Journal of Personality and Social Psychology, 10*(4), 446–454.

Herbst, T. H. H., & Conradie, P. D. P. (2011). Leadership effectiveness in higher education: Managerial self-perceptions versus perceptions of others. *Journal of Industrial Psychology, 37*(1), 1–14.

Hertzman, M., & Festinger, L. (1940). Shifts in explicit goals in a level of aspiration experiment. *Journal of Experimental Psychology, 27*(4), 439–452.

Hesselbein, F., & Johnston, R. (2002). *On leading change: A leader to leader guide.* San Francisco, CA: Jossey-Bass.

Heuven, E., & Bakker, A. (2003). Emotional dissonance and burnout among cabin attendants. *European Journal of Work and Organizational Psychology, 12*(1), 81–100.

Hewitt, P. (2009). *Oxford handbook of positive psychology.* Oxford: Oxford University Press.

Higgins, E. T. (1987). Self-discrepancy: A theory relating self and affect. *Psychological Review, 94*(3), 319–340.

Higgins, E. T., Bond, R. N., Klein, R., & Strauman, T. (1986). Self-discrepancies and emotional vulnerability. How magnitude, accessibility, and type of discrepancy influence affect. *Journal of Personality and Social Psychology, 51*(1), 5–15.

Higgins, J. P. T., & Green, S. (2006). Cochrane handbook for systematic reviews of interventions 4.2.6 [updated September 2006]. Retrieved September 1, 2015, from http://community.cochrane.org/sites/default/files/uploads/Handbook4.2.6Sep2006.pdf

Hogg, M. A., & Terry, D. J. (2000). Social identity and self-categorization processes in organizational contexts. *Academy of Management Review, 25*(1), 121–140.

Hoijer, B. (2011). Social representations theory. *Nordicom Review, 32*(1), 3–16.

Holdford, D., & Lovelace-Elmore, B. (2001). Applying the principles of human motivation to pharmaceutical education. *Journal of Pharmacy Teaching, 8*(4), 1–18.

Holland, D. (1997). Selves as cultured: As told by an anthropologist who lacks a soul. In: R. D. Ashmore, & L. Jussim (Eds.), *Self and identity: Fundamental issues* (pp. 160–190). New York, NY: Oxford University Press.

Hollinger, R. C., & Clark, J. P. (1982). Formal and informal social controls of employee deviance. *Sociological Quarterly, 23*, 333–343.

Holt-Lunstad, J., Smith, T. B., Baker, M., Harris, T., & Stephenson, D. (2015). Loneliness and social isolation as risk factors for mortality: A meta-analytic review. *Perspectives on Psychological Science, 10*(2), 227–237.

Holten, A.-L., & Brenner, S. O. (2015). Leadership style and the process of organizational change. *Leadership & Organization Development Journal, 36*(1), 2–16.

Holwerda, T. J., Deeg, D. J., Beekman, A. T., van Tilburg, T. G., Stek, M. L., Jonker, C., & Schoevers, R. A. (2012). Feelings of loneliness, but not social isolation, predict dementia onset: Results from the Amsterdam Study of the Elderly (AMSTEL). *Journal of Neurology, Neurosurgery & Psychiatry, 85*(2), 135–142.

Horstmeier, C. A., Boer, D., Homan, A. C., & Voelpel, S. C. (2017). The differential effects of transformational leadership on multiple identifications at work: A meta-analytic model. *British Journal of Management, 28*(2), 280–298.

Hoyt, C. L., Simon, S., & Innella, A. N. (2011). Taking a turn toward the masculine: The impact of mortality salience on implicit leadership theories. *Basic and Applied Social Psychology, 33*(4), 374–381.

Huang, G., Ashford, S. J., Wellman, N., Lee, C., & Wang, L. (2017). Deviance and exit: The organizational costs of job insecurity and moral disengagement. *Journal of Applied Psychology, 102*(1), 26–42.

Huang, J.-W. (2013). The effects of transformational leadership on the distinct aspects development of social identity. *Group Processes & Intergroup Relations, 16*(1), 87–104.

Hudson, D. L. (2013). Attachment theory and leader-follower relationships. *The Psychologist-Manager Journal, 16*(3), 27(2), 147–159.

Hull, C. L. (1943). *Principles of behavior: An introduction to behavior theory.* Oxford: Appleton-Century.

Ibarra, H. (2015). *Act like a leader, think like a leader.* Boston, MA: Harvard Business Review Press.

Jacobsen, C. B., & Andersen, L. B. (2017). Leading public service organizations: How to obtain high employee self-efficacy and organizational performance. *Public Management Review, 19*(2), 253–273.

Janis, I. L. (1972). *Victims of groupthink.* Boston, MA: Houghton Mifflin Company.

Janis, I. L. (1982). *Groupthink: Psychological studies of policy decisions and fiascos.* Boston, MA: Houghton Mifflin Company.

Jayawardana, A., & O'Donnell, M. (2010). Social exchange, organizational support and employee performance in Sri Lanka's Garment Industry. *South Asian Journal of Management, 17*(2), 7–28.

Jehn, K. A., & Mannix, E. A. (2001). The dynamic nature of conflict: A longitudinal study of intra-group conflict and group performance. *Academy of Management Journal, 44*(2), 238–251.

Jimmieson, N. L., Peach, M., & White, K. M. (2008). Utilizing the theory of planned behavior to inform change management: An investigation of employee intentions to support organizational change. *Journal of Applied Behavioral Science, 44*(2), 237–262.

Jimmieson, N. L., Rafferty, A. E., & Allen, J. E. (2013). Change communication and employee responses. In: S. Oreg, A. Michel, & R. T. By (Eds.), *The psychology of organizational change: Viewing change from the employee's perspective.* Cambridge: Cambridge University Press.

Johnson, B. T., & Eagly, A. H. (1989). Effects of involvement on persuasion: A meta-analysis. *Psychological Bulletin, 106*(2), 290.

Johnson, D. W., & Johnson, R. T. (1989). *Cooperation and competition: Theory and research.* Edina, MN: Interaction Book Company.

Johnson, D. W., Johnson, R. T., & Smith, K. (2007). The state of cooperative learning in postsecondary and professional settings. *Educational Psychology Review, 19*(1), 15–29.

Jonas, E., Kauffeld, S., Sullivan, D., & Fritsche, I. (2011). Dedicate your life to the company! A terror management perspective on organizations. *Journal of Applied Social Psychology, 41*(12), 2858–2882.

Jones, E. E. (1990). *A series of books in psychology. Interpersonal perception.* New York, NY: W H Freeman/Times Books/ Henry Holt & Co.

Jordan, M. R., Jordan, J. J., & Rand, D. G. (2017). No unique effect of intergroup competition on cooperation: Non-competitive thresholds are as effective as competitions between groups for increasing human cooperative behavior. *Evolution of Human Behavior, 38*(1), 102–108.

Jost, J. T., & Banaji, M. R. (1994). The role of stereotyping in system-justification and the production of false consciousness. *British Journal of Social Psychology, 33*(1), 1–27.

Jost, J. T., Banaji, M. R., & Nosek, B. A. (2004). A decade of system justification theory: Accumulated evidence of conscious and unconscious bolstering of the status quo. *Political Psychology, 25*(6), 881–919.

Jost, J., & Hunyady, O. (2003). The psychology of system justification and the palliative function of ideology. *European Review of Social Psychology, 13*(1), 111–153.

Jost, J. T., Ledgerwood, A., & Hardin, C. D. (2008). Shared reality, system justification, and the relational basis of ideological beliefs. *Social and Personality Psychology Compass, 2*(1), 171–186.

Jost, J. T., Pelham, B. W., Sheldon, O., & Ni Sullivan, B. (2003). Social inequality and the reduction of ideological dissonance on behalf of the system: Evidence of enhanced system justification among the disadvantaged. *European journal of Social Psychology, 33*(1), 13–36.

Jovchelovitch, S. (1996). In defence of representations. *Journal of the Theory of Social Behaviour, 26*(2), 121–135.

Jovchelovitch, S. (2007). *Knowledge in context: Representations, community culture.* London: Routledge.

Judge, T. A., & Bono, J. E. (2001). Relationship of core self-evaluations traits— Self-esteem, generalized self-efficacy, locus of control, and emotional stability— With job satisfaction and job performance: A meta-analysis. *Journal of Applied Psychology, 86*(1), 80–92.

Judge, T. A., Erez, A., & Bono, J. E. (1998). The power of being positive: The relation between positive self-concept and job performance. *Human Performance, 11*(2/3), 167–187.

Kamdar, D., & Van Dyne, L. (2007). The joint effects of personality and workplace social exchange relationships in predicting task performance and citizenship performance. *Journal of Applied Psychology, 92*(5), 1286–1298.

Karatepe, O. M. (2011). Do job resources moderate the effect of emotional dissonance on burnout?: A study in the city of Ankara, Turkey. *International Journal of Contemporary Hospitality Management, 23*(1), 44–65.

Kay, A. C., & Friesen, J. (2011). On social stability and social change: Understanding when system justification does and does not occur. *Current Directions in Psychological Science, 20*(6), 360–364.

KC, D., Staats, B. R., & Gino, F. (2013). Learning from my success and from others' failure: Evidence from minimally invasive cardiac surgery. *Management Science, 59*(11), 2435–2449.

Kelley, H. H. (1967). Attribution theory in social psychology. In: D. Levine (Ed.), *Nebraska symposium on motivation* (Vol. 15, pp. 192–238). Lincoln, NE: University of Nebraska Press.

Kelley, H. H., Berscheid, E., Christensen, A., Harvey, J. H., Huston, T. L., Levinger, G., . . . Peterson, D. R. (1983). *Close relationships.* New York, NY: Freeman.

Kelloway, E. K., & Barling, J. (2000). What we have learned about developing transformational leaders. *Leadership & Organizational Development Journal, 21*(7), 355–362.

Kelman, H. C. (1958). Compliance, identification, and internalization: Three processes of attitude change. *Journal of Conflict Resolution, 2*(1), 51–60.

Kendra, C. (2017). What is social exchange theory? Retrieved March 16, 2017, from www.verywell.com/what-is-social-exchange-theory-2795882

Khalifa, M. H. E. (2011). Perceptions of Equity and job satisfaction: A study of university employees in Egypt. *International Journal of Management, 28*(4), 130–143.

Khalifa, M. H. E., & Trong, Q. (2011). The effects of internal and external equity on components of organizational commitment: An empirical study in the Egyptian hotel sector. *International Journal of Management, 28*(1), 306–315.

Kickul, J., Lester, S. W., & Finkl, J. (2002). Promise breaking during radical organizational change: Do justice interventions make a difference? *Journal of Organizational Behavior, 23*(4), 469–488.

Kim, K.-H., & Tsai, W. (2012).Social comparison among competing firms. *Strategic Management Journal, 33*(2), 115–136.

Kim, M., & Shin, Y. (2015). Collective efficacy as a mediator between cooperative group norms and group positive affect and team creativity. *Asia Pacific Journal of Management, 32*(3), 693–716.

Kim, T.-Y., Aryee, S., Loi, R., & Kim, S.-P. (2013). Person–organization fit and employee outcomes: Test of a social exchange model. *The International Journal of Human Resource Management, 24*(19), 3719–3737.

Kirkpatrick, L. A., & Ellis, B. J. (2004). An evolutionary-psychological approach to self-esteem: Multiple domains and multiple functions. In: M. B. Brewer & M. Hewstone (Eds.), *Perspectives on social psychology: Self and social identity* (pp. 52–77). Malden, MA: Blackwell Publishing.

Kistruck, G. M., Lount, R. B., Jr., Smith, B. R., Bergman, B. J., Jr., & Moss, T. W. (2016). Cooperation vs. competition: Alternative goal structures for motivating groups in a resource scarce environment. *Academy of Management Journal, 59*(4), 1174–1198.

Knoll, M., Lord, R. G., Petersen, L., & Weigelt, O. (2016). Examining the moral grey zone: The role of moral disengagement, authenticity, and situational strength in predicting unethical managerial behaviour. *Journal of Applied Social Psychology, 46,* 65–78.

Kong, D. T., Dirks, K. T., & Ferrin, D. L. (2014). Interpersonal trust within negotiations: Meta-analytic directions, critical contingencies, and directions for future research. *Academy of Management Journal, 57*(5), 1235–1255.

Konovsky, M. A., & Pugh, S. D. (1994). Citizenship behaviour and social exchange. *Academy of Management Journal, 37*(3), 656–669.

Kotter, J. P. (2008). *A sense of urgency.* Boston, MA: Harvard Business Review Press.

Kotter, J. P. (2012). *Leading change.* Boston, MA: Harvard Business Review Press.

Kouzes, J. M., & Posner, B. Z. (2012). *The leadership challenge: How to make extraordinary things happen in organizations.* Hoboken, NJ: John Wiley & Sons.

Kramer, R. M. (1993). Cooperation and organizational identification. In: J. K. Murnighan (Ed.), *Social psychology in organizations: Advances in theory and research* (pp. 244–268). Englewood Cliffs, NJ: Prentice Hall.

Kriegel, R. J., & Brandt, D. (1996). *Sacred cows make the best burgers.* New York, NY: Warner Books, Inc.

Krohne, H. W. (2001). Stress and coping theories. In: *International encyclopedia of the social & behavioral sciences* (pp. 15163–15170). New York, NY: Elsevier.

Kwang, T., & Swann, W. B., Jr. (2010). Do people embrace praise even when they feel unworthy? A review of critical tests of self-enhancement versus self-verification. *Personality and Social Psychology Review, 14*(3), 263–280.

Kyei-Poku, I. (2013). The benefits of belongingness and interactional fairness to interpersonal citizenship behavior. *Leadership & Organization Development Journal, 35*(8), 691–709.

Lai, M.-C., & Chen, Y.-C. (2012). Self-efficacy, effort, job performance, job satisfaction, and turnover intention: The effect of personal characteristics on organization performance. *International Journal of Innovation, Management & Technology, 3*(4), 387–391.

Laloux, F. (2014). *Reinventing organizations: A guide to creating organizations inspired by the next stage of human consciousness.* Brussel, BE: Nelson Parker.

Lamb, M. E., Thompson, R. A., Gardner, W. P., Charnov, E. L, & Estes, D. (1984). Security of infantile attachment as assessed in the "strange situation": Its study and biological interpretation. *The Behavioral and Brain Sciences, 7*(1), 127–171.

Landen, S. M., & Wang, C.-C. D. C. (2010). Adult attachment, work cohesion, coping, and psychological well-being of firefighters. *Counselling Psychology Quarterly, 23*(2), 143–162.

Lane, R. (1991). Love: Emotion, myth and metaphor. *Analytic Philosophy, 32*(4), 243–244.

Laroche, H. (1995). From decision to action in organizations: Decision-making as a social representation. *Organizational Science, 6*(1), 62–75.

Latané, B. (1981). The psychology of social impact. *American Psychologist, 36*(4), 343–356.

Latané, B. (1996). Dynamic social impact. In: R. Hegselmann, U. Mueller, & K. G. Troitzsch (Eds.), *Modelling and simulation in the social sciences from the philosophy of science point of view.* Theory and Decision Library. Springer Science+Business Media, NL: Dordrecht.

Latané, B., & Bourgeois, M. J. (2001). Successfully simulating dynamic social impact: Three levels of prediction. In: J. P. Forgas & K. D. Williams (Eds.), *The Sydney symposium of social psychology: Social influence: Direct and indirect processes* (pp. 61–76). New York, NY: Psychology Press.

Latané, B., Nowak, A., & Liu, J. H. (1994). Measuring emergent social phenomena: Dynamism, polarization, and clustering as order parameters of social systems. *Behavioral Science, 39*(1), 1–24.

Lazarus, R. S. (1966). *Psychological stress and the coping process.* New York, NY: McGraw-Hill.

Lazarus, R. S. (1974). Psychological stress and coping in adaptation and illness. *The International Journal of Psychiatry in Medicine, 5*(4), 321–333.

Lazarus, R. S. (2000). Toward better research on stress and coping. *American Psychologist, 55*(6), 665–673.

Lazarus, R. S., & Folkman, S. (1984). *Stress, appraisal, and coping.* New York, NY: Springer Publishing.

Leakey, R. E., & Lewin, R. (1977). *Origins.* New York, NY: Dutton.

Leary, M. R., Tambor, E. S., Terdal, S. K., & Downs, D. L. (1995). Self-esteem as an interpersonal monitor: The sociometer hypothesis. *Journal of Personality and Social Psychology, 68*(3), 518–530.

Lecky, P. (1945). *Self-consistency; A theory of personality.* Washington, DC: Island Press.

Ledgerwood, A., & Chaiken, S. (2007). Priming us and them: Automatic assimilation and contrast in group attitudes. *Journal of Personality and Social Psychology, 93*(6), 940–956.

Lee, A. Y., Aaker, J. L., & Gardner, W. L. (2000). The pleasures and pains of distinct self-construals: The role of interdependence in regulatory focus. *Journal of Personality and Social Psychology, 78*(6), 1122–1134.

Lee, E. S., Park, T. Y., & Koo, B. (2015). Identifying organizational identification as a basis for attitudes and behaviors: A meta-analytic review. *Psychological Bulletin, 141*(5), 1049.

Lent, R. W., & Brown, S. D. (2006). Integrating person and situation perspectives on work satisfaction: A social-cognitive view. *Journal of Vocational Behavior, 16*(2), 236–247.

Lent, R. W., & Brown, S. D. (2008). Social cognitive career theory and subjective well-being in the context of work. *Journal of Career Assessment, 16*(1), 6–21.

Lent, R. W., Brown, S. D., & Hackett, G. (1994). Toward a unifying social cognitive theory of career and academic interest, choice, and performance. *Journal of Vocational Behavior, 45*(1), 79–122.

Lent, R. W., Lopez, A. M. Jr., Lopez, F. G., & Sheu, H.-B. (2008). Social cognitive career theory and the prediction of interests and choice goals in the computing disciplines. *Journal of Vocational Behavior, 73*(1), 52–62.

Leonard, A., & Gobler, A. F. (2006). Exploring challenges to transformational leadership communication about employment equity: Managing organizational change in South-Africa. *Journal of Communication, 10*(4), 390–406

Leonard, H. S., Lewis, R., Friedman, A. M., & Passmore, J. (2013). *The Wiley-Blackwell handbook of the psychology of leadership, change and organizational development.* Hoboken, NJ: Wiley-Blackwell.

Leventhal, G. S. (1980). What should be done with equity theory? New approaches to the study of fairness in social relationships. In: K. Gergen, M. Greenberg, & R. Willis (Eds.), *Social exchange: Advances in theory and research* (pp. 27–55). New York, NY: Plenum Press.

Levine, M., & Tompson, K. (2004). Identity, place, and bystander intervention: Social categories and helping after natural disasters. *Journal of Social Psychology, 144*(3), 229–245.

Lewig, K. A., & Dollard, M. F. (2003). Emotional dissonance, emotional exhaustion and job satisfaction in call centre workers. *European Journal of Work and Organizational Psychology, 12*(4), 366–392.

Lewin, K. (1943a). Defining the "Field at a given time". In: D. Cartwright (Ed.; 1952), *Field theory in social science: Selected Theoretical Papers by Kurt Lewin* (pp. 43–59). London: Social Science Paperbacks.

Lewin, K. (1943b). Forces behind food habits and methods of change. *Bulletin of the National Research Council, 108,* 35–65.

Lewis, J. D., & Weigert, A. (1985). Trust as a social reality. *Social Forces, 63*(4), 967–985.

Lin, C.-C., Kao, Y.-T., Chen, Y.-L., & Lu, S.-C. (2016). Fostering change-oriented behaviors: A broaden and-build model. *Journal of Business and Psychology, 31*(3), 399–414.

Lippitt, L. L. (1999). Preferred futuring: The power to change whole systems of any size. In: P. Holman & T. Devane (Eds.), *The change handbook* (pp. 159–174). San Francisco, CA: Berrett-Koehler.

Little, L. M., Nelson, D. L., Wallace, C., & Johnson, P. D. R. (2011). Integrating attachment style, vigor at work, and extrarole performance. *Journal of Organizational Behavior, 32*(3), 464–484.

Loi, R., Chan, K. W., & Lam, L. W. (2014). Leader—Member exchange, organizational identification, and job satisfaction: A social identity perspective. *Journal of Occupational and Organizational Psychology, 87*, 42–61.

Loi, R., Lai, J. Y. M., & Lam, L. W. (2012). Working under a committed boss: A test of the relationship between supervisors' and subordinates' affective commitment. *Leadership Quarterly, 23*(3), 466–475.

Luchman, J. N., & González-Morales, M. G. (2013). Demands, control and support: A meta-analytic review of work characteristics interrelationships. *Journal of Occupational Health Psychology, 18*(1), 37–52.

Madden, T. J., Ellen, P. S., & Ajzen, I. (1992). A comparison of the theory of planned behavior and the theory of reasoned action. *Personality and Social Psychology Bulletin, 18*(1), 3–9.

Madsen, S. R., Miller, D., & John, C. R. (2005). Readiness for organizational change: Do organizational commitment and social relationships in the workplace make a difference. *Human Resource Development Quarterly, 16*(2), 213–233.

Mael, F., & Ashforth, B. E. (1992). Alumni and their alma mater: A partial test of the reformulated model of organizational identification. *Journal of Organizational Behavior, 13*(2), 103–123.

Manz, C. C., & Sims, H. P. Jr. (1987). Leading workers to lead themselves: The external leadership of self-managing work teams. *Administrative Science Quarterly, 106*–129.

Markus, H. (1978). The effect of mere presence on social facilitation: An unobtrusive test. *Journal of Experimental Social Psychology, 14*(4), 389–397.

Martins-Silva, P. O., Silva-Junior, A. D., Peroni, G. G. H., De Medeiros, C., & Vitória, N. O. D. (2016). The social representation theory in Brazilian organizational studies: A bibliometric analysis from 2001 to 2014. *Cadernos EBAPE. BR, 14*(4), 891–919.

Maslow, A. H. (1943). A theory of human motivation. *Psychological Review, 50*, 370–396.

Maslow, A. H. (1971). *The farther reaches of human nature.* New York, NY: Arkana/Penguin Books.

Matela, F., & Ryan, R. M. (2016). Prosocial behavior increases well-being and vitality even without contact with the beneficiary: Causal and behavioral evidence. *Motivation and Emotion, 40*(3), 351–357.

Maurer, R. (2010). *Beyond the wall of resistance: Why 70% of all changes still fail—And what you can do about it.* Austin, TX: Bard Press.

Mayer, R. C., Davis, J. H., & Schoorman, F. D. (1995). An integrative model of organizational trust. *Academy of Management Review, 20*, 709–734.

McCall, G. J., & Simmons, J. L. (1966). *Identities and interactions*. New York, NY: The Free Press.

McCormick, M. J. (2001). Self-efficacy and leadership effectiveness: Applying social cognitive theory to leadership. *The Journal of Leadership Studies*, 8(1), 22–33.

McGraw, K. O. (1978). The detrimental effects of reward on performance: A literature review and a prediction model. In: M. Lepper & D. Greene (Eds.), *The hidden costs of reward: New perspectives on the psychology of human motivation* (pp. 33–60). London: Psychology Press.

McLeod, S. (2007). Moscovici and minority influence. Retrieved November 9, 2017, from www.simplypsychology.org/minority-influence.html

Meeker, G. B. (1971). Fade-out joint venture. *Thunderbird International Business Review*, 13(3), 17–18.

Meneghel, I., Salanova, M., & Martinez, I. M. (2016). Feeling good makes us stronger: How team resilience mediates the effect of positive emotions on team performance. *Journal of Happiness Studies*, 17(1), 239–255.

Mercy, O. N., & Peter, A. S. (2014). Risky sexual behaviours among female in-school adolescents in delta, Nigeria: Self-esteem, parental involvement and religiosity as predictors. *European Scientific Journal*, 10(31), 1857–7431.

Miao, C., Qian, M. S., & Ma, D. (2016). The relationship between entrepreneurial self-efficacy and firm performance: A meta-analysis of main and moderator effects. *Journal of Small Business Management*, 55(1), 87–107.

Michel, A., & González-Morales, M. (2013). Reactions to organizational change: An integrated model of health predictors, intervening variables, and outcomes. In: S. Oreg, A. Michel, & R. By (Eds.), *The psychology of organizational change: Viewing change from the employee's perspective* (pp. 65–92). Cambridge: Cambridge University Press.

Michel, A., Stegmaier, R., Meiser, D., & Sonntag, K. (2009). Der Elfenbeinturm öffnet sich—Veränderungsprozesse im Hochschulbereich: Werden Commitment to Change und Person-Organisations-Passung durch Prozessmerkmale bestimmt? *Zeitschrift für Personalpsychologie*, 8(1), 1–13.

Mikkelsen, M. F., Jacobsen, C. B., & Andersen, L. B. (2017). Managing employee motivation: Exploring the connections between managers' enforcement actions, employee perceptions, and employee intrinsic motivation. *International Public Management Journal*, 20(2), 183–205.

Mikulincer, M., & Florian, V. (1998). The relationship between adult attachment styles and emotional and cognitive reactions to stressful events. In: J. A. Simpson & W. S. Rholes (Eds.), *Attachment theory and close relationships* (pp. 143–165). New York, NY: Guilford Press.

Mikulincer, M., Florian, V., & Weller, A. (1993). Attachment styles, coping strategies, and posttraumatic psychological distress: The impact of the Gulf War in Israel. *Journal of Personality and Social Psychology*, 64(5), 817–826.

Mikulincer, M., & Shaver, P. R. (2007). *Attachment in adulthood: Structure, dynamics, and change*. New York, NY: Guilford Press.

Mishra, A. K., & Spreitzer, G. M. (1998). Explaining how survivors respond to downsizing: The roles of trust, empowerment, justice, and work redesign. *Academy of Management Review*, 23(3), 567–588.

Mishra, S., & Bhatnagar, D. (2010). Linking emotional dissonance and organizational identification to turnover intention and emotional well-being: A study of medical representatives in India. *Human Resource Management*, 49(3), 401–419.

Mishra, S. K., & Kumar, K. K. (2016). Minimizing the cost of emotional dissonance at work: A multi sample analysis. *Management Decision, 54*(4), 778–795.

Moher, D., Liberati, A., Telzlaff, J., & Altman, D. G. (2009). Preferred reporting items for systematic reviews and meta-analyses: The PRISMA statement. *PloS Med, 6*(7).

Moon, K., Lee, K., Lee, K., & Oah, S. (2017). The effects of social comparison and objective feedback on work performance across different performance levels. *Journal of Organizational Behavior Management, 37*(1), 63–74.

Moore, C., Detert, J. R., Klebe Treviño, L., Baker, V. L., & Mayer, D. M. (2012). Why employees do bad things: Moral disengagement and unethical organizational behavior. *Personnel Psychology, 65*(1), 1–48.

Moore, D. A. & Healy, P. J. (2008). The trouble with overconfidence. *Psychological Review, 115*(2), 502–517.

Mor Barak, M. E., Travis, D. J., Pyun, H., & Xie, B. (2009). The impact of supervision on worker outcomes: A meta-analysis. *Social Service Review, 83*(1), 3–32.

Moscovici, S. (1961). *La psychanalyse, son image et son public.* Paris, FR: Presses Universitaires de France.

Moscovici, S. (1963). Attitudes and opinions. *Annual Review of Psychology, 14*(1), 231–260.

Moscovici, S. (1973). Introduction. In: C. Herzlich (Ed.), *Health and illness: A social psychological analysis.* London: Academic Press.

Moscovici, S. (1984). The phenomenon of social representation, In: R. Farr & S. Moscovici (Eds.), *Social representations.* Cambridge: Cambridge University Press.

Moscovici, S. (1988). Notes towards a description of social representations. *European Journal of Social Psychology, 18*(3), 211–250.

Mourier, P., & Smith, M. R. (2001). *Conquering organizational change: How to succeed were most companies fail.* Hoboken, NJ: John Wiley & Sons.

Mühlhaus, J., & Bouwmeester, O. (2016). The paradoxical effect of self-categorization on work stress in a high-status occupation: Insights from management consulting. *Human Relations, 69*(9), 1823–1852.

Mullen, B. (1985). Strength and immediacy of sources: A meta-analytic evaluation of the forgotten elements of social impact theory. *Journal of Personality and Social Psychology, 48*(6), 1458–1466.

Mullen, B., Anthony, T., Salas, E., & Driskell, J. E. (1994). Group cohesiveness and quality of decision making: An integration of tests of the groupthink hypothesis. *Small Group Research, 25*(2), 189–204.

Murray, S., MacDonald, G., & Holmes, J. G. (1998). Through a looking glass darkly? When self-doubts turn into relationship insecurities. *Journal of Personality and Social Psychology, 75*(6), 1459–1480.

Na'im, A. (2004). Intragroup cooperation vs. intragroup competition: A meta-analytical study. *Gadjah Mada International Journal of Business, 6*(3), 309–322.

Nebergall, R. E. (1966). The social judgment-involvement approach to attitude and attitude change. *Western Speech, 30,* 209–215.

Nemeth, C. J., Personnaz, M., Personnaz, B., & Goncalo, J. A. (2004). The liberating role of conflict in group creativity: A study in two countries. *European Journal of Social Psychology, 34*(4), 365–374.

Neumann, Y. (1980). A contingency approach for understanding equity theory and its predictions. *Social Behavior and Personality, 8*(2), 153–159.

Neves, P. (2011). Building commitment to change: The role of perceived supervisor support and competence. *European Journal of Work and Organizational Psychology, 20*(4), 437–450.

Neves, P., & Caetano, A. (2006). Social exchange processes in organizational change: The roles of trust and control. *Journal of Change Management, 6*(4), 351–364.

Ng, K. Y., & Van Dyne, L. (2001). Individualism—Collectivism as a boundary condition for effectiveness of minority influence in decision making. *Organizational Behavior and Human Decision Processes, 84*(2), 198–225.

Ng, T. W. H. (2015). The incremental validity of organizational commitment, organizational trust, and organizational identification. *Journal of Vocational Behavior, 88*, 154–163.

Ng, T. W. H., & Sorensen, K. L. (2008). Toward a further understanding of the relationships between perceptions of support and work attitudes. *Group & Organization Management, 33*(3), 243–268.

Nijstad, B. A. (2013). Performance. In: J. M. Levine (Ed.), *Frontiers of social psychology: Group processes* (pp. 193–213). New York, NY: Psychology Press.

Novak, D. (2012). *Taking people with you: The only way to make big things happen*. New York, NY: Portfolio and Penguin.

Oc, B., & Bashur, M. R. (2013). Followership, leadership and social influence. *The Leadership Quarterly, 24*, 919–934.

Offermann, L. R., Schroyer, C. J., & Green, S. K. (1998). Leader Attributions for subordinate performance: Consequences for subsequent leader interactive behaviors and ratings. *Journal of Applied Social Psychology, 28*(13), 1125–1139.

O'Keefe, D. J. (1990). *Current communication: An advanced text series, Persuasion: Theory and research* (Vol. 2). Thousand Oaks, CA: Sage Publications, Inc.

Onorato, R. S., & Turner, J. C. (2004). Fluidity in the self-concept: The shift from personal to social identity. *European Journal of Social Psychology, 34*(3), 257–278.

Oreg, S. (2003). Resistance to change: Developing an individual differences measure. *Journal of Applied Psychology, 88*(4), 680.

Oreg, S., Michel, A., & Todnem, R. (2013). *The psychology of organizational change: Viewing change from the employee's perspective*. Cambridge: Cambridge University Press.

Ouweneel, E., Le Blanc, P. M., Schaufeli, W. B., & Van Wijhe, C. I. (2012). Good morning, good day: A diary study on positive emotions, hope, and work engagement. *Human Relations, 65*(9), 1129–1154.

Paglis, L. L., & Green, S. G. (2002). Leadership self-efficacy and managers' motivation for leading change. *Journal of Organizational Behavior, 23*(2), 215–235.

Pajares, F., Prestin, A., Chen, J. A., & Nabi, R. L. (2009). Social cognitive theory and mass media effects. In: *Handbook of media processes and effects* (pp. 283–297). Thousand Oaks, CA: Sage Publications, Inc.

Petticrew, M., & Roberts, H. (2006). *Systematic reviews in the social sciences: A practical guide*. Malden, MA: Blackwell Publishing.

Pettigrew, A. M. (1979). On studying organizational cultures. *Administrative Science Quarterly, 24*(4), 570–581.

Petzall, B. J., Parker, G. E., & Stoeberl, P. A. (2000). Another side to downsizing: Survivor' behavior and self-affirmation. *Journal of Business and Psychology*, 14(4), 593–603.

Phelan, J. E., & Rudman, L. A. (2011). System justification beliefs, affirmative action, and resistance to equal opportunity organizations. *Social Cognition*, 29(3), 376–390.

Pittman, T. S., & Heller, J. F. (1987). Social motivation. *Annual Review of Psychology*, 38(1), 461–490.

Postmes, T., Spears, R., & Cihangir, S. (2001). Quality of decision making and group norms. *Journal of Personality and Social Psychology*, 80(6), 918–930.

Pouliakas, K. (2010). Pay enough, don't pay too much or don't pay at all? The impact of bonus intensity on job satisfaction. *Kyklos, International Review for Social Sciences*, 63(4), 597–626.

Pratt, M. G. (1998). To be or not to be? Central questions in organizational identification. In: D. A. Whetten & P. C. Godfrey (Eds.), *Identity in organizations: Building theory through conversations* (pp. 171–207). Thousand Oaks, CA: Sage.

Pratto, F., Sidanius, J., Stallworth, L. M., & Malle, B. F. (1994). Social dominance orientation: A personality variable predicting social and political attitudes. *Journal of Personality and Social Psychology*, 67(4), 741–763.

Proudfoot, D., & Kay, A. C. (2014). System justification in organizational contexts: How a motivated preference for the status quo can affect organizational attitudes and behaviors. *Research in Organizational Behavior*, 34, 173–187.

Putra, E. D., Cho, S., & Liu, J. (2017). Extrinsic and intrinsic motivation on work engagement in the hospitality industry: Test of motivation crowding theory. *Tourism and Hospitality Research*, 17(2), 1–14.

Rafferty, A. E., & Restubog, S. L. D. (2009). When leadership meets organizational change: The influence of the top management team and supervisory leaders on change appraisals, change attitudes, and adjustment to change. Retrieved July 15, 2017, from www.cambridge.org/core/books/the-psychology-of-organizational-change/when-leadership-meets-organizational-change-the-influence-of-the-top-management-team-and-supervisory-leaders-on-change-appraisals-change-attitudes-and-adjustment-to-change/0A0E697AB140632FF459D39B6109E6AE

Rafferty, A. E., & Restubog, S. L. D. (2017). Why do employees' perceptions of their organization's change history matter? *Human Resource Management*, 56(3), 533–550.

Reinharth, L., & Wahba, M. A. (1975). Expectancy theory as a predictor of work motivation, effort expenditure, and job performance. *The Academy of Management Journal*, 18(3), 520–537.

Rempel, M. W., & Fisher, R. J. (1997). Perceived threat, cohesion, and group problem solving in intergroup conflict. *International Journal of Conflict Management*, 8(3), 216–234.

Renko, M., Kroeck, K. G., & Bullough, A. (2012). Expectancy theory and nascent entrepreneurship. *Small Business Economics*, 39(3), 667–684.

Riccobono, F., Bruccoleri, M., & Größler, A. (2015). Groupthink and project performance: The influence of personal traits and interpersonal ties. *Production and Operations Management*, 25(4), 609–629.

Ridgeway, C. L. (2001). Gender, status and leadership. *Journal of Social Issues*, 57(4), 637–655.

Rijsman, J., & Poppe, M. (1977). Power difference between players and level of matrix as determinants of competition in a MDG. *European Journal of Social Psychology*, 7(3), 347–367.

Rijsman, J. B. (1990). How European is social psychology in Europe? In: P. Drenth, J. Sergeant, & R. Takens (Eds.), *European perspectives in psychology*. Chichester: John Wiley & Sons.

Rijsman, J. B. (1997). Social diversity: A social psychological analysis and some implications for groups and organizations. *European Journal of Work and Organizational Psychology*, 6(2), 139–152.

Riketta, M. (2002). Attitudinal organizational commitment and job performance: A meta-analysis. *Journal of Organizational Behavior*, 23(3), 257–266.

Riketta, M. (2005). Organizational identification: A meta-analysis. *Journal of Vocational Behavior*, 66(2), 358–384.

Riketta, M., & Van Dick, R. (2005). Foci of attachment in organizations: A meta-analytic comparison of the strength and correlates of workgroup versus organizational identification and commitment. *Journal of Vocational Behavior*, 67(3), 490–510.

Rise, J., Sheeran, P., & Hukkelberg, S. (2010). The role of self-identity in the theory of planned behavior: A meta-analysis. *Journal of Applied Psychology*, 40(5), 1085–1105.

Rivis, A., Sheeran, P., & Armitage, C. J. (2009). Expanding the affective and normative components of the theory of planned behavior: A meta-analysis of anticipated affect and moral norms. *Journal of Applied Social Psychology*, 39(12), 2985–3019.

Riyanto, Y. E., & Zhang, J. (2013). The impact of social comparison of ability on pro-social behaviour. *The Journal of Socio-Economics*, 47(c), 37–46.

Robak, R. W., Ward, A., & Ostolaza, K. (2005). Development of a general measure of individuals' recognition of their self-perception processes. *North American Journal of Psychology*, 7(3), 337–344.

Rosenberg, M. J., Rosenthal, R., & Rosnow, R. L. (1969). The conditions and consequences of evaluation apprehension. In: *Artifacts in behavioral research* (pp. 211–263). New York, NY: Oxford University Press Inc.

Ross, L., Greene, D., & House, P. (1977). The 'false consensus effect': An egocentric bias in social perception and attribution processes. *Journal of Experimental Social Psychology*, 13(3), 279–301.

Rubin, M., & Hewstone, M. (2004). Social identity, system justification, and social dominance: Commentary on Reicher, Jost et al., and Sidanius et al. *Political Psychology*, 25(6), 823–844.

Rummel, A., & Feinberg, R. (1988). Cognitive evaluation theory: A meta-analytic review of the literature. *Social Behavior and Personality: An International Journal*, 16(2), 147–164.

Ryan, C. G., Grant, P. M., Tigbe, W. W., & Granat, M. H. (2006). The validity and reliability of a novel activity monitor as a measure of walking. *British Journal of Sports Medicine*, 40(9), 779–784.

Ryan, R. M. (1982). Control and information in the intrapersonal sphere: An extension of cognitive evaluation theory. *Journal of Personality and Social Psychology*, 43(3), 450.

Ryan, R. M., & Deci, E. I. (2000). Intrinsic and extrinsic motivations: Classic definitions and new directions. *Contemporary Educational Psychology*, 25, 54–67.

Ryan, R. M., & Deci, E. L. (2011). A self-determination theory perspective on social, institutional, cultural, and economic supports for autonomy and their importance for well-being. In: V. I. Chirkov, R. M. Ryan, & K. M. Sheldon (Eds.), Cross-cultural advancements in positive psychology: *Vol. 1. Human autonomy in cross-cultural context: Perspectives on the psychology of agency, freedom, and well-being* (pp. 45–64). New York, NY: Springer Science + Business Media.

San Martin, A., Swaab, R. I., Sinaceur, M., & Vasiljevic, D. (2015). The double-edged impact of future expectations in groups: Minority influence depends on minorities' and majorities' expectations to interact again. *Organizational Behavior and Human Decision Processes, 128*, 49–60.

Saruhan, N. (2014). The role of corporate communication and perception of justice during organizational change process. *Business and Economics Research Journal, 5*(4), 143–166.

Schein, E. H. (1985). *Organizational culture and leadership*. San Francisco, CA: Jossey-Bass.

Schein, E. H. (1999). *Process consultation revisited: Building the helping relationship*. London: Pearson Education.

Schein, E. H. (2001). *De bedrijfscultuur als ziel van de onderneming; zin en onzin over cultuurverandering*. Schiedam, NL: Scriptum.

Schein, E. H. (2013). *Humble inquiry: The gentle art of asking instead of telling*. San Francisco, CA: Berrett-Koehler.

Schiefer, D., & Van Der Noll, J. (2016). The essentials of social cohesion: A literature review. *Social Indicators Research, 132*(2), 579–603.

Schultz, K., & Weingast, B. (1994). The democratic advantage: The institutional sources of state powers in international competition. *International Organization, 57*, 3–42.

Schweiger, D. M., Sandberg, W. R., & Ragan, J. W. (1986). Group approaches for improving strategic decision making: A comparative analysis of dialectical inquiry, devil's advocacy, and consensus. *Academy of Management Journal, 29*(1), 51–71.

Scott, B. A., & Colquitt, J. A. (2007). Are organizational justice effects bounded by individual differences? *Group & Organization Management, 32*(3), 290–325.

Shadish, W. R., Cook, T. D., & Campbell, D. T. (2002). *Experimental and quasi-experimental designs for generalized causal inference*. Boston, MA: Houghton Mifflin Company.

Shah, J., & Higgins, E. T. (1997). Expectancy X value effects: Regulatory focus as determinant of magnitude and direction. *Journal of Personality and Social Psychology, 73*(3), 447–458.

Shah, J., &, Higgins, E. T. (2001). Regulatory concerns and appraisal efficiency: The general impact of promotion and prevention. *Journal of Personality and Social Psychology, 80*(5), 693–705.

Shah, J., Higgins, E. T., & Friedman, R. S. (1998). Performance incentives and means: How regulatory focus influences goal attainment. *Journal of Personality and Social Psychology, 74*(2), 285–293.

Shaver, K. G. (2015). *Principles of social psychology* (Vol. 3). Hove: Psychology Press.

Shaver, P. R., & Mikulincer, M. (2013). Attachment theory. In: P. A. Van Lange., A. W. Kruglanski, & E. T. Higgins (Eds.), *Handbook of theories of social psychology* (Vol. 2). Thousand Oaks, CA: Sage Publications, Inc.

Sheppard, B. H., Hartwick, J., & Warshaw, P. R. (1988). The theory of reasoned action: A meta-analysis of past research with recommendations for modifications and future research. *Journal of Consumer Research*, *15*(3), 325–343.

Sherif, C. W., Kelly, M., Rodgers, H. L., Jr., Sarup, G., & Tittler, B. I. (1973). Personal involvement, social judgment, and action. *Journal of Personality and Social Psychology*, *27*(3), 311–328.

Sherif, M. (1935). A study of some social factors in perception. *Archives of Psychology*, *27*, 187.

Sherif, M. (1936). *The psychology of social norms*. Oxford, UK: Harper.

Sherif, M., & Hovland, C. I. (1961). *Social judgment: Assimilation and contrast effects in communication and attitude change*. Oxford: Yale University Press.

Sherif, M., Sherif, C. W., & Nebergall, R. (1965). *Attitude and attitude change: The social judgment involvement approach*. Philadelphia, PA: W.B. Saunders.

Sherman, D. K., & Cohen, G. L. (2002). Accepting threatening information: Self-affirmation and the reduction of defensive biases. *Current Directions in Psychology Science*, *11*(4), 119–123.

Sherman, D. K., & Cohen, G. L. (2006). The psychology of self-defense: Self-affirmation theory. In: *Advances in experimental social psychology* (pp. 183–242). Cambridge, MA: Academic Press.

Shore, T. H. (2004). Equity sensitivity theory: Do we all want more than we deserve? *Journal of Managerial Psychology*, *19*(7), 722–728.

Shu, L., Gino, F., & Bazerman, M. H. (2009). Dishonest deed, clear conscience: Self-preservation through moral disengagement and motivated forgetting. *Harvard Business Review (working paper 09–078)* Retrieved July 18, 2017, from www.hbs.edu/faculty/Publication%20Files/09-078.pdf

Sidanius, J., Levin, S., Federico, C., & Pratto, F. (2001). Social dominance approach. *The psychology of legitimacy: Emerging perspectives on ideology, justice, and intergroup relations*. Cambridge: Cambridge University Press.

Sidanius, J., Levin, S., & Pratto, F. (1996). Consensual social dominance orientation and its correlates within the hierarchical structure of American society. *International Journal of Intercultural Relations*, *20*(3–4), 385–408.

Sidanius, J., & Pratto, F. (2011). Social dominance theory. In: P. A. Van Lange, A. W. Kruglanski, & E. T. Higgins (Eds.), *Handbook of theories of social psychology* (Vol. II). Thousand Oaks, CA: Sage Publications, Inc.

Sidanius, J., & Pratto, F. (1999). *Social dominance: An intergroup theory of social hierarchy and oppression*. New York, NY: Cambridge University Press.

Simmons, A. L., & Umphress, E. E. (2015). The selection of leaders and social dominance orientation. *Journal of Management Development*, *34*(10), 1211–1226.

Sims, H. P. (1977). The leader as a manager of reinforcement contingencies: An empirical example and a model. In: J. G. Hunt & L. L. Larson (Eds.), *Leadership: The cutting edge*. Carbondale, IL: Southern Illinois University Press.

Sinek, S. (2014). *Leaders eat last: Why some teams pull together and others don't*. London: Penguin Books Ltd.

Sivanathan, N., Molden, D. C., Galinsky, A. D., & Ku, G. (2008). The promise and peril of self-affirmation in de-escalation of commitment. *Organizational Behavior and Human Decision Processes*, *107*(1), 1–14.

Smircich, L., & Morgan, G. (1982). Leadership: The management of meaning. *The Journal of Applied Behavioral Science*, *18*(3), 257–273.

Smith, C. A., & Lazarus, R. S. (1990). Emotion and Adaptation. In: L. A. Pervin (Ed.), *Handbook of personality: Theory and research* (pp. 609–637). New York, NY: Guilford Press.

Smith, E. R., Mackie, D. M., & Claypool, H. M. (2014). *Social psychology* (4th ed.). Abingdon: Taylor & Francis Ltd.

Smith, G. E., Thomas, E. F., & McGarty, C. (2015). "We must be the change we want to see in the world": Integrating norms and identities through social Interaction. *Political Psychology, 36*(5), 543–557.

Solomon, S., Greenberg, J., & Pyszczynski, T. (1991). A terror management theory of social behavior: The psychological functions of self-esteem and cultural worldviews. *Advances in Experimental Social Psychology, 24*(C), 93–159.

Sowislo, J. F., & Orth, U. (2013). Does low self-esteem predict depression and anxiety? A meta-analysis of longitudinal studies. *Psychological Bulletin, 139*(1), 213–240.

Spence, J. R., Brown, D. J., & Heller, D. (2011). Understanding daily citizenship behaviors: A social comparison perspective. *Journal of Organizational Behavior, 32*(4), 547–571.

Spence, K. W. (1958). A theory of emotionally based drive (D) and its relation to performance in simple learning situations. *American Psychologist, 13*(4), 131–141.

Spreitzer, G. M., & Mishra, A. K. (2002). To stay or to go: Voluntary survivor turnover following an organizational downsizing. *Journal of Organizational Behavior, 23*(6), 707–729.

Stajkovic, A. D., & Fred, L. (1998). Self-efficacy and work-related performance: A meta-analysis. *Psychological Bulletin, 124*(2), 240–261.

Steele, C. M. (1988). The psychology of self-affirmation: Sustaining the integrity of the self. *Advances in Experimental Social Psychology, 21*, 261–302.

Steffens, N. K., Haslam, S. A., Schuh, S. C., Jetten, J., & van Dick, R. (2017). A meta-analytic review of social identification and health in organizational contexts. *Personality and Social Psychology Review, 21*(4), 303–335.

Stone, J., Aronson, E., Crain, A. L., Winslow, M. P., & Fried, C. B. (1994). Inducing hypocrisy as a means of encouraging young adults to use condoms. *Personality and Social Psychology Bulletin, 20*(1), 116–128.

Strauss, B. (2002). Social facilitation in motor tasks: A review of research and theory. *Psychology of Sport and Exercise, 3*(3), 237–256.

Strikwerda, H. (2002). Organisatieverandering: Opgesloten in de verkeerde modellen! Retrieved June 12, 2017, from www.managementsite.nl/organisatieverandering-opgesloten-verkeerde-modellen

Strikwerda, H. (2005). De marginalisering van change management. *Holland Management Review, 101*, 17–31.

Strikwerda, H. (2011). Het realiseren van een cultuuromslag. *Holland Management Review, 135*, 16–23.

Suls, J., Martin, R., & Wheeler, L. (2002). Social comparison: Why, with whom, and with what effect? *Current Directions in Psychological Science, 11*(5), 159–163.

Suls, J., & Wheeler, L. (2012). Social comparison theory. In: P. A. Van Lange, A. W. Kruglanski, & E. T. Higgins (Eds.), *Handbook of theories of social psychology* (Vol. I). Thousand Oaks, CA: Sage Publications, Inc.

Suls, J., & Wheeler, L. (2013). *Handbook of social comparison.* New York, NY: Springer Science+Business Media.

Swann, W. B., Jr. (1983). Self-verification: Bringing social reality into harmony with the self. In: J. Suls & A. G. Greenwald (Eds.), *Psychological perspectives on the self* (Vol. 2, pp. 33–66), Hillsdale, NJ: Erlbaum.

Swann, W. B., Jr. (2012). Self-verification theory. In: P. A. Van Lange, A. W. Kruglanski, & E. T. Higgins (Eds.), *Handbook of theories of social psychology* (Vol. II). Thousand Oaks, CA: Sage Publications, Inc.

Swann, W. B., Jr., & Ely, R. J. (1984). A battle of wills: Self-verification versus behavioral confirmation. *Journal of Personality and Social Psychology, 46*(6), 1287–1302.

Swann, W. B., Jr., Kwan, V. S., Polzer, J. T., & Milton, L. P. (2003). Fostering group identification and creativity in diverse groups: The role of individuation and self-verification. *Personality and Social Psychology Bulletin, 29*(11), 1396–1406.

Swann, W. B., Jr., Milton, L. P., & Polzer, J. T. (2000). Should we create a niche or fall in line? Identity negotiation and small group effectiveness. *Journal of Personality and Social Psychology, 79*(2), 238–250.

Swann, W. B., Jr., Wenzlaff, R. M., Krull, D. S., & Pelham, B. W. (1992). Allure of negative feedback: Self-verification strivings among depressed persons. *Journal of Abnormal Psychology, 101*(2), 293–306.

Tafarodi, R. W., & Swann, W. B. (1995). Self-linking and self-competence as dimensions of global self-esteem: Initial validation of a measure. *Journal of Personality Assessment, 65*(2), 322–342.

Tajfel, H. (1978). *Differentiation between social groups: Studies in the social psychology of intergroup relations.* London: Academic Press.

Tajfel, H. (1982). Social psychology of intergroup relationships. *Annual Reviews Psychology, 33,* 1–39.

Tajfel, H., & Turner, J. C. (1979). *An integrative theory of intergroup conflict* (Chapter 3). England: University of Bristol.

Tajfel, H., & Turner, J. C. (1986). The social identity theory of intergroup behavior. In: S. Worchel & W. G. Austin (Eds.), *Psychology of intergroup relations* (2nd ed., pp. 7–24). Chicago, IL: Nelson-Hall.

Tasa, K., & Whyte, G. (2005). Collective efficacy and vigilant problem solving in group decision making: A non-linear model. *Organizational Behavior and Human Decision Processes, 96*(2), 119–129.

Tauer, J. M., & Harackiewicz, J. M. (2004). The effects of cooperation and competition on intrinsic motivation and performance. *Journal of Personality and Social Psychology, 86*(6), 849–861.

Taylor, S., Neter, E., & Wayment, H. A. (1995). Self-evaluation processes. *Personality and Social Psychology Bulletin, 21*(12), 1278–1287.

ten Have, S., ten Have, W. D., Huijsmans, A.-B., & Otto, M. (2016). *Reconsidering change management: Applying evidence-based insights in change management practice.* New York, NY: Routledge.

ten Have, S., ten Have, W. D., Huijsmans, A.-B., & Van der Eng, N. (2015). *Change competence: Implementing effective change.* New York, NY: Routledge.

ten Have, S., ten Have, W. D., & Rijsman, J. (2018). Naar een sociale psychologie voor gedragsverandering in organisaties. *Holland Management Review, 177.*

Terpstra, D. E., & Honoree, A. L. (2003). The relative importance of external, internal, individual and procedural equity to pay satisfaction. *Compensation and Benefits Review, 35*(6), 67–74.

Terry, D. J. (2003). A social identity perspective on organizational mergers: The role of group status, permeability, and similarity. In: S. A. Haslam, D. van Knippenberg, M. J. Platow, & N. Ellemers (Eds.), *Social identity at work: Developing theory for organizational practice* (pp. 223–240). New York, NY: Psychology Press.

Terry, D. J., Carey, C. J., & Callan, V. J. (2001). Employee adjustment to an organizational merger: An intergroup perspective. *Personality and Social Psychology Bulletin, 27*(3), 267–280.

Thau, S., Aquino, K., & Poortvliet, P. M. (2007). Self-defeating behaviors in organizations: The relationship between thwarted belonging and interpersonal work behaviors. *Journal of Applied Psychology, 92*(3), 840–847.

Thibaut, J. W., & Walker, L. (1975). *Procedural justice: A psychological analysis.* Hillsdale, NJ: Erlbaum.

Thornton, D. A., & Arrowood, A. J. (1966). Self-evaluation, self-enhancement, and the locus of social comparison. *Journal of Experimental Social Psychology, 1*(1), 40–48.

Thyler, B. A., & Myers, L. L. (1998). Social learning theory: An empirically-based approach to understanding human behavior in the social environment. *Journal of Human Behavior in the Social Environment, 1*(1), 33–52.

Tice, D. M., & Bratslavsky, E. (2000). Giving in to feel good: The place of emotion regulation in the context of general self-control. *Psychological Inquiry, 11*(3), 149–159.

Titmuss, R. M. (1970). The gift relationship: From human blood to social policy. Bristol: Bristol University Press.

Topa, G., Morales, J. F., & Moriano, J.-A. (2009). Psychological contract breach and social identity: Their influences on Spanish soldiers' job satisfaction and organizational citizenship behaviour. *Estudios de Psicología, 30*(3), 303–315.

Triplett, N. (1898). The dynamogenic factors in pacemaking and competition. *The American Journal of Psychology, 9*(4), 507–533.

Trompenaars, F., & Hampden-Turner, C. (2012). *Riding the waves of culture: Understanding diversity in global business* (3rd ed.). London: McGraw-Hill.

Turner, J. C. (1985). Social categorization and the self concept: A social cognitive theory of group behavior. In: E. J. Lawler (Ed.), *Advances in group process* (Vol. 2, pp. 77–122). Bingley: Emerald Group Publishing.

Turner, J. C., Hogg, M. A., Oakes, P. J., Reicher, S. D., & Wetherell, M. S. (1987). *Rediscovering the social group: A self-categorization theory.* Cambridge, MA: Basil Blackwell.

Turner, M. E., Pratnakis, A. R., Probasco, P., & Leve, C. (1992). Threat, cohesion, and group effectiveness: Testing a social identity maintenance perspective on groupthink. *Journal of Personality and Social Psychology, 63*(5), 781–796.

Turner, J. C., & Reynolds, K. J. (2012). Self-categorization theory. In: P. A. M. Van Lange, A. W. Kruglanski, & E. T. Higgins (Eds.), *Handbook of theories of social psychology* (Vol. 2). Thousand Oaks, CA: Sage Publications, Inc.

Tyler, T. R., & De Cremer, D. (2005). Process-based leadership: Fair procedures and reactions to organizational change. *The Leadership Quarterly, 16*(4), 529–545.

Tziner, A., Ben-David, A., Oren, L., & Sharoni, G. (2014). Attachment to work, job satisfaction and work centrality. *Leadership & Organization Development Journal, 35*(6), 555–565.

Umphress, E. E., & Simmons, A. L. (2008). Managing discrimination in selection: The influence of directives from an authority and social dominance orientation. *Journal of Applied Psychology, 93*(5), 982–993.

Useem, M. (1975). *Protest movement in America.* New York, NY: Bobbs-Merill.

Uziel, L. (2007). Individual differences in the social facilitation effect: A review and meta-analysis. *Journal of Research in Personality, 41*(3), 579–601.

Valtorta, N. K., Kanaan, M., Gilbody, S., Ronzi, S., & Hanratty, B. (2016). Loneliness and social isolation as risk factors for coronary heart disease and stroke: Systematic review and meta-analysis of longitudinal observational studies. *Hearth, 102*(13), 1009–1016.

Van den Bos, K., & Miedema, J. (2000). Toward understanding why fairness matters: The influence on mortality salience on reactions to procedural fairness. *Journal of Personality and Social Psychology, 79*(3), 355–366.

Van der Linden, D., Beckers, D. G. J., & Taris, T. W. (2007). Reinforcement Sensitivity theory at work: Punishment sensitivity as a dispositional source of job-related stress. *European Journal of Personality, 21*(7), 889–909.

Van Dierendonck, D., & Jacobs, G. (2002). Survivors and victims, a meta-analytical review of fairness and organizational commitment after downsizing. *British Journal of Management, 23*(1), 96–109.

Van Knippenberg, B., Martin, L., & Tyler, T. (2006). Process-orientation versus outcome-orientation during organizational change: The role of organizational identification. *Journal of Organizational Behavior, 27*(6), 685–704.

Van Lange, P. A. M., Kruglanski, A. W., & Higgins, E. T. (2012a). *Handbook of theories of social psychology* (Vol. 1). London: Sage Publications, Inc.

Van Lange, P. A. M., Kruglanski, A. W., & Higgins, E. T. (2012b). *Handbook of theories of social psychology* (Vol. 2). London: Sage Publications, Inc.

Vancouver, J. B., & Kendall, L. N. (2006). When self-efficacy negatively relates to motivation and performance in a learning context. *Journal of Applied Psychology, 91*(5), 1146–1153.

Veldsman, D., & Coetzee, M. (2014). People performance enablers in relation to employees' psychological attachment to the organization. *Journal of Psychology in Africa, 24*(6), 480–486.

Vella, J., Caruana, A., & Pitt, L. F. (2012). Perceived performance, equity sensitivity and organizational commitment among bank managers. *Journal of Financial Service Marketing, 17*(1), 5–18.

Verkuyten, M., Rood-Pijpers, E., Elffers, H., & Hessing, D. J. (1994). Rules for breaking formal rules: Social representation and everyday rule-governed behavior. *The Journal of Psychology, 128*(5), 485–497.

Vidyarthi, P. R., Anand, S., & Liden, R. C. (2014). Do emotionally perceptive leaders motivate higher employee performance? The moderating role of task interdependence and power distance. *The Leadership Quarterly, 25*, 232–244.

Viswesvaran, C., & Ones, D. S. (2002). Examining the construct of organizational justice: A meta-analytic evaluation of relations with work attitudes and behaviors. *Journal of Business Ethics, 38*(3), 193–203.

Vroom, V. H., & Jago, A. G. (2007). The role of the situation in leadership. *American Psychologist, 62*(1), 17–24.

Wagner, J. A., & Lepine, J. A. (1999). Effects of participation on performance and satisfaction: Additional meta-analytic evidence. *Psychological Reports, 84*(3), 719–725.

Walczak, D. (2015). The process of exchange, solidarity and sustainable development in building a community of responsibility. *Mediterranean Journal of Social Sciences, 6*(1), 506–512.

Walton, G. M., Cohen, G. L., Cwir, D., & Spencer, S. J. (2012). Mere belonging: The power of social connections. *Journal of Personality and Social Psychology, 102*(3), 513–532.

Wanous, J. P., Reichers, A. E., & Austin, J. T. (2000). Cynicism about organizational change: Measurement, antecedents, and correlates. *Group & Organization Management, 25*(2), 132–153.

Waters, E., Corcoran, D., & Anafarta, M. (2005). Attachment, other relationships, and the theory that all good things go together. *Human Development, 48*(1–2), 80–84.

Watkins, M. D. (2013). *The first 90 days: Proven strategies for getting up to speed faster and smarter, updated and expanded.* Boston, MA: Harvard Business Review Press.

Weibel, A., Rost, K., & Osterloh, M. (2009). Pay for performance in the public sector—Benefits and (hidden) costs. *Journal of Public Administration Research and Theory, 20*(2), 387–412.

Weick, K. E. (1979). *The social psychology of organizing.* New York, NY: McGraw-Hill.

Weick, K. E. (1993). The collapse of sensemaking in organizations: The Mann Gulch disaster. *Administrative Science Quarterly, 38*(4), 628–652.

Weick, K. E. (1995). *Sensemaking in organisations.* London: Sage Publications, Inc.

Weisenfeld, B. M., Brockner, J., & Martin, C. (1999). A self-affirmation analysis of survivors' reactions to unfair organizational downsizings. *Journal of Experimental Social Psychology, 35*(5), 441–460.

Weiss, H. M., & Cropanzano, R. (1996). Affective events theory: A theoretical discussion of the structure, causes and consequences of affective experiences at work. *Research in Organizational Behavior, 18*, 1–74.

Welsh, D. H. B., Bernstein, D. J., & Luthans, F. (1992). Application of the premack principle of reinforcement to the quality performance of service employees. *Journal of Organizational Behavior Management, 13*(1), 9–32.

Whelpley, C. E., & McDaniel, M. A. (2016). Self-esteem and counterproductive work behaviors: A systematic review. *Journal of Managerial Psychology, 31*(4), 850–863.

Whyte, W. H., Jr. (1956). *The organization man.* New York, NY: Touchstone/Simon & Schuster.

Wilensky, H. L. (1964). The professionalization of everyone? *American Journal of Sociology, 70*(2), 137–158.

Wills, T. A. (1981). Downward comparison principles in social psychology. *Psychological Bulletin, 90*(2), 245–271.

Won-Woo, P. (2000). A comprehensive empirical investigation of the relationships among variables of the groupthink model. *Journal of Organizational Behavior, 21*(8), 873–887.

Wood, J. V. (1989). Theory and research concerning social comparisons of personal attributes. *Psychological Bulletin, 106*(2), 231–248.

Wood, J. V., Taylor, S. E., & Lichtman, R. R. (1985). Social comparison in adjustment to breast cancer. *Journal of Personality and Social Psychology, 49*(5), 1169–1183.

Wood, W., Lundgren, S., Ouellette, J. A., Busceme, S., & Blackstone, T. (1994). Minority influence: A meta-analytic review of social influence processes. *Psychological Bulletin*, *115*(3), 323–345.

Wu, C. (2012). Longitudinal reciprocal relationships between core self-evaluations and job satisfaction. *Journal of Applied Psychology*, *97*(2), 331–342.

Yen, C.-L., & Lin, C.-Y. (2012). The effects of mortality salience on escalation of commitment. *International Journal of Psychology*, *47*(1), 51–57.

Yigit, I. (2016). The effect of organizational commitment on the social exchange and organizational socialization: A study in research and practice hospital of Kocaeli university. *KAUJEASF*, *7*(12), 24–50.

Yip, J. J., & Kelly, A. E. (2013). Upward and downward social comparisons can decrease prosocial behaviour. *Journal of Applied Social Psychology*, *43*(3), 591–602.

Zaccaro, S. J., & McCoy, M. C. (1988). The effects of task and interpersonal cohesiveness on performance of a disjunctive group task. *Journal of Applied Social Psychology*, *18*(10), 837–851.

Zaffron, S., & Logan, D. (2009). *The three laws of performance: Rewriting the future of your organization and your life*. San Francisco, CA: Jossey-Bass.

Zajonc, R. B. (1965). Social facilitation. *Science*, *149*(3681), 269–274.

Zajonc, R. B. (1972). *Compresence*. Unpublished ms. University of Michigan.

Zhang, Y., & Chen, C. C. (2013). Developmental leadership and organizational citizenship behavior: Mediating effects of self-determination, supervisor identification, and organizational identification. *The Leadership Quarterly*, *24*(4), 534–543.

Zhou, Y., Tsang, A. S. L., Huang, M., & Zhou, N. (2014). Group service recovery strategies effectiveness: The moderating effects of group size and relational distance. *Journal of Business Research*, *67*(11), 2480–2485.

Zuckerman, M., Porac, J., Lathin, D., & Deci, E. L. (1978). On the importance of self-determination for intrinsically-motivated behavior. *Personality and Social Psychology Bulletin*, *4*(3), 443–446.

Index

Page numbers in *italics* indicate figures and in **bold** indicate tables on the corresponding pages.

Printed in the United States
by Baker & Taylor Publisher Services